# THE PSYCHOLOGY
# OF LEARNING AND MOTIVATION

## Advances in Research and Theory

*VOLUME 5*

# CONTRIBUTORS TO THIS VOLUME

*John Robert Anderson*

*Sheldon M. Ebenholtz*

*Murray Glanzer*

*G. Robert Grice*

*Bennet B. Murdock, Jr.*

*H. S. Terrace*

# THE PSYCHOLOGY
# OF LEARNING AND MOTIVATION

## Advances in Research and Theory

EDITED BY GORDON H. BOWER

STANFORD UNIVERSITY, STANFORD, CALIFORNIA

*Volume 5*

1972

**ACADEMIC PRESS**    New York · London

ACADEMIC PRESS, INC.
111 Fifth Avenue, New York, New York 10003

*United Kingdom Edition published by*
ACADEMIC PRESS, INC. (LONDON) LTD.
24/28 Oval Road, London NW1 7DD

LIBRARY OF CONGRESS CATALOG CARD NUMBER: 66-30104

PRINTED IN THE UNITED STATES OF AMERICA

# CONTENTS

## CONDITIONING AND A DECISION THEORY OF RESPONSE EVOCATION

### G. Robert Grice

## SHORT-TERM MEMORY

### Bennet B. Murdock, Jr.

## STORAGE MECHANISMS IN RECALL

### Murray Glanzer

# BY-PRODUCTS OF DISCRIMINATION LEARNING

## H. S. Terrace

# SERIAL LEARNING AND DIMENSIONAL ORGANIZATION

## Sheldon M. Ebenholtz

# FRAN: A SIMULATION MODEL OF FREE RECALL

*John Robert Anderson*

# LIST OF CONTRIBUTORS

Numbers in parentheses indicate the pages on which the authors' contributions begin.

**John Robert Anderson,** Stanford University, Stanford, California (315)

**Sheldon M. Ebenholtz,**[1] University of Wisconsin, Madison, Wisconsin (267)

**Murray Glanzer,** New York University, New York, New York (129)

**G. Robert Grice,** University of New Mexico, Albuquerque, New Mexico (1)

**Bennet B. Murdock, Jr.,** University of Toronto, Toronto, Ontario, Canada (67)

**H. S. Terrace,** Columbia University, New York, New York (195)

[1] Present address: Dalhousie University, Halifax, N.S., Canada.

# CONTENTS OF
# PREVIOUS VOLUMES

## Volume 4

# CONDITIONING AND A DECISION THEORY OF RESPONSE EVOCATION[1]

## G. Robert Grice

UNIVERSITY OF NEW MEXICO, ALBUQUERQUE, NEW MEXICO

[1] This research was supported by PHS Research Grant No. MH 16400 from the National Institute of Mental Health. Portions of the experimental work were conducted at the University of Illinois, and were supported by Grant No. MH 08033, also from the National Institute of Mental Health. The writer wishes to express indebtedness to his colleague Frank A. Logan, who has listened patiently and provided helpful suggestions and items of information.

1

# I. Introduction

## A. THEORETICAL BACKGROUND

Under some circumstances, at least, a conditioned or voluntary response, which is evoked by a strong stimulus, will occur with a higher probability or a shorter latency than when the response is evoked by a weaker stimulus. However, functions which relate these behavioral measures to the intensity of the eliciting stimulus are by no means consistent, but vary widely in slope or form, dependent upon the accompanying circumstances under which the relationship is observed. In other words, the relation between response and stimulus intensity interacts to varying degrees with a number of additional variables. What was originally an attempt to understand and provide a theoretical account of this state of affairs has led to the present theoretical developments. These efforts now seem to be taking the form of a general reformulation of the type of behavior theory initiated by Hull and extended by Spence. But, while the basic ancestry is clear, the approach has other readily identifiable sources. It relies heavily, as did Hull for a time, on the scaling theory of Thurstone. And, in particular, it draws from some of the more recent developments in decision theory — especially the Theory of Signal Detection (TSD) and the stochastic latency model of McGill (1963).

Decision theories vary in the nature and complexity of the decision rules leading to the occurrence of some specified behavior. The version employed here is of a very simple variety. The state leading to the instigation of a response on a particular trial or at a particular point in time is thought of as existing in some degree of strength. This instigating state may be simple or consist of multiple components, but in the present approach it is initiated by stimulation. There is then another value which is a momentary property of the behaving individual usually called the criterion. When the strength of the instigating state is greater than the criterion, a response will occur, and when it is less than the criterion, there will be no response. Following Hull and Spence we shall call the instigating state excitatory strength (E) and its strength will be indicated on a scale based on Thurstonian theory. The criterion, or as we shall usually call it, the threshold, is also a value on this scale. It comes as a surprise to some that the theory of Hull and Spence was also a decision theory in this same sense. Their concept of reaction threshold (L) served just the function described above. The writer has indicated elsewhere (Grice, 1968, 1971) the mathematical identity of L and the criterion of TSD. The chief difference between their theory and ones explicitly identified as decision theories is a concern with potential dynamic properties of the criterion. Decision theorists frequently regard the criterion as manipulatable by such things as motivation, payoff, risk, and expectancy, or, at least, evaluatable by such devices as certainty ratings. Hull and Spence typically regarded the threshold as a fixed value, the primary (and certainly important) function of which was its effect on the form of learning functions. Actually, Spence (1960, Ch. 22) may have been moving in the direction of more use of the concept when he suggested that a long jump by a rat might have a higher reaction threshold than a short jump. Variation and manipulation of the threshold play a central role in the present formulations.

The variability of behavior being what it is, any adequate theory must contain a probabilistic component. We have chosen to assume that the threshold is a random variable. In this respect the approach differs from its forebears. The original theory of signal detectability was, of course, a model for the stimulus in which the probability distribution was produced by a noisy background. Later application which did not involve noise in the stimulus used similar mathematics but assumed that a distribution of "noise" was produced by the S (e.g., see Weintraub & Hake, 1962). While variation in the criterion is essential for the construction of a Receiver Operating Characteristic (ROC), the criterion is typically treated as constant at any particular value. Hull and Spence postulate a normally distributed, inhibitory, oscillation function (O) which is subtracted from the value of E. Thus, both TSD and Hull-Spence utilize a function which is the algebraic sum of a normal distribution and a constant strength value. In both cases, probability of response is determined by the scale distance of this function from the criterion or threshold. McGill derives variability in latency from postulated stochastic properties of sensory inputs and assumes the criterion to be constant. The writer's preference for assuming that random variability is associated with the threshold is based on conceptual and psychological, rather than mathematical grounds. In the first place, it is conceived as much more multiply determined than the sensory and associative concepts employed in the theory. Describing the state of readiness of the individual to respond, it is thought of as dependent on such factors as motivation, incentive, emotional state, set, attention, sequence effects, adaptation, and individual differences. It appears rather compelling to view such a state as labile and a major source of response variability. Treating, as we do, the threshold as the sole source of variability does not mean that we must believe that other biological processes are literally free of variability. It merely means that other sources may be effectively and parsimoniously treated as trivial in their effects on behavior variability. The threshold is represented as a normal distribution with a mean and standard deviation which are parameters for an individual with respect to a specific response under a specified set of experimental conditions. When analyses are made of groups, the mean is the group mean, and the variance is the appropriately weighted sum of individual difference and within-individual variance. To place this treatment in the Thurstonian context, it is mathematically equivalent to a conceptualization of the law of categorical judgment in which the scale value is viewed as fixed and all variability is associated with the category boundary. The assumption of normality has, so far, worked very well, but, in any case, the methods used permit evaluation of this assumption.

Our current interest in stimulus intensity effects originated with demonstrations in the writer's laboratory (Beck, 1963; Grice & Hunter, 1964) that much steeper conditioned stimulus (CS) intensity effects are obtained in within-$S$ investigations in which the intensities are presented in an irregular order, than in between-$S$ conditions in which separate groups of $S$s each receive a single intensity. After an initial interest in adaptation level (AL) theory as a potential explanation of this phenomenon, the writer (Grice, 1968) turned to decision theory as a more powerful approach which was more amenable to the prediction of response evocation and more readily integratable with other theoretical structures. We began with a modification of McGill's latency model in which the criterion was allowed to vary and were soon led to see the relationships and features in common among the various theoretical approaches mentioned above. The initial assumption was that adaptation, other than pure sensory adaptation, affects the level of the criterion. The mean of the criterion distribution, then, is a function of the intensity of stimulation to which $S$ is exposed, and the relationship is positive − more intense stimulation leading to higher criteria. Thus, in the between-$S$ intensity experiment, the groups would be expected to have different criteria. With irregular presentation, on the other hand, $S$ must respond to each intensity with the same mean criterion level. We then showed that this state of affairs leads to the deduction of a steeper intensity function in the within-$S$ condition.

The next step (Grice, 1968) was an analysis of Beck's (1963) data in which she manipulated CS intensity in combination with unconditioned stimulus (UCS) intensity and anxiety, presumed to be drive variables. A model analogous to the TSD decision axis was used with four scale values representing her four motivational conditions and one scale distance representing the CS intensity effect. Using the normal assumption, this accounted for practically all of the between-cells variance, and implied an additive relation between stimulus intensity and motivational effects rather than the multiplicative relation assumed by Hull. Further analyses also suggested an additive relation between CS intensity and associative or habit strength (H), and suggested threshold variation as the major source of individual differences.

A considerable amount of the work stemming from this approach has been with simple reaction time (RT). Originally, it was shown (Grice, 1968) that the effects upon RT of preadaptation to various stimulus intensities (Kohfeld, 1968; Murray & Kohfeld, 1965) behave as criterion manipulations should. More generally we have been working on the assumption that variation in the height and slope of signal intensity — RT functions are typically criterion phenomena. At latest count, in published and unpublished research, the writer and his students, mostly the latter, have discovered 15 experimental variables which influence the criterion as judged by overall effects on mean RT and the production of predicted changes in the slopes of stimulus intensity functions. But this work is not the concern of the present paper.

Recently, the writer (Grice, 1971) has explored more fully the hypothesis that variables commonly regarded as manipulating drive (D) may be regarded as controlling the reaction threshold. This hypothesis was proposed as an alternative to the multiplicative theory (H x D) favored by Hull and Spence. The data from several eyelid conditioning experiments, which were conceived in the context of multiplicative theory, and in which such variables were manipulated, were analyzed. In all cases, it was possible to account for the acquisition curves in satisfactory detail with the threshold assumption. When groups were conditioned with drive differences, it was assumed that they shared a common associative or habit growth function. It was possible to secure estimates of these functions from the data. Also, parameters of the hypothetical threshold distributions were estimated. In all cases the mean threshold values were obtained, and in some instances, when the assumption of equal variability did not apply, it was necessary to estimate the standard deviations as well. Threshold variability has pronounced effects on both the form and terminal level of conditioning curves. These analyses provided promising initial support for the threshold model of drive effects, which is additive rather than multiplicative. Progress was also made in the development of analytic methods suggested by the model.

## B. THE EFFECT OF FACILITATIVE AND INHIBITORY INSTRUCTIONS ON CONDITIONING: AN ILLUSTRATIVE EXAMPLE

Several investigators have shown that sets induced by the instructions have a substantial effect on human eyelid conditioning. For example, in one of these experiments (Nicholls & Kimble, 1964), the $S$s in an inhibitory condition were told, "Concentrate on not blinking until you feel the puff of air. That is, try not to blink after the light comes on until you feel the air puff." In a facilitative condition the $S$s were told, "Relax and let your eye reactions take care of themselves. If you feel your eye close or about to close, do nothing to stop it." As is typical in such experiments, conditioning was obtained under both conditions, but there was large difference between them. Now, if anything has obvious face validity as a means of influencing the $S$'s criterion for response, or reaction threshold, it must be this sort of manipulation. We shall now present an analysis of the Nicholls and Kimble data in terms of the threshold model. This analysis will serve a twofold function. In the first place, it will provide a test of the adequacy of the theory in a rather obvious application. It will also serve as an introduction to some of the details of the model itself and methods for applying it.

We shall begin with the assumption that the two groups are the same with respect to the growth of associative strength (H), and differ only in their threshold distribution (T). The basic model is then:

$$E_F = H - T_F \tag{1}$$

and

$$E_I = H - T_I \tag{2}$$

$E_F$ and $E_I$ are the suprathreshold excitatory strengths for the two groups and are estimated by the normal deviate $(z)$ corresponding to the percentage of conditioned responses (CRs) for a given block of trials. H is the habit or associative strength, and is the same for the two groups at any level of training. $T_F$ and $T_I$ are the means of the threshold distribution for the two conditions. From Eqs. (1) and (2) we may readily write two additional equations:

$$T_I - T_F = E_F - E_I \tag{3}$$

and

$$H - (T_F + T_I)2 = (E_F + E_I)/2 \tag{4}$$

Equation (3) is the scale distance between the two threshold distributions, and, as will be apparent, corresponds to the TSD measure, $d'$, which we shall call simply $d$. If we now select as our working scale, one with zero midway between the two threshold distributions, $(T_F + T_I)/2 = 0$, and Eq. (4) reduces to

$$H = (E_F + E_I)/2 \tag{5}$$

Thus, an estimate of H is simply the mean of the two E values at a particular stage of training. Also, on this scale $T_I = +d/2$ and $T_F = -d/2$. Thus the terms of the basic model of Eqs. (1) and (2) may be estimated, but now it is necessary to consider the question of the equivalence of the units.

Nicholls and Kimble presented their data for 40 conditioning trials plotted in blocks of five trials; however, these data points behaved somewhat erratically. In order to reduce the variability of the points, display the basic trends more clearly, and simplify the solution, we have reduced their conditioning curves to four blocks of 10 trials each. In this analysis and in subsequent ones, such data are treated and plotted with respect to the midpoint of the trial block. These data for the two conditioning curves are presented in Fig. 1. The percentages of CRs have first been converted to $z$ or E values. Then, $z_F$ has been plotted as a function of $z_I$ for each of the four blocks of trials. The trial blocks are in order from left to right. This figure is equivalent to an ROC of TSD plotted in normal-normal units.

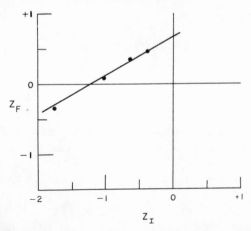

Fig. 1. REC relating acquisition data of facilitative and inhibitory conditions from the Nicholls and Kimble experiment. See text for further explanation.

However, since ROC is not descriptive here, the writer (Grice, 1971) has suggested that this application be termed Response Evocation Characteristic (REC). As previously noted (Grice, 1968, 1971), there are two psychologically meaningful dimensions in this figure. In this instance, distances parallel to the minor diagonal are related to $d$ the scale distance attributable to the instructions. Distances parallel to the major diagonal are related to response strength, and since this variation is produced here by trials, to associative strength or H. This becomes especially clear when one considers a 45° counterclockwise rotation of the axes, and, in fact, the mathematics of Eqs. (1)–(5) are derivable in this way. However, this was discussed in the just cited references, and the exercise will not be repeated here.

The fact that the points of the REC are well fitted by a straight line implies that the data may be desribed by a model based on the normal distribution. However, the fact that the slope, .589, departs markedly from unity, introduces complications. It would have unit slope under conditions in which habit grows at the same rate for both groups and the standard deviations (SD) of the two threshold distributions are equal. Therefore, one of these conditions is not fulfilled. Since the slope is less than one, if one accepted the differential habit growth rate alternative, one would be forced to accept the somewhat improbable conclusion that habit grows more slowly with the facilitative instructions than with the inhibitory ones. The interpretation usually drawn in the TSD applications, and that previously used by the writer (Grice, 1971) is that slopes other than one indicate unequal variability. Under these circumstances as in TSD, the slope is an estimate of the ratio of the SDs. Here $\sigma_I/\sigma_F = .589$. Actually, we were committed to this choice by our initial assumption that H would be unaffected by the instructions. However, it does make sense that Ss instructed to "concentrate" should be less variable than Ss instructed to "relax."

The unequal $\sigma$ condition means the $E_F$ and $E_I$ are in different units with the ratio .589. This creates a problem since it is clear that the operations of Eqs. (3) and (5) are meaningless unless the two E values are in the same units. This means that an unequal $\sigma$ scaling solution is necessary. Since the ratio of the $\sigma$s are given by the slope of the REC, it is possible to choose either $\sigma$ as the working unit and convert the values for the other condition to this unit. The logic of this procedure was originally described by Thurstone (1925, 1927b), who at that time used the equivalent of an ROC for the purpose. More recently, it has been used in other scaling contexts by Saffir (1937), and also has been described by Torgerson (1958, pp.

221-227). In the present context, the procedure has previously been used by the writer (Grice, 1971). In this instance, the values of $E_F$ were converted to the units of the inhibitory group by dividing by .589. This has the effect of rotating the REC to a slope of one around the $z_F$ intercept. The value of $d$ is assumed to be constant over trials and is obtained by averaging Eq. (3) over all trial blocks.

$$d = T_I - T_F = \left[ \Sigma_1^n \left( E_{F_i} - E_{I_j} \right) \right] / n \qquad (6)$$

where $n$ is the number of trial blocks. The value of $d$ is 1.183 in units of the inhibitory group $\sigma$.

The next step is to estimate the function for habit growth common to the two conditions. Estimates of points on the function are now obtained by the application of Eq. (5) to the values of $E_F$ and $E_I$, now in common units. These are the plotted points in Fig. 2. The points are then fitted by a smooth function. In each of our

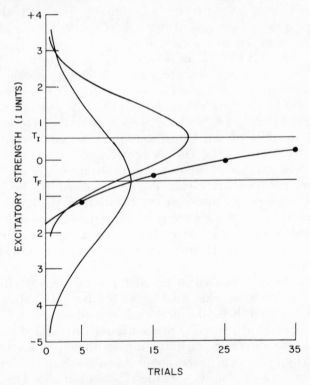

Fig. 2. Habit function derived from the Nicholls and Kimble data. Threshold levels and their distributions are also indicated.

analyses, so far, an exponential growth function of the type used by
Hull and Spence to describe habit growth has been quite satisfactory
for this purpose. This instance is no exception, and the fitted
function indicated by the smooth curve of Fig. 2 has the equation

$$H = .5 - 2.24(10)^{-.0253N} \tag{7}$$

where $N$ is the number of trials. We now have the estimated values of
$d$, $\sigma_I / \sigma_F$, and habit growth function — all of the information
necessary to calculate predicted conditioning curves for the two
groups.

The model and the logic of the calculations is shown graphically in
Fig. 2. Along with the H function, the location of the mean
threshold values is indicated by horizontal lines at $\pm d/2$. The normal
curves indicate the two threshold distributions. Since the ordinate is
in $I$ units, $SD_I = 1$, and $SD_F = 1/.589$. The probability of response at
any level of training is estimated by obtaining the distance from that
point on the curve to the appropriate threshold (H–T) and
ascertaining the proportion of the area of the distribution below that
value. For example, the calculated value of H at five trials from Eq.
(7) is $-1.16$. This is 1.75 units below $T_I$. ($z = -1.16-.59 = -1.75$.)
From the normal distribution function, the corresponding area is .04,
which is the predicted value for the inhibitory condition. $H_5$ is .57
units below $T_F$. [$z = -1.16-(-.59) = -.57$.] At this point it must be
remembered that this value is in units of $SD_I$. Therefore, it must be
returned to units of the F distribution to obtain the correct area.
($z = -.57 \times .589 = -.34$.) The area corresponding to this value of $z$ is
.37 which is the predicted response probability for the facilitative
condition. This procedure may also be visualized. If a horizontal line
is passed through any point on the H function, the areas of the two
distributions below it are the predicted response probabilities for the
corresponding number of trials. If these calculations are repeated for
a number of values of H, smooth, predicted conditioning curves will
be generated.

The model is presented in another way in Fig. 3. This is in the
form of a decision axis analogous to that of TSD. The chief
difference is that here the probability distributions are associated
with the thresholds, whereas in applications of TSD the criterion is
treated as fixed and probability distributions are associated with
sensory strength, or in some applications associative strength. Here
the abscissa is in units of the I distribution. The threshold
distributions, each with the appropriate SD, are separated by the
distance $d$. The vertical lines are at locations calculated from Eq. (7)

for the four trial blocks analyzed. A response occurs when the threshold is below the level of excitatory strength produced by habit growth (T < H). The probability of this is predicted by the areas of the two normal distributions which lie below (to the left of) the four levels of habit strength. Thus, the four values on each conditioning curve are predicted by the eight such areas represented in the figure.

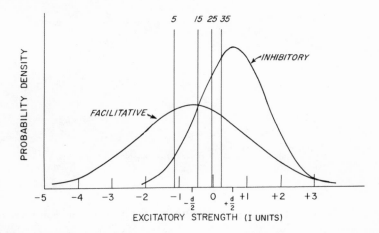

Fig. 3. Decision axis for the Nicholls and Kimble data based on estimated values of H, $d$, and $\sigma_I/\sigma_F$.

The final fit of the model to the experimental data is presented in Fig. 4. The data points plotted are the percentages of conditioned responses obtained by Nicholls and Kimble. The two smooth curves are the predicted conditioning functions calculated in the manner just described. It is apparent that the model describes these data with considerable precision. Not only are the forms of the conditioning curves accurately predicted, but none of the predicted values differ from the obtained ones by more than a single percentage point. The results of the experiment, then, are consistent with the interpretation that facilitative or inhibitory instructions do not affect conditioning in the sense of influencing the development of associative strength, but have their effect upon $S$'s readiness to respond or his reaction threshold. Apparently, however, the effect was not limited to the obvious one of determining the mean level of the threshold, but also affected its variability. This may be sensibly interpreted as reflecting states of concentration or relaxation also induced by the instructions. The assumption of normally distributed thresholds was also supported.

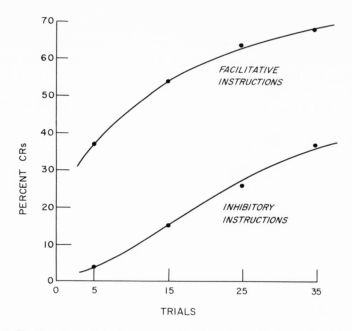

Fig. 4. Predicted conditioning curves fitted to the Nicholls and Kimble data.

## II. Differential Conditioning to Stimulus Intensity: Experimental Research[2]

### A. INTRODUCTION

There has been surprisingly little work on differential classical conditioning to stimuli which differ only in intensity. Moore (1964) has certainly demonstrated that the phenomenon does occur in eyelid conditioning with either the stronger or the weaker of two stimuli positive, and that differentiation is greater when it is the positive stimulus which is stronger. In other words, there was evidence for both associative and stimulus intensity effects in operation. From the writer's point of view, however, the results of Moore's experiments were not sufficiently clear-cut or consistent to provide an adequate basis for a full and quantitative theoretical

[2] Appreciation is expressed to the research assistants who conducted these experiments. They are Rona Roydes and Richard Araway at the University of Illinois, and Jeffrey M. Speiss and Kermit F. Henricksen at the University of New Mexico.

analysis. Therefore, it was determined to conduct such an experiment employing a larger difference in stimulus intensity, in the hope that its effect would be large in relation to error, and in relation to associative effects.

Differential conditioning to stimulus intensity differences is of special interest in the present theoretical context. In the first place, it is a procedure which inherently involves within-$S$ presentation of more than one intensity. This should make possible an analysis of the relation between the effects of intensity and associative process under conditions of a single criterion or threshold. In the Grice and Hunter (1964) experiment presentation of a soft tone produced a significant rise in response to a loud tone, even though there were 50 percent fewer reinforcements to the loud tone than in a control condition. It seemed possible that even nonreinforced presentations of a soft tone might have quite a different effect on the level of response to the positive, loud tone than the evidence for generalization of inhibition obtained by Gynther (1957) in differential conditioning on a nonintensity dimension. For purposes of such comparisons, control conditions were run with simple 100 percent reinforcement to each stimulus intensity. To extend the scope of the experiment a bit further, 50 percent partial reinforcement conditions were also run with each intensity. Partial reinforcement is operationally the same as differential conditioning, except that the same stimulus is presented on reinforced and nonreinforced trials rather than different stimuli. Possible relationships between CS intensity and partial reinforcement have not been investigated. Theoretical analysis should also give at least preliminary evidence as to whether the typical decrement in acquisition is associatively or nonassociatively determined.

## B. METHOD

### 1. Apparatus and General Procedures

The research was conducted in the writer's laboratories at the University of Illinois and the University of New Mexico. In both instances the eyelid response was transduced by a low torque potentiometer attached to $S$'s head. In the Illinois laboratory it was recorded by a Hunter Motions Recorder in combination with a Brush inkwriting oscillograph. Timing and circuitry control was by Hunter Decade Timers and relay circuitry. Automatic control of the experimental session was accomplished by a stepping-switch system.

At New Mexico, a Beckman Type RS Dynograph was used for recording. Control was by solid state (BRS) logic components. Timing of critical intervals was by binary coded decimal counters driven by a free-running precision time base. Sessions were controlled by paper-tape readers.

Auditory stimuli (1000 Hz tones) were produced by a Hewlett-Packard audio-oscillator and switched by a Grayson-Stadler electronic switch. The tones were presented by calibrated, Telephonics TDH-39 earphones. Air-puff stimuli were controlled by a Matheson low pressure regulator, and released by a solenoid valve. At Illinois, the warning signal was a buzzer, and at New Mexico it was produced by a BRS click generator adjusted to give a similar sound. Ss were instructed to blink once at the onset of the warning signal. Standard neutral instructions for eyelid conditioning were used. Ss were seated in sound-attenuating compartments.

## 2. Subjects

The Ss were 200 undergraduate women enrolled in introductory psychology, and received course credit for participation. There were 20 Ss in each experimental condition and 20 in each replication of a condition.

## 3. Experimental Parameters and Variables

The CSs and, in the case of differential conditioning, the negative stimuli were 1000 Hz tones of either 100 or 50 dB SPL. Their duration was .5 second and they were switched with rise and decay times of 30 msec. The onset of the air-puff UCS was at the termination of the UCS and its duration was 40 msec. Its intensity was 1.0 psi measured at the solenoid valve. The warning signal, with a duration of .5 second, preceded the CS or negative stimulus by 2, 3, or 4 seconds in an irregular order. The intertrial interval was 15, 20, or 25 seconds also in an irregular order. Anticipatory blinks resulting in a pen deflection of 1 mm or more were scored in the interval from 150 to 528 msec which does not include latency of the UCR. Recorder paper speed was 125 mm/second. When latency data are presented, latencies were read to the nearest mm, i.e., 8 msec.

In the initial research at Illinois there were six experimental conditions. At New Mexico three of these conditions were replicated and one additional condition was introduced. The experimental conditions were as follows:

$L^+ S^-$: Differential conditioning in which the loud (100 dB) tone was paired with the UCS and the soft (50 dB) tone was never reinforced. There were 100 trials, 50 to each stimulus, presented in an irregular order. In each block of 20 trials there were 10 presentations of each tone.

$S^+ L^-$: The reverse arrangement in which the UCS accompanied the soft tone.

$L_{100}$: 50 paired conditioning trials to the loud tone.

$S_{100}$: 50 paired conditioning trials to the soft tone.

$L_{50}$: A partial reinforcement condition in which the loud tone was presented for 100 trials and paired with the UCS on half of these. The order of reinforced and nonreinforced trials was the same as in the differential conditioning groups.

$S_{50}$: A similar partial reinforcement condition with the soft tone as CS.

$L_{100D}$: 50 trials of 100% reinforcement with the loud CS but with distributed trials. The average *temporal* distribution of trials was identical to that of the *reinforced* trials of the differential conditioning and partial reinforcement conditions. This was the new condition introduced at New Mexico.

The conditions replicated at New Mexico were $L^+ S^-$, $L_{100}$, and $L_{50}$.

## C. RESULTS AND GENERAL DISCUSSION

### 1. Differential Conditioning

Acquisition curves for the differential conditioning groups are presented in Fig. 5. Data for the full experiment, conducted at Illinois, are indicated by the points connected by the solid lines. It is clear that differentiation is much greater when the loud stimulus is positive than when soft is positive, both functions for $S^+ L^-$ lying intermediate between the positive and negative functions for $L^+ S^-$. In terms of total CRs, both the effects of intensity and reinforcement (+ *vs.* −) are highly significant. For reinforcement, $F$ $(1,38) = 76.6$, $p < .001$. For stimulus intensity, $F$ $(1,38) = 19.2$, $p < .001$. The reinforcement × intensity interaction, which is also the between groups effect is not significant. $F$ $(1.38) = .21$, n.s. This implies that the effects of intensity and differential reinforcement may be regarded as additive.

The New Mexico replication of $L^+ S^-$ is indicated by the points connected by dashed lines. This replication with a sample from a

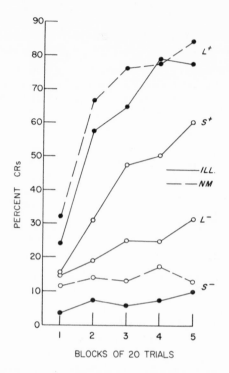

Fig. 5. Acquisition of differential conditioning to stimuli differing in intensity. L, loud stimulus; S, soft stimulus. Dashed lines are the replication of the L⁺S⁻ condition. Ill., studies done at Illinois; NM, studies done at New Mexico.

different population, conducted with different equipment, by different *E*s, resulted in a somewhat higher level of response. However, the *F* for replications did not reach statistical significance. $F$ (1,38) = 2.52, $p > .10$. The combined effect for stimuli in the two replications, which involved differential reinforcement and intensity acting in the same direction was obviously highly significant. $F$ (1,38) = 227.5, $p < .001$. The replications × stimuli interaction was very small and not significant. $F$ (1,38) = .003, n.s. Replication of this sort is an encouraging state of affairs for a moving *E*.

A preliminary insight into the nature of the underlying process in this experiment is given by an examination of the distributions of the latencies of response to the two stimuli in each condition. These distributions for all trials combined are presented, in cumulative form, in Fig. 6. Inspection of these functions leads one to conclude that associative and stimulus intensity process act independently and

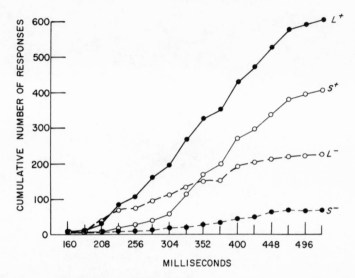

Fig. 6. Cumulative distributions of latency of response in the differential conditioning experiment.

follow different time courses in their effects on response evocation. Of particular interest are the two distributions for the $S^+ L^-$ condition where the directions of the two effects are opposed. Until about 330 msec, there are more responses to the unreinforced, loud stimulus than to the reinforced, soft stimulus, and it is only after this that response to the reinforced stimulus moves ahead. This certainly suggests something about the temporal relations of these processes. These latency data will provide a basis for a theoretical investigation of the relationships.

## 2. Differential Conditioning, Continuous Reinforcement, and Partial Reinforcement, Compared

Acquisition curves to the loud stimulus for the differential conditioning, 100 percent reinforcement, and 50 percent reinforcement conditions are presented in Fig. 7. Data from the original Illinois experiment are indicated by the points connected by solid lines. There were equal numbers of reinforcements to the loud tone in each of these three conditions, and the data are plotted in blocks of 10 reinforced trials. Of course, in the differential conditioning group, there were an equal number of interspersed unreinforced presentations of the soft tone, and in the partial reinforcement condition, there were equal nonreinforced presentations of the CS

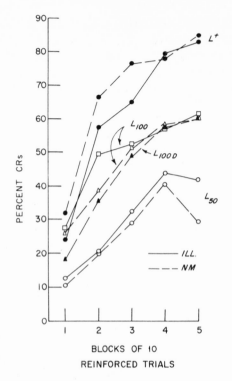

Fig. 7. Acquisition curves for continuous reinforcement, the positive stimulus in differential conditioning, and partial reinforcement. Data are for the loud stimulus.

itself. The difference between the $L_{100}$ and $L_{50}$ curves represents the acquisition decrement commonly found in partial reinforcement. Since these conditions were replicated, the replications have been analyzed together in terms of total CRs. The partial reinforcement decrement is significant. $F$ (1,76) = 13.5, $p < .001$. The effect of replication is not significant. $F$ (1,76) = .58, n.s. Also, the interaction of the replications by reinforcement condition is not significant. $F$ (1,76) = .004, n.s.

It is also apparent from Fig. 7 that there was substantially more responding to the loud tone when it was positive in the $L^+ S^-$ differential conditioning group than there was to the same stimulus in the straight 100 percent reinforcement condition. This is a finding of considerable importance and theoretical significance. It was largely because of this importance, and the fact that, from some points of view, this result is unpredictable that these conditions were replicated. The difference is statistically reliable. $F$ $(1,76) = 8.93$, $p < .005$. Neither the effect of replications nor the conditions $\times$ replications was significant. For replications: $F$ $(1,76) = .08$, n.s. For conditions $\times$ replications: $F$ $(1,76) = 1.07$, n.s.

While $L^+$ and $L_{100}$ received equal reinforcements, there is one difference in the procedures which logically could have produced the difference rather than the unreinforced presentations of the soft tone. This is the fact that the temporal distribution of reinforced trials was twice as great for $L^+$ as it was for $L_{100}$, due to the time required for $S^-$ trials. It is, therefore, logically possible that the effect was produced by something like a distributed practice effect. It is for this reason that condition $L_{100D}$ was run along with the replications. This 100% reinforcement condition had the same temporal distribution of reinforcement as $L^+$. However, it is apparent from Fig. 7 that this variable was ineffective and this is supported by statistical analysis. This condition did not differ significantly from the more massed 100% condition in either replication. It should be noted that, because of potentially possible population and other differences in the replications, the comparisons with the New Mexico conditions are the more appropriate. For Illinois and New Mexico respectively: $t$ $(38) = .82$, n.s.; and $t$ $(38) = .34$, n.s. It was also significantly below $L^+$ for both replications. Again for Illinois and New Mexico, respectively: $t$ $(38) = 2.15$, $p < .05$; and $t$ $(38) = 3.20$, $p < .01$. It now appears that we must conclude that the superiority of $L^+$ over the continuous reinforcement conditions is attributable to the unreinforced presentations of the soft tone.

Not only would most theoretical treatments of differential conditioning fail to predict this result, but they would, in fact, predict the reverse. For example, generalized inhibition from the nonreinforced soft tone would be expected to decrease response to $L^+$ when compared to a control. Of particular relevance here is the theory of Perkins (1953) and Logan (1954) which accounts for the effects of stimulus intensity entirely in associative terms. These effects are assumed to be the result of generalized inhibition from the unreinforced background intensity. Employing their concepts, the introduction of an additional nonreinforced stimulus, even closer in similarity to the CS than the zero background intensity, could have only one effect. The theory would unambiguously predict decreased responding to $L^+$. In view of the present and other accumulated evidence (Grice & Hunter, 1964; Grice, Masters, & Kohfeld, 1966), the writer believes that this theory now should be regarded as untenable. There are chiefly two things with which the

Perkins-Logan theory deals rather successfully, which have made the theory attractive, but which have been regarded mistakenly as strong evidence for it. One of these is the approximately equivalent effects of stimulus onset and cessation in response evocation. Here the writer believes that criterion effects apply equally to the detection of, and response to, both increases and decreases in stimulus intensity. It is not true that equal stimulus increases and decreases always result in equivalent behavior (e.g., see Grice *et al.,* 1966; Woodworth & Schlosberg, 1954, Ch. 2). Also the writer will shortly publish reaction time data where equal increases and decreases in auditory signal intensity have different consequences. The other fact commonly cited as evidence for the theory is that, under some circumstances, intensity effects occur only under conditions of differential reinforcement (Gray, 1965; Perkins, 1953). Under the present view, the intensity of a stimulus will have an effect only when it is the occasion for evoking a response. In other current language, the response must be under the control of the stimulus. Differential reinforcement is a way of bringing about this state of affairs.

Hull's theory would also fail to predict the present finding. The stimulus intensity dynamism (V) would be equal for $L^+$ and $L_{100}$ as should H. However, generalized inhibition from $S^-$ should introduce some tendency to reduce response to $L^+$. In a typical application of stimulus sampling theory, elements in common to the stimuli should be deconditioned as the result of $S^-$ trials. This should also result in decreased probability of response to $L^+$. It appears that some such process as adaptation, contrast, or criterion effect is necessary to account for these data. Analysis in terms of the present model will be presented later.

Comparable data comparing response to the soft tone are presented in Fig. 8. Here the picture is quite different than for the loud tone. Response to $S^+$ and $S_{100}$ is approximately equivalent and does not differ significantly. $t$ (38) = .43, n.s. If the effect found in the case of the loud tone were symmetrical, one would be led to expect less responding to $S^+$ than to $S_{100}$. Clearly, this did not occur. The analysis (Grice, 1968) of the Grice and Hunter LS condition, with both stimuli reinforced, indicated that the criterion was closer to that determined by the S condition alone than by the L condition alone. This also seems to be the case here. This suggests, in somewhat cognitive language, that the S "adopts" a criterion which will permit a substantial number of anticipatory responses to the weakest, reinforced stimulus. The result of this is an increased

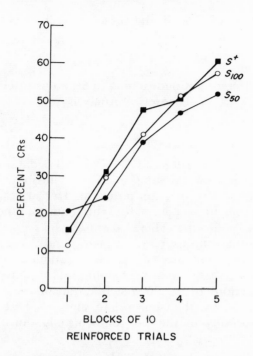

Fig. 8. Acquisition curves for continuous reinforcement, the positive stimulus in differential conditioning, and partial reinforcement. Data are for the soft stimulus. See text for further explanation.

number of responses to the stronger stimuli. It is clear, however, that criterion level is not determined only by the reinforced stimuli, because of the difference between $L^+$ and $L_{100}$ .

In the case of the partial reinforcement effect, the 50% group is only slightly below the 100% condition, and the difference is not significant. $t$ $(76) = .20$, n.s. The entire partial reinforcement experiment for both stimuli has also been analyzed. Here, the combined effect for both stimuli reaches only borderline significance. $F$ $(1.76) = 3.79$, $.10 > p > .05$. However, the significance of the effect for the loud stimulus only has been demonstrated in replication. The interaction of the reinforcement condition x stimulus intensity also reaches borderline significance. $F$ $(1,76) = 2.75$, $.10 > p > .05$. This suggested dependence of the acquisition partial reinforcement effect upon CS intensity should be pursued further, but, so far, this has not been done. It might be noted that a significant partial reinforcement decrement has not always been obtained — as in the very first such eyelid conditioning experiment (Humphreys, 1939).

## III. Differential Conditioning to Stimulus Intensity: Theoretical Analysis

### A. ACQUISITION OF DIFFERENTIAL CONDITIONING TO A STIMULUS INTENSITY DIFFERENCE

Our analysis (Grice, 1968) of Beck's (1963) data suggested that associative strength and stimulus intensity contribute independent, additive components to reaction potential. This suggests that quite a simple model might account for the data of the differential conditioning experiment. There are two sources of associative strength, resulting from reinforcement and nonreinforcement, respectively; and there are two levels of stimulus intensity. The suggested hypothesis is that probability of response in the four acquisition functions of Fig. 5 is a function of the suprathreshold strength produced by the appropriate sums of these components. This model is specified by the four following equations:

$$E_{L^+} = H^+ + V_L - T_1 \qquad (8)$$

$$E_{S^-} = H^- + V_S - T_1 \qquad (9)$$

$$E_{S^+} = H^+ + V_S - T_2 \qquad (10)$$

$$E_{L^-} = H^- + V_L - T_2 \qquad (11)$$

Equations (8) and (9) apply to the $L^+ S^-$ condition and Eqs. (10) and (11) apply to $S^+ L^-$. E refers to suprathreshold excitatory strength at any particular level of practice, the subscripts indicating loud or soft tone, positive or negative. These values are estimated by normal deviates $(z)$ corresponding to the percentage of CRs. $H^+$ is the associative strength resulting from reinforcement and is independent of stimulus intensity. At a given level of practice, it is the same for the two conditions, and, over trials, $H^+ = f(N)$ where $N$ is the number of reinforced trials. Presumably, this function should be of the form obtained in the previous example. $H^-$ is the associative strength associated with nonreinforcement, and, over trials, $H^- = f(\overline{N})$ where $\overline{N}$ is the number of nonreinforced trials. There is nothing within the present model to predict the form of this function, so it must be estimated from the data. In the present experiment, response to the negative stimulus increases monotonically, as it has in some others. However, in some experiments response to the negative stimulus has decreased. Following Hull, the symbol V, with the appropriate subscript, is the component of excitatory strength contributed by stimulus intensity. It should be remembered, however, that it does not have the multiplicative relationship of Hull's stimulus intensity dynamism. $T_1$ is the mean of the threshold distribution for the $L^+ S^-$ condition, and $T_2$ is the threshold for $S^+ L^-$. As in other within-$S$ experiments with irregular presentation of stimuli, a single threshold distribution may be ascribed to a group. Between groups, however, they are likely to differ, not only because of sampling error, but because they may also be affected by the experimental treatments. We shall assume normality, and, in this instance, equal variability. The analysis is based on the Illinois data which involve a complete orthogonal manipulation of stimulus intensity and differential reinforcement.

At first glance, the possibility of testing the adequacy of the model by estimation of all values in Eqs. (8)–(11) appears unpromising since there are four equations with six unknowns. However, with additional aids provided by the model, a solution is possible. The first step is estimation of the threshold values. From Eqs. (8)–(11) it is possible to derive:

$$T_1 - T_2 = [(E_{L^+} + E_{S^-}) - (E_{S^+} + E_{L^-})]/2 \qquad (12)$$

This is the value $d$ for the difference in the group thresholds and may be estimated for any block of trials for which percentages of CRs, and hence E, are available, or it may be estimated for all trials combined which is what was done here. Actually $d$ was quite constant over trials, and the estimates differ only slightly. Here, $d = T_1 - T_2 = -.114$. As in the previous example, we employ a working scale with zero at $(T_1 + T_2)/2$. Then, $T_1 = +.057$, and $T_2 = -.057$.

The next step is to estimate the magnitude of the intensity effect, and from the four basic equations we derive:

$$V_L - V_S = [(E_{L^+} - E_{S^+}) + (E_{L^-} - E_{S^-})]/2 \qquad (13)$$

This difference also differed only slightly over trials, and the estimate used is from all trials combined.[3] The estimate is:

$$V_L - V_S = .616 \qquad (14)$$

This is the difference in contribution to excitatory strength produced by the two stimulus intensities. The values of $V_L$ and $V_S$ cannot be

[3] It is possible to obtain this estimate and estimates of T by weighting each block of trials equally. However, it was necessary to have identical estimates here and in the analysis in the following section, and the one based on total responses is more appropriate there.

estimated separately from Eqs. (8)–(11), but must be obtained in another way.

The two functions relating associative strength to trials must now be obtained.

From Eqs. (8)–(11):

$$H^+ + (V_L + V_S)/2 = (E_{L^+} + E_{S^+})/2 \tag{15}$$

and

$$H^- + (V_L + V_S)/2 = (E_{L^-} + E_{S^-})/2 \tag{16}$$

Thus, the two estimates, which are obtainable from the data, are the values of the positive and negative associative strengths, plus a

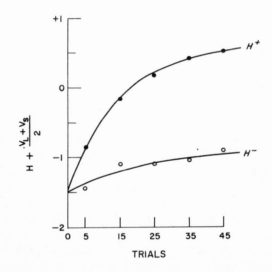

Fig. 9. Estimated functions for the growth of associative strength to positive and negative stimuli. The estimates are from loud and soft stimuli combined.

constant, which is the mean of the two intensity values. These two estimates were obtained for each of the five blocks of trials, and are the plotted points in Fig. 9. It is reasonable to assume that, prior to conditioning, the *associative* strength of the two stimuli should be equal and zero. The points of Fig. 9 estimate the two desired functions plus the constant which is their common intercept at $(V_L + V_S)/2$. Curve fitting was then carried out with the restriction that the functions have the same intercept, and this was by no means an unreasonable restriction. The function for reinforced stimuli was fitted by the same type of growth function used previously and resulted in the relation:

$$H^+ = 2.14(1 - 10^{-.0276N}) - 1.49 \qquad (17)$$

The function for nonreinforced stimuli was fitted with a function of the same type with a slower growth rate:

$$H^- = .63(1 - 10^{-.018\bar{N}}) - 1.49 \qquad (18)$$

The equations for the absolute contributions of $H^+$ and $H^-$ are merely Eqs. (17) and (18) with the intercept constant deleted.

From Eqs. (15)-(18) we may now conclude:

$$(V_L + V_S)/2 = -1.49 \qquad (19)$$

or

$$V_L + V_S = -2.98 \qquad (19a)$$

At this point, Eqs. (14) and (19a) may be solved simultaneously to provide the estimates of the two intensity effects separately. These values are $V_L = -1.182$, and $V_S = -1.798$. There should be no confusion regarding the fact that these values are negative, remembering that they are points on a scale with zero at an arbitrary location. The problem of absolute zero reaction potential need not be faced here.

All of the values necessary are now available for the use of Eqs. (8)-(11) in calculating predicted values of E. The procedure is now similar to that of the previous example. The appropriate values of V, T, and calculated values from the two H functions are used in the four equations to generate the four relations of E to the number of trials. These calculated values of suprathreshold excitatory strength are then transformed to predicted probability of response by use of the normal probability function. In this instance, under the assumption of equal variability, all conditions are in the same units. These calculated functions and the obtained data points are presented in Fig. 10. The predicted functions are based on seven, nonredundant parameters estimated from the data, so 13 degrees of freedom remain after fitting the model. It is clear that the course of differential conditioning is quite consistent with this simple additive model.

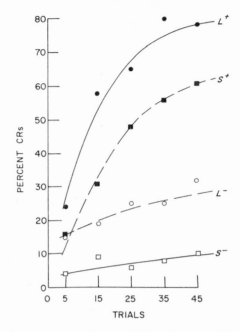

Fig. 10. Fit of the model to the acquisition data for differential conditioning to the stimulus intensity difference.

## B. Intratrial Events: The Temporal Course of Associative and Stimulation Effects

One of the useful functions of a model with analytic capabilities is in the exploration of data in an effort to formulate hypotheses about the nature of underlying processes. The cumulative distributions of latencies presented in Fig. 6 suggest the possibility of such an application here. As was pointed out, these distributions provide evidence that associative strength and stimulus intensity involve independent and different functions of time as determiners of response probability. An attempt will be made here to separate these functions and to determine their form.

In this effort we shall begin with the simple assumption that these functions provide estimates of the recruitment of suprathreshold excitatory strength within the interstimulus interval (ISI). In other words, a point on one of the functions at $t_i$ means, that by $t_i$, sufficient excitatory strength has developed to have produced $n$ responses. The basic rationale is that, following the onset of the CS, E undergoes a process of temporal recruitment. When, and if, E reaches the momentary threshold level, a response will occur. The value of E, as it depends upon the individual recruitment functions of its components, in combination with the mean and variability parameters of the threshold, will then generate the distribution of latencies.

The first step in the analysis is to transform the functions into the terms of the theory. Each point in the four distributions was first converted to percent CRs. These percentages were then transformed to their normal deviates. In this form, the four functions are now interpretable as indicating the cumulative temporal growth of E, suprathreshold excitatory strength. The model expressed in Eqs. (8)-(11) now applies to these values. The threshold values $T_1$ and $T_2$ are assumed to be constant throughout the ITI, and have already been estimated in the analysis of acquisition. The effect of the stimulus intensity difference $(V_L - V_S)$ may now be estimated throughout the scoring interval by the application of Eq. (13) to the four E values for each class interval. The resulting values are the points plotted in Fig. 11. These values provide an encouragingly orderly picture. This difference in E attributable to the difference in intensity increases from the beginning of the scoring interval to a maximum at about 280 msec, and then decreases to a terminal level at about 400 msec, where it is approximately constant for the remainder of the interval. Is it possible to infer the separate time functions for $V_L$ and $V_S$ from this difference function? This function would be obtained if the loud tone function $(V_L)$ increased rapidly to a constant level, and $V_S$ increased more slowly to a lower constant level. It is possible to derive linear approximations of these functions. The process was begun by fitting the three lines indicated in Fig. 11. The final constant level is located at $V_L - V_S = .616$, which is the value estimated in the previous analysis. This estimate was based on all trials combined, and is for the entire scoring interval, which is, of course, the final level of the cumulative distributions. The other lines are linear approximations of the increasing and decreasing segments of the difference function and were obtained by least squares fits to visually selected points. The increasing function was fitted to the first six points and has the equation:

$$V_L - V_S = .00335t - .052 \tag{20}$$

The decreasing segment was fitted to points 6-10 and is:

$$V_L - V_S = -.002t + 1.393 \tag{21}$$

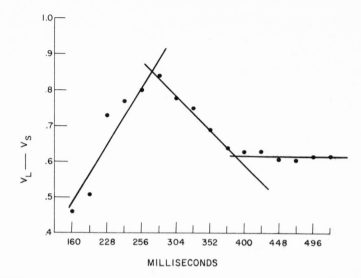

Fig. 11. The difference in E attributable to the stimulus intensity effect as a function of time within the scoring interval. See text for further explanation.

The individual recruitment functions for $V_L$ and $V_S$ may now be obtained. The values of $V_L$ and $V_S$ derived in the acquisition analysis are the constant terminal levels. The slopes and intersections of the three lines of Fig. 11 provide the remaining information necessary to determine these functions. The rising segments of the functions are:

$$V_L = .00535t - 2.627 \tag{22}$$

$$V_S = .002t - 2.567 \tag{23}$$

$V_L$ reaches a constant value of $-1.182$ at 270 msec, and $V_S$ reaches its terminal level of $-1.798$ at 389 msec. These two functions are presented in Fig. 12. This, then, represents the temporal recruitment of the stimulation component of excitatory strength as it depends upon the intensity of the stimulus.

Comparable time functions for the associative component of reaction potential must now be estimated, and for this purpose we return to the basic model. Eqs. (15) and (16) may be rewritten as follows:

$$H^+ = (E_L{}^+ + E_S{}^+)/2 - (V_L + V_S)/2 \tag{24}$$

and

$$H^- = (E_L{}^- + E_S{}^-)/2 - (V_L + V_S)/2 \tag{25}$$

The values of E are the points of the transformed cumulative distributions and are available for each class interval. The value $(V_L + V_S)/2$ may be computed for each interval from the functions of Fig. 12. Thus, from Eqs. (24) and (25) estimates of $H^+$ and $H^-$ may be obtained throughout the interval. The results of these

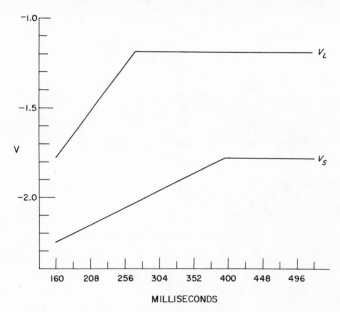

Fig. 12. Derived functions indicating the growth of the stimulus intensity component of E for each stimulus separately. See text for further explanation.

computations are the points plotted in Fig. 13. These computed points also indicate orderly functions, both increasingly monotonically with negative acceleration It is also of interest to note that the *difference* between them also increases monotonically — a situation quite different from the intensity difference function of Fig. 11, which had a maximum of 270 msec. The points under 200 msec are clearly not sufficiently reliable to be included in a curve-fitting analysis. They are based on such low probability values that a difference of one or two responses produces a large change in the $z$ transformation. It is assumed that the initial inversion is the result of this unreliability. This was dealt with, arbitrarily, by omitting the initial points from the curve-fitting solutions, and treating the H values below 200 for both functions as equal to that at the point of intersection. Both functions were then fitted by exponential growth

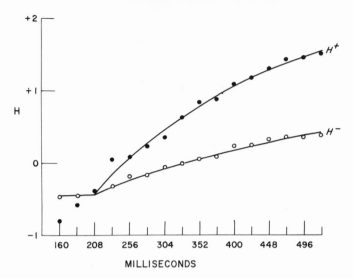

Fig. 13. Derived functions indicating the temporal recruitment of positive and negative associative strength ($H^+$ and $H^-$).

functions of time, which are the curves indicated in Fig. 13. The equations are:

$$H^+ = 6.501(1 - 10^{-.00181t}) - 4.201 \tag{26}$$

and

$$H^- = 2.692(1 - 10^{-.0013t}) - 1.692 \tag{27}$$

where $t$ is in milliseconds. Calculated values of H are not absolute, but indicate locations on the working scale.

This completes the analysis into hypothetical functions describing the temporal course of associative and stimulation factors as they affect response probability. This effort may be partially evaluated by use of these derived functions in attempting to reconstruct the distributions with which the derivation began. This is done with calculated values from Fig. 12 and Eqs. (26) and (27) together with the two threshold values. Eqs. (8)–(11) are then solved for each class interval, yielding predicted values of E for each condition. These E values are then converted to probability by the normal distribution. Presented in terms of percent CRs, the result of this reconstruction is given in Fig. 14, where the smooth curves are the calculated values. The fit is remarkably good and there are no serious distortions. It is clear that the data of this experiment are quite consistent with this analysis in terms of the model.

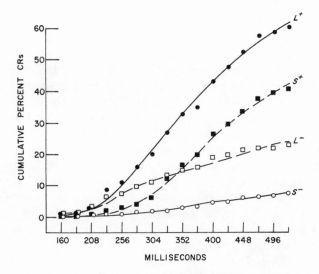

Fig. 14. Fit of the model to the cumulative latency distributions.

Analysis followed by successful resynthesis, without losing anything of value, leads to confidence in the validity of both processes. Probably the important thing here is that the component functions appeared in the analysis in orderly form. If this were not so, these functions could not have been well described by simple mathematical expressions and the accurate fit of the model to the data would have been impossible. While we are inclined to feel rather strongly that we have, indeed, learned something about the underlying processes, these are internal criteria. We should still ask, "Do these derived, hypothetical processes make other sense?"

The stimulus intensity functions imply that, in conditioning experiments in which CS intensity and ISI are both varied, the effect of intensity should be greater for shorter ISIs. This should be particularly true in the range of 300 msec. This prediction has been confirmed by Fishbein, Jones, and Silverthorne (1969). This is the only experiment of this type which the writer has found, but the approach should be carried further. In two experiments with a fixed, 500 msec ISI, the effect of CS intensity has been examined separately in early and late portions of the interval (Beck, 1963; Walker, 1960). In both of these experiments the intensity effect was more pronounced early in the interval. Thus, implications of the intensity functions do have some confirmation from other conditioning experiments.

It certainly appears that the intensity function should be related to the findings of experiments more directly concerned with the investigation of sensory processes. These functions are, indeed, very similar in form to those presented by John (1967) as representative of the "build-up" time of sensory processes. John presented these functions in the context of a theory of reaction time very similar to the writer's approach. It is tempting to speculate that the functions should be the same as, or at least closely related to, the results of psychophysical experiments concerned with the recruitment of loudness or the detection of auditory signals as a function of duration. The writer has no special competence in this area, and it will not be reviewed here. The present functions are not dissimilar in form from some of these findings, and are within the time range indicated by some. However, it is the writer's conclusion that there is not, at this time, a picture of sufficient consistency to provide the basis for much more than speculation about the relationship. Figure 12 is volunteered for consideration for membership in this literature.

The associative functions of Fig. 13 lead to one prediction which has been confirmed in the literature. The difference between these functions increases monotonically. This implies that if the ISI is varied, the degree of differential conditioning should increase with increasing duration of the ISI. This was the finding of Hartman and Grant (1962). In this connection it is interesting to speculate what would be the effect of different ISIs upon the form of these hypothetical processes. Since the intensity functions are presumed to depend on primary sensory processes, one is inclined to guess that they might be independent of the ISI. The data from simple conditioning experiments, however, suggest the possibility that the rate of rise of H may vary with the ISI, being the most rapid for short intervals and decreasing as intervals become longer. This is suggested by the longer latencies and greater variability of latency with longer intervals. This possibility is not necessarily so, however, since similar results could be produced by dependence of the threshold parameters upon the ISI. Also relevant here, is the typical finding that conditioning is optimal with an ISI of about .5 second or less. This has typically been viewed as an associative phenomenon and as evidence concerning the nature of learning. This is possible. However, it is also possible that it may be a criterion effect, resulting from an influence of the ISI upon the threshold. It is significant, and perhaps a bit discouraging, that even such a simple model as this points to such complexities and dangers in the interpretation of data. If one admits that differences in responsiveness and variability do play a role in behavior, then one is forced to conclude that experiments concerned with the ISI may have contributed no evidence at all concerning the purely *associative* efficacy of these arrangements. It is to be hoped that future research and theoretical analysis can answer this question.

Taken together, the sensory and habit functions are capable of predicting the kind of bimodal distributions of latencies sometimes seen in eyelid conditioning experiments (e.g., see Boneau, 1958). The notion is that there might be an initial mode associated with the initial phase of sensory recruitment and a second associated with the later rise of associative strength. Whether or not bimodality is obtained would depend upon the particular experimental parameters. It should be most likely with long ISIs, which agrees with Boneau's finding. Since the second mode would be dependent on the acquisition of habit strength, it should be most pronounced later in training. This also agrees with Boneau's result. The early mode did not vary in a systematic fashion with stage of training. Certainly, a question which should be investigated is the relation of the temporal functions to stage of conditioning. The present analysis was for all trials combined, and the terminal levels of the H functions were the averages over trials. Investigation of the possibility that either the V or H functions may not be invariant with trials will be difficult because of the low level of response early in the interval.

## C. Analysis of the Relations of Continuous Reinforcement to Differential and Partial Reinforcement

### 1. Differential Reinforcement

The initial reason for providing an experimental comparison of differential conditioning with continuous reinforcement was the possibility that unreinforced presentations of the negative stimulus might affect the threshold and thus influence the level of response to the positive stimulus in an interesting way. This type of result was limited to the $L^+ S^-$ condition, where response to $L^+$ was significantly elevated. It is possible to employ the results of the analysis of the acquisition curves for the differential conditioning experiment to evaluate the threshold interpretation of this finding. The implication of this view is that the associative function for $H^+$, i.e. Eq. (17), which was estimated for the differential conditioning experiment, should be the same for the continuous reinforcement condition, $L_{100}$. Also, the intensity component, $V_L$, should be the same for both conditions. It should then be possible to predict the acquisition curve for $L_{100}$, merely by the estimation of new threshold parameters from the data.

The procedure used for securing the necessary estimates was to first construct an REC, similar to Fig. 1, relating the acquisition curves of $L^+$ and $L_{100}$. The resulting function was linear, but the slope indicated that the SD of the $L_{100}$ threshold distribution was greater than that of the $L^+$ condition by a ratio of 1.674:1. This is a substantial difference and implied that an unequal $\sigma$ solution would be necessary in order to estimate the difference between their means. The value of $z$ for total CRs for $L_{100}$ was then converted to $L^+$ units by multiplying by 1.674. In this unit the $d = E_L - E_{L_{100}} = .274$. Since the $L^+$ threshold $(T_1)$ is .057, this places the threshold for $L_{100}$ $(T_{100})$ at +.351, on the scale of the original analysis. Equation (8) was then solved using $H^+$ values from Eq. (17), $V_L = -1.182$, and substituting the estimated value of $T_{100}$. This yielded an estimated acquisition curve for $E_{100}$, but in units of the original analysis. These values were then converted to units of the $L_{100}$ distribution by dividing by 1.674, and predicted probability values were obtained from the normal probability function. This predicted acquisition function is the middle curve of Fig. 15 plotted with the actual data points. The upper curve provides the comparison with $L^+$ and is the same as in Fig. 10.

It appears that differences in threshold parameters do adequately describe the difference between the continuous reinforcement condition and response to the positive stimulus in the differential reinforcement condition. The data are consistent with the interpretation that the unreinforced presentation of $S^-$ did lower the threshold and result in increased response to $L^+$. However, the analysis also indicates that variability was lower in the differential conditioning experiment. This was not predicted and is subject only to *post hoc* interpretation. Perhaps it is reasonable that the variety of stimulation or the process of differential reinforcement itself may produce a somewhat more consistently attentive $S$.

## 2. Partial Reinforcement

A similar analysis has been performed to test the hypothesis that the acquisition partial reinforcement decrement, obtained for the loud CS, can be attributed to threshold factors. The first step here, also, was to map the data into the analysis of the differential conditioning experiment by the construction of an REC relating them to the $L^+$ condition. In this case the slope indicated that the

SD of $L_{50}$ was also greater than that of $L^+$ by a ratio of 1.359:1. Thus the variability was intermediate between that of $L^+$ and $L_{100}$. In units of the $L^+$ distribution the threshold was at 1.022 on the original scale. This compares with .057 for $L^+$, and .351 for the continuous reinforcement condition. A solution similar to that above, using the $H^+$ function and $V_L$ from the preceding analysis yielded the predicted function for $L_{50}$ also presented in Fig. 15.

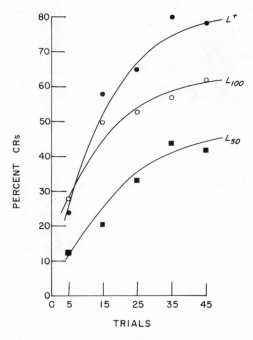

Fig. 15. Fit of the model to the three acquisition functions for the loud stimulus.

The fit is sufficiently adequate to establish the credibility of the hypothesis that the effect of nonreinforced presentations of the CS is to raise the reaction threshold. This is a nonassociative interpretation, and differs from some of the other possible views of this process. For example, a natural explanation from the point of stimulus sampling theory would be to assume that elements from the CS set become deconditioned on nonreinforced trials.

It is of interest now, to point out that the function for $H^+$, Eq. (17) has been used successfully in the prediction of four quite different acquisition curves. Originally derived from $L^+$ and $S^+$ in combination, it has now been found applicable to $L^+$, $S^+$, $L_{100}$, and

$L_{50}$. Within the context of the model, this implies that the acquisition of associative strength was uninfluenced by the experimental variables differentiating these conditions. While not presented, the model has also been applied to the data of the New Mexico replication of condition $L^+ S^-$ with the estimation of a single new parameter for the mean threshold level. For acquisition, the fit of $L^+$ was excellent. The form of the $S^-$ function was correct, but averaged about 3.5 percentage points too low, suggesting that the estimate of $V_S$, was slightly low for these data. The model also provided an excellent description of the latency distributions — $S^-$ again being slightly low.

## IV. Differential Conditioning and Drive Variables

### A. INTRODUCTION

Our recent analyses of simple conditioning experiments involving drive variables (Grice, 1971) were quite successful in indicating that these variables may be regarded as influencing the reaction threshold. The variables manipulated in these experiments were anxiety measured by the Manifest Anxiety Scale (MAS), UCS intensity, and threat of electric shock. There were also manipulations of these variables in combination. In no instance did the multiplicative theory (H x D) produce a better fit to the data than the threshold model. In other cases, the fit of the threshold theory was either superior, or the multiplicative theory was entirely inapplicable and provided no basis for comparison. One class of experiments not included were differential conditioning experiments involving drive manipulation. There is some interest in this kind of experiment, because the multiplicative theory has two predictions to make about them, one of which differs from that made by the threshold theory. The most obvious prediction is that with high drive there will be more responding to both the positive and negative stimuli than with low drive. This is not at issue here since it is also implied in the threshold model. The other prediction of the multiplicative theory is that the amount of differentiation, at least when measured in E units, will be greater under high drive conditions. This differs from the prediction of the threshold theory which implies that differentiation, measured in the same units, should be independent of drive. In order to evaluate the adequacy of the present model, it has been applied to the acquisition data of two experiments of this class. The analyses are similar to those of the preceding examples.

## B. Anxiety as a Threshold Variable

The first experiment analyzed is one by Spence and Farber (1954) in which differential conditioning was conducted with two groups of Ss selected on the basis of high and low scores on the MAS. The acquisition functions were not included in the original paper, but were later published by Rundquist, Spence, and Stubbs (1958). The CS was a tone of 500 Hz and the negative stimulus was 5000 Hz. The ISI was 500 msec, and the UCS was an air puff of 1.0 psi. There were 50 trials with each stimulus. In order to increase the stability of the trends, the present analysis is based on 20 trial moving averages of percent CRs.

To begin the analysis, data from the four acquisition functions are presented in Fig. 16 in the form of a single REC. Plotted in terms of the $z$, or E, transformation of percent CRs, values on the ordinate represent the acquisition functions for the high anxious (HA) group. On the abscissa are the corresponding values for the low anxious (LA) group. The solid points represent response to the positive stimulus and the four successive trial blocks are in order from left to right. The open circles are for the negative stimulus and also fall in

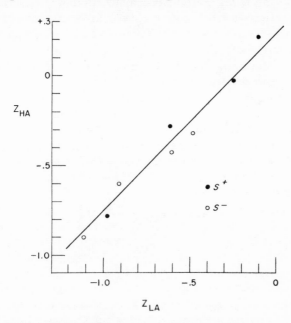

Fig. 16. REC relating high anxious ($Z_{HA}$) and low anxious ($Z_{LA}$) acquisition data from the Spence and Farber differential conditoning experiment.

the order of trial blocks from left to right. The entire plot is well fitted by a single linear function with a slope of unity. This, in itself, is a fact of considerable interest and significance. The multiplicative hypothesis requires that the slope be greater than one. That is, as strength is increased by training (H) along the responsiveness dimension, the effect of drive should increase along the drive difference dimension parallel to the minor diagonal. The fact that this is not so implies that the anxiety difference is not produced by a multiplicative relationship and that a solution in terms of the theory would be impossible. No multiplicative factor sensibly different from one could be estimated from the data. The fit does imply that the anxiety difference can be satisfactorily described by a constant, $d$, at all levels of training and for both the positive and negative stimuli. In the present model, this is the difference between the two threshold levels.

The fact that response to both the positive and negative stimuli falls along a single axis of response strength is also significant. It implies not merely that there are two, but that there are only two dimensions in the REC. For example, if there were an inhibitory factor, resulting from nonreinforcement, that was related to drive in a manner different from positive associative strength, two oblique functions would have resulted. This is a fact to be kept in mind in future theoretical efforts.

The unit slope of the REC implies that an equal variability solution is appropriate. The value of $d = T_{HA} - T_{LA}$ was computed by averaging the scale separation due to anxiety over all points of the REC. This is merely extending Eq. (6) to include both positive and negative stimuli. The value of $d$ was .256. If $(T_{HA} + T_{LA})/2 = 0$, $T_{HA} = -.128$, and $T_{LA} = +.128$. Estimates of positive and negative associative strength were made by the use of appropriate adaptations of Eq. (5).

$$H^+ = (E^+_{HA} + E^+_{LA})/2 \qquad\qquad (28)$$

and

$$H^- = (E^-_{HA} + E^-_{LA})/2 \qquad\qquad (29)$$

This was done for each block of trials and the resulting points are plotted in Fig. 17. The next step was to estimate the development of positive and negative associative strength by fitting a growth function to these points. Since stimulus intensity was not manipulated in this experiment, it was not necessary for V to enter the computations.

However, the stimuli were not counterbalanced, and probably were not strictly equal in loudness. For this reason the functions were not fitted with the restriction of equal intercepts, since this is where such an effect would appear. The two functions, represented by the smooth curves are:

$$H^+ = 1.977(1 - 10^{-.0182N}) - 1.557 \qquad (30)$$

and

$$H^- = 1.365(1 - 10^{-.0185\overline{N}}) - 1.515 \qquad (31)$$

The mean threshold levels are also indicated in Fig. 17, although the

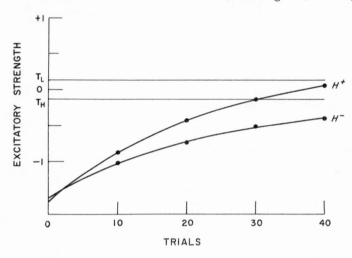

Fig. 17. Estimated functions describing the acquisition of positive and negative associative strength ($H^+$ and $H^-$) in the Spence and Farber experiment. See text for further explanation.

distributions are not. In this instance they are equal and their standard deviation, the unit of measurement, is one. The interpretation of this figure is the same as that of Fig. 2, but in this instance four acquisition functions in terms of probability of response are implied. These predicted functions are presented in Fig. 18, along with the data points obtained by Spence and Farber. The calculated functions describe the data with sufficient accuracy and detail to justify some confidence in the underlying assumptions. These were simply that the high and low anxious groups shared common functions for the growth of associative strength to the positive and negative stimuli and differed only in mean threshold level.

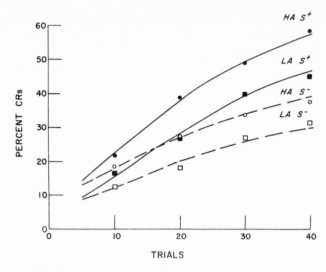

Fig. 18. Fit of the model to the Spence and Farber data on differential conditioning with groups differing in anxiety.

## C. DIFFERENTIAL CONDITIONING AND THE INTENSITY OF THE UCS

One of the experimental variables which our earlier analyses of simple conditioning indicated could consistently be interpreted as controling the threshold was the intensity of the UCS. This has also been studied in a differential conditioning experiment by Rundquist *et al.* (1958). These data provide the basis for another test of the threshold model with this kind of experiment. This experiment was similar to the Spence and Farber experiment. The same auditory stimuli were used and the ISI was 500 msec in the case of CS⁺. However, the CS⁻ was also followed by the UCS at 2500 msec. This stimulus was considered unreinforced since the scoring interval was limited to 500 msec. One group (S) was conditioned with an air-puff UCS of 2.0 psi. For the second group (W), the UCS was .3 psi. There were a total of 120 trials. The present analysis is based on blocks of 20 trials to each stimulus.

The REC relating the acquisition functions of Group S to those of Group W is presented in Fig. 19. Again the data for both stimuli are well described by a single straight line with a slope of one. Thus, the remarks made about this state of affairs in the anxiety experiment are also applicable here to UCS intensity The remainder of the analysis is the same. The value $d = T_S - T_W = .412$. Thus, $T_S = -.206$ and $T_W = +.206$. The estimated functions for $H^+$ and $H^-$ and the

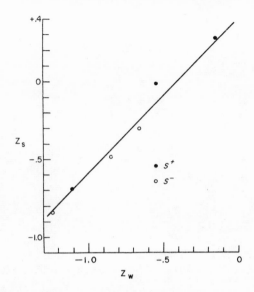

Fig. 19. REC relating acquisition data for strong UCS ($Z_S$) to that for weak UCS ($Z_W$). Data from Rundquist, Spence, and Stubbs.

points from which they were estimated are presented in Fig. 20. The equations are:

$$H^+ = 1.86(1 - 10^{-.014N}) - 1.43 \qquad (32)$$

and

$$H^- = .95(1 - 10^{.0232\bar{N}}) - 1.43 \qquad (33)$$

In this instance the equal intercepts appeared so naturally that the restriction was retained. The fit of the data to the calculated acquisition functions is presented in Fig. 21. The threshold theory of UCS intensity effects is again supported by this fit.

These results are consistent with those of our previous analyses of simple conditioning experiments with UCS intensity variation (Grice, 1971). Probably, the most significant thing here is the implication that habit growth is independent of UCS intensity. Spence believed it to be a determinant of habit strength (e.g., see Trapold & Spence, 1960). The evidence he accumulated was rather convincing, but was not conceived with threshold theory in mind. Of course, our analyses do not prove that habit growth was unaffected by UCS intensity, but they are certainly consistent with this. The writer believes that this question should be reopened, both experimentally and theoretically.

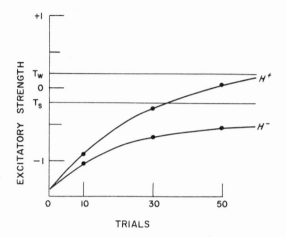

Fig. 20. Derived functions indicating the acquisition of positive and negative associative strength (H⁺ and H⁻) in Rundquist, Spence, and Stubbs experiment.

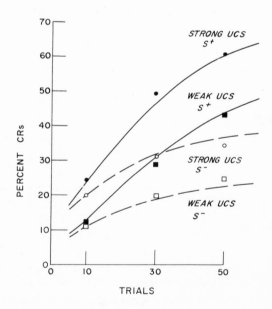

Fig. 21. Fit of the model to data from Rundquist, Spence, and Stubbs experiment on differential conditioning with variation in UCS intensity.

The truth is we really do not yet know enough about the properties of the threshold concept to evaluate the relevance of Spence's evidence to this interpretation. For example, the writer now doubts the applicability of crossover and other shift designs. While the effects of the threshold are assumed to be nonassociative insofar as the CS-UCS relation is concerned, there is certainly no reason to assume that it is independent of S's history. In fact, the evidence is clearly to the contrary.

Taken together, these two analyses of differential conditioning complement and extend our previous findings supporting a threshold interpretation of motivational variables.

## V. Stimulus Generalization and Drive

### A. A REEVALUATION OF THE NEWMAN AND GRICE EXPERIMENT

A stimulus generalization experiment conducted in the writer's laboratory (Newman & Grice, 1965) was interpreted as supporting the multiplicative theory of habit and drive. In view of the doubts now cast upon that hypothesis by our analyses of conditioning experiments, it now seems appropriate that these data should be reconsidered from the point of view of the threshold theory. Such an analysis will also have the advantage of providing a start, at least, on the task of relating the model to a dependent variable other than probability of response — in this case, response latency. The Newman and Grice experiment was conducted with rats who were trained to obtain food by approaching a white, circular disk of 79 cm$^2$. Generalization tests were conducted with separate groups of Ss, either to the training stimulus (CS) or to one of three smaller test stimuli, which were 50, 32, and 20 cm$^2$ in size. Original training was conducted with 24 hours of food deprivation. In testing, high drive animals were under 48 hours of deprivation and low drive animals were under 12 hours. There were eight groups in all, with 15 Ss per group. The response measure most directly related to the theoretical predictions was the speed of the first test response.

As Spence (1958) has pointed out, the multiplicative theory predicts that generalization gradients, obtained under high drive conditions, should be higher and of steeper slope than those obtained under low drive conditions. This is just what was obtained in the experiment. In fact, when a function was fitted to one of the gradients, a simple multiple of it provided a good fit to the other.

Given Spence's (1956) assumption that E and speed of response evocation are linearly related, this is good evidence for the multiplicative theory. The interpretation depends, however, upon the validity of this assumption, and, actually, there has never been any strong evidence for it. At one time, Spence (1954) derived the relation from theoretical considerations. Later, though, he abandoned a key assumption which had made the derivation possible (Spence, 1956, p. 100). At this point, the linear relation of E and speed reverted to the status of stimple assumption. As part of a new analysis of the Newman and Grice data, we shall attempt to evaluate its validity.

The relationships of the present theory are in terms of hypo-thetical excitatory strength, and, so far, there is no basis for assuming any particular mathematical function relating it to response latency or speed. However, an approach to investigating this relationship is possible. In this experiment, there are eight experimental groups for which suprathreshold excitatory strength (E) must be estimated. E is the algebraic sum of H, a parameter for a condition, and a normally distributed threshold value. This is the kind of theoretical variable for which Thurstone scaling procedures are appropriate. If we merely assume that latency is monotonically related to E, then a scaling operation applied to latency should produce a valid scale of E. This is similar to the approach of Hull, Felsinger, Gladstone, and Yamaguchi (1947). In the present instance, the latency data have been scaled by the method of categorical judgment applied to ranked data. Latencies of all 120 Ss were ranked, and reduced to five categories in the solution. The solution used is described by Torgerson (1958) as Class II, Condition D, which involves the assumption of equal variance. Parenthetically, it is of methodological interest to note that a preliminary solution using only two categories with an arbitrary boundary produced nearly the same result. The obtained scale values for the eight experimental groups are presented in Table I. To

Table I

Categorical Scale Values for Each Condition

| Stimulus area (cm$^2$) | Hours of deprivation | |
|---|---|---|
| | 48 | 12 |
| 79 | 1.637 | .593 |
| 50 | .690 | .023 |
| 32 | −.053 | −.984 |
| 20 | −.554 | −1.354 |

facilitate later analyses, the zero point of the scale is at the mean. Interpreted in terms of the present model, the unit of the scale is the SD of the threshold distribution which is assumed to be equal for the high and low drive conditions. Each scale value estimates:

$$E = H_i - T_j \qquad (34)$$

where $H_i$ is the generalized associative strength of a particular test stimulus, and $T_j$ is the threshold determined by either 48-hour or 12-hour deprivation. From Table I and the eight equations implied by Eq. (34), $d = T_{12} - T_{48} = .860$. Also, $(T_{48} + T_{12})/2 = 0$, and $T_{48} = -.430$, and $T_{12} = +.430$.

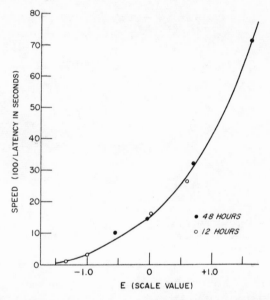

Fig. 22. Median speed of each group in the Newman and Grice experiment as a function of E value derived from categorical scaling.

Evaluation of the relative adequacy of the multiplicative theory and the threshold model for these data is approached from several points of view. First, is a direct examination of the relation between response speed and the scale values of E. In Fig. 22, median speed is plotted as a function of the scale values of the eight experimental groups. It is obvious that the function is not linear and the fitted smooth function is represented by the exponential equation:

$$\text{Speed} = 21.43 \times 10^{.341E} - 6.4 \qquad (35)$$

Unfortunately, this function has not been derived from theory and is purely descriptive. However, considerable doubt is cast on any interpretation of the data based on the assumption of a linear relationship. It was upon the basis of this assumption that the analysis of Newman and Grice was based.

The eight scale values are presented in a different way in Fig. 23. Here the 48-hour scale values are plotted as a function of the

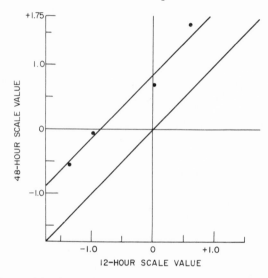

Fig. 23. Forty-eight hour scale value as a function of the corresponding 12-hour scale value for each test stimulus in the Newman and Grice generalization experiment.

corresponding 12-hour values, each point representing the data for one of the test stimuli. The top point is that for the CS and those descending to the lower left are for the progressively less similar stimuli. While these values are from the scaling procedure, this figure closely resembles the REC functions previously considered in both form and interpretation. This includes its bidimensionality. Parallel to the major diagonal, is the response strength axis determined by varying amounts of generalization. The orthogonal dimension is the difference produced by the two drive levels. The points are fitted by a straight line with a slope of one, which approximates a line of best fit. This implies that the effect produced by the drive variable is approximately constant at all levels of generalization. As in the previous examples, this is contrary to the expectation of the multiplicative theory which implies that the difference due to drive should increase with associative response strength. Since the slope is one, both intercepts are at the value of $d$, just as they would be $d'$ in an ROC. A possible model for this "REC" will be presented later. Meanwhile, it is sufficient to indicate that it is more consistent with an additive than with a multiplicative relation of generalization and drive.

The two generalizations gradients, in E units, are presented in Fig. 24. Since the data did not provide a particularly good fit to any

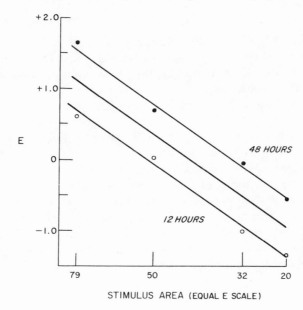

Fig. 24. Newman and Grice generalization gradients in scale units of E.

simple function, they are presented in linear form with an equal-E spacing of the stimuli. This scaling of the stimuli was performed with respect to the means of the two drive levels for each stimulus. These means lie on the middle line of the figure. The procedure was the simple graphical method described by Anderson (1970). The upper and lower lines which pass through the points are parallel to the line joining the means, and are located ± 1/2 $d$ from it. That is, they are parallel lines separated by the distance $d$. The fits of these lines to the points are nearly identical to those of least square lines of best fit. This picture is again contrary to the multiplicative theory which predicts that these lines should systematically converge as generalized response strength decreases. This analysis is consistent with the

threshold model or other possible additive models. In terms of the
threshold model, the line joining the means is the estimated function
for generalized habit strength (H) from Table I, and Eq. (34). The
other two functions are the estimated functions for E, suprathreshold excitatory strength. This implies that the eight scale values
are well described by the relation of Eq. (34) when the four values of
H and the value of $d$ are estimated from them.

## B. THE RELATION OF SCALE VALUES TO THE DECISION MODEL

Using the values from the scaling procedure and Eq. (34), it is
possible to construct a decision axis for this experiment in the same
way, and of the same form, as that presented in Fig. 3 for the
Nicholls and Kimble experiment on the effect of instructions on
eyelid conditioning. This has been done, and the resulting axis is
presented in Fig. 25. The two threshold distributions are separated
by the calculated distance, $d$. The vertical lines represent the
calculated values of H for the CS and the three generalized stimuli.
The four values of H mark off eight areas of the two distributions
corresponding to the eight experimental conditions. These areas
estimate a probability that the threshold is below the associative
strength of the stimulus, and, hence, a probability related to response
evocation. But the response measure here was not all-or-none
occurrence, but latency, and the interpretation of these predicted
response probabilities is not immediately obvious.

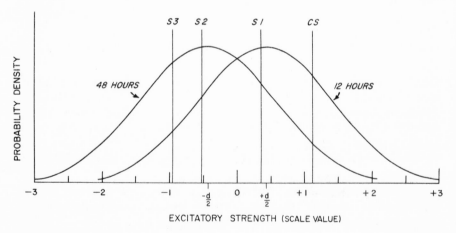

Fig. 25. Decision axis for Newman and Grice experiment based on estimates
of H and $d$ calculated from scale values.

In order to arrive at the proper interpretation of the predicted probabilities, it is necessary to consider further the meaning of the scale values produced by the ranking procedure. The scale value for each condition indicates the location of the distribution of that condition in relation to the general distribution for all groups combined. The scale values used here are actually $z$ values expressing the deviations of the means of each condition from the mean of the total scale. Since the scale was based on ranks, the latency corresponding to the mean of the scale is the general median. The areas of Fig. 25 predict the probability of response faster than the general median latency which was 5.7 seconds. The accuracy with which this prediction is achieved is a test of the *combined* adequacy of three basic assumptions or restrictions imposed by the model. These are (*a*) the two component model of habit and threshold with the relation described by Eq. (34); (*b*) the assumption of normality; and (*c*) the assumption of equal variance. An evaluation of the prediction is indicated in Fig. 26. The ordinate is the obtained

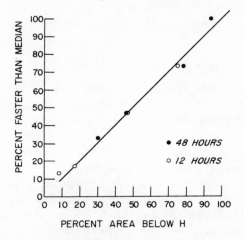

Fig. 26. Percent of each group faster than the general median as a function of the area of the normal threshold distribution below H.

percentage of response faster than the general median for each condition and the abscissa is the area of the normal distributions below the four H values. The line drawn through the points is simply the line of equality, $P_o = P_c$. There are no discrepancies from equality greater than that produced by a single $S$.

This internal consistency of the data with the assumptions of the model appears to justify some confidence in our interpretation of the relation between generalization and drive, and in the evidence for the nonlinear relation of E and response speed. It also provides an additional basis for understanding Fig. 23. This may now be regarded as an REC based on probability of response faster than the median. Its underlying model is the decision axis of Fig. 25.

It is of historical interest to note that, almost 25 years ago, Hull presented a figure which could now be called an ROC or REC (Hull *et al.*, 1947, Fig. 3). This figure was based on paired comparison scaling of learning data, and, in it, data for one trial were plotted on a function of another trial. The value of *d* for this figure was the basis of Hull's estimate of the E difference between the two trials. The orthogonal dimension was habit growth over all trials. This figure was based on an earlier suggestion of Thurstone (1927a) that such a plot provided a test of the assumptions of normality and homogeneous variance. At that time, this was regarded purely as a test of scaling assumptions and no criterion or threshold model was involved. It is well for the modern reader to keep in mind that, while these concepts provide a sensible and productive model, they are not a necessary part of the interpretation of an ROC.

## C. LATENCY AND THE RECRUITMENT OF HABIT

It is obvious that the present model deals most handily with response measures which are all-or-none, and whose frequency can be directly considered as estimates of response probability. To achieve generality, however, it must be extended to consider other response measures. Response latency, employed in this experiment, is one of the most obvious of these. Our analysis of the differential conditioning experiment suggested that the growth or recruitment of habit within the trial was a major determinant of latency. In the Newman and Grice animal experiment the latencies were sufficiently long, that it seems unlikely that latency distributions are influenced by the initial growth of a purely sensory component, although stimulus intensity may still be involved as a constant. This suggests that in situations such as this the temporal recruitment of habit in combination with the threshold distribution may be the primary determinant of latency. We believe that this is likely to turn out to be the correct approach. Spence (1954), in his derivation of the relation between speed and E, assumed that H was constant for the duration of a trial and deduced an expected value of latency upon the basis of a rapid fluctuation of the oscillation component (O). However, this implies an exponential distribution of latencies — an incorrect prediction.[4] Approaches which have been more successful in the prediction of latency distribution have assumed a recruitment process in one form or another. Bush and Mosteller (1955) suggested recruitment with respect to components of the response itself until it reached the scoring criterion. La Berge (1962), in the context of stimulus sampling theory, suggested that conditioned elements sampled were accumulated until their number reached a criterion value resulting in response. Both of these approaches differ from the present one in that the probabilistic component was attributed to properties of the recruitment process itself, rather than to criterion variability. However, their success in the prediction of latency distributions suggests that the assumption of a recruitment process is the correct approach.

The present model contains no assumptions leading to a prediction of the specific form which the temporal recruitment of habit might take. On common sense grounds, we might expect it to be some sort of negatively accelerated growth function beginning at, or shortly after, exposure to the stimulus. This is what was indicated in the eyelid conditioning data. In the absence of a specific prediction, an alternative approach is to utilize the latency distributions in an effort to infer the nature of this function. Confidence in the outcome of such an analysis is encouraged by the remarkable consistency with which the model's assumptions apply to the present set of data.

This analysis is similar to that of the differential conditioning data, and begins with the construction of the cumulative distributions of latency for the eight conditions. This was done for successive fifths of each distribution. (Because of a special procedure used by Newman and Grice, it was not possible to use data with latencies greater than 30 seconds. In order to obtain both latency and resistance to extinction measures, they terminated the trial and began a new one if no response had occurred in 30 seconds. Longer latencies were cumulated until a response occurred. While this latency measure is monotonically related to E, it is not appropriate as an index of habit recruitment. Since there were no points falling between 20 and 30 seconds, the analysis is actually terminated at 20 seconds.) The cumulative frequencies of the eight distributions were converted to percent response, and then to the corresponding normal deviates. At this point the functions indicated the cumulative growth

---

[4] This deficiency of Spence's derivation was originally pointed out to the writer by F. A. Logan. The rapid oscillation of O within the trial was the assumption later abandoned by Spence (1956).

of E, suprathreshold excitatory strength, with respect to each group's individual threshold.

The next step was to reduce these eight distributions to a single array. According to the model, there should be only four habit recruitment functions, one for each stimulus; and there should be only two thresholds, one for each drive level. The reduction was accomplished by transforming all of the data to the original scale of Table I which was used in the preceding analyses. It will be remembered that on this scale the thresholds were at $\pm\frac{1}{2}d$, i.e. $T_{48} = -.43$ and $T_{12} = +.43$. The scale transformation was made simply by subtracting the constant .43 from all points in the 48-hour distributions and adding it to all points in the 12-hour distributions. This moves the two functions for each stimulus together by the distance, $d$, the estimated size of the drive effect. The resulting points derived from the eight distributions are plotted in Fig. 27. The solid points indicate data from the high drive condition, and open points are from the low drive groups. While there is some irregularity, it should be kept in mind that each point represents the addition of only three $S$s to the cumulative distributions. The fact is that, in a fairly convincing manner, the high and low drive conditions combined describe a single function for each of the four stimuli. This supports the implication of the theory that there should be a single habit recruitment function for each stimulus. The result is also significant because of the fact that units involved in the derivation came from different sources. The value $d$ is in the $\sigma$ unit derived from the categorical scaling procedure with the application of Eq. (34). The units, in which the individual distributions were plotted, were those indicated by the application of the $z$ transformation to each distribution separately. Under the assumptions of the model and the scaling procedure, these units should be the same. Figure 27 suggests that they are, in fact, interchangeable. This is an additional confirmation of the consistent picture indicated by the analysis of Figs. 25 and 26.

The habit recruitment functions have been estimated by fitting exponential growth functions of time to the data for each of the four stimuli. Probably the most reasonable assumption to make is that it is the asymptote of habit recruitment which is determined by the amount of generalized associative strength and that the rate of approach is constant. For this reason the restriction of an equal exponential constant was imposed in fitting the four equations. However, we have not achieved exactly equal growth rates because we did not also impose the restriction of equal intercepts. While this could have been done with little change in the appearance of the fit, it was not done for several reasons. Aside from technical difficulties, it would not be justified if there are small stimulus intensity differences. Also, it seems likely that the proper common origin of the curves is not at the intercept but at some time slightly greater than zero. An analysis of such a degree of refinement really requires more precise data, based on a larger $N$. The equations of the four fitted functions are:

$$H_{79} = 4.688(1 - 10^{-.09t}) - 2.111 \tag{36}$$

$$H_{50} = 3.829(1 - 10^{-.09t}) - 2.296 \tag{37}$$

$$H_{32} = 2.535(1 - 10^{-.09t}) - 2.266 \tag{38}$$

$$H_{20} = 2.109(1 - 10^{-.09t}) - 2.410 \tag{39}$$

The two threshold levels are also indicated in Fig. 27. To summarize,

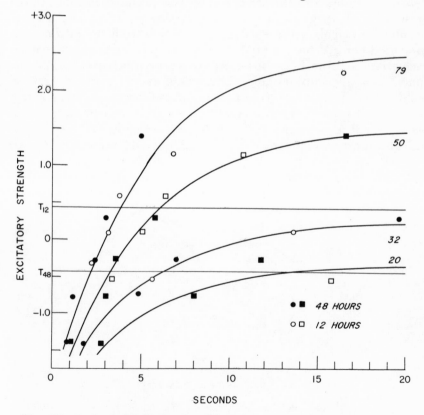

Fig. 27. Derived functions describing the temporal recruitment of habit strength for each test stimulus.

this hypothesis states that habit grows following the onset of the trial. When the momentary threshold of an $S$ is reached, a response occurs. The momentary threshold is a function of $S$'s mean level of responsiveness and his own variability. This model suggests that the relation between latency and measures of E is considerably more complex than Spence's assumption. It implies that latency is an increasing function of the ratio of the amount habit must grow in order to reach the threshold to the maximum it is approaching. Thus, latency is determined not only by the difference between habit and the threshold, but by their absolute level as well

Analysis of the decision axis in the preceding section indicated that the original scale values measured each condition with respect to the general median latency, 5.7 seconds. The analysis also indicated that the scale could be treated as values of E and analyzed into associative and threshold components with the use of Eq. (34). Figure 27 shows the threshold values, and purports to indicate the growth of H with respect to time. It should, therefore, also be possible to calculate these values of H and E from the information presented here. Values of H at 5.7 seconds have been calculated for each stimulus from Eqs. (36)–(39). These are plotted in Fig. 28 as a function of the corresponding H values obtained from the original scale values by Eq. (34). The straight line indicates equality, and it is seen that the values are essentially the same. The eight scale values were treated as suprathreshold excitatory strength, $E = H - T$. This has also been computed from Fig. 27 at 5.7 seconds for each

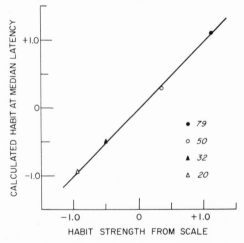

Fig. 28. Values of H at 5.7 seconds calculated from the recruitment functions as a function of H calculated from scale values by Eq. (34).

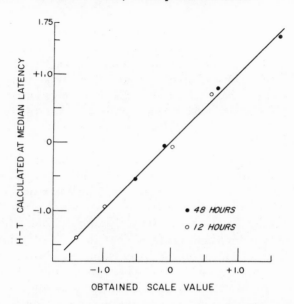

Fig. 29. Values of suprathreshold excitatory strength calculated from recuitment functions at 5.7 seconds as a function of corresponding initial scale values.

condition. These values are plotted in Fig. 29 as a function of the original scale values, and, again, the two estimates of E are approximately equal.

The present analysis is only beginning in the task of establishing a relation between the decision model and response latency. The habit recruitment hypothesis is just that and no more. However, the high degree of internal consistency in these applications suggests that it may be a fruitful approach in the analysis of other instrumental learning situations.


## VI. Conditioning Curves for Individuals

All of the analyses in terms of the threshold model, which have been presented so far, have been of data for groups of Ss. However, the model is also intended to be a theory of individual behavior, and it is clearly desirable to extend the application to this area. This is more difficult because of the instability of data based upon individual Ss, and fits of the quality obtainable with groups are not to be expected. However, because of the importance of the problem, we have attempted to determine if the assumptions of the model are capable of describing the conditioning curves of individuals to at least a reasonable degree. The data analyzed were collected in the writer's laboratory by Walker (1960). This was a simple eyelid conditioning experiment with human Ss. For the group analyzed, the CS was a 1000 Hz tone with a sensation level of 30 dB. The UCS was an air puff of .5 psi. The ISI was .5 second. There were 80 conditioning trials.

The basic assumption here is that individual differences in conditioning are primarily attributable to differences in responsiveness, as reflected in the parameters of the individual's threshold distribution. These parameters are the mean, indicating the average level of responsiveness and the SD reflecting the individual's degree of variability. We have also assumed that the rate of habit growth is the same for all Ss. This is an unusual assumption, but, in the writer's opinion, not an unreasonable one. There is no compelling reason to believe that, in normal human adults, there should be significant individual differences in a task so simple as learning to associate a tone and a puff of air. In any case, the assumption can be at least partially evaluated by the results of the analysis.

The solution to this problem is essentially the same as that of our initial example involving the Nicholls and Kimble experiment on the effect of instructions. Groups are replaced by individuals. The task is to obtain estimates of the threshold parameters for each S, and of the habit growth function assumed to be common to all. The analysis was based on blocks of 16 trials. There were 40 Ss, in the group from Walker's experiment; however, it was possible, with the methods used, to analyze the data for only 34 of these. Two Ss who made only two and three CRs were eliminated. The remaining four Ss eliminated were ones who showed no increase in response frequency during conditioning. While, under the assumptions of the model it is perfectly reasonable that such cases should occur, it was not possible to obtain variability estimates for them. This state of affairs would be expected sometimes with Ss at the extremes of variability. At the low extreme it would be possible for an S to be at asymptotic performance in the first block of trials. On the other hand, if variability were very large in relation to habit growth, only random performance might appear. Since the evidence from the remaining 34 Ss indicated that the distribution of SDs was positively skewed, this latter explanation is regarded as the more probable. The difficulty here is that the effect of habit growth must not be totally obscured by variability if estimation is to be based on an REC. Slopes of zero order do not yield meaningful estimates.

Frequencies of response for each $S$ were expressed as percent CRs in each trial block, and, as in the preceding analyses, were converted to normal deviates. These $z$ values then indicated suprathreshold excitatory strength (E) with respect to each $S$'s mean threshold level, and in units of the SD of his personal threshold distribution. It was then necessary to transform the data for all $S$s into common units, in order to continue the solution. This was accomplished by transforming the data for each $S$ into units of the between-$S$ distribution. The growth of E, in terms of between-$S$ units, was estimated just as previously done for group data. The mean percentage of CRs for each block of trials was converted to normal deviates. RECs were then constructed relating the growth of E for each of the 34 $S$s to the group data. As might be anticipated, some of these were fairly erratic, but all contained evidence of a linear trend, and a mutual regression line was fitted to each. Naturally, for some $S$s there were zero and 100 per cent values which could not be transformed to $z$. Estimated values for such points were obtained by extrapolation. Since the RECs were constructed with group data as the abscissa and the individual as the ordinate, the slopes of the regression lines estimated the ratio of the group $\sigma$ to that of the individual. Since we ordinarily believe within-$S$ variability to be less than that between individuals, the variability interpretation of these functions is encouraged by noting that the slope was greater than one in 31 of the 34 instances. The alternative interpretation would have to be that the average rate of learning for the group was slower than that of the individuals comprising it.

The data for each $S$ were next converted into the theoretical units of the between-$S$ distribution. The values for the five blocks of trials for each $S$ were multiplied by the slope of the REC. At this stage, all data were in common E units, and it was now possible to estimate the growth function for H, and the value of T for each $S$. The data may be arranged in a Trial Blocks (5) × $S$s (34) table. Each entry would now be, in terms of the model:

$$E_{ij} = H_i - T_j \tag{40}$$

$E_{ij}$ is suprathreshold excitatory of $S_j$ on trial $i$. $H_i$ is the habit on trial $i$, and $T_j$ is the threshold of $S_j$. These are values on a scale where zero is the mean of $T_j$. In estimating the values of T, it was assumed that each block of trials contains an estimate of T, and they

**G. Robert Grice**

were weighted equally. From Eq. (40) it can be shown that the threshold can be estimated by subtracting $S$'s mean from the general mean.

$$T_j = \left[ \sum_1^{34} \sum_1^5 E_{ij}/(34 \times 5) \right] - \left( \sum_1^5 E_{ij}/5 \right) \tag{41}$$

Values of H disappear in this derivation. Since the mean of $T_j$ is zero, values of $H_i$ are estimated simply by the mean of each block of trials.

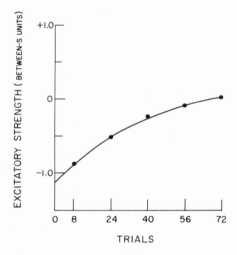

Fig. 30. Estimated habit growth function for 34 Ss from Walker's data.

The estimated values of H are plotted in Fig. 30, where the fitted function for habit growth is represented by the equation:

$$H = 1.39(1 - 10^{-.0108N}) - 1.14 \tag{42}$$

It would be possible to add to Fig. 30, 34 horizontal lines indicating the mean thresholds of each $S$, and also their distributions with appropriate SDs. This would portray the model in a form identical to that of Fig. 2, and indicate the nature of the computations required to obtain the predicted conditioning curves for each $S$. Using Eq. (42) for H and the estimates of T for each $S$, functions indicating the growth of E were computed by Eq. (40). These functions were in between-$S$ units. In order to obtain the predicted values of $p$, these suprathreshold values of E were returned to units of the individual $S$ distribution by dividing by the slopes of the RECs. The final predicted functions and the obtained data points in terms of percent CRs are presented in Figs. 31a and 31b.

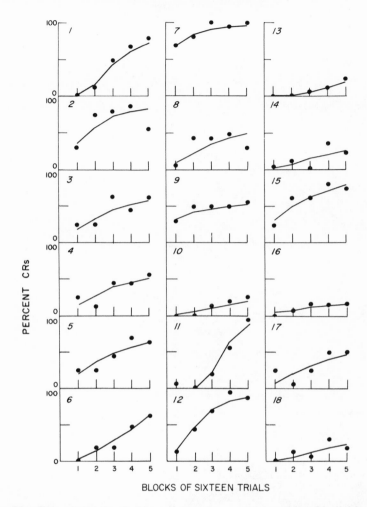

Fig. 31a. Fits of the threshold model to the acquisition data of individual Ss.

Considering the unreliability of individual data, it is the writer's impression that the fits are about as good as could be expected. When the experiment is viewed as a Ss x Trials analysis of variance the fit of the model to the individual Ss accounts for 90% of the total variance. Since 71 constants were estimated there remain 98 degrees of freedom. In terms of variance components the fit accounts for essentially 100 percent of the variance due to Ss and of variance due to trials. Statistically, neither of these is a remarkable achievement since transformations of the S means were used in estimating T,

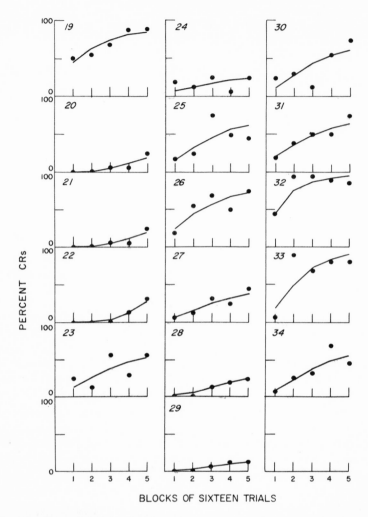

Fig. 31b. Fits of the threshold model to the acquisition data of individual Ss.

and three constants were estimated in the habit function. However, the habit function did fit, and, in principle, the use of the normal assumption and the calculations implied by the model could have introduced systematic distortions. Obviously, this did not occur. That it did not, is well illustrated by the group conditioning curve presented in Fig. 32. Here, the smooth curve connects points which are the means of the predicted percentages for all Ss. The plotted points are the obtained mean percentages.

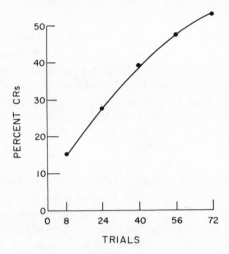

Fig. 32. Group conditioning curve for the 34 *S*s. The line connects the means of the estimates for each *S*, and points are the obtained mean percentages. Residuals are all less than one percent.

The variance component which reflects individual differences in the *shape* of the separate functions is the *S*s x Trials interaction. The fits account for 44 percent of this variance. Of course, error variance is heavily weighted in this component. Since we have no independent estimate of error, we cannot fully evaluate this achievement. However, inspection of the individual graphs suggests, with a few possible exceptions, that the residuals are related more to irregularity of the data, than to systematic errors in goodness of fit. We are encouraged to believe that the model has accounted for a rather high proportion of the nonerror variance. One interesting observation is the wide variety in the forms of the individual functions produced by variation in the two parameters. A discussion of the relation of the form of conditioning curves to these parameters has been given previously (Grice, 1971). In general, the slope and the asymptote are negatively related to both variables, but the relationships are interdependent. Variations in curvature are produced by the normal distribution function and depend upon its SD and its distance from the habit function.

No claim is made that the estimation procedures used here are the best for the purpose. Blocks of 16 trials are obviously rather crude units of analysis. Yet, without crude units, it is difficult to see the form of individual conditioning functions. Also, a reasonable number of trials are needed for the estimation of response probability.

Perhaps estimates based on response sequences will turn out to be preferable. With the present methods, applications must be limited to sets of data where intermediate levels of conditioning are obtained and the frequency of zero and 100 percent entries are fairly low.

Many modern behavioral scientists have as one of their goals the integration of information from traditional experimental psychology and from the study of individual differences. The present approach appears to be a step in that direction. A single model with the same relationships and the same theoretical concepts has been capable of describing both the results of research with experimentally manipulated variables and a rather complex pattern of individual differences. Obviously, this approach should be pushed further. One matter of immediate interest would be further investigation of the two individual difference parameters which purport to measure responsiveness and its variability. Are they related in meaningful and interesting ways to various psychometric or physiological measures which might be obtained? While considering the possible psychometric properties of these values, it should be mentioned that the estimated threshold levels were normally distributed in the present sample. This confirms the consistent, but less direct, evidence for this which has been obtained in all of our analyses of group data. The distribution of the individual SDs was positively skewed.

The fits obtained with this analysis are of sufficient quality that they do not seriously endanger our initial assumption that individual differences in human conditioning are attributable to differences in responsiveness and its variability rather than to differences in associative processes. This assumption has been shown capable of accounting for differences in the form of conditioning functions as well as in their level. The interpretation is quite different from most other current views, and it needs much further exploration.

## VII. Concluding Remarks

All but one of the applications in this paper of this decision theory of response evocation have been limited to human eyelid conditioning. Previously presented applications have dealt either with conditioning or simple reaction time. Yet, the model has been able to deal effectively with a variety of experimental variables, and is potentially capable of shedding light on their mode of operation. These successes and the hope for considerable future extension seem to rest primarily upon the analytic methods, inherent in the model, which make it possible to obtain estimates of the strength of theoretical processes and states. This represents an advance over the similar approach of Hull and Spence. While their theories were formulated in terms of the strength of theoretical entities and their relationships, neither of these theories had yet reached the state where these values of strength could be separately estimated and entered into the theoretical equations. While we have not gone very far in this direction, at least a beginning has been made which suggests the possible direction of future progress.

The present theory, with its emphasis on describing the strength of hypothetical states, differs from many of the more recent approaches to quantitative learning theory. Based on modern mathematics and probability theory, the emphasis has been upon the estimation of probability states descriptive of an individual, combined with attempts to estimate, and specify the rules for, transitions in probability. To state that these developments have proceeded with no interest in the nature of underlying processes would not be accurate, but an effort to describe their strength has not been the emphasis. In the meantime, a large number, and perhaps the majority, of $E$s and less mathematical theorists in the learning area have continued to base their thinking and research upon inferences about the strength of a number of inferred processes. It seems to the writer that this is an inevitable approach to psychological theory, and it is hoped that the present efforts will help to redirect attention toward the use of more quantitative and powerful analytic procedures in connection with this mode of thought.

This model is clearly not a general theory of learning of the sort conceived by Hull. We have not touched such favorite issues as the nature of reinforcement, inhibition, or even of association itself. The threshold theory, however, is in itself a principle of psychological significance, and potential generality. This principle, together with the methods of analysis should provide avenues of approach, which have not previously been available, to the investigation of other variables. Further theoretical progress may be possible in several directions.

### REFERENCES

Anderson, N. H. Functional measurement and psychophysical judgment. *Psychological Review*, 1970, 77, 153–170.

Beck, S. B. Eyelid conditioning as a function of CS intensity, UCS intensity, and Manifest Anxiety Scale score. *Journal of Experimental Psychology*, 1963, **66**, 429–438.

Boneau, C. A. The interstimulus interval and the latency of the conditioned eyelid response. *Journal of Experimental Psychology*, 1958, 56, 464–471.

Bush, R. R., & Mosteller, F. *Stochastic models for learning.* New York: Wiley, 1955.

Fishbein, H. D., Jones, P. D., & Silverthorne, C. CS intensity and CS-UCS interval effects in human eyelid conditioning. *Journal of Experimental Psychology*, 1969, 81, 109–114.

Gray, J. A. Relation between stimulus intensity and operant response rate as a function of discrimination training and drive. *Journal of Experimental Psychology*, 1965, 69, 9–24.

Grice, G. R. Stimulus intensity and response evocation. *Psychological Review*, 1968, 75, 359–373.

Grice, G. R. A threshold model for drive. In H. H. Kendler & J. T. Spence (Eds.), *Essays in neobehaviorism: A memorial volume to Kenneth W. Spence.* New York: Appleton-Century-Crofts, 1971.

Grice, G. R., & Hunter, J. J. Stimulus intensity effects depend upon the type of experimental design. *Psychological Review*, 1964, 71, 247–256.

Grice, G. R., Masters, L., & Kohfeld, D. L. Classical conditioning without discrimination training: A test of the generalization theory of CS intensity effects. *Journal of Experimental Psychology*, 1966, 72, 510–513.

Gynther, M. D. Differential eyelid conditioning as a function of stimulus similarity and strength of response to the CS. *Journal of Experimental Psychology*, 1957, 53, 408–416.

Hartman, T. F., & Grant, D. A. Differential eyelid conditioning as a function of the CS-UCS interval. *Journal of Experimental Psychology*, 1962, 64, 131–136.

Hull, C. L., Felsinger, J. M., Gladstone, A. I., & Yamaguchi, H. G. A proposed quantification of habit strength. *Psychological Review*, 1947, 54, 237–254.

Humphreys, L. G. The effect of random alternation of reinforcement on the acquisition and extinction of conditioned eyelid reactions. *Journal of Experimental Psychology*, 1939, 25, 141–158.

John, I. D. A statistical decision theory of simple reaction time. *Australian Journal of Psychology*, 1967, 19, 27–34.

Kohfeld, D. L. Stimulus intensity and adaptation level as determinates of simple reaction time. *Journal of Experimental Psychology*, 1968, 76, 468–473.

La Berge, D. A recruitment theory of simple behavior. *Psychometrika*, 1962, 27, 375–396.

Logan, F. A. A note on the stimulus intensity dynamism (V). *Psychological Review*, 1954, 61, 77–80.

McGill, W. J. Stochastic latency mechanisms. In R. D. Luce, R. R. Bush, & E. Galanter (Eds.), *Handbook of mathematical psychology.* Vol. I. New York: Wiley, 1963. Pp. 309–360.

Moore, J. W. Differential eyelid conditioning as a function of the frequency and intensity of auditory CSs. *Journal of Experimental Psychology*, 1964, 68, 250–259.

Murray, H. G., & Kohfeld, D. L. Role of adaptation level in stimulus intensity dynamism. *Psychonomic Science*, 1965, 3, 439–440.

Newman, J. R., & Grice, G. R. Stimulus generalization as a function of drive level, and the relation between two measures of response strength. *Journal of Experimental Psychology*, 1965, 69, 357–362.

Nicholls, M. F., & Kimble, G. A. Effect of instruction upon eyelid conditioning. *Journal of Experimental Psychology*, 1964, 67, 400–402.

Perkins, C. C., Jr. The relation between conditioned stimulus intensity and response strength. *Journal of Experimental Psychology*, 1953, 46, 225–231.

Rundquist, W. N., Spence, K. W., & Stubbs, D. W. Differential conditioning and intensity of the UCS. *Journal of Experimental Psychology*, 1958, 55, 51–55.

Saffir, M. A comparative study of scales constructed by three psychophysical methods. *Psychometrika*, 1937, 2, 179–198.

Spence, K. W. The relation of response latency and speed to the intervening variables and N in S-R theory. *Psychological Review*, 1954, 61, 209–216.

Spence, K. W. *Behavior theory and conditioning.* New Haven, Conn.: Yale University Press, 1956.

Spence, K. W. Behavior theory and selective learning. In M. R. Jones (Ed.), *Nebraska symposium on motivation.*Lincoln, Neb.: University of Nebraska Press, 1958. Pp. 73–107.

Spence, K. W. *Behavior theory and learning.* Englewood Cliffs, N.J.: Prentice-Hall, 1960.

Spence, K. W., & Farber, I. E. The relation of anxiety to differential eyelid conditioning. *Journal of Experimental Psychology*, 1954, 47, 127–134.

Thurstone, L. L. A method of scaling psychological and educational tests. *Journal of Educational Psychology*, 1925, 16, 433–451.

Thurstone, L. L. Psychophysical analysis. *American Journal of Psychology*, 1927, 38, 368–389. (a)

Thurstone, L. L. The unit of measurement in educational scales. *Journal of Educational Psychology*, 1927, 19, 505–524. (b)

Torgerson, W. S. *Theory and methods of scaling.* New York: Wiley, 1958.

Trapold, M. A., & Spence, K. W. Performance changes in eyelid conditioning as related to the motivational and reinforcing properties of the UCS. *Journal of Experimental Psychology*, 1960, 59, 209–213.

Walker, E. G. Eyelid conditioning as a function of intensity of conditioned and unconditioned stimuli. *Journal of Experimental Psychology*, 1960, 59, 303–311.

Weintraub, D., & Hake, H. W. Visual discrimination, an interpretation in terms of detectability theory. *Journal of the Optical Society of America*, 1962, 52, 1179–1184.

Woodworth, R. S., & Schlosberg, H. *Experimental psychology.* (Rev. ed.) New York: Holt, 1954.

# SHORT-TERM MEMORY[1]

## Bennet B. Murdock, Jr.

UNIVERSITY OF TORONTO
TORONTO, ONTARIO, CANADA

## I. Introduction

In this paper I would like to survey and discuss some of the research in human short-term memory done over approximately the last 10 years. I shall consider recent trends (Section II), methods and designs (Section III), empirical phenomena (Section IV), and models of memory (Section V). I shall be particularly concerned to present a finite-state decision model (Section V,B), an expanded version of the fluctuation model previously described (Murdock, 1967c, 1970). The

[1] Over the past 10 years this work has been supported by Research Grants MH3330 and MH10882 from the National Institute of Mental Health, U.S. Public Health Service, Grant GB 4545 from the National Science Foundation, Grant APA 146 from the National Research Council of Canada, and Grant OMHF 164 from the Ontario Mental Health Foundation.

purpose of this monograph series is to allow individual research workers a chance to provide a systematic integration of their work in a field, and I hope that the finite-state model will be useful in this regard. While I intend to emphasize problems that I have worked on, for a more rounded presentation I shall draw freely on the work of others.

My general concern has been to try to understand the basic mechanisms and processes by which the human brain encodes, stores, and retrieves information. I believe that our understanding of human memory can most effectively be approached by studying short-term memory before long-term memory. The latter presumably depends on the former; also, experimental work on long-term memory is much harder to perform. The time periods involved are longer, and the amount of possible experimental control is weaker. When there is so much that we do not know, it seems important to take the first feeble steps as quickly as possible.

## II. Recent Trends

It seems to me that the basic change that has occurred in the field of human verbal learning and memory over the past decade is that we now routinely take the single item rather than the entire list of items as the unit of analysis. Ten years ago, studies of memory went under the title of "verbal learning," and the usual measure of performance was trials to criterion. Retention measures would be expressed in terms of total number of correct responses or total number of errors after specified retention intervals, and the independent variables were introduced following the end of learning.

Today, the basic datum instead seems to be probability of recall (or recognition). The analysis focuses on the individual item, not the list as a whole. With this change in the unit of analysis has come a rather different orientation. Many investigators now agree that what we are studying in these laboratory tasks is memory, regardless of the terms one uses to describe the phenomenon. Thus, when an item is presented on Trial $n$ and subsequently tested (either in the anticipation method or the study–test method) on Trial $n + 1$, this is a measure of intertrial retention (Bernbach, 1965; Mandler, 1967b; Murdock, 1963; Tulving & Arbuckle, 1963). After each presentation there is some residual retention, and it appears that this residual retention (asymptote) increases rather consistently with repetition. What has traditionally been called a "learning curve" reflects the change (increase) in the amount of residual retention as a function of repetition. Thus, as has been said many times, what has been studied in the laboratory as "verbal learning" is essentially resistance to forgetting.

Along with (or perhaps as a result of) this shift in the unit of analysis has come a change in the methods and techniques of studying memory, a plethora of new experimental phenomena, and a new set of concepts, assumptions, and models. Ten years is a rather short time given that the field started with the work of Ebbinghaus in the latter part of the last century, but the changes have been considerable. Ten years ago it was reasonable to make the claim that "Interference theory occupies an unchallenged position as the only major significant analysis of the process of forgetting" (Postman, 1961). Today, the basic emphasis is more on the encoding, storage, and retrieval of information, and there are now a variety of techniques for studying these phenomena. There are numerous theoretical models which have been developed in the past few years, many of which are contained in a recent book edited by Norman (1970).

What are the factors that brought about such a change in this area of experimental psychology? Without pretending to be an historian, in retrospect several main contributions can be noted. The first is the filter theory of Broadbent (1958). This was an attractive and compelling argument for considering the human organism as an information processing system, and it seemed to provide a consistent and useful explanation for a large number of experimental facts that were then known. A second line, experimental in nature, was the distractor technique of short-term memory, developed concurrently by J. Brown (1958) in England and Peterson and Peterson (1959) in the United States. Here was an experimental technique that brought short-term memory under experimental control in the laboratory and was able to reproduce, in a span of a few seconds, the whole gamut of forgetting that previously had taken weeks or months to observe. One only needs to look at recent journals to note the many and varied uses to which this technique has been put.

A third main factor (which should not be minimized) was the very influential paper of Melton (1963). In effect, he put the seal of respectability on the newly developing field of short-term memory, and from the "revolutionary" point of view (Kuhn, 1962) this paper was a critical factor. He interrelated the traditional area of verbal learning and the newer work in short-term memory and indicated clearly the promise that the latter held for increasing our understanding of the former. Then, of course, there were other main contributions such as the work on iconic memory by Sperling (1960), the distinction between Primary Memory and Secondary Memory (Waugh & Norman, 1965), the multicomponent model of Bower (1967), the buffer model of Atkinson and Shiffrin (1965, 1968), the work on acoustic confusions by Conrad (1964), the work of Mandler (1967a) and Tulving (1968) on organization and retrieval processes, and the application of signal-detection theory to memory (Murdock, 1965b; Norman & Wickelgren, 1965).

## III. Methods and Designs

In the last 10 years of research on short-term memory we have learned quite a bit about conducting proper experiments, both in terms of what to do and what not to do. Furthermore, there has been enough work so some of the important methods and designs seem to have emerged quite clearly. As a consequence, it might be useful to try to outline some of the important concepts and principles.

### A. METHODS

Recall and recognition are the two main methods used in studying short-term memory. The old method of rearrangement could be, but seldom is used, while relearning simply uses derived measures based on recall (generally using the anticipation technique). The basic difference between recall and recognition is probably whether or not the $S$ can readily generate all possible alternatives. If he can, or if they are physically present, then the method would be recognition. If he cannot, and they are not physically present, then the method would be recall.

For recall, there must be some pointer to designate the target information, and this pointer is generally either temporal or associative. Thus in the Peterson and Peterson (1959) task the $S$ is always to recall the most recently presented trigram, so the pointer is temporal. With paired associates or sequential probes, the pointer is obviously associative, except that there is also an implicit temporal designation. That is, in the typical memory experiment, the $S$ is to recall that item most recently presented paired with or following the probe item. In single-trial free recall the pointer is obviously temporal, as the S is told to report all items in the most recently presented list.

Recognition can be tested by a yes–no, an m-alternative forced choice, or a batch-testing procedure. In the first procedure, one alternative is presented for decision (and the two alternative responses may be supplemented by confidence judgments). In the second procedure, one target and m−1 lures are presented, and in the third procedure all targets and many lures are presented as in tests of recognition of list membership. Also, one can use a discrete-trials procedure or a continuous task. A continuous yes–no procedure was used by Shepard and Teghtsoonian (1961), a continuous m-alternative forced choice task was used by Shepard and Chang (1963), a discrete yes–no procedure was used by Murdock (1968a), and a discrete m-alternative forced choice procedure was used by Schwartz and Rouse (1961).

For studies of long-term memory, the two standard techniques are the method of anticipation and the study-test procedure. In short-term memory there is the Brown-Peterson distractor technique (J. Brown, 1958; Peterson & Peterson, 1959) and the probe technique (Anderson, 1960; Murdock, 1961c; Sperling, 1960; Waugh & Norman, 1965). There is some reason to hope (Murdock, 1967d) that the probe and the distractor techniques can yield equivalent results in studies of short-term memory.

## B. Measures

Sometimes investigators of memory do not distinguish between the slope, intercept, and asymptote of a curve. It is of considerable importance that these distinctions be preserved, since there are reasons to believe that certain experimental variables might affect one and not the other. As a simple example, it is sometimes claimed that repetition affects the rate of forgetting. However, data for the Vocal Group as shown in Table I of Peterson and Peterson (1959), p. 197, suggest that repetition affects the asymptote instead. The forgetting curves can be well approximated by exponential equations of the form $y = ae^{-bt} + c$. Semilog plots [log $(y-c)$ as a function of $t$] for the three groups are essentially parallel for appropriate values of $c$, thus suggesting that in fact repetition has no effect on the numerical value of the rate constant $b$.

It seems, therefore, most consistent with everyday use as well as scientific custom to define forgetting as the slope of the curve which plots retention as a function of time. This curve will typically have

an intercept or starting value, a slope, and an asymptote which may
or may not be zero. Learning is the other side of the coin, wherein
acquisition is plotted with some performance measure as a function
of practice. Again it seems most consistent if learning be defined as
the slope of the acquisition curve.

Such a definition, of course, is most appropriate if one takes an
incremental view of learning. If one believes in a finite-state model,
then learning would be a change of state and would be a
discontinuous rather than a continuous process. One's theoretical
position on this issue does not, however, affect the basic argument.

A very contentious point in the history of the short-term memory
work has been the issue of the degree of original learning
(Underwood, 1964). The argument advanced therein would seem to
be that one could not compare groups on forgetting whose initial
acquisition differed. This point may be wrong. It can be quite proper
to compare two curves to find out whether or not they have the
same slope (forgetting) regardless of whether or not they have the
same starting value. The slopes and the starting values may or may
not be independent, and the final conclusion will obviously be
tempered by this interrelationship. But, whether or not they are
independent is quite a different matter from slope differences per se.
The problem lies in the interpretation of slope differences, if any are
found.

## C. EXPERIMENTAL DESIGN

I have become convinced of the desirability of using as an
experimental design a classificatory system wherein every single
observation is preserved as a unique datum. In general, the crossed
classifications of factorial design are most suitable for this problem,
and the advantages from both the point of view of design and
statistical analysis have been set forth elsewhere (Murdock & Ogilvie,
1968). While the data matrices can become enormous, this size
presents no problem with computer analysis of the data. One of the
advantages lies in the fact that, once the original data are transcribed
into a form suitable for computer analysis, any analysis is possible
that one is capable of programming. In fact, sometimes the
temptation to do analysis simply because they can be done proves
almost irresistible, so one should temper one's enthusiasm for data
analysis by asking first the question of thereotical relevance.

Perhaps a more important reason for this type of analysis is the fact that an exact test of the underlying model is possible. If one assumes a binomial model, then the expected mean squares value will tell to what extent the obtained precision of the experiment approaches the theoretical precision possible. In effect, one has a figure of merit by means of which one can assess the amount of unexplained or residual variance. There have been several times I have been saved from wrong conclusions by detecting errors in computer programs which showed up with unusually large discrepancies between obtained and expected results. Unless one has such a rational "figure of merit" in the first place, some comparisons are not possible.

It is generally assumed that there are subject–item interactions with paired-associate material. That is, it is assumed that certain pairs are particularly easy, and others rather hard, for a given $S$, and that this variation is purely idiosyncratic. As a consequence, many conditional probability analyses are suspect because, it is felt, one has introduced a selection bias in the conditionalizing. This subject–item interaction is more often assumed than determined. The binomial model described in Murdock and Ogilvie (1968) makes possible a statistical test of this assumption, and it may come as a surprise to know how often the data show no evidence for the existence of this alleged interaction. I have yet to encounter extreme subject–item interactions; whether moderate interactions do not exist or whether the statistical test is insensitive has not been investigated.

As a consequence of this type of detailed analysis, it is necessary to take great pains in data analysis and tabulation. We have developed systems for error detection which are time consuming in the extreme but necessary if one is to have errorfree data. Essentially, the absolutely necessary precaution is to get some sort of arithmetic check on the raw data as obtained from the individual protocols and compare it with totals obtained by the computer from the analysis of the data. Thus, in a free recall experiment, one might score the serial position data by hand. (If it were done by computer, then other considerations would prevail.) Having done so, one then adds up the totals for each $S$ for each list and then sums over the $S$s, sessions, and lists. The data are punched for computer analysis in terms of input as a function of output order, and the check totals from the computer analysis are obtained. It will take a considerable period of rather trying checking and rechecking before the totals agree, but no data analyses on the computer should even be considered before the totals match perfectly. This is an elementary and obvious point which may be apparent to all researchers in the field, but somehow I am not convinced that people are as careful about their data as they might be.

Finally, to conclude this section, let me mention one other strong personal bias of mine. I think it important that investigators working in short-term memory make a serious attempt to sample stimulus material across lists. That is, it is very desirable to have a basic word pool from which one samples to obtain lists, and under many conditions one should sample randomly for each $S$ for each list. Only when the canons of random sampling are observed can one generalize to a known population. While we have long been advised to observe principles of sampling in regard to $S$s, it seems to me equally important to observe these principles in regard to stimuli.

## D. SIGNAL-DETECTION METHODS

I do not intend to review here at any depth the matter of signal-detection applications to memory. However, I would like to reiterate a main conclusion from a recent article on this topic (Lockhart & Murdock, 1970). The contention is that signal-detection theory is not a theoretically neutral way of analyzing data. Quite the contrary; one either has an explicit model wherein the analysis is proper and sensible, or one accepts uncritically the host of assumptions that are embodied in signal-detection theory as it is generally known among psychologists. The conclusions that one draws from such an analysis will in turn be dependent upon the basic assumptions from which one starts. One can use signal-detection methods to separate sensitivity and response bias only if one is willing to make certain assumptions about what sensitivity and bias are.

This issue becomes particularly thorny when one is attempting Type II analyses. As I choose to make the distinction, when one is analyzing recognition memory one is doing a Type I or stimulus-conditional analysis whereas in recall one is doing a Type II or response-conditional analysis. In Type I situations, the *a priori* probabilities are under the control of the experimenter, but in Type II situations they are so only indirectly. If one believes in a strength theory of memory, one should probably not do Type II analyses at all. However, as I have argued elsewhere (Murdock, 1970), there are cases where a Type II analysis may be quite useful.

## IV. Empirical Phenomena

A. ENCODING

The single most important finding from all the work on short-term memory is that items are "learned" or encoded in a single brief presentation. This point is so obvious and fundamental that it is difficult to imagine that any proof would be needed. I am sure that any reasonable man in the street would accept this argument without being confronted with masses of data. An item is a single unit such as a digit, letter, or word; a CCC nonsense syllable is three units (Murdock, 1961b).

The reason that this point is so basic and so fundamental is that it changes the conceptual framework for understanding associations and memory traces. The general point of view must be that associations and memory traces are laid down in a single brief presentation and decay (in a theoretically neutral sense) thereafter. Thus, as mentioned in Section II, what remains subsequently is that which has resisted forgetting. Rather than conceive of associations gradually being strengthened by repetition, it is more nearly correct to say that associations become progressively more resistant to forgetting as repetition increases.

This fact constrains any theory of learning or memory. An acceptable theory must both be able to cope with the immediate changes which follow shortly after presentation and the residual effects which are manifest after longer periods of time. Said one way, this means that theories must explain the transition from short-term to long-term memory; said another way, theories of memory and association must cope with short-term memory. Regardless of whether one thinks of memory as a continuous process or as composed of separate states for short-term and long-term periods, one must include short-term effects within a long-term theory.

It seems to me that this point on initial encoding presents serious problems for some of the early learning and memory models. I have in mind such models as the one-element model of Bower (1962), its extension to a three-state model by Kintsch and Morris (1965), and the EPAM model of Feigenbaum and Simon (1962). If one starts with the view that learning is the formation or strengthening of associations over trials, how does one explain the immediate memory changes that are so pronounced? It could be, of course, that the proper model for short-term memory would be like the perceptual enrichment hypothesis of Gibson and Gibson (1955) wherein the richness and diversity of the memory trace increased with exposure. However, the data on short-term memories for simple verbal material do not really seem consistent with such a view.

Of course, it is possible to change or reconstruct learning models so they are consistent with the immediate memory effects. This has been done, for instance, by Atkinson and Crothers (1964), Bjork (1966), and Kintsch (1967) by considering the learned state as a long-term memory state and introducing an intermediate or short-term memory state. However, it seems to me that the more fruitful approach is to start directly with memory rather than learning and consider learning effects as derivable from memory residues.

## B. Recency Effect

The recency effect refers to the positive relationship between recency of presentation and memory. The effect is large in magnitude, reliable, and occurs in most short-term memory tasks. It can be found in recall tasks, recognition tasks, paired associates, free recall, the distractor technique, and the probe technique. The chief exception seems to be in the serial position curves of memory span, where (particularly for visual presentation) the required forward order of recall pretty much eliminates the recency effect.

In single-trial free recall, the recency effect generally spans about the last eight items when the lists are constructed of randomly selected common English words. This can be seen in Fig. 1, where

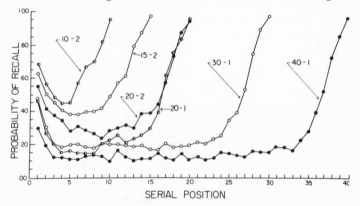

Fig. 1. Serial position curves for single-trial free recall (data from Murdock, 1962).

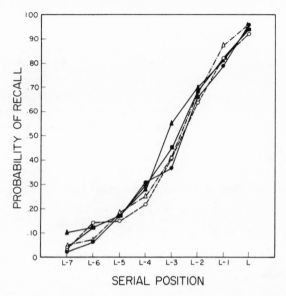

Fig. 2. Normalized echo-box curves (data from Murdock, 1962). *Key:* 15-2 = ●——●; 20-2 = ○— — —○; 20-1 = ▲——▲; 30-1 = △— · — · △; 40-1 = ■——■

serial position curves are shown. If one normalizes these curves (brings the flat middle section or asymptote to zero) the curves more or less fall on top of one another. This can be seen in Fig. 2, where five of the six curves of Fig. 1 are reproduced in normalized form. In the terminology of Waugh and Norman (1965), the correction factor used was

$$P(i) = \frac{R(i) - S(i)}{1 - S(i)} \tag{1}$$

where the terms $R(i)$, $P(i)$ and $S(i)$ are, for Item $i$, the probability of recall, the probability of being in Primary Memory, and the probability of being in Secondary Memory, respectively.

The normalized curves of Fig. 2 seem quite similar to the Primary Memory functions obtained by Waugh and Norman (1965) using a sequential probe in a serial list of digits. This Primary Memory or recency curve can best be described by the double-exponential Gompertz function given in Murdock (1962). This function also turns up in various theoretical formulations. One example is in Eq. (1) of Atkinson, Brelsford, and Shiffrin (1967) where probability of a correct response from long-term memory is a double-exponential function of the interval between displacement from the buffer and the test. A similar equation is given by Shiffrin for a memory search model (see Shiffrin, 1970, Appendix, p. 443).

It is possible to give a Gompertz double-exponential function for the recency effect in single-trial free recall which (a) is reasonably accurate in describing the data and (b) has no free parameters. If one examines the numerical values of the constants in Table II of Murdock (1962, p. 484) it can be seen that, for the six groups, $g$ is approximately the reciprocal of list length $L$, and $h$ is approximately .5. So, as a first approximation we have

$$P(i) = 1 - (1/L)^{.5^i} \tag{2}$$

where $i$ is the number of subsequent items. For

$$15 \leqslant L \leqslant 40, \sum_{i=0}^{7} P(i) \approx 3.0.$$

That is, over this range of list lengths, there are three words (±10%) in the "echo-box."


## C. Asymptote

After the recency effect is expended the probability of recall stays approximately constant at some value greater than zero. This value is the asymptote of the retention curve (e.g., Fig. 1). Experimentally this phenomenon is found with single-trial free recall (Murdock, 1962), noncontingent, multitrial free recall (Murdock, Penney, & Aamiry, 1970), and probe paired associates (Murdock, 1963). It probably does not occur in tasks with serial order (Murdock, 1968c).

These last two phenomena (the recency effect and the asymptote) seem to have been of considerable importance in determining current concepts and models of memory (e.g., Atkinson & Shiffrin, 1965, 1968; Waugh & Norman, 1965). That is, these dichotomous models assume that the recency effect reflects loss from a short-term buffer, while the asymptote reflects that which persists in a longer term or Secondary Memory. The indepedence assumption suggests a transfer process, and is corroborated by the experimental separation which has been demonstrated by Glanzer and Cunitz (1966).

It is important from a theoretical point of view to understand that these theories have not "explained" Primary Memory and Secondary Memory. They have postulated on the basis of data that there are these underlying stores and these stores have the characteristics required by the data. It is a mistake, therefore, to think that these models explain the asymptote; they have instead simply assumed as an underlying process a storage system which has the necessary characteristics. By contrast, Bernbach (1969) and Murdock (1967c) have developed models wherein Secondary Memory or the asymptote is a consequence of more molecular processes. In the Bernbach model, the asymptote is the outcome of the probability fluctuations in the classical "gambler's ruin" paradigm as described in Feller (1968). In the Murdock model, it occurs when the number of items being forgotten is the same as the number of items undergoing "spontaneous recovery."

Is the asymptote a "within-trials" or a "between-trials" phenomenon? That is, if it is the former the stability would only hold up within the framework of a single presentation and test; if it is the latter, it would hold up across lists. As a very simple test, we ran a standard single-trial free-recall experiment wherein Ss were given lists one at a time to recall, each such presentation and test being one "cycle." Lists were presented visually at a rate of 30 words/minute, and each word list was 20 words long. Computer-generated lists were used; from a 100-word pool, each S was given unique lists (sampling without replacement from the pool). Spoken recall was recorded by E. After five such cycles we asked for final recall; i.e., Ss were to recall as many words as they could from the entire five lists. The mean number of words recalled were 1.8, 1.9, 2.4, 2.6, and 3.8 for Lists 1–5, respectively. Thus, there was a recency effect, suggesting that the asymptote is a within-trials phenomenon and not a between-trials phenomenon. This finding has also been reported for categorized word lists by Tulving and Psotka (1971), so Secondary Memory does not seem to be all that permanent.

## D. DISCRIMINABILITY

A fourth major finding from studies of short-term memory is the high level of discriminability of memory traces. Subjects are able to examine or observe their own memory and report their degree of certainty about its contents. The fact that they are not only able to do so, but also able to do so with rather considerable accuracy has been revealed by applying methods of signal detection to the study of memory. The basic paradigm consists of testing old (presented) or new (nonpresented) items and asking Ss both to respond "yes" or "no" and to assign a confidence judgment about their certainty. The $d'$ of signal detection theory is one measure of discriminability, and the greater its value the more discriminable are the two distributions.

It is probably better to interpret $d'$ as a measure of discriminability rather than as a measure of strength, since in the field of memory the term "strength" has considerable surplus meaning.

The accuracy of the confidence judgments can be assessed by the *a posteriori* probability curves and they are impressive indeed (e.g., Lockhart & Murdock, 1970). The probability that an item was in fact old given a particular confidence judgment is generally of the order of .95 for "certain old" judgments, perhaps .05 for "certain new" judgments, and intermediate judgments are ordered appropriately.

The idea of having Ss make such judgments might have been anathema to strict behaviorists several decades ago. It does indeed smack of a little homunculus sitting in judgment and making decisions about memory processes. However, these experimental facts are clear and cannot be avoided. Somehow the central processor is, in fact, able to examine the contents of the store and make a report on what it finds.

One of the discriminability issues not yet resolved is whether the S responds on the basis of a likelihood ratio (which, of course, would first have to be computed) or whether, instead, he makes it on some direct measure such as "strength." In other words, what is the decision axis? In a doctoral dissertation, Donaldson (1967) attempted to get experimental separation of $d'$ and $\beta$ in one experimental paradigm. To manipulate $\beta$, he introduced a standard experimental variable which, according to the theory of the ideal observer, should affect the criterion according to a likelihood ratio rule. In a yes–no continuous recognition memory task he varied both the lag between the presentation of an item and its test and the *a priori* probabilities. These probabilities were .5 and .2 for the main experimental considerations of interest. The probabilities varied across (but not within) sessions, and Ss were informed. According to a maximum likelihood rule, assuming a symmetric pay-off matrix, the criterion should have shifted from 1.0 to 4.0 as the probability of occurrence of an old signal decreased.

The results were quite clear. In general Ss did not shift their criterion in the way expected by a maximum likelihood rule. Instead, the results were more consistent with the idea that the S was making his judgment on the basis of a direct observation of the memory trace and using exactly the same criterion under the two *a priori* probabilities. The *a posteriori* probability curves went down considerably, as one would expect under this assumption.

A simple numerical example can demonstrate what happens when

$d'$ stays constant, the cut-off points have the same $z$ scores on the decision axis, and only the *a priori* probabilities change. Such an example is given in Table I, where $d' = 1.0$ and the two distributions (S and N) have the same variance. It can be seen that the main effect of the experimental manipulation (i.e., varying *a priori* probabilities) is to decrease the *a posteriori* probabilities.

### E. MODALITY EFFECTS

A fifth main phenomenon is the existence of large differences between auditory and visual presentation in the studies of short-term memory. The main results are quite clear: retention of verbal material presented auditorily is better than retention of the same material presented visually, but (at least for free recall and paired associates) the effect is restricted to the recency part of the curve.

As an example, Figs. 3 and 4 show data from a master's thesis of Walker (1967). Ten-word serial lists were presented at a rate of 2 words/second and (the five) visual and (the five) auditory words were interleaved randomly. Thus, modality was a within-lists rather than a between-lists variable. The modality of the probe and the modality of the target were combined factorially (2 x 2). For a probe recall test (Fig. 3) the results confirmed a previous finding of Murdock

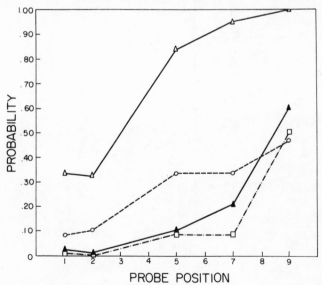

Fig. 3. Probe recall in mixed-mode auditory-visual serial lists (data from Walker, 1967). *Key:* A-A = △——; V-V = ▲—; A-V = □—·—·; V-A = ○- - -.

TABLE I

Numerical Example to Show Effect of *a Priori* Probability on *a Posteriori* Probability

| Prior | | Decision axis | | | | | | | Totals |
|---|---|---|---|---|---|---|---|---|---|
| .5 | S | 228 | 440 | 919 | 1498 | 1915 | 1915 | 3085 | 10,000 |
| | N | 1587 | 1498 | 1915 | 1915 | 1498 | 919 | 668 | 10,000 |
| | Posterior | .126 | .227 | .324 | .439 | .561 | .676 | .822 | |
| .2 | S | 228 | 440 | 919 | 1498 | 1915 | 1915 | 3085 | 10,000 |
| | N | 6348 | 5992 | 7660 | 7660 | 5992 | 3676 | 2672 | 40,000 |
| | Posterior | .035 | .068 | .107 | .164 | .242 | .342 | .536 | |

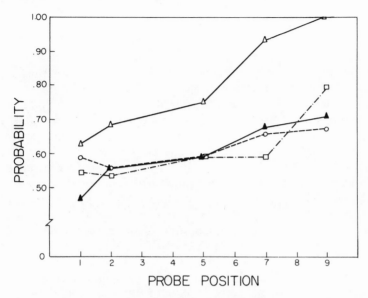

Fig. 4. Probe recognition in mixed-mode auditory-visual serial lists (data from Walker, 1967). *Key:* A-A = △—; V-V = ▲—; A-V = □—.—.; V-A = ○- - -.

(1967a, Exp. 3). The same general results occurred under a recognition (A-B *vs.* A-X) paradigm. Thus, both for recall and for recognition the best performance occurs when both the probe and the target had been presented auditorily. When either one (or both) had been presented visually, performance was greatly impaired. These data demonstrate that (*a*) the modality effect can be large indeed, and (*b*) the modality effect is not a retrieval phenomenon (Murdock, 1968a).

The modality effect clearly interacts with presentation rate. It is most pronounced at a fast rate and decreases at slower rates (Laughery & Pinkus, 1966; Murdock & Walker, 1969). This interaction poses something of a dilemma for research on the problem. If one presents material at too fast a rate, perceptual problems are encountered, but if one presents it at too slow a rate, there will be no modality effects remaining. For unrelated words, I feel that a presentation rate of 2 words/second is a reasonable compromise. There are clearly no perceptual difficulties at this rate, yet the modality effects are large enough to provide one with some experimental elbow room. In fact, one can even have mixed mode lists presented at this rate, where the S must switch randomly back and forth across modes. While Ss report that it is taxing, the difficulties still do not seem to be perceptual in nature.

There are some obvious explanations of modality effects which do not hold up under scrutiny. One explanation might be as follows: Since auditory simple reaction time is faster than visual simple reaction time, information presented in an auditory mode is processed more rapidly than information presented in a visual mode, and therefore the direction of the difference reflects no more than the greater rehearsal time available for auditory material. This explanation is clearly false. As described in the discussion of Murdock and Walker (1969), it takes longer to process (as measured by a simple categorization technique) spoken words than written words. The reason, of course, is probably obvious; the presentation of a spoken word extends over time, and if the reaction time is measured from onset of the stimulus to onset of the response, the obtained 200-msec difference is probably largely if not exclusively absorbed by differences in presentation time. In any event, this finding means that the differential rehearsing bias if anything goes the other way, so if one were to equate functional time rather than nominal time, the modality effects might even be larger.

Another explanation sometimes suggested is that these differences reflect intensity differences; somehow spoken words are greater in amplitude than written words. While Murray (1965) has found effects in short-term memory using intensity of articulation, we are talking here instead about the intensity of the stimulus input. In one study where S/N ratio was experimentally manipulated (Murdock, 1967b), we had to get down nearly to a S/N ratio of zero dB before any memory effects were obtained. Even then the memory effects were slight. Also, they occurred in that part of the curve where the modality effects are not obtained, so all things considered this explanation seems most unlikely.

A third explanation might be in terms of S-R compatibility. As discussed in a previous paper (Murdock, 1969), most studies on verbal short-term memory test for temporal associations, and the auditory mode might be better designed than the visual mode to cope with temporal relationships. We attempted to test this by using a spatial display for both visual and auditory presentation, and probed to see if the Ss could remember *where* the target item had been presented rather than *when* it had been presented. Even under these conditions, auditory presentation was superior to visual presentation.

However, analysis of the intrusion data suggested that the basic format of storage was temporal and spatial information was extracted by reconstruction. What this experiment may have demonstrated, then, is that under this particular set of display conditions the Ss were unwilling or unable to use a spatial format and had no recourse but to fall back on the same temporal format used in standard short-term memory experiments. In retrospect, then, it is not clear that this experiment gave a final answer to exclude the S-R compatibility interpretation of modality effects.

As has been stated elsewhere (Murdock & Walker, 1969; Tulving & Madigan, 1970), these results on modality differences are something of a puzzle for theorists of memory. For Sperling's model (Sperling, 1963, 1967), one would expect all information regardless of presentation mode to be coded into an auditory information store, given the relatively slow presentation rate used. If it were, then such large differences would not be expected. A tagging notion could explain the organization in retrieval (see Murdock & Walker, 1969), but the main effect is still unexplained. To say that auditory words are better recalled than visual words because the "tags" denoting auditory presentation are more visible or more legible after a period of time than the tags denoting visual presentation is simply describing the results. Also, the data of Sternberg (1969b) argue against a tagging model. If Ss simply examined the trace of an item to determine whether or not it had been presented in the list, time to respond to the nonpresented items (negative probes) should not vary systematically with set size.

Additional evidence against a tagging notion comes from a master's thesis by Colotla (1969). Short lists of digits were presented to the S for either temporal or numerical recall. For temporal recall, 623159 should be reported as 623159, while for numerical recall it should be reported as 123569. Thus, temporal recall was recall in the order presented, while numerical recall was recall in ascending numerical order. If items go into an "event store" (Buschke, 1966), temporal recall should be easier than numerical recall because the latter could only be effected by a transformation of the former. However, if list presentation simply tagged the representation of each digit in long-term memory, then it should be at least as easy to read off the tagged items in ascending numerical order as to parrot them back. In fact, both for auditory and visual presentation, numerical recall was in general slower to initiate and less accurate than temporal recall.

The general problem for any two-store model is to account for the *lack* of difference in the asymptote of the serial position curve given the appreciable differences in the recency effect. If items enter Secondary Memory through Primary Memory, how can this be? The buffer model of Atkinson and Shiffrin (1965, 1968) is a case in point. If it were simply the case that the buffer was smaller for visual than for auditory presentation, one would expect a *shorter* recency effect. However, the data show the recency effect still to extend over eight terminal positions for both auditory and visual presentation; only the starting point for visual is lower. One would have to postulate, probably, two processes involved: one handling the differences in the rehearsal buffer and the other compensating for this difference to yield no differences in the asymptote of the curve.

The Crowder and Morton (1969) model is probably the most adequate model to deal with these modality effects, but it too has problems. They say that the information in an auditory precategorical store has a maximum useful life of perhaps two seconds, whereas in the comparable visual store it is essentially zero. Data showing recency differences as a function of modality when serial recall is used are clearly inconsistent with the model, so it has been suggested (Crowder & Raeburn, 1970) that Ss engage in a private "run through" before commencing recall. With mixed-mode free recall lists, the modality differences span too long a time to be consistent with the numerical estimates of temporal duration given above; this point is discussed in Murdock and Walker (1969). Finally, in an undergraduate honors thesis Mann (1970) used 20-word mixed mode (randomized) auditory-visual lists with postcued recall instructions. The Ss were either to recall all the visual words they could before reporting the auditory words, or vice versa. Given that a word was recalled, with probability .98 it was assigned to the proper modality. Such veridical reporting seems difficult to reconcile with the notion of transient echoic and iconic stores. Perhaps even more important, when output interference was held constant the number of words recalled in the *second* modality was still greater for auditory than for visual words. This finding also seems counter to the Crowder and Morton (1969) model. For further discussion on modality effects, see Murdock (1971b).

## F. ACCESSIBILITY

The work of Tulving has provided us with some clear implications for the problem of accessibility in short-term memory. He has been able to show that the difference between cued and noncued recall lies in the different number of categories recalled rather than the number of items per category (Tulving & Pearlstone, 1966). Thus, once access to a category is gained, the number of items per category will be constant regardless of whether or not a retrieval cue has been provided by the $E$. However, what the $E$ is capable of manipulating (thereby demonstrating large effects) is the presence or absence of retrieval cues themselves.

One of the findings that has emerged from this research is the fact that a retrieval cue must be stored with the target information at the time of presentation in order to be effective (Tulving & Osler, 1968). Thus, it might be thought that the word "dog" would be an effective retrieval cue for the word "cat." However, if it had not been presented at the time of presentation, "dog" would be no more effective in eliciting "cat" at the time of retrieval than in a control group which had not been presented with the retrieval cue at presentation at all. Furthermore, if weak and strong cues are present or absent at input or output in a 2 x 2 orthogonal design, it is even the case the strong cues at output (e.g., dog-cat) are deleterious compared to no cue at all. Thus, our associative network (whose existence is so clearly demonstrated in word association studies) is surprisingly insular, and access to information is far from automatic.

Another aspect of this problem of accessibility is the interpretation of retroactive inhibition phenomena. It has been shown (e.g., Postman & Keppel, 1967; Tulving & Psotka, 1971; Tulving & Thornton, 1959) that retroactive inhibition effects do occur in free recall. That is, if one varies either the number of lists learned or the number of trials on a given list preceding a final total recall, performance demonstrates graded interference effects. It has also been shown (Tulving & Psotka, 1971) that, in a categorized word list, it is the number of categories recalled that decreases, but the number of items per category remains constant. Thus, the implication drawn by these authors is that retroactive inhibition effects in free recall (and perhaps in other types of recall tasks as well) results from loss of accessibility to information in the store rather than decreased availability of mnemonic information.

There are several measures which can demonstrate the efficacy of retrieval cues in recall. One method is to compare performance on cued vs. noncued recall (e.g., Tulving & Pearlstone, 1966). Another method is to look at the slope of the function relating number of items recalled to total presentation time. At least within limits this function seems to be reasonably linear both for single-trial free recall (e.g., Murdock, 1960) and for probe paired associates (e.g., Murdock, 1967d). The slope for paired associates is generally at least twice that of the slope for single-trial free recall. This difference presumably reflects the fact that one member of a pair is a more effective retrieval cue for an item than whatever retrieval cues there are for conventional single-trial free recall procedures. Comparable slope differences can also be found in the data of Tulving and Pearlstone (1966) by comparing cued and noncued recall.

## G. Temporal Format

The seventh and final empirical phenomenon has been placed last because I believe firmly in the importance of recency effects. As anyone who has worked in the short-term memory area can report, the data of short-term memory experiments are always consistent with the idea of temporally structured memory traces. Not only is the recency effect temporally defined but also the pattern of intrusions one gets with a probe technique is temporally ordered. This fact is so obvious and so consonant with our expectations that it is all too easy not to give it the theoretical attention it deserves.

As one example, order of recall in "free" recall is temporally structured. Analysis of data from a previous experiment (Murdock, 1962) showed that, if the first two words recalled had been adjacent in presentation, the odds that they were recalled in a forward order rather than in a backward order were approximately 5:1. For words in the middle of the list that were both adjacent in presentation and consecutive in recall the comparable odds were about 2:1; this effect (i.e., odds favoring forward recall) occurred in 100 out of 103 Ss.

With ordered recall of trigrams, adjacent transpositions are at least five times as common as remote transpositions (Murdock & vom Saal, 1967), even though on a chance basis the expectation is 3:2 in the other direction. Intrusions in paired-associate probe experiments always show strong temporal generalization gradients. Even serial-order intrusions show this effect. Data from Table III of Conrad (1959) show that if an intrusion came from the prior list, the probability that it was from the corresponding serial position was .88. Analyses of some of our own data show this effect equally clearly.

Loss of order information may precede loss of item information. In studies of memory span and in studies using the Brown-Peterson distractor technique (e.g., Murdock & vom Saal, 1967), one does find cases of errorless transpositions. These are cases where all items are correctly recalled, but the order is rearranged. The separability of item and order information has been discussed by Crossman (1961). And of course the Colotla (1969) finding of the superiority of temporal over numerical recall provides further evidence for the importance of the temporal format in short-term memory.

This conviction of the importance of the temporal dimension is reinforced whenever I read discussions of similarity effects in short-term memory. The work of Conrad (1964), Wickelgren (1965), and others has clearly demonstrated the existence of acoustic similarity effects in short-term memory. The initial evidence demonstrating these effects was the similarity between intrusion errors and correct responses. The similarity was acoustic or articulatory in nature (Hintzman, 1965; Levy & Murdock, 1968) in that the pattern of errors demonstrated in a memory task paralleled the pattern of errors in a confusion matrix obtained from a listening task.

As a result of such data, some people have adopted the point of view that information in short-term or Primary Memory is coded primarily in an acoustic or articulatory format, and information in long-term or Secondary Memory is coded primarily in semantic fashion (Baddeley & Dale, 1966; Kintsch & Buschke, 1969). One should also say that items in short-term memory are coded in a temporal format. After all, there are intrusion errors along a temporal dimension, and to be consistent the reasoning must be that that dimension which shows similarity effects must be represented in the coding format. Although a strict comparison might be a bit like comparing apples and oranges, I would imagine that in terms of the magnitude of the effects, the temporal intrusion errors are appreciably larger than the acoustic confusion errors.

Another line of reasoning which has strengthened and given support to the notion of encoding and similarity effects in short-term memory is the Wickens (1970) work on "release from proactive inhibition." In effect, Wickens has argued that those stimulus attributes which can demonstrate a release from proactive inhibition (PI) must be represented in the encoding format. Again, the temporal dimension would seem to qualify. For one thing, the intrusion errors in a Peterson and Peterson technique do demonstrate a marked temporal gradient, intrusions from immediately prior trigrams being most common (Murdock, 1961b). Furthermore, for the release effect one would change the dimension not by changing the stimulus material but by changing the length of the intertrial interval. Such an effect has already been reported; Loess and Waugh (1967) demonstrated that PI decreased as the intertrial interval increased and was essentially absent by two minutes. However, a more thorough test may necessitate a shift design such as that used by Kintsch (1966).

In my opinion, it is misleading to say only that information is stored in short-term memory in an acoustic or articulatory format. It is also misleading to say that acoustic or articulatory errors characterize short-term memory, while semantic errors and confusions characterize long-term memory. There are anecdotes (Woodworth, 1938, p. 37) and evidence (R. Brown & McNeill, 1966) demonstrating acoustic effects in long-term memory. Also, there is evidence demonstrating semantic effects in short-term memory (Murdock & vom Saal, 1967; Tulving & Patterson, 1968). Furthermore, the extensive work of Posner (1969) shows that relative importance of visual and abstract codes in short-term memory.

Where does this leave us? I still believe in an extremely simplistic and, to most of my colleagues, naive view of encoding processes in short-term memory. I believe that there is an initial veridical representation of the stimulus laid down as presented to the S and whatever attributes are present in the stimulus are also initially represented in the trace. In other words, we write little messages in the head which are isomorphic to the physical stimulus. The work of Kabrisky and his colleagues (e.g., Kabrisky, Tallman, Day & Radoy, 1970) suggests that pattern recognition in humans can be based on (Fourier) transforms of veridical stimulus representations in the auditory and visual sensory projection areas. Furthermore, Kabrisky (1971) has suggested that the Fourier metric may provide a useful measure of the similarity among letters, and it is even possible to specify precisely the Gestalt of an individual letter. If this analysis can be extended from pattern recognition to memory, it may provide a powerful way of reconciling the reproductive characteristics of short-term memory with the well-known perceptual invariances of pattern recognition.

## V. Models of Memory

### A. TWO-STORE MODELS

There seems little doubt that some version of a two-store model is currently preeminent in the field of short-term memory. The buffer model of Atkinson and Shiffrin (1965, 1968) is probably the most carefully detailed, documented, and tested model of this type that there is. It seems to me that this model has been an important step forward in our understanding of memory in that it has suggested in considerable detail one possible way in which the memory system might work. Furthermore, it has led to some experimentally interesting problems, and it goes without saying that it is formulated with sufficient rigor and precision so that its predictions are certainly capable of disproof. At the very least, it has demonstrated that a detailed consideration of possible underlying mechanisms and processes can greatly further our understanding of the memory phenomena we obtain in the laboratory.

This particular buffer model is one of a larger class of two-store models which were previously characterized as a "modal model" (Murdock, 1967d). According to this general modal model, there are separate stores or stages of information processing which are represented by an initial sensory store (iconic and echoic memory, as described by Neisser, 1967), a short-term limited-capacity buffer much as described initially by Broadbent (1958), then a more commodious long-term store. [These latter two compartments loosely represent the Primary Memory–Secondary Memory distinction of Waugh and Norman (1965).] The term "two-store" model is applicable because the sensory registers are generally considered not to play an important role in short-term memory experiments, and the distinguishing characteristic of such models is the dichotomizing of short- and long-term memory. Forgetting occurs by decay, displacement, and interference in the sensory store, the buffer, and long-term memory, respectively. It seems likely that this view of memory has gained considerable strength from the recent work of Sternberg (1969a) in terms of his "stages of processing" analysis.

I suspect that more people are coming to accept this general point of view. In fact, one sometimes reads articles in which this compartmentalization of memory is simply assumed without question. I think this point of view is wrong, and I think it is important to consider alternatives. The arguments which have been presented in its favor are not unanswerable, as I would like to point out in the next few paragraphs. Then, I would like to suggest a finite-state decision model as an alternative to a two-store model.

The main reason why such a modal model must be wrong is that in a very general sense it is incompatible with what we know about understanding grammatical utterances. Such models posit perfect memory for a very small number of items, while the redundancy of language demands a short-term memory system capable of holding imperfectly a large number of items. To comprehend written or spoken language one must keep in memory fairly large segments of unprocessed or partly processed information before making linguistic decisions, and these decisions may be made at a fairly slow rate (e.g., Miller, 1962). A simple demonstration of the persistence of information is the writing-righting example of Lashley (1951, p. 120). In general, if our short-term buffer was as restricted as modal models say it is, then it is unlikely that our language would have evolved as it has. For additional arguments against a buffer model, see Murdock (1968c).

The basic arguments that support a two-store model have been presented by Atkinson and Shiffrin (1968) and by Baddeley and Warrington (1970). Atkinson and Shiffrin (1968) say that, ". . . the single most convincing demonstration of a dichotomy in the memory system [is] the effects of hippocampal lesions . . . [p. 97]." These patients apparently have a normal memory span (as measured by their ability to repeat back immediately short lists of items), yet they seem unable to enter anything into a "long-term" store. In support of this argument, a recent study by Baddeley and Warrington (1970) on amnesiac patients similar to the hippocampal cases of Milner (1966) would seem to provide confirming evidence obtained under a variety of standardized short-term memory tasks.

However, one could also argue that this evidence suggests retrieval difficulties from a unitary store. The fact that the amnesic patients in the Baddeley and Warrington study showed no deficit in a Hebb (1961) repetition-technique experiment goes against the alleged long-term deficit postulated by a two-store model. Moreover, a recent study by Robbins and Meyer (1970) revealed the startling finding that retrograde amnesia effects were more dependent on "context" than on temporal factors. Weiskrantz (1966) has also pointed out the importance of retrieval problems in studies of amnesia. And, as called to my attention by Gordon Bower (personal communication), a recent study by Warrington and Shallice (1969) reported the case of a patient with an auditory memory span of one who was able to learn a 10-item free recall list within the normal range of trials. It does not seem that this could happen if information only gets into long-term memory through a short-term buffer.

A second argument for two-store models is based on the experimental separation of the recency effect and the asymptote in studies of short-term memory. Thus, in one study, Glanzer and Cunitz (1966) were able to show that interpolated activity eliminated the recency effect, but the presentation rate affected only the asymptote (see also Glanzer, 1968). While it is certainly true that, *if* there are separate short-term and long-term stores, then experimental separation should be possible, it does *not* follow that if the recency effect and the asymptote are experimentally separable then there must be a dichotomous memory system. In fact, the model which I shall describe shortly is a one-store model whose validity requires such an experimental separation.

A variant of this basic argument rests on the findings of acoustic and semantic similarity effects in short- and long-term memory. This relationship and the interpretative difficulties have already been discussed, so the point will not be pursued further.

There must be other arguments too, but they may be more indicative of our naive enthusiasm than our scientific maturity. The case must rest, after all, not on such general pretheoretical assumptions and arguments, but on the ability of any theory, one store or many stores, to describe and predict the experimental findings. All I would wish to convince the reader of so far is that arguments presented in the literature to date do not compel one to accept some version of the modal model.

However, before turning to the next section, let me make two more general comments. The first concerns the wisdom of applying concepts and mechanisms from information processing systems such as computers to human information processing and memory. It can certainly be provocative, stimulating, instructive, and amusing. Concepts such as buffer stores and work space, associative memory, access time, storage and control processes, push-down stacks, and all the rest are certainly too useful and even powerful to do without. In moments of weakness it is tempting to start speculating about how human short-term memory might really be like the accumulator, say, of a PDP computer in the laboratory; one has displacement, overwriting, transfer, limited capacity, coding, and, with a little imagination, one could probably even generate U-shaped serial position curves and transpositions.

These computer concepts may or not be more than metaphors. The important point, however, is that there is only one sure thing we can take as a guiding principle from computer analogies. It is that relatively complex processes can be obtained by concatenating very simple and fundamental logical properties. This point is not new; see, for instance, Suppes (1969) and Wooldridge (1963, p. 236).

The second general point is that we may be too casual in our use of the notion of "stages of processing." Suppose one has a model with two "stages" such as short-term memory and long-term memory. Two questions about transfer of which information should be but seldom are asked are: (a) What is the change in redundancy from one stage to the next? (b) What is the transfer function involved? Briefly, let me amplify.

If there is a change in redundancy, then presumably information available at one stage is not available at the other stage. (Obviously, the direction of change can be either way, depending upon whether redundancy is seen as increasing or decreasing.) If redundancy is seen as increasing, then it must be recognized that this is an uneconomical operation from the point of biological utility, and some justification must be provided. On the other hand, if redundancy is seen as decreasing, then information available at one stage must not be available at a later stage. With modality comparisons it often is.

Point (b) above seems seldom to be appreciated. If we have a "stage" of processing, and if we take the black-box approach (as we almost must), then we must have an input to this black box and an output from it. Furthermore, there must be a transfer function involved that maps the input into the output. "Electrical communication involves the generation and processing of random signals: waveforms are transformed by modulation, detection, filtering, and so forth. As a consequence, many of the communication applications of probability theory involve the generation of new random variables by means of transformations applied to given ones [Wozencraft & Jacobs, 1965, p. 58]." From knowing the input function and the output function, one may try to infer the transfer function. This transfer function then tells you something about the mode of operation of the unknown in the system; namely, the black box.

The effect of a given transfer function upon a given input function is not always obvious. To take a simple example, suppose the input is a ramp function, $f(x) = 2x$, $0 \leqslant x \leqslant 1$, and the black box simply squares the input, so $y = h(x) = x^2$. This situation is depicted in Fig. 5. Imagine, for instance, that on each trial some value between 0 and 1.0 is fed into the black box, and the output is the square of the input. The ramp function simply describes the distribution of inputs over trials. I ask the reader to predict what the output distribution will be. The answer is given in Fig. 6, and I will be surprised if you are not surprised.

What does this example have to do with human memory? Suppose one believes in a strength theory of memory, and there is a decision system that maps the strength of the memory trace into some observable response such as a confidence judgment. Then memory

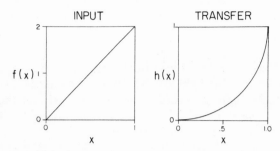

Fig. 5. Ramp input and "squarer" transfer function.

trace strength would be the input, the decision system the black box, and the confidence judgments the output. We must be careful not to place too much trust in our intuitions. Suppose we do an experiment to find out what the distribution of confidence judgments is. What will this experiment tell us about the underlying trace-strength distribution or the transfer function of the decision system — without knowing one or the other, very little.

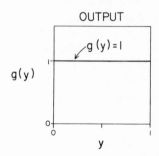

Fig. 6. Rectangular output from ramp input to "squarer" transfer function.

These comments should not be construed as opposition to the "stages of processing" concept. It is a powerful and widely used tool in other disciplines, and it has already been used to good advantage in psychology in interpreting data from reaction time studies (e.g., Sternberg, 1969a) and in applications of signal-detection theory to memory (e.g., Lockhart & Murdock, 1970). Furthermore, in the next section I shall suggest a model based directly on a separation of the memory and decision components of the system. The caution is meant to apply to the intuitive use of this concept. If the distributions and relationships are not explicitly specified, the predictions are not always as obvious as one might think.

Let me summarize what I have tried to say. I do not think that the case for a two-store model is yet proved. The reasons for dividing the human information processing system into sensory registers, a short-term buffer, and a longer term memory are not compelling. In the following section, I shall try to present a viable alternative to a two-store model. It is an elaboration and extension of the fluctuation model that I have previously suggested (Murdock, 1967c, 1970). There is no partitioning of the memory space into temporally distinct subsets. It is a finite-state representation of memory, and the concept of trace strength is not used.

## B. FINITE-STATE DECISION MODEL

Performance on a recognition-memory task involves basically two components of the human information processing system: comparison and decision. When the probe is presented, some representation is compared against representations of the possible alternatives from which a choice is to be made. This comparison is one main stage of processing, and the output from this stage becomes the input to the decision system. The actual observed response is the output from the decision stage, so these processes are the main components of performance in recognition memory. A similar view is suggested in Kintsch (1970). Parenthetically, it might be mentioned that the fact that reaction time in studies of recognition memory increases in linear fashion as a function of set size does not necessitate the assumption of an underlying serial comparison process (Atkinson, Holmgren, & Juola, 1969; Murdock, 1971a).

In recall there is an additional process or stage which we can loosely call "search." I have nothing very useful or novel to say about search here, but it does seem that its existence should be noted. The main point is that recall may fail because an item is inaccessible even though available. Whether or not a similar failure can occur in recognition is currently a moot point; Tulving and Thomson (1971) argue that it can, but the logic of their argument is not impeccable. In any case, it still seems a likely possibility that recall involves an additional process or stage not present in recognition.

Elsewhere (Murdock, 1970) I have made some suggestions as to how the output from the memory system might be mapped by the decision process into observable responses. However, this application was very restricted, dealing only with single-trial probe paired associates. Here I would like to concentrate on extending the model to additional tasks; in particular, multitrial paired associates, single-trial free recall, and judgments of recency. I shall, however, start with the previous single-trial paired-associate application, presenting this material as background and also including some new parameter estimates.

The emphasis here, then, will be on the memory aspects of the system, and little more will be said about decision processes. I would suggest that short-term memory can be viewed as a stochastic process in which the state of items in memory fluctuates over time. More specifically, when an item (a single unit such as a word or a single paired associate) is first presented to $S$ it may be encoded into memory, and the probability that it will be so encoded is $p_0$. As each subsequent item is presented there is a certain probability that the target item will be forgotten, and this probability is $\alpha$. Items which have been forgotten may recover, and this probability is $\beta$. In other words, there are two states, an item is either available or unavailable, forgetting occurs when an item moves from the former to the latter state, recovery occurs when an item moves from the latter to the former state, and $\alpha$ and $\beta$ are simply the transition probabilities. Every time a new item is presented or an old item is tested, changes of state can occur. Whether or not a given item does in fact change state is, of course, probabilistic rather than deterministic.

The longer the initial presentation time and/or the greater the number of presentations, the larger the numerical value of $\beta$, the recovery parameter. The exact relationship between presentation time and $\beta$ is determined by the parameter $\gamma$, and this relationship seems to be slightly different for multitrial paired associates and single-trial free recall. In general, though, increasing total presentation time does not "strengthen the memory trace," whatever that means, instead, it increases the probability that an item, once forgotten, will recover.

In a multitrial learning task such as paired associates, an important determinant of performance is the number of times the item in question has been correctly recalled (anticipated). In the model, each successful recall is presumed to decrease subsequent forgetting. In particular, the numerical value of $\alpha$ decreases geometrically as a function of the number of prior correct recalls, and the rate at which it decreases is determined by the parameter $\delta$. Thus, we have a nonhomogeneous Markov process in which the transition parameters $\alpha$ and $\beta$ vary with practice, and the parameters which determine how they vary with practice are $\delta$ and $\gamma$, respectively.

The problem of accessibility seems to be most serious in free recall. Therefore, it will be necessary to introduce yet another parameter, $\theta$, the probability that an available item will actually be recalled. There must also be problems with accessibility in paired associates. If so, then this parameter would be relevant there too. However, this application has not yet been attempted.

If the reader is disturbed by the apparent proliferation of parameters, it might be noted that the buffer model of Atkinson and Shiffrin (1968) requires about the same number of parameters to account for the diverse empirical phenomena to which the model has been applied. Also, in the present case one or more parameters may often be regarded as fixed or determined, so in any specific application the number of free parameters is not quite so large. Given the wide variety of empirical effects that we know about, the best strategy would seem to be to postulate processes and parameters which can account for some of the main effects taken individually. Then, one can work out the interrelationships to see how well the interactions can be explained.

Let me call the two states A and N. An item in State A is available, while an item in State N is not. [In Murdock (1970), the states denoted accessibility, but with the introduction of the retrieval parameter $\theta$ they now are better described in terms of availability.] To keep track of changes in state it is useful to have a transition matrix $T$ which gives the probability that an item will or will not change state as each new item is presented (or as each old item is tested). This matrix is simply

$$T = \begin{bmatrix} 1-\alpha & \alpha \\ \beta & 1-\beta \end{bmatrix} \tag{3}$$

In addition to $T$ one needs the vector

$$s = (p_0 \quad 1-p_0) \tag{4}$$

for the starting states; with probability $p_0$, an item which is presented starts in State A, and with probability $1-p_0$ it starts in State N. The parameter $p_0$ is for initial encoding, and it appears to relate to memory processes rather than perception (as measured, say, by $S$'s ability to repeat a word he has just seen or heard).

The probability that an item is available after $i$ units of interference is

$$P_A(i) = \frac{\beta}{\alpha+\beta} + \left( p_0 - \frac{\beta}{\alpha+\beta} \right)(1-\alpha-\beta)^i \tag{5}$$

Thus, when $i = 0$ then $P_A(i) = p_0$ and when $i$ is very large $P_A(i)$ approaches $\beta/(\alpha+\beta)$ as an asymptote. If one normalizes the recency effect as in Eq. (1) and calls this $y$ then

$$\log y = i \log (1-\alpha-\beta) \qquad (6)$$

where

$$y = \frac{P_A(i)-\beta/(\alpha+\beta)}{p_0-\beta/(\alpha+\beta)} \qquad (7)$$

Thus, on a semilog plot, the recency effect should be linear with a slope of $\log (1-\alpha-\beta)$.

To give the reader some familiarity with the model, Fig. 7 shows

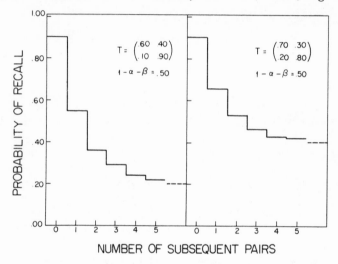

Fig. 7. Illustration of retention curves differing only in asymptote.

two short-term retention curves which differ only in asymptote (.20 and .40 for the left and right panels, respectively). Figure 8 shows two curves with the same asymptote and intercept but quite different slopes. The encoding parameter $p_0$ determines the intercept or starting value, and its effect will be illustrated later. It should be noted that in the model the slope, asymptote, and intercept are three independent aspects of short-term retention curves in that each is free to vary without affecting either of the other two.

To date, I have tried to apply this basic model to single-trial paired associates, multitrial paired associates, single-trial free recall, and judgments of recency. Although the basic framework is the same, the

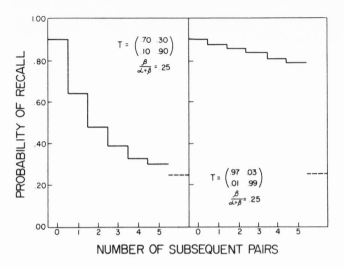

Fig. 8. Illustration of retention curves differing only in slope.

details vary somewhat according to the application. Therefore, these applications will be discussed in turn.

### 1. Single-Trial Paired Associates

In this task a short list of paired associates is presented once, and then the $S$ is probed with one word of a pair to see if he can recall its mate. Typical data are shown in Fig. 9, where the vertical bars represent means and standard deviations across $S$s. Probability of correct recall is plotted as a function of input interference. The values of $\alpha$, $\beta$, and $p_0$ were .39, .13, and .90, respectively. The staircase shows the retention curve predicted by the model given these parameters, and the numerical value of the asymptote is .25 (for additional details, see Murdock, 1970).

As has already been discussed (see this same reference) the model predicts the major empirical effects found in single-trial paired associates; namely, the shape of the recency effect, the existence of an asymptote, the absence of a primacy effect, the RTT data, and the linear relationship between list length and number of words recalled. In addition, confidence judgment data, *a posteriori* probabilities, and Type II ROC curves can be given a rational interpretation within the model provided one is willing to make additional assumptions about the decision processes involved in short-term memory experiments; again see this same reference.

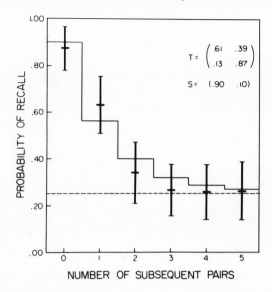

Fig. 9. Recall probability in a single-trial paired-associate probe experiment; data and model.

Thus, qualitatively speaking, the model is reasonably consonant with experimental data. More stringent tests are now appropriate; namely, experimental separation of parameters. As the model now stands, there are three parameters: $\alpha$, $\beta$, and $p_0$. It would be desirable to find experimental variables which would uniquely affect individual parameters. Two such attempts will be reported, one varying presentation time and the other varying modality of presentation.

The first experiment tested four paid $S$s on one practice session and 12 test sessions. On each session, each $S$ was given 60 lists, each of six pairs, and the items were common English words. It was a probe study, and each possible position was tested once in each block of six lists. The presentation time was one, two, three, or four seconds/pair, constant within a session but varied across sessions. Presentation was visual, each $S$ was tested individually, computer-generated lists were used, the recall interval was 15 seconds, omissions were proscribed, and across sessions each $S$ cycled through the four different presentation times in the same order but with a unique starting value. Confidence judgments were obtained but not analyzed.

The main results (pooled over the four $S$s) are shown in Fig. 10, where probability of recall is plotted as a function of numbers of

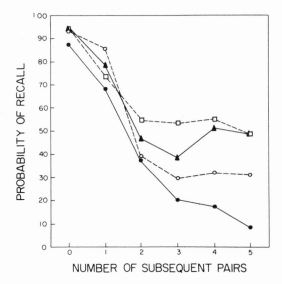

Fig. 10. Recall probability in single-trial paired-associate probe experiment with four presentation times. *Key:* 4 seconds = □– – –□; 3 seconds = ▲——▲; 2 seconds = ○– – –○; 1 second = ●——●.

subsequent pairs. Generally speaking, the curves seem to differ primarily in asymptote, a result consistent with a previous finding (see Murdock, 1970, Fig. 3, p. 289).

To estimate parameters, a simplex method for function minimization as described by Nelder and Mead (1965) was used. Minimum $\chi^2$ values are given in Table II, which shows the values of $\alpha$, $\beta$, $p_0$, and $\chi^2$ for each of the four presentation times (data pooled over $Ss$). The conclusion that I would like to draw from these data is that presentation time affects $\beta$ but not $\alpha$ or $p_0$.

TABLE II

Parameter Estimates and $\chi^2$ for Paired-Associate Probe
Experiment with Different Presentation Times
(Fluctuation Model)

|        | 1 second | 2 seconds | 3 seconds | 4 seconds |
|--------|----------|-----------|-----------|-----------|
| $\alpha$  | .345     | .295      | .301      | .271      |
| $\beta$   | .000     | .065      | .225      | .259      |
| $p_0$     | .891     | .945      | .955      | .943      |
| $\chi^2$  | 7.29     | 30.0      | 16.4      | 2.53      |

## TABLE III

Parameter Estimates and $\chi^2$ for Paired-Associate Probe
Experiment for Each of the Four $Ss$ (Fluctuation Model)

| Subject | Time (seconds) | $\alpha$ | $\beta$ | $p_0$ | $\chi^2$ |
|---------|------|------|------|------|------|
| A.K. | 1 | .382 | .009 | .940 | 6.06 |
|      | 2 | .279 | .038 | .918 | 7.29 |
|      | 3 | .383 | .241 | .970 | 15.65 |
|      | 4 | .344 | .234 | 1.000 | 5.85 |
| L.K. | 1 | .257 | .000 | .911 | 4.52 |
|      | 2 | .310 | .213 | .967 | 1.63 |
|      | 3 | .223 | .453 | .936 | 3.22 |
|      | 4 | .373 | .853 | .969 | 19.78 |
| B.L. | 1 | .386 | .000 | .857 | 4.38 |
|      | 2 | .335 | .064 | 1.000 | 20.50 |
|      | 3 | .305 | .242 | 1.000 | 5.23 |
|      | 4 | .178 | .000 | .975 | 3.74 |
| C.M. | 1 | .367 | .000 | .862 | 6.09 |
|      | 2 | .294 | .035 | .897 | 17.38 |
|      | 3 | .273 | .017 | .912 | 4.97 |
|      | 4 | .178 | .000 | .848 | 5.09 |

The results of comparable analyses for individual $Ss$ are shown in Table III. Here, the results are not quite so uniform. Subjects A. K. and L. K. clearly showed the desired effects; namely, a systematic change only in $\beta$. It is this increase in $\beta$ with presentation time that results in the higher asymptote. However, C. M. showed instead a decrease in $\alpha$, while B. L. showed a little of both. Until more evidence is available, I would like to think that the original conclusion still might possibly be correct.

For comparative purposes, we also fit the buffer model of Atkinson $et\ al.$ (1967) to the data. The three equations used were

$$\beta_j = \begin{cases} 1-\alpha, & j = 0 \\ (1-\beta_0)(1-\alpha/r)^{j-1}\alpha/r, & j > 0 \end{cases} \tag{8}$$

$$\Pr(C_i) = \left[1 - \sum_{k=0}^{i} \beta_k\right] + \left[\sum_{k=0}^{i} \beta_k \rho_{ik}\right] \tag{9}$$

$$\rho_{ij} = 1-(1-g) \exp\left[-j\theta(\tau^{i-j})\right] \tag{10}$$

where $r$ is buffer size, $\alpha$ is the probability that an item (pair) enters the buffer, $\theta$ is the transfer rate from the buffer to long-term memory, and $\tau$ is the decay parameter for information that has been displaced from the buffer but exists in long-term memory. The guessing value $g$ was set to zero since words rather than digits were used as the stimulus material, and for the same reason $(s-r)/s$ was taken as unity. Since the intertrial interval was short (15 seconds), it was assumed that the buffer was already full at the start of each trial. Finally, $r$ was restricted to integer values, and $\alpha$, $\theta$, and $\tau$ were restricted to the range 0–1. [While some values of $\theta$ in Table I of Atkinson *et al.* (1967) exceed unity, this parameter is treated as a probability in Atkinson and Shiffrin (1965).]

The parameter estimates and $\chi^2$ are shown in Table IV, summed over Ss, and in Table V separately for each S. A comparison of Tables II and IV indicates that the goodness of fit of the two models is comparable, though the buffer model has one more free parameter than the fluctuation model. If the parameters are reestimated with $r$ fixed at 3, then for the one-second group the values of $\alpha$, $\theta$, $\tau$, and $\chi^2$ are .895, .000, .913, and 15.53, respectively. While the fit worsens, the overall pattern of results becomes more regular. With $r = 3$, the buffer model says that increasing the presentation time has as its main effect increasing the rate at which information is transferred from the buffer to long-term memory.

TABLE IV

Parameter Estimates and $\chi^2$ for Paired-Associate Probe
Experiment with Different Presentation Times
(Buffer Model)

|          | 1 second | 2 seconds | 3 seconds | 4 seconds |
|----------|----------|-----------|-----------|-----------|
| $r$      | 2        | 3         | 3         | 3         |
| $\alpha$ | .879     | .945      | .952      | .941      |
| $\theta$ | .516     | .074      | .204      | .275      |
| $\tau$   | .000     | 1.000     | 1.000     | 1.000     |
| $\chi^2$ | 3.99     | 30.0      | 17.54     | 2.78      |

However, this pattern does not hold up for individual Ss. A look at Table V shows that $\theta$ and $\tau$ vary widely both within and between Ss. In addition, $r$ varied somewhat too. (The parameter $\alpha$ in the buffer model is comparable to $p_0$ in the fluctuation model; in both cases they are heavily determined by performance on the last pair in the

TABLE V

Parameter Estimates and $\chi^2$ for Paired-Associate Probe Experiment for
Each of the Four $Ss$ (Buffer Model)

| Subject | Time (seconds) | $r$ | $\alpha$ | $\theta$ | $\tau$ | $\chi^2$ |
|---------|------|-----|------|------|------|------|
| A.K. | 1 | 2 | .933 | .325 | .091 | 6.30 |
|      | 2 | 3 | .909 | .314 | .000 | 7.75 |
|      | 3 | 3 | .965 | .143 | 1.000 | 18.60 |
|      | 4 | 3 | 1.000 | .166 | 1.000 | 7.13 |
| L.K. | 1 | 3 | .908 | .241 | .000 | 4.49 |
|      | 2 | 4 | .951 | .083 | 1.000 | 3.31 |
|      | 3 | 4 | .926 | .433 | 1.000 | 3.70 |
|      | 4 | 2 | .903 | .898 | 1.000 | 27.4 |
| B.L. | 1 | 1 | .841 | 1.000 | .398 | 2.45 |
|      | 2 | 2 | 1.000 | .266 | .744 | 23.1 |
|      | 3 | 3 | 1.000 | .207 | 1.000 | 5.64 |
|      | 4 | 4 | .968 | .983 | .000 | 0.97 |
| C.M. | 1 | 2 | .863 | .368 | .000 | 4.83 |
|      | 2 | 3 | .891 | .161 | .000 | 17.79 |
|      | 3 | 3 | .908 | .205 | .000 | 5.08 |
|      | 4 | 4 | .845 | .247 | .000 | 5.10 |

list.) All in all, I would say that the fluctuation model is somewhat more economical than the buffer model in describing the data of this experiment.

The second set of data to establish parameter separation comes from a previous study of response latencies (Murdock, 1968b). It was a standard paired-associate probe experiment in which one of the experimental variables was the length of time allowed for recall. Another variable was modality of presentation. The recall data from this experiment (partitioned on modality but pooled over recall times) are shown in Fig. 11. As can be seen, modality of presentation seems to affect the recency part of the curve but not asymptote (see also Murdock & Walker, 1969).

Parameter estimates are given in Table VI. The technique used here was a grid search which explored progressively smaller regions of the parameter space as each global minimum was found. The largest effect of modality is on the encoding parameter $p_0$; by comparison $\alpha$ and $\beta$ do not seem to be much affected by the auditory-visual manipulation.

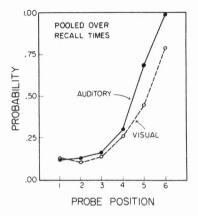

Fig. 11. Recall probability as a function of modality of presentation (data from Murdock, 1968b).

TABLE VI

Parameter Estimates and $\chi^2$ for Fluctuation Model

| Modality | $\alpha$ | $\beta$ | $p_0$ | $\chi^2$ |
|----------|----------|---------|-------|----------|
| Auditory | .432 | .026 | 1.00 | 6.23 |
| Visual | .485 | .048 | .80 | 1.74 |

Note: Data from Murdock (1968b).

## 2. Multitrial Paired Associates

To extend the fluctuation model from the single presentation and probe to the multitrial situation necessitates assumptions about the effects of repeated presentations and correct recalls (anticipations). As stated above, the assumptions are that repeated presentations increase the probability of recovery and that each correct recall of a pair decreases the probability of subsequent forgetting of that pair. Thus, each repetition increases $\beta$, and each correct recall decreases $\alpha$. Some evidence for the first assumption does exist. In two studies, Postman (1963) varied the number of presentations of paired associates before giving a series of test trials. The data (see particularly Figs. 8-2, 8-3, and 8-4) show that the NC responses (correct on a second test given not correct on the first) increased with the number of presentations.

More specifically, let us assume that

$$\beta = 1 - e^{-\gamma t} \tag{11}$$

and

$$\alpha_k = \alpha_0 e^{-\delta k} \tag{12}$$

Equation (11) says that $\beta$ increases in negatively accelerated fashion with (functional) study time, and the rate parameter is $\gamma$. [The distinction between nominal and functional study time, as in Cooper and Pantle (1967), might become important at slow presentation rates.] Equation (12) says that the forgetting parameter $\alpha$ decreases geometrically to zero from an initial value of $\alpha_0$ as a function of $k$ where $k$ is the number of prior correct recalls. The rate parameter here is $\delta$.

A Monte Carlo simulation was run on the computer to see if the data it generated could bear a reasonable resemblance to data from human Ss. The "real" data came from an old study (Murdock, 1961a) which had used a study-test procedure. There were 20 paired associates consisting of Thorndike-Lorge (Thorndike & Lorge, 1944) A and AA words, 10 trials, a presentation time of two seconds/pair, and 32 Ss from the subject pool at the University of Vermont. Given the heterogeneity of Ss and pairs, I analyzed here only the data from the middle 10 Ss and the middle six pairs. The Monte Carlo simulation was run on 1000 statistical Ss.

It is possible to find parameter values such that the data from the simulation are much like the data from the experimental Ss. Figure 12 shows a typical multitrial paired-associate acquisition ("learning")

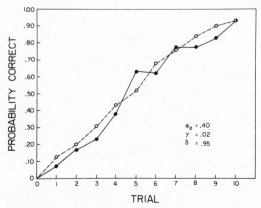

Fig. 12. Paired-associate acquisition curve for human subjects and Monte Carlo simulation. *Key:* subjects = ●——●; Monte Carlo = ○– – –○.

curve; that is, probability correct as a function of trials. The values of the parameters are shown in the graph; $p_0$ was held at 1.0.

In case it is not clear, for the Monte Carlo we actually "ran" 1000 $S$s each for 10 trials, incrementing $\beta$ appropriately over trials, decreasing $\alpha_k$ for each correct recall, using a standard pseudo-random number generator to determine "correct" and "incorrect" responses, and scoring data exactly as one would with human $S$s. For description of computer simulation techniques see Naylor, Balintfy, Burdick, and Chu (1966) or Martin (1968).

A more detailed comparison of the two sets of data is shown in Fig. 13, where the probability of a first correct anticipation on Trial $n$ is plotted as a function of $n$, both for the human $S$s and for the Monte Carlo. At each trial, only those pairs were tabulated which had not, on any previous trial, been correctly recalled. The increase in this conditional probability over trials reflects the effect of study time on $\beta$. And, of course, this increase would be inconsistent with a single-stage all-or-none model (see Restle, 1965).

Finally, for the Monte Carlo data I determined the probability of a correct recall on that trial immediately following the first correct anticipation. The values were .36, .44, .51, .50, .59, .54, .63, .70, and .76 for Trials 2–10, respectively. A comparison of these values with those of Fig. 13 will show the potency of reinforcement. One correct

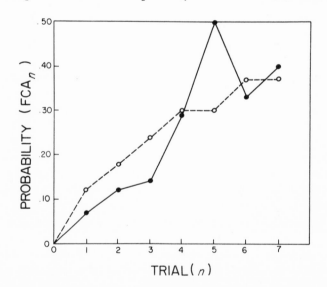

Fig. 13. Probability of first correct anticipation on trial $n$ for human subjects and Monte Carlo simulation. *Key:* subjects = ●——●; Monte Carlo = ○- - -○.

recall appreciably increases the probability of another. For the human $S$s, the probability (summed over all trials because of insufficient data) was .68.

This is as far as I have gone in extending the fluctuation model to the multitrial situation. It seems promising in that it can generate data which, superficially at least are like real data. It accommodates the effects of repetition and reinforcement. The fact that one can trade repetitions for presentation time in a probe experiment (Murdock, 1965c) is quite consistent with the model. However, difficulties may be experienced with the lag effect (Bjork, 1970; Greeno, 1964; Peterson, Wampler, Kirkpatrick, & Saltzman, 1963), and whether the model can account for some of the really detailed features of the data (e.g., Bower, 1961) remains to be seen.

### 3. Single-Trial Free Recall

The extension of the fluctuation model to single-trial free recall is somewhat different from the extension to paired-associate learning. This difference reflects the basic difference between cued and noncued recall. In single-trial free recall, $S$ must report as many of the items as he can remember, and generally he is not provided either with probes or with retrieval cues.

There is clearly a retrieval problem here. As discussed in Section IV, F items may be available but not accessible. That items can be available but not retrieved was demonstrated in a study by Tulving (1967) where three outputs followed each input. Although the total number of words recalled stayed approximately constant over each set of three outputs (see Tulving, 1967, Fig. 2, p. 178), only about 50% of the words were recalled in all three output phases. In the model, the probability that an available item will be recalled is $\theta$.

Single-trial free recall studies typically show a primacy effect (e.g., Murdock, 1962), but single-trial paired-associate probe studies do not (e.g., Murdock 1967c). Furthermore, in free recall, the $S$ probably groups or organizes the material somehow during list presentation. At the beginning of the list there are only a few items to work with, but as each additional item is presented the load increases. To reflect these processes it will be assumed that the numerical value of the recovery parameter $\beta$ assigned to each item decreases during list presentation. More specifically, since organization requires rehearsal, rehearsal takes time and the amount of time available for each new item presented decreases the larger the number of other items currently available. So, the value of $\beta$ assigned to each item is simply the starting value, $\beta_1$, divided by the number of currently available items. That differential rehearsal is a factor of some importance in single-trial free recall is suggested by the results of Rundus and Atkinson (1970) and Bruce and Papay (1970).

In reporting the analyses, we shall give the numerical values of $\gamma$ rather than $\beta$. The relationship between these two parameters is given in Eq. (11) provided one remembers that here this equation determines the starting value $\beta_1$. As noted above, $\beta_1$ must be attenuated by the number of prior available items.

Finally, from what we know about order of output in single-trial free recall, the regularities in the data clearly seem to preclude any *simple* random-sampling model. With considerable uniformity, practiced Ss recall the last few items first [usually in a forward order, though this may depend upon modality of presentation (see Murdock & Walker, 1969)]. However, the interresponse time data do suggest a random-sampling process (e.g., Murdock & Okada, 1970). As an attempt to represent these features of the data in the model, it will be assumed that recall proceeds as follows: the $S$ outputs the last chunk with probability 1, then randomly samples with probability $\theta$ from the remaining pool of available items. The last chunk will be an unbroken terminal string of available items. Thus, if available and unavailable items are represented by 1 and 0, respectively, at the end of list presentation the availability of a 20-item list might be 10110001011011101111. Then, chunk size would be four. These last four items would be recalled with probability 1, while the probability of recalling any of the remaining items would be $\theta$.

As evidence for the psychological reality of the concept of the last chunk, let me mention one additional analysis of data reported in Murdock and Okada (1970). Look at only those cases where Ss recall 17, 18, 19, 20, 00 in order. That is, they run out the string by recalling the items which had been presented in these serial positions (20-word lists), and "00" designates some nonterminal list item. For 103 such cases, mean inter-response times were 426, 639, 752, and 2830 msec for serial positions 17-18, 18-19, 19-20, and 20-00, respectively. Thus, after Ss have recalled the last chunk, there seems to be a discontinuity in the retrieval process.

We may, then, define the following four terms: $w_j(i)$ is the probability that an item is available, $x(n)$ is the chunk size distribution, $y(j)$ is the probability that an item is available outside the last chunk, and $z(j)$ is the probability of recall of an item. We have four parameters: $\alpha, \beta_1, p_0$, and $\theta$ where $\beta_1$ is the initial value of the recovery parameter at the start of the list. As mentioned, $\theta$ is the retrieval parameter; $\alpha$ and $p_0$ are as defined previously. Then, the equations are

$$w_j(i) = \frac{\beta_j}{\alpha+\beta_j} + \left(p_0 - \frac{\beta_j}{\alpha+\beta_j}\right)(1-\alpha-\beta_j)^i$$

$$\beta_j = \begin{cases} 1-e^{-\gamma t}, & j = 1 \\ \dfrac{\beta_1}{\displaystyle\sum_{k=1}^{j} w_k(j-k)}, & j > 1 \end{cases} \tag{13}$$

$$x(n) = \begin{cases} 1-p_0, & n = 0 \\ \left(\displaystyle\prod_{i=0}^{n-1} w_{L-i}(i)\right)[1-w_{L-n}(n)], & n > 0 \end{cases} \tag{14}$$

$$y(j) = \begin{cases} 0, & j = L \\ \displaystyle\sum_{n=0}^{n=L-(j+1)} x(n), & j < L \end{cases} \tag{15}$$

$$z(j) = w_j(L-j)\{[1-y(j)] + \theta y(j)\} \tag{16}$$

where $L$ is list length, the subscripts $j$ and $k$ are for serial position, and $i$ is the number of subsequent items. Equation (13) must be computed recursively; the rule used was to increment the value of $i$ before assigning the value of $\beta_j$ to the current item. Also, $y(j)$ is a conditional probability; given that an item is available, $y(j)$ is the probability that it is available outside the last chunk.

The model was first fitted to the serial position data of Murdock (1962). The actual numbers used are those shown in Norman (1970, Table II, p. 514). Although it is not stated there, these data are based on only the first 15 Ss per group; having equal N's for all six groups makes comparison easier. In fitting, the simplex method was used; the parameter estimates and the minimum $\chi^2$ value for each group are shown in Table VII. As noted above, Eq. (13) computes with $\beta_j$ but $\beta_1$ is determined from Eq. (11). Consequently, the appropriate parameter to report is $\gamma$.

It is obvious from Table VII that the numerical values of $\chi^2$ are very large. However, in evaluating the fit it must be remembered that the number of subject lists per group is also quite large (i.e., 1200). When one considers the number of data points involved, the worst fit

TABLE VII

Parameter Estimates and $\chi^2$ for Serial Position Curves of Single-Trial
Free Recall

| Group | $\alpha$ | $\gamma$ | $p_0$ | $\theta$ | $\chi^2$ |
|-------|------|------|-------|------|------|
| 10-2 | .143 | .192 | .955 | .949 | 46.5 |
| 15-2 | .120 | .241 | .983 | .800 | 26.6 |
| 20-2 | .124 | .235 | .954 | .684 | 80.5 |
| 20-1 | .135 | .200 | .963 | .622 | 206.7 |
| 30-1 | .125 | .502 | .977 | .520 | 230.6 |
| 40-1 | .096 | .397 | .944 | .350 | 281.5 |

Note: Data from Murdock (1962).

is group 20-1. For a visual evaluation, the model predictions and the data for this group are shown in Fig. 14. The first serial position is badly off, but otherwise the fit does not seem too unreasonable. Quantitative comparisons with other models are much to be desired. However, while everyone seems to fit these data, they seldom report numerical measures of goodness of fit.

As the predicted curve in Fig. 14 shows, the model is quite capable of generating serial position curves for single-trial free recall which

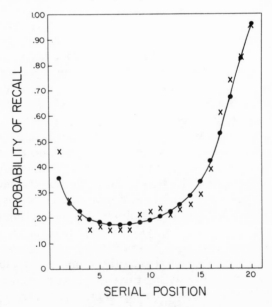

Fig. 14. Serial position curve for Group 20-1 with parameter estimates for model from Table VII. *Key:* Data = X; model = ●——●.

have the necessary characteristics; namely, an S-shaped recency effect, a small primacy effect, and an asymptote that is (more or less) flat. The parameter estimates, however, are not completely unambiguous. While $\alpha$ and $p_0$ seem quite constant across the six groups, both $\gamma$ and $\theta$ vary. The problem in interpreting these trends is that no estimate of error is readily available; also, at times the parameter space is quite flat. Appreciable changes in a parameter value can occur with very small effect on the overall goodness of fit.

I think that the best way to make sense out of these findings is to do parameter estimates for each S individually. Hopefully, the parameter space will not be so flat as for data averaged over many Ss and, of course, estimates of variability will then be available. Work on this problem is currently under way.

However, as a provisional attempt, we reestimated the parameters with $\alpha$, $\gamma$, and $p_0$ fixed across groups but $\theta$ free to vary. The rationale was that perhaps the variations in $\gamma$ reported in Table VII were spurious. The parameter estimates that then resulted were .119, .318, and .962 for $\alpha$, $\gamma$, and $p_0$, respectively, and .772, .760, .624, .495, .574, and .438 for $\theta$ for Groups 1–6, respectively. Since the lists in Groups 1–3 were presented for two seconds per word but the lists in Groups 4–6 were presented for one second per word, and since the numerical estimates for $\theta$ seem to break accordingly, one interpretation of these findings would be that increased presentation time increased the probability of retrieval for each item, but list length does not affect retrieval probability *per se*.

The $\chi^2$ goodness of fit value was 1019. Since the value with all four parameters free to vary was 872 (the sum of the six numbers in the last column of Table VII), reducing the number of free parameters from 24 to 9 only results in an increase of 17% in $\chi^2$. If the provisional interpretation suggested above turns out to be correct, then one could further reduce the number of parameters from 9 to 5 (one value of $\theta$ for each of the two presentation rates used, plus one each for $\alpha$, $\gamma$, and $p_0$). If past experience is any guide, further increases in $\chi^2$ would be trivial.

Given that the model can describe serial position curves of single-trial free recall, do the parameters change reasonably with experimental manipulation? Two attempts to answer this question will be reported, one varying modality and presentation rate, the second introducing the use of a subsidiary task. The data for the former come from Experiment I of Murdock and Walker (1969), where presentation of 20-word lists was either auditory or visual and (orthogonally) at a presentation rate of either one or two words/second.

The parameter estimates (simplex method) are shown in Table VIII. The value of $p_0$ is lower for auditory than visual and this difference is greater at the fast presentation rate than at the slow presentation rate. Both these effects were anticipated. What was not expected were the changes in $\theta$. What these changes mean is not yet clear.

TABLE VIII

Parameter Estimates and $\chi^2$ for Serial Position Curves as a Function of Mode and Rate of Presentation

| Condition | $\alpha$ | $\gamma$ | $p_0$ | $\theta$ | $\chi^2$ |
|---|---|---|---|---|---|
| Auditory-fast | .174 | .188 | .933 | .769 | 19.51 |
| Visual-fast | .216 | .195 | .742 | 1.000 | 20.59 |
| Auditory-slow | .136 | .162 | .945 | .638 | 26.56 |
| Visual-slow | .149 | .121 | .860 | .778 | 41.08 |

Note: Data from Murdock & Walker (1969).

The second manipulation involves the use of a subsidiary task. In the experiments, Ss sorted playing cards at the same time that they were listening to the presentation of the free-recall lists (Murdock, 1965a). In Experiment I, Ss either sorted the cards on the basis of color (red and black) or suit (a relatively incompatible ordering of diamonds, spades, clubs, and hearts) or simply (in the "plain" condition) turned them over one at a time and put them on a pile. In Experiment II, all Ss sorted by suit using the same incompatible arrangement; only the pay-off was varied. Under free recall emphasis, Ss were encouraged to do as well as they could on the recall task, while under card sorting emphasis they were told the card sorting was more important.

The serial position curves are shown in the original article, and the parameter estimates (simplex method) given here in Table IX. Variations in $\theta$ occur in Experiment I but not in Experiment II; however, they are irregular with respect to the experimental conditions. The main effect of the subsidiary task seems to be on $\gamma$. The change (Experiment I) from dealing to sorting seems to reduce the numerical value of the recovery parameter by a factor of four, and if in addition one puts a premium on the sorting it is reduced again by more than a factor of two (Experiment II).

Finally, the parameters reestimated with $\alpha$, $p_0$, and $\theta$ fixed but $\gamma$ free to vary across groups. For Experiment I the estimates were .17,

.87, and .46 for $\alpha$, $p_0$, and $\theta$, respectively, and .71, .20, and .12 for $\gamma$ for the three different experimental conditions. For Experiment II, the estimates were .17, .93, and .46 for $\alpha$, $p_0$, and $\theta$, respectively, and .16 and .06 for $\gamma$. In neither case did the $\chi^2$ go up much from the estimation shown in Table IX; specifically, in Experiment I it increased from 88.7 to 92.2, while in Experiment II it increased from 113.3 to 124. It seems reasonable to suggest that variations in the difficulty of a subsidiary task has its effect largely on the recovery process. This then is a somewhat more explicit statement of what a "limited capacity" hypothesis might mean.

TABLE IX

Parameter Estimates and $\chi^2$ for Serial Position Curves as a Function of the Nature (Exp. I) and Relative Importance (Exp. II) of the Subsidiary Task

| Experiment | Condition | $\alpha$ | $\gamma$ | $p_0$ | $\theta$ | $\chi^2$ |
|---|---|---|---|---|---|---|
| I | Plain | .15 | .60 | .84 | .47 | 32.1 |
| | Color | .20 | .15 | .87 | .61 | 28.4 |
| | Suit | .16 | .16 | .89 | .38 | 28.2 |
| II | FR emphasis | .15 | .15 | .95 | .43 | 55.1 |
| | CS emphasis | .19 | .06 | .93 | .49 | 58.2 |

Note: Data from Murdock (1965a).

Obviously, much remains to be done. The explanation of the variation in parameters with experimental conditions is clearly somewhat *ad hoc,* and we are far from a theory of parameters which is a reasonable long-range goal. In fact, we have not yet even deduced the linear relationship between recall and total presentation time (Murdock, 1967d) which, at least within limits, so frequently occurs in single-trial free recall. However, the model does seem of generating reasonable serial position curves which vary in reasonable ways with experimental manipulations — and without postulating separate short- and long-term stores.

## 4. Judgments of Recency

The basic experimental paradigm is one where a list of items is presented and followed by a probe whose relative ordinal position is to be judged. Thus, the list might be GALLANT, LEGEND, INSPIRE, FOOTBALL, STANDING followed by the probe

LEGEND. The correct judgment would be "four." Either a continuous or discrete trial procedure can be used, and the independent variable is sometimes reported in terms of lag (number of intervening items between presentation and probe; in the above example, three).

The unexpected finding in these studies is an overestimation at short lags followed by an underestimation at long lags. Figure 3 from a recent article by Hinrichs (1970) is reproduced here as Fig. 15 to

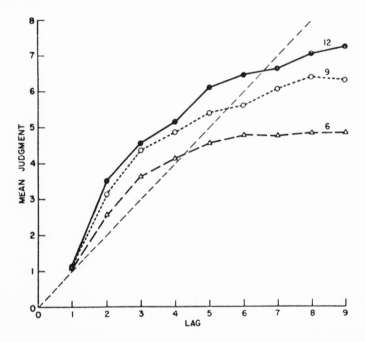

Fig. 15. Judgments of recency under three instructed maximum lag conditions (reproduced from Hinrichs, 1970, Fig. 3, with permission of the American Psychological Association). *Key:* Condition: 6 = – –△– –; 9 = – – – ○ – – –; 12 = –●–.

illustrate this phenomenon. In his study, the experimental manipulation was the "instructed" maximum lag; the true maximum lag was always nine. This finding has also been reported by Lockhart (1969) and Peterson (1967).

To account for this effect, assume the following: When the probe is presented, the S makes a backward scan of his memory system, counting available items until he comes to the trace of the probe. If the probe (i.e., its trace) is available, he increments the count (to convert lag into relative ordinal position) and reports this value as his judgment of recency. If the probe is not available, he reports $d/2$ where $d$ is the "functional" maximum delay.

To develop the equations, the probability that any given item is available is given by Eq. (5). For the sake of simplicity, assume that $p_0 = 1.0$ and $\beta = 0$ so Eq. (5) reduces to

$$P_A(j) = p^{j-1} \tag{17}$$

where $p = 1-\alpha$ and $j$ is relative ordinal position. Thus, the probability that an item is available is a simple geometric function, starting at unity for lag 0 and approaching zero asymptotically as lag increases.

For any given delay, we need to know the number of other available items intervening between the presentation of an item and its subsequent test. Stated as an urn problem, imagine that there are $n$ urns each with a different proportion of black and white marbles. With one draw from each urn, how many white marbles should you get? The probability of exactly $r$ successes with $n$ urns can be written as

$$f_{r,n} = \sum_{j=r}^{n} \left\{ (-1)^{j+r} \binom{j}{r} \Sigma\pi_j \right\} \tag{18}$$

where $\Sigma\pi_j$ refers to the sum of all $\binom{n}{j}$ combinations of products of the individual probabilities taken $j$ at a time. Also $\Sigma\pi_0 \equiv 1$. Thus, if $r = 1$, $n = 3$, and $p_1$, $p_2$, and $p_3$ denote the probabilities associated with each urn, we have

$$
\begin{aligned}
f_{1,3} &= 3\Sigma\pi_1 - 3\Sigma\pi_2 + \Sigma\pi_3 \\
&= 3(p_1 + p_2 + p_3) - 3(p_1 p_2 + p_1 p_3 + p_2 p_3) + p_1 p_2 p_3 \tag{19}
\end{aligned}
$$

To find the mean and variance of this distribution, we can write the moment-generating function as

$$M_r(\theta) = \sum_{r=0}^{n} e^{\theta r} f_{r,n} = \sum_{r=0}^{n} e^{\theta r} \sum_{j=r}^{n} \left\{ (-1)^{j+r} \binom{j}{r} \Sigma\pi_j \right\} \tag{20}$$

which looks more formidable than it really is. It turns out the first two moments of the distribution are very simple; specifically,

$$\mu = \Sigma\pi_1 = p_1 + p_2 + p_3 + \ldots + p_n \tag{21}$$

and

$$\sigma^2 = \Sigma\pi_1 - \Sigma(\pi_1)^2 = (p_1 + p_2 + \cdots + p_n) - (p_1^2 + p_2^2 + \cdots + p_n^2) \tag{22}$$

Thus, the mean is simply the sum of the individual probability values. If all probabilities are equal, Eq. (21) reduces to $\mu = np$, the mean of binomial distribution.

Given this result, we can easily write an expression for recency judgments. It is

$$Y(j) = P_A(j)(1 + \Sigma\pi_1) + (1 - P_A(j))(d/2) \qquad (23)$$

Verbally, the recency judgment will be an average of two cases. One is where the item is available, in which case over the long run the $S$ will report the average number of intervening available items incremented by one to convert lag to relative ordinal position. The other case is where the item is unavailable, in which case he will guess. His best guess is $d/2$.

Illustrative values are shown in Fig. 16 for functional lags of 6, 9, and 12 to parallel the Hinrichs (1970) data shown in Fig. 15. To generate these curves, we arbitrarily set the value of $p$ in Eq. (17) to 2/3 and, given Eq. (23), everything else followed. Not only do these curves show the basic overshoot-undershoot effect characteristic of judgments of recency in general, but they also seem to show much the same variation with instructed lag that the real data show.

It does not take too much imagination to extend the model so that it can make a prediction about latency data. Assume that the backward scan examines items one by one in serial fashion, and that

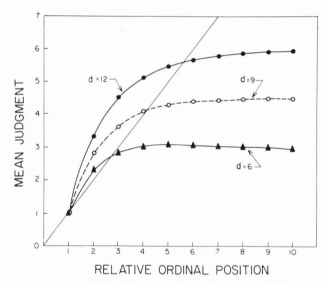

Fig. 16. Predicted recency judgments when $p = 1 - \alpha = 2/3$.

the time to examine each available item is the same. Then, it follows that, for lag $i$,

$$T_i \sim \sum_{j=0}^{i} p^j, \qquad i = 0, 1, 2, \ldots, d \qquad (24)$$

That is, the latency at any lag should be proportional to the number of items scanned, which will simply be the sum of the first $i$ terms of a geometric series. Probably, this prediction could also be deduced from a parallel-processing model (e.g., Murdock, 1971a).

Confirming evidence comes from a recent study by Okada (1970), and his Fig. 4 is reproduced here as Fig. 17. The experiment was

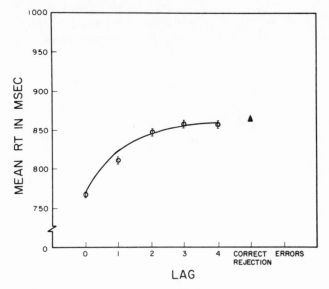

Fig. 17. Mean latencies as a function of lag in a continuous recognition memory experiment (data from Okada, 1970). *Key:* O = observed RTs for hits; — = exponential; $y = 861 - 91e^{-.84x}$; □ = miss; ■ = false alarm.

simply a continuous recognition memory task where latencies of "yes" and "no" responses were obtained. As can be seen, the data are well approximated by the appropriate exponential function.

## IV. Summary

In closing, let me paint with a broad brush. In a very general way, I would like to interrelate theory and data; specifically, the empirical phenomena of short-term memory and the finite-state decision model presented in the last section.

Items as presented are generally encoded into memory. Later items interfere with earlier items, but the loss of availability reflects interference rather than decay. The recency effect reflects the interference gradient, and will be S-shaped as a function of the greater accessibility of the terminal chunk. The asymptote reflects the equilibrium of two opposing processes, forgetting and recovery.

In principle, the recency effect, the asymptote, and the primacy effect of single-trial free recall are all experimentally separable. The area under the curve (though not its span) will be determined by the value of the encoding parameter $p_0$ and this is how modality effects are manifest. The size and extensiveness of the primacy effect reflects $\beta_1$, and the asymptote reflects the joint effects of $\alpha$ and $\beta_1$. Recognition would presumably be better than recall, and cued better than noncued recall through the operation of the retrieval parameter $\theta$. Increased presentation time increases the value of the recovery parameter $\beta$ and in cued recall tasks successful retrievals reduce $\alpha$, the probability of subsequent forgetting. The search through recent memory is along a temporally ordered dimension, and the overt response is a function of memory and decision processes.

In conclusion, it must be admitted that the model as presented here is far from complete; many details remain to be worked out, and on many points the model is vague or perhaps even wrong. Hopefully, however, it captures some of the major processes and is capable of explaining some of the main empirical findings that we know about today. Finally, let me close with a comment about an attitude that one hears not infrequently these days. The attitude can be labeled "model pessimism," and it refers to the following state of affairs: It often happens that models which as formulated sound quite different actually lead to similar or identical predictions. As a consequence, one might feel pessimistic about the potential contribution of theoretical models.

In reply, two points should be kept in mind: (a) It would be surprising if different models didn't lead to the same predictions, sometimes. After all, we are all working with the same corpus, and some theoretical convergence is surely both predictable and desirable. (b) It has not been demonstrated that different models *always* lead to the same predictions; presumably they don't. One may have to concentrate on finding those cases where differential predictions emerge. The history of science should teach us that this problem may not be trivial. In my opinion, model pessimism is unwarranted and deplorable. Sooner or later a generally acceptable model of memory and human information processing will emerge, and we should expend every effort to bring it about sooner rather than later.

## ACKNOWLEDGMENTS

I should like to thank the many members of the Ebbinghaus Empire for their interest and participation in all aspects of this research. Also, I owe a special debt of gratitude to my father for frequent and invaluable mathematical tutelage, and to Elisabeth Wells for assistance with parameter estimation.

## REFERENCES

Anderson, N. S. Poststimulus cueing in immediate memory. *Journal of Experimental Psychology, 1960,* 60, 216–221.

Atkinson, R. C., Brelsford, J. W., & Shiffrin, R. M. Multiprocess models for memory with applications to a continuous presentation task. *Journal of Mathematical Psychology,* 1967, 4, 277–300.

Atkinson, R. C., & Crothers, E. J. A comparison of paired-associate learning models having different acquisition and retention axioms. *Journal of Mathematical Psychology,* 1964, 1, 285–315.

Atkinson, R. C., Holmgren, J. E., & Juola, J. F. Processing time as influenced by the number of elements in a visual display. *Perception & Psychophysics,* 1969, 6, 321–326.

Atkinson, R. C., & Shiffrin, R. M. Mathematical models for memory and learning. Technical Report No. 79, 1965, Institute for Mathematical Studies in the Social Sciences, Stanford University.

Atkinson, R. C., & Shiffrin, R. M. Human memory: A proposed system and its control processes. In K. W. Spence & J. T. Spence (Eds.), *The psychology of learning and motivation: Advances in research and theory.* Vol. 2. New York: Academic Press, 1968. Pp. 89–195.

Baddeley, A. D., & Dale, H. C. The effect of semantic similarity on retroactive interference in long- and short-term memory. *Journal of Verbal Learning and Verbal Behavior,* 1966, 5, 417–420.

Baddeley, A. D., & Warrington, E. K. Amnesia and the distinction between long- and short-term memory. *Journal of Verbal Learning and Verbal Behavior,* 1970, 9, 176–189.

Bernbach, H. A. A forgetting model for paired-associate learning. *Journal of Mathematical Psychology,* 1965, 2, 128–144.

Bernbach, H. A. Replication processes in human memory and learning. In G. H. Bower & J. T. Spence (Eds.), *The psychology of learning and motivation: Advances in research and theory.* Vol. 3. New York: Academic Press, 1969. Pp. 201–239.

Bjork, R. A. Learning and short-term retention of paired associates in relation to specific sequences of interpresentation intervals. Technical Report No. 106, 1966, Mathematical Studies in the Social Sciences, Stanford University.

Bjork, R. A. Repetition and rehearsal mechanisms in models for short-term memory. In D. A. Norman (Ed.), *Models of human memory.* New York: Academic Press, 1970. Pp. 307-330.

Bower, G. H. Application of a model to paired-associate learning. *Psychometrika,* 1961, 26, 255-280.

Bower, G. H. An association model for response and training variables in paired-associate learning. *Psychological Review,* 1962, 69, 34-53.

Bower, G. H. A multicomponent theory of the memory trace. In K. W. Spence & J. T. Spence (Eds.), *The psychology of learning and motivation: Advances in research and theory.* Vol. 1. New York: Academic Press, 1967. Pp. 229-325.

Broadbent, D. E. *Perception and communication.* New York: Pergamon, 1958.

Brown, J. Some tests of the decay theory of immediate memory. *Quarterly Journal of Experimental Psychology,* 1958, 10, 12-21.

Brown, R., & McNeill, D. The "tip of the tongue" phenomenon. *Journal of Verbal Learning and Verbal Behavior, 1966,* 5, 325-337.

Bruce, D., & Papay, J. P. Primacy effects in single-trial free recall. *Journal of Verbal Learning and Verbal Behavior,* 1970, 9, 473-486.

Buschke, H. Types of immediate memory. *Journal of Verbal Learning and Verbal Behavior,* 1966, 275-278.

Colotla, X. Scanning processes in numerical recall. Unpublished master's thesis, University of Toronto, 1969.

Conrad, R. Errors of immediate memory. *British Journal of Psychology,* 1959, 50, 349-359.

Conrad, R. Acoustic confusions in immediate memory. *British Journal of Psychology,* 1964, 55, 75-84.

Cooper, E. H., & Pantle, A. J. The total-time hypothesis in verbal learning. *Psychological Bulletin,* 1967, 68, 221-234.

Crossman, E. R. F. W. Information and serial order in human immediate memory. In C. Cherry (Ed.), *Information theory: Fourth London symposium.* Washington: Butterworth, 1961. Pp. 147-159.

Crowder, R. G., & Morton, J. Precategorical acoustic storage (PAS). *Perception & Psychophysics,* 1969, 5, 365-373.

Crowder, R. G., & Raeburn, V. P. The stimulus suffix effect with reversed speech. *Journal of Verbal Learning and Verbal Behavior,* 1970, 9, 342-345.

Donaldson, W. An examination of false positives in short-term recognition memory. Unpublished doctoral dissertation, University of Toronto, 1967.

Feigenbaum, E. A., & Simon, H. A. A theory of the serial position effect. *British Journal of Psychology,* 1962, 53, 307-320.

Feller, W. *An introduction to probability theory and its applications.* (3rd ed.) Vol. I. New York: Wiley, 1968.

Gibson, J. J., & Gibson, E. J. Perceptual learning: Differentiation or enrichment? *Psychological Review,* 1955, 62, 32-41.

Glanzer, M. Storage mechanisms in free recall. *Transactions of the New York Academy of Sciences,* 1968, 30, 1120-1129.

Glanzer, M., & Cunitz, A. R. Two storage mechanisms in free recall. *Journal of Verbal Learning and Verbal Behavior,* 1966, 5, 351-360.

Greeno, J. G. Paired-associate learning with massed and distributed repetitions of items. *Journal of Experimental Psychology,* 1964, 67, 286-295.

Hebb, D. O. Distinctive features of learning in the higher animal. In J. F. Delafresnaye (Ed.), *Brain mechanisms and learning.* New York: Oxford University Press, 1961. Pp. 37-46.

Hinrichs, J. V. A two-process memory-strength theory for judgment of recency. *Psychological Review,* 1970, 77, 223–233.

Hintzman, D. L. Classification and aural coding in short-term memory. *Psychonomic Science,* 1965, 3, 161–162.

Kabrisky, M. Psychologically testable correlates of a mathematical model of the human visual system. Paper presented at the fourth annual Winter Conference on Brain Research, Snowmass-at-Aspen, Colorado, January 1971.

Kabrisky, M., Tallman, O., Day, C. M., & Radoy, C. M. A theory of pattern perception based on human physiology. In A. T. Welford & L. H. Houssiadas (Eds.), *Contemporary problems in perception.* London: Taylor & Francis, 1970. Pp. 129–147.

Kintsch, W. Recognition learning as a function of the length of the retention interval and changed in the retention interval. *Journal of Mathematical Psychology,* 1966, 3, 412–433.

Kintsch, W. Memory and decision aspects of recognition learning. *Psychological Review,* 1967, 74, 496–504.

Kintsch, W. Models for free recall and recognition. In D. A. Norman (Ed.), *Models of human memory.* New York: Academic Press, 1970. Pp. 331–373.

Kintsch, W., & Buschke, H. Homophones and synonyms in short-term memory. *Journal of Experimental Psychology,* 1969, 80, 403–407.

Kintsch, W., & Morris, C. J. Application of a Markov model to free recall and recognition. *Journal of Experimental Psychology,* 1965, 69, 200–206.

Kuhn, T. S. *The structure of scientific revolutions.* Chicago: University of Chicago Press, 1962.

Lashley, K. S. The problem of serial order in behavior. In L. A. Jeffress (Ed.), *Cerebral mechanisms in behavior.* New York: Wiley, 1951.

Laughery, K. R., & Pinkus, A. L. Short-term memory: Effects of acoustic similarity, presentation rate and presentation mode. *Psychonomic Science,* 1966, 6, 285–286.

Levy, B. A., & Murdock, B. B., Jr. The effects of delayed auditory feedback and intra-list similarity in short-term memory. *Journal of Verbal Learning and Verbal Behavior,* 1968, 7, 887–894.

Lockhart, R. S. Recency discrimination predicted from absolute lag judgments. *Perception & Psychophysics,* 1969, 6, 42–44.

Lockhart, R. S., & Murdock B. B., Jr. Memory and the theory of signal detection. *Psychological Bulletin,* 1970, 74, 100–109.

Loess, H., & Waugh, N. C. Short-term memory and intertrial interval. *Journal of Verbal Learning and Verbal Behavior,* 1967, 6, 455–460.

Mandler, G. Organization and memory. In K. W. Spence & J. T. Spence (Eds.), *The psychology of learning and motivation: Advances in research and theory.* Vol. 1. New York: Academic Press, 1967. Pp. 327–372. (a)

Mandler, G. Verbal learning. In *New directions in psychology. Vol. III.* New York: Holt, Rinehart & Winston, 1967. (b)

Mann, J. E. Modality effects in free recall ordered by presentation mode. Unpublished bachelor's thesis, University of Toronto, 1970.

Martin, F. F. *Computer modeling and simulation.* New York: Wiley, 1968.

Melton, A. W. Implications of short-term memory for a general theory of memory. *Journal of Verbal Learning and Verbal Behavior,* 1963, 2, 1–21.

Miller, G. A. Decision units in the perception of speech. *IRE Transactions on Professional Group Information Theory,* 1962, **IT-8,** 81–83.

Milner, B. Amnesia following operation on the temporal lobes. In C. W. M. Whitty and O. L. Zangwill (Eds.), *Amnesia.* London: Butterworth, 1966. Pp. 109-133.

Murdock, B. B., Jr. The immediate retention of unrelated words. *Journal of Experimental Psychology.* 1960, **60**, 222-234.

Murdock, B. B., Jr. Repetition in paired-associate learning. Paper presented at the Eastern Psychological Association, Philadelphia, April 1961. (a)

Murdock, B. B., Jr. The retention of individual items. *Journal of Experimental Psychology,* 1961, **62**, 618-625. (b)

Murdock, B. B., Jr. Short-term retention of single paired associates. *Psychological Reports,* 1961, **8**, 280. (c)

Murdock, B. B., Jr. The serial position effect of free recall. *Journal of Experimental Psychology,* 1962, **64**, 482-488.

Murdock, B. B., Jr. Short-term memory and paired-associate learning. *Journal of Verbal Learning and Verbal Behavior,* 1963, **2**, 320-328.

Murdock, B. B., Jr. Effects of a subsidiary task on short-term memory. *British Journal of Psychology,* 1965, **56**, 413-419. (a)

Murdock, B. B., Jr. Signal-detection theory and short-term memory. *Journal of Experimental Psychology,* 1965, **70**, 443-447. (b)

Murdock, B. B., Jr. A test of the "limited capacity" hypothesis. *Journal of Experimental Psychology,* 1965, **69**, 237-240. (c)

Murdock, B. B., Jr. Auditory and visual stores in short-term memory. *Acta Psychologica,* 1967, **27**, 316-324. (a)

Murdock, B. B., Jr. The effects of noise and delayed auditory feedback on short-term memory. *Journal of Verbal Learning and Verbal Behavior,* 1967, **6**, 737-743. (b)

Murdock, B. B., Jr. A fixed-point model for short-term memory. *Journal of Mathematical Psychology,* 1967, **4**, 501-506. (c)

Murdock, B. B., Jr. Recent developments in short-term memory. *British Journal of Psychology,* 1967, **58**, 421-433. (d)

Murdock, B. B., Jr. Modality effects in short-term memory: Storage or retrieval? *Journal of Experimental Psychology,* 1968, **77**, 79-86. (a)

Murdock, B. B., Jr. Response latencies in short-term memory. *Quarterly Journal of Experimental Psychology,* 1968, **20**, 79-82. (b)

Murdock, B. B., Jr. Serial order effects in short- term memory. *Journal of Experimental Psychology,* 1968, **76**, Part 2 (Monogr. Suppl.), 1-15. (c)

Murdock, B. B., Jr. Where or when: Modality effects as a function of temporal and spatial distribution of information. *Journal of Verbal Learning and Verbal Behavior,* 1969, **8**, 378-383.

Murdock, B. B., Jr. Short-term memory for associations. In D. A. Norman (Ed.), *Models of human memory.* New York: Academic Press, 1970. Pp. 285-304.

Murdock, B. B., Jr. A parallel-processing model for scanning. *Perception & Psychophysics,* 1971, **10**, 289-291. (a)

Murdock, B. B., Jr. Four-channel effects in short-term memory. *Psychonomic Science,* 1971, **24**, 197-198. (b)

Murdock, B. B., Jr., & Ogilvie, J. C. Binomial variability in short-term memory.*Psychological Bulletin,* 1968, **70**, 256-260.

Murdock, B. B., Jr., & Okada, R. Interresponse times in single-trial free recall. *Journal of Experimental Psychology,* 1970, **87**, 263-267.

Murdock, B. B., Jr., Penney, C., & Aamiry, A. Interactive presentation in multi-trial free recall. *Journal of Verbal Learning and Verbal Behavior,* 1970, **9**, 679-683.

Murdock, B. B., Jr. & vom Saal, W. Transpositions in short-term memory. *Journal of Experimental Psychology*, 1967, 74, 137-143.

Murdock, B. B., Jr., & Walker, K. D. Modality effects in free recall. *Journal of Verbal Learning and Verbal Behavior*, 1969, 8, 665-676.

Murray, D. J. Vocalization-at-presentation and immediate recall, with varying presentation-rates. *Quarterly Journal of Experimental Psychology*, 1965, 17, 47-56.

Naylor, T. H., Balintfy, J. L., Burdick, D. S., & Chu, K. *Computer simulation techniques.* New York: Wiley, 1966.

Neisser, U. *Cognitive psychology.* New York: Appleton-Century-Crofts, 1967.

Nelder, J. A., & Mead, R. A simplex method for function minimization. *Computer Journal*, 1965, 7, 308-313.

Norman, D. A. (Ed.) *Models of human memory.* New York: Academic Press, 1970.

Norman, D. A., & Wickelgren, W. A. Short-term recognition memory for single digits and pairs of digits. *Journal of Experimental Psychology*, 1965, 70, 479-489.

Okada, R. Decision latencies in short-term recognition memory. Unpublished doctoral dissertation, University of Toronto, 1970.

Peterson, L. R. Search and judgment in memory. In B. Kleinmuntz (Ed.), *Concepts and the structure of memory.* New York: Wiley, 1967. Pp. 153-180.

Peterson, L. R., & Peterson, M. J. Short-term retention of individual verbal items. *Journal of Experimental Psychology*, 1959, 58, 193-198.

Peterson, L. R., Wampler, R., Kirkpatrick, M., & Saltzman, D. Effect of spacing presentations on retention of a paired associate over short intervals. *Journal of Experimental Psychology*, 1963, 66, 206-209.

Posner, M. I. Abstraction and the process of recognition. In G. H. Bower & J. T. Spence (Eds.), *The psychology of learning and motivation: Advances in research and theory.* Vol. 3. New York: Academic Press, 1969. Pp. 43-100.

Postman, L. The present status of interference theory. In C. N. Cofer (ed.), *Verbal learning and verbal behavior.* New York: McGraw-Hill, 1961. Pp. 152-179.

Postman, L. One-trial learning. In C. N. Cofer & B. S. Musgrave (Eds.), *Verbal bahavior and learning.* New York: McGraw-Hill, 1963, Pp. 295-321.

Postman, L., & Keppel, G. Retroactive inhibition in free recall. *Journal of Experimental Psychology*, 1967, 74, 203-211.

Restle, F. Significance of all-or-none learning. *Psychological Bulletin*, 1965, 64, 313-325.

Robbins, M. J., & Meyer, D. R. Motivational control of retrograde amnesia. *Journal of Experimental Psychology*, 1970, 84, 220-225.

Rundus, D., & Atkinson, R. C. Rehearsal processes in free recall: A procedure for direct observation. *Journal of Verbal Learning and Verbal Behavior*, 1970, 9, 99-105.

Schwartz, F., & Rouse, R. O. The activation and recovery of associations. *Psychological Issues*, 1961, 3, No. 1 (Monogr. 9).

Shepard, R. N., & Chang, J. Forced-choice tests of recognition memory under steady-state conditions. *Journal of Verbal Learning and Verbal Behavior*, 1963, 2, 93-101.

Shepard, R. N., & Teghtsoonian, M. Retention of information under conditions approaching a steady state. *Journal of Experimental Psychology*, 1961, 62, 302-309.

Shiffrin, R. M. Memory search. *Models of human memory.* New York: Academic Press, 1970. Pp. 375-447.

Sperling, G. The information available in brief visual presentations. *Psychological Monographs,* 1960, 74,(11, Whole No. 498).

Sperling, G. A model for visual memory tasks. *Human Factors,* 1963, 5, 19-31.

Sperling, G. Successive approximations to a model for short-term memory. *Acta Psychologica,* 1967, 27, 285-292.

Sternberg, S. The discovery of processing stages: Extensions of Donders' method. *Acta Psychologica,* 1969, 30, 276-315. (a)

Sternberg, S. Memory-scanning: Mental processes revealed by reaction-time experiments. *American Scientist,* 1969, 57, 421-457. (b)

Suppes, P. Stimulus-response theory of finite automata. *Journal of Mathematical Psychology,* 1969, 6, 327-355.

Thorndike, E. L., & Lorge, I. *The teacher's word book of 30,000 words.* New York: Teachers College, Columbia University, Bureau of Publications, 1944.

Tulving, E. The effects of presentation and recall of material in free-recall learning. *Journal of Verbal Learning and Verbal Behavior,* 1967, 6, 175-184.

Tulving, E. Theoretical issues in free recall. In T. R. Dixon & D. L. Horton (Eds.), *Verbal learning and general behavior theory.* Englewood Cliffs, N.J.: Prentice-Hall, 1968. Pp. 2-36.

Tulving, E., & Arbuckle, T. Y. Sources of intratrial interference in immediate recall of paired associates. *Journal of Verbal Learning and Verbal Behavior,* 1963, 1, 321-334.

Tulving, E., & Madigan, S. W. Memory and verbal learning. *Annual Review of Psychology,* 1970, 21, 437-484.

Tulving, E., & Osler, S. Effectiveness of retrieval cues in memory for words. *Journal of Experimental Psychology,* 1968, 77, 593-601.

Tulving, E., & Patterson, R. D. Functional units and retrieval processes in free recall. *Journal of Experimental Psychology,* 1968, 77, 239-248.

Tulving, E., & Pearlstone, Z. Availability versus accessibility of information in memory for words. *Journal of Verbal Learning and Verbal Behavior,* 1966, 5, 381-391.

Tulving, E., & Psotka, J. Retroactive inhibition in free recall: Inaccessibility of information available in the memory store. *Journal of Experimental Psychology,* 1971, 87, 1-8.

Tulving, E., & Thomson, D. M. Retrieval processes in recognition memory: Effects of associative context. *Journal of Experimental Psychology,* 1971, 87, 116-124.

Tulving, E., & Thornton, G. B. Interaction between proaction and retroaction in short-term retention. *Canadian Journal of Psychology,* 1959, 13, 255-265.

Underwood, B. J. Degree of learning and the measurement of forgetting. *Journal of Verbal Learning and Verbal Behavior,* 1964, 3, 112-129.

Walker, K. D. Some tests of the two-store hypothesis. Unpublished master's thesis, University of Toronto, 1967.

Warrington, E. K., & Shallice, T. The selective impairment of auditory verbal short-term memory. *Brain,* 1969, 92, 885-896.

Waugh, N. C., & Norman, D. A. Primary memory. *Psychological Review,* 1965, 72, 89-104.

Weiskrantz, L. Experimental studies of amnesia. In C. W. M. Whitty & O. L. Zangwill (Eds.), *Amnesia.* London: Butterworth, 1966. Pp. 1-35.

Wickelgren, W. A. Acoustic similarity and intrusion errors in short-term memory. *Journal of Experimental Psychology*, 1965, 70, 102–108.

Wickens, D. D. Encoding categories of words: An empirical approach to meaning. *Psychological Review*, 1970, 77, 1–15.

Woodworth, R. S. *Experimental psychology*. New York: Holt, 1938.

Wooldridge, D. E. *The machinery of the brain*. New York: McGraw-Hill, 1963.

Wozencraft, J. M., & Jacobs, I. M. *Principles of communication engineering*. New York: Wiley, 1965.

# STORAGE MECHANISMS IN RECALL[1]

## Murray Glanzer

NEW YORK UNIVERSITY, NEW YORK, NEW YORK

## I. Introduction

Information on the recall of words has been organized according to several theoretical views. My own view, and that of a number of other workers, is that recall is a process involving two or more distinct storage mechanisms. This view has been developed recently

[1] This paper was written at The Hebrew University in Jerusalem during the author's holding of a Guggenheim Fellowship. Experimental work by the author was carried out under Contract No. DA 49 193 MD 2496 with the Office of The Surgeon General and RO1 HD 04213 with the National Institute of Child Health and Human Development. The author thanks Doris Aaronson and Micha Razel for their critical comments on an earlier draft of this paper.

in the work of several investigators (Atkinson & Shiffrin, 1968; Glanzer & Cunitz, 1966; Waugh & Norman, 1965). I will show here how this view of multiple storage mechanisms relates to available data, and what its implications are.

I will start by considering free recall of words and then show that the ideas used in the analysis of free recall can be used to understand recall in general. I will then turn to some of the detailed considerations of recall. Following this, more general characteristics of recall mechanisms will be considered. Through most of the paper I will keep the discussion fairly close to the data and fairly simple. The assumed processing of the items that are presented to Ss in a free recall task is shown in Fig. 1. Variant forms of this flow chart have

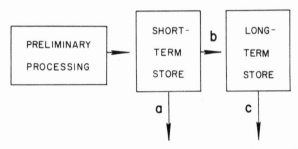

Fig. 1. Flow chart of the processing of items in free recall.

been presented by Atkinson and Shiffrin (1968), Murdock (1967), and Waugh and Norman (1965). An item is viewed here as first going through some preliminary processing at a "sensory" level. This involves some storage of information over very short periods of time (Sperling, 1960). I will not go into this part of the larger system here. The item, that is, information about the item,[2] then appears in short-term store (STS). It resides there for varying periods of time depending on the experimental conditions. Originally it was thought that items were lost from STS because of passage of time — a simple decay notion. It is fairly clear now that displacement by subsequent items is the important factor. Data on this point will be discussed subsequently.

When an item has entered STS it can either stay in or drop out of the system. The loss of the item is indicated by the arrow labeled "a." During its stay in STS a representation of some or all of the information about the item may be registered in long-term store

---

[2] For the sake of brevity I will write "the item" in all cases in which I mean "the information related to the item."

(LTS). This transfer of information to LTS is indicated by the arrow labeled "b" in the figure.

The arrows labeled a and b represent very different functions. Arrow a represents STS information being lost or becoming unavailable. Arrow b represents transmission of information but does not imply removal of that information from STS. The registration of information from STS in LTS is not viewed here as involving the removal or destruction of the item in STS. An item can be represented in both stores at the same time. Arrow "c" represents LTS information being lost or becoming inaccessible. This function will be discussed only briefly in this paper.

I have used above, as equivalent, the terms registration of information in LTS, transmission of information to LTS, and transfer of information to LTS. The process involved will not be examined in detail here. It is likely that it involves not only the storage of information but also the construction of a retrieval procedure. A factor that affects the recall of items from LTS may have its effect on the information that is stored or the retrieval procedure. I will only note here that the possibility for further analysis exists.

Access to information in STS is relatively direct. Access to information in LTS is relatively indirect. This is seen in the temporal characteristics of responses in recall. Items from STS appear early in the recall, in a burst. Items from LTS appear at a slower, steadier rate.

The STS is seen as very limited in its capacity. Most of the experiments reported here indicate that its capacity is from two to three items. The LTS is not limited in this way. Considered in its fullest sense, LTS can contain an unlimited number of items. It is, however, limited in how much it can accept within a given period of time. Each item that is transmitted to LTS requires some processing time. Therefore, if the amount of time is limited, a limited number of items will be registered in LTS.

There are a number of details that can be added to this picture. I will not go into these additions at length here but will indicate some of them briefly.

1. Various types of store may be distinguished in STS according to the sensory mode through which the items are presented. The role of sensory modality will be considered again later.

2. The LTS that is outlined in the figure is a very extensive system. I will consider only part of that system in analyzing recall situations. The role that it plays in different memory tasks,

moreover, varies considerably in ways that cannot be reflected in the figure. In the free recall situation, for example, the S ordinarily faces a number of items which he knows quite well. He is registering in LTS some additional information about these well-known items, namely, that they have just been presented and should be held ready for a recall task. This is probably not the same as what the S does in a paired associates task. It certainly is very different than his learning a new word. The complexity of the LTS and its probable subdivision or layering, although important, are, however, not of immediate interest here.

3. The relations between STS and LTS are a two-way affair. The items that the S deals with in the free recall experiment are usually words. Long-term information of some type has to be called on to carry out this processing. The nature of this interaction has, however, barely been touched on in the literature. The figure omits the arrows that this interaction would require.

4. There are a variety of activities carried out by the S either to maintain an item in STS or to facilitate its transfer to LTS. The term "rehearsal" has been used as a blanket term to refer to both of these possibly very distinct activities. A recursive arrow on the STS box of Fig. 1 would represent the maintenance function.

## II. Interactions with the Serial Position Curve

In the case of free recall, the first reason for assuming such a flow and two separate storage mechanisms may be found in a very prominent and reliable characteristic of free recall — the serial position function. Examples of such curves are shown in Figs. 2 and 3 below.

In the free recall of lists, Ss are more likely to recall the early and late items than the middle items. There are, moreover, a variety of systematic experimental effects that can be worked on this curve. In most cases, the curve is raised or lowered in all positions except the last few. For example, if the rate of presentation is changed, the family of curves seen in Fig. 2 is obtained. There is an interaction between the experimental variable, rate, and serial position. An interaction effect of this type is produced by a number of variables: (1) rate of presentation (Glanzer & Cunitz, 1966; Murdock, 1962; Raymond, 1969); (2) word frequency (Raymond, 1969; Sumby, 1963) (see Fig. 3); (3) list length (Murdock, 1962; Postman &

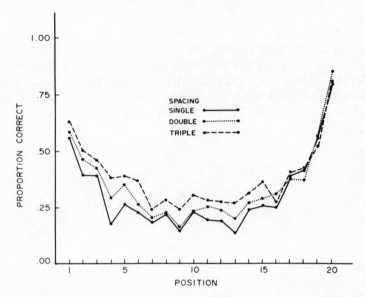

Fig. 2. Serial position curves for three different rates of presentation: single (three seconds); double (six seconds); triple (nine seconds). (After Glanzer & Cunitz, 1966, by permission of Academic Press, Inc., New York.)

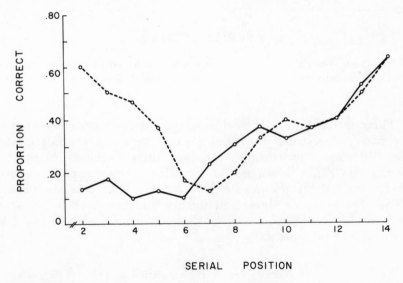

Fig. 3. Serial position curves for high-frequency words (broken line) and low-frequency words (solid line). (After Sumby, 1963, by permission of Academic Press, Inc., New York.)

Phillips, 1965) (see Fig. 4); (4) mnemonic or associative structure
(Glanzer & Schwartz, 1971) (see Fig. 5).

The effects of lengthening the list are particularly striking. One
effect is that the early parts of the list descend as the list increases in
length. Another effect, first noted by Murdock, is that as the list
becomes longer, and the beginning and end peaks are well separated,
it is clear that the middle area of the serial position curve forms a
flat, horizontal line.

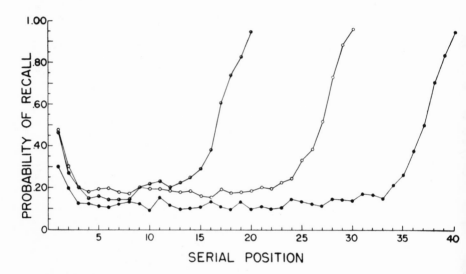

Fig. 4. Serial position curves for three different list lengths. (After Murdock,
1962, by permission of the American Psychological Association, Washington,
D.C.)

These interaction effects, differential effects on the two ends of
the curve, suggest that the serial position curve reflects output from
two different mechanisms. Relating these mechanisms to the
elements in Fig. 1, I will assume that all of the serial position curve
except the last few positions reflect output primarily or wholly from
LTS.[3] The evidence above and further evidence cited below show
that the last few positions reflect output from both STS and LTS
with the STS dominant.

---

[3] Craik (1970) has recently carried the separation of STS and LTS effects a
step farther. He has demonstrated that the final list items are recalled best with
immediate recall but are recalled most poorly when S recalls several preceding
lists.

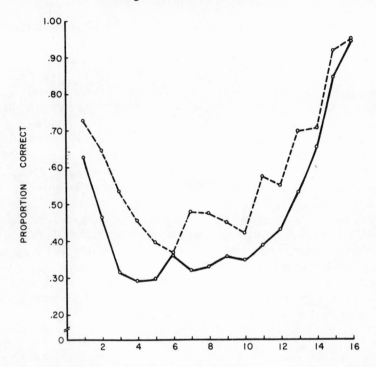

Fig. 5. Serial position curves for high- (broken line) and low- (solid line) mnemonic or associative structure. (After Glanzer & Schwartz, 1971, by permission of Academic Press, Inc., New York.)

I have made two identifications in the statements above. The first identification is that of the early part of the serial position curve with LTS. Assuming that there is a separate store, and assuming that STS is short-term, the identification seems reasonable. Early items in a list would not be expected to be held over in STS. The second identification is that of the experimental variables previously listed with factors affecting LTS. This identification has an interesting characteristic. A few words should be devoted to this.

The list of variables above contains very familiar names. They are the names of the classic variables that are effective in rote learning situations. But it is, of course, LTS that is addressed in a rote learning experiment. This leads to the following generalization. *Any variable that is effective in rote learning will affect all but the last few positions of the free recall serial position curve.* This statement is not completely satisfactory for two reasons. First, it is based on a crude method of separating LTS and STS effects. This method will, however, be replaced by a more refined method. Second, there is at least one exception to the statement. I will touch on this exception later in the discussion of grouping effects.

Although the identification of the early portion of the serial position curve with output from the LTS could be argued on the basis of the interactions above, a much stronger case is made if an operation can be applied that would affect only the end peak of the serial position curve. This is the section that I have assumed to be overlaid by output from STS. There is such an operation, one that is suggested by the literature on short-term memory (Brown, 1958; Peterson & Peterson, 1959). It is delayed recall with some task carried out during the delay. When such a delay is introduced, a dramatic effect appears. In one experiment (Glanzer & Cunitz, 1966), the Ss were given free recall lists and after each list had to wait 0, 10, or 30 seconds before being permitted to recall. During the 10- and 30-second delays they carried out a simple counting task. The results are shown in Fig. 6. With a 30-second delay task the serial position curve flattens out completely. All of the postulated STS seems to be wiped out. The same effect was found by Postman and Phillips (1965) using a very different theoretical approach.

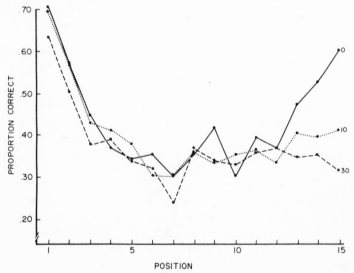

Fig. 6. Serial position curves for three delay periods — 0, 10, and 30 seconds. (After Glanzer & Cunitz, 1966, by permission of Academic Press, Inc., New York.)

## III. Estimation of STS

The use of a delay has been developed as the basis of a standard technique for estimating the amount of output from STS and the amount of output from LTS. I noted earlier that changes in the rate of presentation give curves that show an interaction of serial position with rate. Increased rate lowers all but the last few serial positions. Raymond gave lists with fast and slow presentation rates, one and three seconds between successive words, and replicated the findings displayed in Fig. 2. She also used the same presentation rates with a delay task following the lists. The serial position curves obtained are shown in the top panel of Fig. 7. It is clear then that rate continues

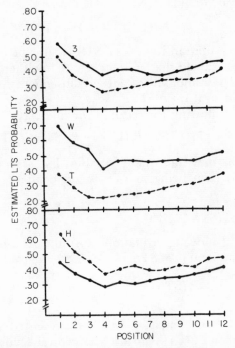

Fig. 7. Serial position curves for three pairs of conditions under delay. Top: fast (one second) *versus* slow (three seconds) presentation rate. Middle: words (W) *versus* trigrams (T). Bottom: high-frequency (H) *versus* low-frequency (L) items. (After Raymond, 1969, by permission of Academic Press, Inc., New York.)

to have its effect through the final list positions, although this steady-state effect is ordinarily concealed by output from STS under no-delay conditions (see Fig. 2).

The experiment by Raymond included two other variables both of which produced the same effect as rate under standard, no-delay conditions. These variables, words *versus* nonsense syllables, and high-*versus* low-frequency words, produce serial position curves that are separate across all but the last few positions. Again, the imposition of delay produces curves that are separate across all positions. These curves are shown in the remaining panels of Fig. 7.

The combined information from the delay and no-delay conditions can be used to get further information about the STS. This is done in the following way. Output from LTS is identified with the output obtained after a delay task. Thus, the delay curves in Fig. 7 are identified as output from LTS, and the probability that an item in list position $i$ is recalled after delay, D, is equated with the probability that the item is in LTS.

$$P_i(\text{LTS}) = P_i(\text{D}) \tag{1}$$

The probability that an item is in STS cannot be estimated quite so directly. It is assumed that an item can be in either STS or LTS or both until the delay imposed by either subsequent list items or the postlist task removes it from STS.

This gives the following for recall in the no-delay (ND) condition:

$$P_i(\text{ND}) = P_i(\text{STS}) + P_i(\text{LTS}) - P_i(\text{STS} \cap \text{LTS}). \tag{2}$$

This equation may be made usable by assuming that the probability of an item being in STS is independent of its being in LTS or that

$$P_i(\text{STS} \cap \text{LTS}) = P_i(\text{STS}) \cdot P_i(\text{LTS}).$$

This gives the following equation for the estimation of the probability that an item is in STS.

$$P_i(\text{STS}) = \frac{P_i(\text{ND}) - P_i(\text{D})}{1 - P_i(\text{D})} \tag{3}$$

The basic form of this equation was first presented and applied by Waugh and Norman (1965) who use the central section of the serial position curve to estimate $P_i$ (LTS). The use of information from both delay and no-delay conditions, as above, was introduced by Raymond (1969). Applying Eq. (3) to the curves in the three panels of Fig. 7, and to their corresponding no-delay curves, the three curves in Fig. 8 were derived by Raymond (1969), for the effect of presentation rate, of words *versus* nonsense syllables, and high-frequency *versus* low-frequency items.

Now that the effects of STS and LTS are separated, a very striking fact becomes clear. All three variables produce a strong effect across all serial positions in LTS (Fig. 7). All three variables produce no effect on STS (Fig. 8).

In this study and others cited below, the estimation of LTS and STS was carried out for each individual $S$, and the results were

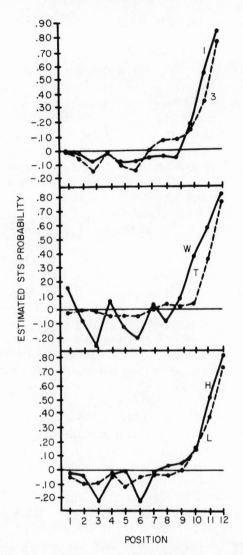

Fig. 8. Derived STS curves for the three pairs of conditions in Fig. 7. Top: fast (one second) *versus* slow (three seconds) presentation rate. Middle: words (W) *versus* trigrams (T). Bottom: high-frequency (H) *versus* low-frequency (L) items. (After Raymond, 1969, by permission of Academic Press, Inc., New York.)

averaged across *S*s. The no-delay curves which show the interaction with serial position seen in Figs. 3 – 6 are not shown here. The reader can, however, construct a close approximation to the no-delay curves for each set of data by adding the corresponding p's in the paired curves according to Eq. (2) with $P_i(\text{STS} \cap \text{LTS})$ set equal to $P_i(\text{STS}) \cdot P_i(\text{LTS})$.

At this point, a large amount of information about both STS and LTS has been developed. I will review this information.

1. As successive list items are presented the probability of registering an item in LTS goes into a steady state which persists for the course of the presentation. The asymptote (see Fig. 4) that develops was noted by Murdock (1962). It shows up clearly as a horizontal function across the middle sections of the serial position curve when long recall lists are used. It shows up even more clearly when a delay task is used. The overlay of output from STS is then eliminated and the asymptote is revealed as continuing through the final list positions. This asymptote indicates that transfer of information from STS to LTS settles down to a fixed rate after the first few list items.

2. Increasing the length of the list lowers the LTS component of the serial position curve. The lowering can be seen very clearly in comparing Postman and Phillips' (1965) serial position curves for 10- and 30-word lists under delay. This indicates a retroactive effect of subsequent LTS registrations on earlier registrations. This effect is a very different one than that obtained in STS with a delay task. In the case of LTS, a large number of items produces a relatively small, evenly distributed effect across all list positions. In the case of a delay task acting on STS, a small number of items produces a large effect that is restricted to the last few list positions.

3. The effect of rate on LTS suggests that the transfer of information to LTS requires a certain amount of time. Restriction in time reduces the possibility of transfer. I will not distinguish here the transfer of item information from the setting up of retrieval routines.

4. The STS is unaffected by a wide variety of factors that affect LTS. This was particularly fortunate for the initial stages of work concerned with the separation of these two mechanisms. If there had been many cases in which the two had been similarly affected, the analysis would have been much more difficult to make.

## IV. Details of the Storage Process

I will examine in detail some of the points touched on above. In particular, three questions will be considered.

1. How are items removed from STS?

2. What occurs during an item's stay in STS?

The STS functions as an input buffer, holding the items temporarily. While the item is in STS, it is available for further processing, e.g., recoding, computation, transmission of its information to LTS. There are several reasons why it is advantageous to have a temporary store in the system. One is that since processing of the items takes some time, it is useful to be able to hold them until the processing is completed. Second, if there is some inherent relation between successive items, sequences of items may be encoded more efficiently. Third, the operations required for a task may involve several items. It is useful, therefore, to accumulate sets of items. Work will be presented that shows that the STS plays an important role in the processing of sequences of items.

## A. How Items Are Removed From STS

It seems most likely at the present time that STS is cleared by subsequent events. The nature of this clearing mechanism will be discussed now because decisions about it will simplify the further discussion of the functions of the STS.

In a series of studies the following factors were examined with respect to their role in the clearing of STS (Glanzer, Gianutsos, & Dubin, 1969): (1) information load or difficulty of subsequent activity, i.e., the delay task; (2) similarity of items involved in subsequent activity; (3) simple number of items processed during subsequent activity; (4) passage of time.

The second and third factors are used in retroactive inhibition (RI) explanations of forgetting. The third factor might be labeled displacement. The fourth factor is used in both trace decay and proactive inhibition explanations.

The first pair of experiments was on the role of information load or difficulty. In both experiments, Ss were given 12 common English words and then delayed in their recall for 1, 5, or 10 seconds. During the delay, the Ss were shown a number to which they added by 1's, 4's, or 7's. These three addition tasks are measurably different in their difficulty for Ss. Their use can, moreover, be rationalized as producing varying degrees of information reduction, along lines suggested by Posner and Rossman (1965). If items in STS are affected by amounts of subsequent information processed, then the elimination of items from STS should be fastest for the adding of 7's and slowest for the adding of 1's.

The experiment was performed twice, once with the Ss pacing their additions during the delay intervals, a second time with the Ss paced by a metronome through the delay interval at one addition per second. The results are virtually identical in the two experiments. They indicate that there is no overall effect of information load or difficulty of subsequent activity on the STS. The curves for the second experiment, with paced addition, are shown in Fig. 9. If the

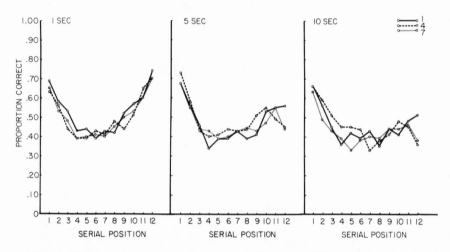

Fig. 9. Serial position curves for 1-, 5-, and 10-second delay at three levels of delay task difficulty — adding 1's, 4's, or 7's. (After Glanzer *et al.*, 1969, by permission of Academic Press, Inc., New York.)

information load had had an effect, then the curves for additions by 1, 4, and 7, should have fanned out at the end positions sometime between the 1- and the 10-second delay. There is little evidence of such an effect in either the figures or the statistical analysis. The results were surprising because Posner and Rossman (1965) have presented evidence that information load plays a major role in short-term memory. The relation of these findings to theirs will be considered below.

The second possible factor in the clearing of STS is similarity of the delay task to the list items. There are two forms of RI explanation that might be entertained. One is a strong RI explanation. It asserts that any postlist item that is similar to a list item has an adverse effect on that list item. Therefore, if a block of postlist items could be constructed with the items similar to the items in positions 1 - 4, the probability of recall of items 1 - 4 would be depressed. If delay task items similar to the items in positions 5 - 8 would be constructed, the probability of recall of those items would be lowered. The reason why the delay task ordinarily affects only the last few positions might be that delay task items are not ordinarily designed to be closely similar to any specific list items. They are, therefore, similar only to the items at the end of the list, on the basis of their temporal position.

A weak RI explanation restricts the RI effect to a limited set of items near the end of the recall list. According to this explanation, when the end of the list is reached, the probability of recall of early list items is already driven down by RI from later list items. The only items that have not already suffered the effects of RI are the end items. They are more likely, therefore, to show the effects of delay items. It would be expected, however, that similarity would have a differential effect on the end items.

To test both of these explanations, Ss were given 12-word lists of common English nouns followed by either a delay task or no delay. The delay task consisted simply of reading aloud four words. The four words were constructed by rearranging the consonants and vowels of either the first, second, or third series of four words in the list. Thus, for example, the following list — soil, life, news, pair, crowd, night, shape, snow, week, car, moon, hill — could be followed by either no delay or a 5-second delay period in which the S read one of the three following delay tetrads:

| | | |
|---|---|---|
| poise | crate | mere |
| safe | showed | cool |
| lure | snipe | win |
| kneel | now | hawk |

The first delay set — poise, safe, lure, kneel — is obtained by reordering the phonemes of the first four list items — soil, life, news, pair. The second and third delay sets are obtained in the same way from the subsequent list items. The experiment was carried out twice — once with the Ss reading the delay list three times during the delay period, the other time with them reading it just once. The results of both experiments were the same. There was no differential effect of the composition of the delay list on either early or late positions. All three delay tasks, whatever their construction, cleared the items held in the STS in the same way (see Fig. 10).

It may be that some other form of similarity should be used to get an effect. The general type of similarity used here, sometimes called "formal similarity," has been used effectively in older work on rote learning with interpolated tasks (Melton & von Lackum, 1941). It

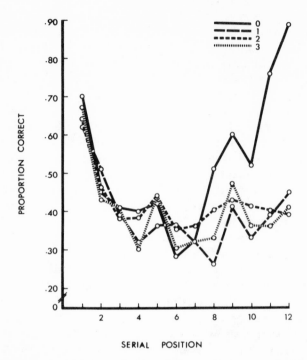

Fig. 10. Serial position curves for four delay conditions: 0, no delay; 1, delay task words similar to first four words; 2, delay task words similar to second four words; 3, delay task similar to third four words. (After Glanzer *et al.*, 1969, by permission of Academic Press, Inc., New York.)

has also been used effectively in more recent work on short-term memory (Wickelgren, 1965). This type of similarity is one that is based on the reordering of elements that make up either the list or units in the list. In the present case, the phonemes making up list words were reordered.

The effectiveness of a particular type of similarity is likely to be determined by the characteristics of the task involved. The free recall task is different from those in which formal similarity has been shown to play a role. It is possible, however, that other types of similarity might be shown to have an effect on STS. Some additional experiments have, however, been completed in which similarity manipulations were based on the distinctive features of phonemes. These experiments display marked similarity effects on LTS but none on STS (Glanzer, Koppenaal, & Nelson, in preparation).

At this point, neither information load nor similarity look

effective as factors in the clearing of STS. The two remaining factors are number of items and time.

There are two sources that indicate that time per se does not play an important role in the clearing of STS. Waugh and Norman (1965) have analyzed a free recall experiment by Murdock that indicates the same amount in STS after slow and fast list presentation. Raymond (1969) has shown by comparison of delay and no-delay conditions that the amount in STS is the same with variations in the rate of list presentation (see Fig. 8).

The effect of time was tested in a different way in the following experiment. Both the duration of the delay task and the number of items in it were varied. Each $S$ was presented with 12-word lists. After each list there was either a 2-second or a 6-second delay. During the delay period, the $S$ read either two or six words. This 2 by 2 factorial arrangement permits the separation of the effects of sheer passage of time and number of items. The results are shown in Fig. 11. The number of items has a clear effect. The length of the delay period has none.

This experiment does not eliminate another interpretation of decay effects. Items might be lost from STS by decay only during the time in which rehearsal is totally blocked, e.g., while the delay task words are being read. On this basis, both a decay and a displacement explanation lead to the same prediction here. It is possible to examine the loss of items from STS so as to separate this view of decay from displacement. The length of the words read during the delay task could be varied. Under this last interpretation of decay, six long words should produce a greater loss from STS than six short words. This experiment has not been carried out. A related experiment has, however, been carried out. Craik (1968) estimated the amount held in STS for lists consisting of short words and lists consisting of long words. He found that STS holds the same number of words whether the words are long or short. This would fit in with a simple displacement view. I will therefore hold to this view.

At this point, the following factors have been demonstrated to have an effect on LTS but not STS — word frequency, rate of presentation, and length of list. I will now turn to check another variable that has an effect on the serial position curve — associative or mnemonic structure. An early attempt had been made to show, by examining the interaction of associative structure with serial position, that the presence of associative relations in the list had no effect on STS (Glanzer & Meinzer, 1967). The attempt did not succeed primarily, I believe, because the structuring of the lists led $S$s

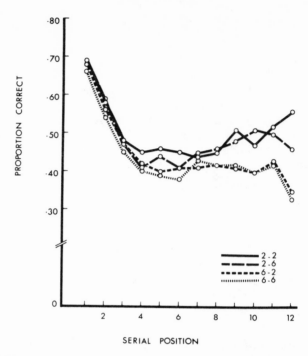

Fig. 11. Serial position curves for four delay conditions: 2-2, two seconds with two words read; 2-6, two seconds, six words; 6-2, six seconds, two words; 6-6, six seconds, six words. (After Glanzer *et al.*, 1969, by permission of Academic Press, Inc., New York.)

to adopt a special grouping strategy. The experiment has recently been repeated with the lists structured to prevent the development of special strategies (Glanzer & Schwartz, 1971). The amount held in STS was estimated by the technique of subtracting delay from no-delay data. In this experiment, Ss were given lists in which low-frequency associates were placed next to each other. These low-frequency associates have a strong effect on overall recall. They consist of word pairs that have an obvious semantic relation to each other, e.g., house–shack, mutton–veal, sleep–slumber, fruit–cherry. Low-frequency rather than high-frequency associates were used to make sure that the Ss could not develop a strategy of recalling what they could and then giving a very likely associate to each recalled word.

The associated pairs were scattered at random through the lists, occupying half the list positions. The mixed lists formed in this manner were followed either by a delay condition or no delay. The delay and no-delay curves are shown in Fig. 12. The derived STS curves are shown in Fig. 13. The results for the associated and unassociated items in the mixed lists have been separated and plotted separately.

It is clear that there is a large, consistent effect of mnemonic structure on the LTS component as seen in the delay curves of Fig. 12. There is, however, no effect on the STS component. Associated

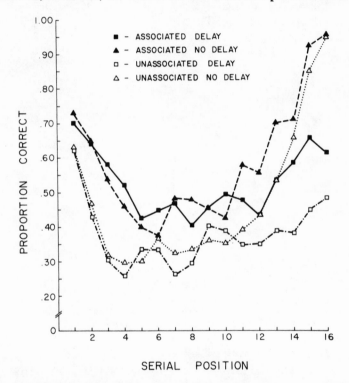

Fig. 12. Serial position curves for the delay and no-delay conditions with associated and unassociated items. (After Glanzer & Schwartz, 1971, by permission of Academic Press, Inc., New York.)

items take up the same space in STS as do unassociated items. This is borne out by the statistical analysis of the data in Fig. 13.

There is one point that should be noted here. The LTS or delay condition curves in Fig. 12 show an end peak. End peaks also appear in other data on delay conditions, e.g., Fig. 7. They mean either that the delay task was not completely effective in clearing STS or that it was less effective than successive list items in preventing transfer of information to LTS before items were cleared from STS. The second alternative seems more likely on the basis of available evidence. It is possible, however, to make sure that the estimate of STS is not distorted whatever the cause of the rise at the end of the delay curve. Following Waugh and Norman's (1965) procedure, it is possible to use the middle section of the curve to estimate the amount in LTS. With this estimate in place of $P_i$ (ND) in Eq. (3), an estimate of STS can be obtained for the last six serial positions. When this is done, a closely overlapping pair of STS curves is again obtained. The curves do not differ significantly.

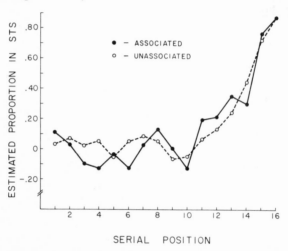

Fig. 13. Derived STS curves for associated and unassociated items. (After Glanzer & Schwartz, 1971, by permission of Academic Press, Inc., New York.)

The results of the studies summarized above can be taken to support a very simple displacement model of STS. All verbal items entering the system remove items from STS. The specific characteristics of the items play no role — their difficulty, length, and similarity to list items. No other factor seems to play a major role. Further work may demonstrate certain limited kinds of similarity effects, but they are not established at present.

Now that the roles of various factors on STS and LTS have been separated and evaluated, I can offer a generalization on STS to match the one given earlier for LTS.

*STS is a very robust, insensitive mechanism that responds to nothing except the passage of items through it.* There are at least two exceptions to this generalization. I will consider both of these later.

## B. WHAT OCCURS IN STS

I will turn now to the actions carried out on items while they are in STS and examine the relations of STS to LTS. In general, the picture of STS is that of an input buffer that can hold a limited number of items. As new items enter, old ones are lost. One function of the STS is to allow time for whatever mnemonic work needs to be done to assure that an item's information is transmitted to LTS. The item, it will be assumed here, can be held in a relatively passive way. It can also have various actions carried out on it either to maintain it in STS or to move it to LTS. Crowder and Morton (1969) and Rundus and Atkinson (1970) have considered some of these activities.

The item can be rehearsed silently either as part of a string of items or by itself. It can be repeated aloud, thus placing it back at the initial input stage, and recycled through the system. It can be put through various types of mnemonic organization at various levels of complexity. The relative frequency and effectiveness of these activities depend on the material and the structure of the task. All three activities have been shown effective. The first two have an effect on maintaining items in STS. Anything that prolongs the stay of an item in STS increases the chance that that item will be transmitted to LTS. If the stay of one item is prolonged without thereby reducing the probability that other items stay in STS, then overall performance on the list will increase. Whether silent rehearsal or repetition aloud do anything beyond increasing the availability of an item in STS for transfer to LTS has not been established.

The setting up of mnemonic structures or the setting up of retrieval routines have an effect on the transfer, registration, and retrieval of items in LTS. The setting up of mnemonic structures may result in a reorganization that helps maintain items in STS. This is relatively unknown territory at this time.

I will now outline one study of free recall that sheds some light on the processing that occurs during an item's stay in STS. My discussion here will not reproduce the logic of the paper as set forth in the original, since a number of factors relevant to the interpretation of the results have come clear through later work.

The study concerned the effect of imposed rehearsal procedures on the $S$. An $S$ will frequently repeat an item or a string of items during list presentations. The repetition may be silent or overt. The main effect of the repetition is presumably to keep the item in STS. The $S$, however, has two jobs to carry out. One is to maintain the item in STS, the other is to transfer information to LTS. If the $S$

were pushed to devote all the time between successive items to the repetition of the list items, he might have less time to devote to the transfer of items to LTS. The last statement assumes that the S, in registering an item in LTS or in setting up its retrieval, does something other than mere repetition of the item.

The experiment (Glanzer & Meinzer, 1967) was simple in form. Fifteen-word lists were presented to Ss with approximately 3 seconds between words. During the 3-second interval a metronome clicked six times. For half the lists, the S repeated aloud the word just presented, six times in time with the clicks. For the other half of the lists he did not do this. It was expected that the repetitions would block the activities that permit items to enter LTS. It was also expected, however, that the repetitions would not disturb the items in STS since these would be maintained by such a rehearsal procedure.

The results shown in Fig. 14 are in line with these expectations. The repetition of the items results in a depression of recall at all positions except the last few. The interaction between the experimental variable and serial position effect is all that is directly

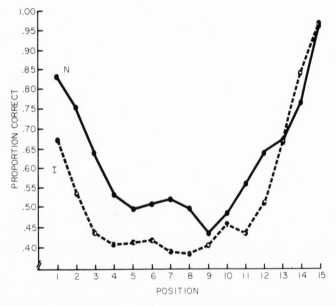

Fig. 14. Serial position curves for repetition (I) and no-repetition (N) condition. (After Glanzer & Meinzer, 1967, by permission of Academic Press, Inc., New York.)

available here. It is possible, however, to obtain an estimate of what is in STS using, as before, the middle items of the list to estimate the amount held in LTS in the final positions. This can be done since the LTS content remains fairly stable after the beginning peak. With this as the basis of estimating LTS, estimates of STS can be obtained. The curves derived on this basis, although rather irregular, show complete overlap. The total of the estimated points is almost the same: 2.26 words for the no-repetition condition, 2.31 for the repetition condition.[4]

There are two points that should be underlined here. One is that the forced repetition has an adverse effect here on overall performance. There are, of course, many situations in which some form of repetition has a positive effect. Indeed, repetition can have a positive, negative, or no effect at all on recall depending on its function in the system. I will try to point out later how repetition varies in its effect depending on how it is applied.

The second point that I will underline is that immediate repetition of individual words has no effect on the total number of different items in STS. This means that repetitions of a word while the word is in STS are not counted by the store as new items. If they were, then multiple repetition of one of the words, as done here, would wipe out all preceding words in STS. This characteristic of not counting repetitions might, on second thought, be a necessary characteristic of a store such as the one I have been describing. If each repetition had the effect of a new separate event, then rehearsal would have in general an adverse rather than beneficial effect. It would not only block transfer to LTS as in this experiment but also clear the STS before much work would be done on any other items.

This characteristic of the STS will appear again as I go over further aspects of the process of transmitting information from STS to LTS. Whether the ignoring of repetitions is a general characteristic of STS or due to a strategy adopted because of the nature of the free recall task cannot be decided now. Those two possibilities remain open.

Several characteristics of STS have been considered thus far. One is its method of entering new items and losing old. Another is its function as an operating register that permits prolonged work on any one item, and work on related sequences of items. The third is its tendency to treat repeated items as single items. The first two characteristics are important in the discussion of the next topic.

---

[4] These figures are obtained by summing the estimate of $P_i$ (STS) over the last five serial positions.

## V. Mnemonically Related Words

If two words are presented successively to the S and these words bear an associative or mnemonic relation to each other, the S may make use of this relation in registering the pair in LTS. I will assume that the STS is the operating register and that it is limited to about three items. The probability that a mnemonic relation can be used depends then on how closely the items follow each other in the sequence of inputs. If the items come one after the other then the probability that they will both be in STS together and available for mnemonic work will be very high.

The total amount of time that they will be in STS together can be obtained from the derived STS curve. As other items enter after the two related items, then the probability that both will remain in STS will decline steeply. If the related items do not enter in immediate succession but are separated by other items, then the probability that both will be in STS together is low from the start. That probability then undergoes further decline as other items enter. The larger the number of intervening items, the lower the initial probability.

It follows then that probability of recall of related items should be a declining function of the number of items between the related items. The asymptote of this function should be near three or four intervening items, since STS curves seem to drop to zero after four or five items (see Fig. 8). The following experiment (Glanzer, 1969) was set up to test this idea. Lists were constructed with mnemonically related, i.e., associated, pairs of words as list members. The distance, that is, the number of items that intervened between these pairs, was systematically varied so that there were either zero, one, three, or seven intervening items. Mnemonic relation was obtained here as indicated earlier by selecting low-frequency associates. The experiment was run at two presentation rates — one second per word and three seconds per word. The results are shown in Fig. 15. These are not serial position curves. They are plots of the overall means for the eight experimental conditions.

As expected, a probability of recall declined as the distance between related words increased. The slower presentation rate increases the time to transfer an item to LTS as an individual item or as a pair of related items. This raises the overall function for the slower rate. To explain the details of the two curves requires working out a much more exact and complex statement about the functions involved than will be attempted here. I will only note that the

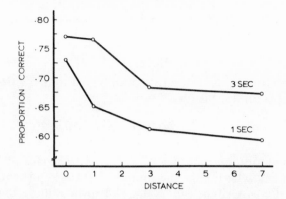

Fig. 15. Proportion of associated words recalled at one- and three-second presentation rates as a function of distance (the number of intervening words). (After Glanzer, 1969, by permission of Academic Press, Inc., New York.)

general shapes of the two curves are what might be expected from the form of the STS serial position curves seen in Figs. 8 and 13.

There have been several studies on the effect of blocking of semantically related words in free recall lists (Dallett, 1964; Puff, 1966; Weingartner, 1964). The results of these studies all show that when semantically related words are close together in a word list, the overall probability of recall increases. These findings would follow from the results and analyses presented above.

## VI. Repeated Words

The general approach used above in the analysis of the processing of mnemonically related words can be used in the analysis of the processing of repeated words. In the case of related words, the subject had an advantage when members of the pair appeared together in STS. In the case of repeated words, however, the S suffers a disadvantage when the word and its repetitions appear together in STS.

I indicated earlier that repetitions are given a single representation in STS. The simplest way of phrasing what happens with repetition of an item is to say that it resets the probability that an item is in STS to its initial value. From that point on, the item's career in STS is the same as if it had not been entered previously. For the sake of clarification, I will assume here that an item's probability of being in STS upon presentation is 1.00. And again, as an example, I will assume that this probability is halved as each successive item is presented to the $S$. The function would then be

$$P_j(\text{STS}) = f(j) = (.50)^j$$

where $j$ goes from zero to the total number of items, $n$, following the item. The area under this function is

$$\sum_{j=0}^{n} P(\text{STS}) = \sum_{j=0}^{n} (.50)^j \approx 2.$$

The total amount of time available for the transfer of the item to LTS is $t \approx 2d$, where $d$ is the amount of time given to each item including the interitem interval. The probability that the first representation of the item is in STS declines to a very small value as $j$, the number of succeeding items, increases. If then the second representation enters after a large number of intervening items, the item receives the benefit of a full stay in STS of the first representation and a full stay of the second representation. The total time that the item is available for transfer to LTS is $t \approx 4d$. If, however, the second representation enters before the $P_i(\text{STS})$ of the first representation is near zero, a different condition results. The second representation replaces the first and sets the loss function back to its value when $j = 0$. From that point on, the same rate of loss obtains. For example, if the first representation is immediately followed by the second representation, then

$$\sum_{j=0}^{n} P(\text{STS}) = 1.00 + \sum_{j=0}^{n} (.50)^j \approx 3.$$

The first term on the left 1.00 or $(.50)^0$ is the contribution of the first representation. The second term is the contribution of the second representation. The total time available for transfer to LTS is $3d$ rather than $4d$, as above. There is then a disadvantage, not an advantage in having an item appear again in STS before its first representation has cleared STS. From this it follows that the $S$ would get the least benefit out of a repetition if it occurred immediately after the first presentation. As the number of intervening items increases, the chances decrease that the second representation will appear in STS before the first clears STS. The chances therefore increase that the $S$ will have double the period of time to transmit the item to LTS.

An experiment with repeated words was run to test these expectations about the effect of spacing of repetitions. $S$s were given word lists at either a fast (one second) or slow (three second) rate.

Each list consisted of 16 words, including four repeated words. The number of words intervening between a word and its repetition was either zero, one, two, or five. It was expected that effect of repetition would be greater as the number of intervening items increased. The results of the experiment are shown in Fig. 16. They agree with the expectations.

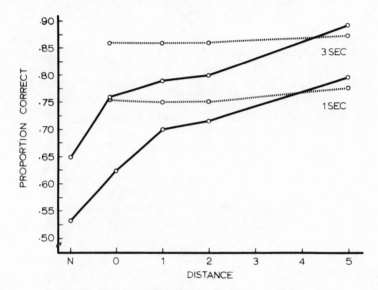

Fig. 16. Proportions of repeated words recalled at one- and three-second presentation rates as a function of distance (the number of intervening words). Also shown are the proportions for unrepeated words (N). The estimated proportions for two independent trials are on the broken lines. (After Glanzer, 1969, by permission of Academic Press, Inc., New York.)

In addition to the plots of recall of repeated items, estimated proportions for two independent transmissions to LTS are shown in the figure. These estimates indicate the probability that an $S$ would transmit information based on the first representation or the second representation or both when the two have appeared at different times in STS. The estimates are based on the proportions of correct unrepeated items in corresponding list positions. These items yield two proportions which are combined according to the equation

$$\text{Estimated } p = p_1 + p_2 - p_1 p_2.$$

It can be seen that the proportion correct of repeated items increases as the number of intervening items increases. The proportions rise to the theoretical asymptotes indicated by the dotted lines. All differences between the observed and corresponding theoretical points are statistically significant except those at distance 5. The fact, however, that both sets of data — those for the fast rate and those for the slow rate — overshoot the theoretical values, may indicate that additional factors are important in the registration of items in LTS. This indication is also found in data of Melton's (1967).

Before turning to other related data, I will draw one implication from what I have summarized above. This implication is analogous to the one drawn concerning the effect of associative relations and tested in the experiment by Glanzer and Schwartz above. It is that the positive effects of repetition are found solely in LTS. To test this it is necessary to carry out an experiment in which repeated items are presented at various list positions. Delay and no-delay conditions would be applied to separate effects on STS from those on LTS. I expect that the positive effect of repetition should be solely in LTS.

The data on spacing of repetitions reported above agree in the main with expectations based on characteristics of STS. There are, however, in the literature three other sets of free recall data, each of which gives a different picture of the effects of spacing of repetitions. Melton (1967) found results similar to those outlined above: increasing distance increases the effect of repetition. The study has been replicated by Madigan (1969). One aspect of the Melton and Madigan data does not fit the picture I have set up. They obtain a continued effect of spacing at distances of 20 and 40 intervening items. The factors that I have considered will cover changes only over much shorter distances. These long-range effects, if supported by further work, would require some special handling. They cannot be handled by available approaches, including the context explanation offered by Melton. This explanation involves, as does the one that I have offered, the assumption that a block of items is held in a limited processor of some type.

Experiments on distance effects in free recall are, however, not univocal. Waugh (1963, 1967) does not find any distance effects. Underwood (1969) finds an increase when the distance between the repeated items is greater than 0, i.e., a gross difference between massed and distributed presentation, but no clear or simple change as the distance increases from 2 to 20 intervening items. The procedures of the experiments above differ in a number of ways. For example, the Melton and the Glanzer experiments use visual presentation. Underwood and Waugh use auditory presentation. The resolution of the differences, however, awaits further exploration. There is sufficient evidence from other sources, e.g., from related paired-associates experiments (Peterson, Wampler, Kirkpatrick, & Saltzman, 1963), that I will hold to the statements above concerning the processing of repeated words.

## VII. Relation of Free Recall and the Model to Other Memory Tasks

In this section I will consider the generality of the information that has been developed up to this point. I will first consider several experimental situations and try to establish the correspondences between them. The relations between the several recall tasks have been pointed out by others. I will try to develop the correspondences further here. In addition to the free recall task, the following types of tasks are used in memory experiments:

1. Distractor task. A single item or string of items is followed by a delay task. The length and the characteristics of the delay task may be varied. This is the Peterson and Peterson (1959) design. The main task is often an arbitrary sequence of three consonants. The Ss' job is ordered recall of the trigram. The delay task may be anything from reading numbers or letters to carrying out complex mental operations.

2. Probe task. A series of items is followed by probes for specific items. This takes three popular forms: sequential probe, position probe, and paired associates. In a sequential probe task the $S$ is given a sequence of items, 1 through $n$, is presented with item $i$ and is asked to recall the following item, $i + 1$. In some cases the preceding item, $i - 1$, is asked for. In a position probe task the item to be recalled is designated by its ordinal position in the sequence, for example, "the third," or by its spatial position (for example, experimenter points to a window or reversed card which displayed the item.) In paired associates, the $S$ is given a sequence of paired items, is then given the first element of the pair, and then asked to recall the second. There are two ways in which the sequential, positional, or paired-associates probes are given to the $S$. One of the ways has been described above, the main task followed by the series of test items. Another way is to mix the items to be recalled with the test items in a running memory task. In this general class of experimental situations, the later items in the sequence may be viewed as delay tasks for the earlier items.

3. Fixed-order recall task. A series of items is presented, all of which are to be recalled in order. The sequence is usually longer than that used in a distractor task. This task is also called a serial recall task or memory span task. This type of task will be considered separately below.

The simplest situation is perhaps 1, the distractor task. The curve derived for this task has been presented by Peterson and Peterson (see Fig. 17). The curve is very clear. It is important to emphasize the following point. The curve has two parts: a descending slope and an

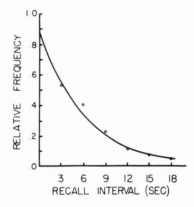

Fig. 17. Proportion of trigrams recalled after varying delay periods. (After Peterson & Peterson, 1959, by permission of the American Psychological Association, Washington, D.C.)

asymptote. The asymptote looks here as if it might be close to zero. According to a formula that Peterson and Peterson derive on the basis of a stimulus sampling model, the asymptote is .0089. This does not, however, tell the full story. The curve in Fig. 17 reflects correct responses made with a latency below 2.83 seconds. If a similar plot is made of correct responses within 14 seconds, a somewhat elevated curve appears that goes to a considerably higher asymptote, approximately .10.

These two parts of the curve, the descending slope and the asymptote, are, I believe, of great importance in the consideration of functions such as that in Fig. 17, and also in the consideration of serial position functions. The asymptote defines what is held in LTS. The peaked part of the curve is a joint function of STS and LTS. The rate at which it descends to an asymptote is an indication of the rate at which STS is cleared.

In some of the cases that I consider below I will discuss an asymptote on the basis of rather incomplete data. I do this with the awareness that more extensive testing would lead to a different definition of the asymptote.

The distractor task bears a double resemblance to the free recall situation. As free recall is ordinarily given, the middle section of the serial position curve corresponds to the asymptote in Fig. 17. The end peak of the serial position curve corresponds to the peak of the curve here. This is the first resemblance. To emphasize the correspondence, the curve in Fig. 17 should be plotted backwards. The second resemblance becomes evident when a delay is imposed after a free recall list. If the probability of recall of the last list item in Fig. 6 is plotted as a function of time, then a curve like Fig. 17 appears. The corresponding descent to an asymptote occurs. This is, of course, the closer correspondence. The drop of probability of the last list item in free recall with delay corresponds most closely to the drop of probability of a trigram with delay in the distractor task.

I will now go over some of the variables that have been shown to affect free recall: rate of presentation, list length, delay. I will bring in data on the effect of these variables in the other classes of memory task listed above. My purpose will be to show that the statements that I have made about free recall can be extended to these other situations. I wish to underline the similarity of the main results. I also wish to stress that the separation of STS and LTS is called for in these other experimental situations. To establish these points, I will try to show that the curves generated with variations of such factors as presentation rate give curves that correspond to those shown in Figs. 2, 3, 4, and 5.

## A. RATE OF PRESENTATION

Murdock (1963) carried out a series of experiments in which he used paired associates to determine the effect of presentation position. In one of the experiments, he varied the rate of presentation of the five pairs given. The results show some evidence of interaction, of merging of the peaks, and clear separation of the asymptotes. This interaction shows up most clearly in the curves for the 3-second and 2-second rate (see Fig. 18). The interaction of rate and serial position (here, subsequent pairs) is statistically significant. This figure should be compared with the results displayed in Fig. 2. Both types of task indicate an effect restricted to LTS.

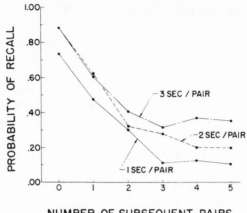

NUMBER OF SUBSEQUENT PAIRS

Fig. 18. Proportion of paired associates recalled as a function of position in sequence and presentation rate. (After Murdock, 1963, by permission of Academic Press, Inc., New York.)

B. LENGTH OF LIST

In the same paper, Murdock reports an experiment with a similar paired-associates procedure, in which the variables are number of items in the series and position in the series. The results are displayed in Fig. 19. These results are to be compared with those in Fig. 4 for free recall. A similar pattern of results is found in a spatial probe

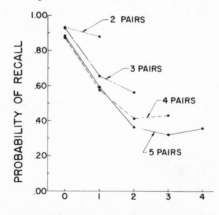

NUMBER OF SUBSEQUENT PAIRS

Fig. 19. Proportion of paired associates recalled as a function in sequence and list length. (After Murdock, 1963, by permission of Academic Press, Inc., New York.)

technique experiment reported by Phillips, Shiffrin, and Atkinson (1967). All three techniques give similar results. The results indicate that length affects only LTS.

## C. Number of Repetitions

There is a third experiment by Murdock (1963) in which the same interactive pattern is displayed. The experimental variable here is the number of repetitions of the item. Again it is clear that the probability of recalling an item repeated one, two, or three times is much the same after a short delay. With an increase in delay, the probability of recall goes to different asymptotes as a function of number of repetitions. The results above are based on repetition of lists of paired associates. They are paralleled by results of increased recall over trials in free recall learning.

Similar results are found with immediate successive repetitions of items in a distractor task (Hellyer, 1962; Peterson & Peterson, 1959). There is then evidence from both the probe and distractor tasks that repetition affects LTS primarily. A similar demonstration is not available for free recall, although it should be easy to carry out.

The role of repetition in recall is complicated. In an earlier section of this paper, I cited findings (Glanzer & Meinzer, 1967) showing that repetition lowered the probability of recall. I subsequently noted that immediate repetition of a free recall item raised its probability of recall, but that this increase was greater if the repetition was spaced (Glanzer, 1969). In the distractor and probe tasks, the effects of repetitions are, in general, to increase probability of recall. There are important differences between the experimental situations that I will point out now.

In the first case (Glanzer & Meinzer, 1967), the S repeated a word during a fixed interitem interval. There was no increase in the total presentation time for the item. The repetition only encroached on the time needed to register the word in LTS. In the second case (Glanzer, 1969), as in most cases in the literature, a repetition meant a doubling of the total presentation time.

There is, however, another important difference between the probe and distractor experiments as opposed to the free recall experiment. This difference will become critical in the further examination of the effects of immediate repetition. In the probe and distractor experiments, the S repeats not a single item but a sequence of units — a pair as in paired-associates probe procedure or a trigram in the distractor tasks. Before he says the first letters of a trigram a second time he has to say two other letters. This means that the appropriate comparison of repetition effects in free recall and other tasks should make use of repeated sequences of items.

### D. Spacing of Repetitions

There are a number of studies using paired-associate probes (Greeno, 1964; Peterson, 1963; Peterson, Wampler, Kirkpatrick, & Saltzman, 1963; Pollatsek, 1969) that show an effect of distribution of repetitions similar to those shown in Fig. 15 for free recall. The Peterson *et al.* data show in their Experiment I a steady increase in recall as the number of intervening items between repetitions goes from 0 to 1, 2, 4, and 8. Although there is a drop in recall with 16 intervening items in this experiment, the drop is probably not significant. In their Experiment II they use 0, 4, and 30 intervening items. They find an increase in recall from 0 to 4, but no further change beyond that.

### E. Delay

The effect of delay is apparent in all three classes of the recall task. The effect, of course, was shown for the distractor task by Peterson and Peterson (1959). It can be found in data for probe recall tasks that involve more than one test in each series of items. In those cases, the first probe corresponds to a no-delay condition, and the later probes correspond to delay conditions. An experiment by Tulving and Arbuckle (1963) gave data on such recall probabilities for paired associates. By using a counterbalanced design, they were able to separate the effect of the serial position of the pair within the list from the effect of delay of the probe. The results are shown in Fig. 20. The early probes gave a serial position function with a high end peak. Later probes gave a serial position function identical in the early positions but with the end peak eliminated. Comparison of Fig. 20 with Fig. 6 shows the similarity of the probe task results to the free recall results. Similar effects of delay on fixed-order recall tasks are cited below.

## VIII. Fixed-Order Recall

In the light of the results on the effects of delay, it is possible to understand the special case of the fixed-order or serial recall task.

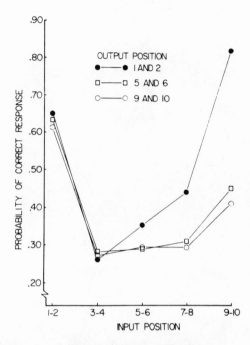

Fig. 20. Proportion of paired associates recalled as a function of serial position and delay. (After Tulving & Arbuckle, 1963, by permission of Academic Press, Inc., New York.)

The information developed so far gives all that is needed to understand that task. In fixed-order recall tasks, the S is required to recall the items in the order in which they are presented. Thus, the S's own responses act as a delay task with respect to the items in STS, the items from the end of the list. On the assumption that order information does not play any further role, it would be expected that serial position curves like the delay curves seen before would be produced by serial recall. These are curves without an end peak. Jahnke (1965) has compared the serial position curves obtained with free and fixed-order or serial recall. The curves obtained for 5, 10, and 15 word lists under these two conditions are shown in Fig. 21. Similar results have been found by Deese (1957). Fixed-order recall gives a lower end peak than free recall.

There is, however, one discrepancy. An end peak still remains in the fixed-order serial position curve. This occurs, I believe, because the experimenter, in this situation, does not have strong control over the time at which the S starts his response. If the S delays without

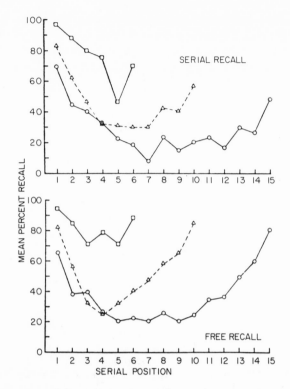

Fig. 21. Serial position curves for free recall and fixed-order, or serial recall, at three list lengths. (After Jahnke, 1965, by permission of the American Psychological Association, Washington, D.C.)

making any overt response, then he can use that empty delay period to register items from the end of the list in LTS.

Two implications about fixed-order recall can be drawn from the last statement.

1. If the experimenter forces the start of recall so that it must be made immediately after the last item, the end peak will disappear. As the $S$ is given more time before the start of recall, the end peak will increase in magnitude. I should underline the fact that the end peak here is all in LTS. It is a conversion of what is held in STS at the end of the presentation. It has to be in LTS because it can only be reported after a number of other items have been reported.

2. A second implication is that the imposition of a delay task immediately after the presentation of the list will also eliminate the end peak. With a delay task, the experimenter would ordinarily make sure that the $S$ responds quickly on the delay task. This operation

has been carried out in an experiment by Jahnke (1968a). The results for a 0-, 3-, 9-, and 18-second delay with a counting task are shown in Fig. 22. The results are very similar to those in Fig. 6 for free recall. Now that the relation of fixed-order recall to free recall has been considered, it is clear why the findings with the two procedures are similar.

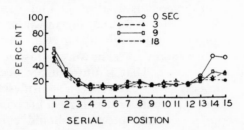

Fig. 22. Serial position curves for fixed-order recall with four delay periods. (After Jahnke, 1968a, by permission of the American Psychological Association, Washington, D.C.)

The following relations have been established by Jahnke. They parallel relations found in free recall and the other memory tasks listed above.

1. Rate of presentation — as in free recall, increase in rate results in a decrease in all serial positions except those at the end of the list (Jahnke, 1968b).

2. List length — as list length increases, the probability of recall decreases in those positions usually associated with LTS, the early and middle list sections (Jahnke, 1963, 1965, 1968a, 1968b). In the case of fixed-order recall, however, the end peak also declines (see Fig. 21). This does not occur to any marked degree in free recall. The reason for this is that in fixed-order recall, the end peak represents items transferred from STS to LTS after the list ends. The factors that lower the probability of registration in LTS with longer lists will also therefore affect end peak items. In free recall, the end peak is obtained in good part from STS which is not affected by list length.

The material presented so far in this section exaggerates the similarities between the several classes of a recall task. There is one extremely important and obvious characteristic in which the free recall task differs from all the rest. It does not require order information. All the rest, including the distractor task, require order information of varying degrees — from the simple order involved in paired associates, to the intermediate order involved in the distractor task to the complex order information required in serial recall.

## IX. Evaluation of Other Findings

It is now possible to review a number of problems in recall and to clarify some points on the basis of a multiple store approach. Before doing this, I should distinguish between two terms — the term STS used here as a construct, a theoretical term, and the term short-term memory. Short-term memory is used in the literature to refer to any one of a number of experimental situations in which the $S$'s final test on an item takes place within a minute or two. The term is neutral with respect to theory. Sometimes, however, this term is used as if it has theoretical significance. That is unfortunate because it leads to confusion. The process that I have been considering involves two storage mechanisms. Alternatives to this should certainly and will certainly be proposed. But the proposal should come with a clear differentiation of experimental task and theoretical construct.

I would recommend further that an explicit analysis be made of the role of STS and LTS in any discussion of a short-term memory experiment. A distinction should be made between effects that result in asymptote (LTS) differences and effects that result in differences in the rate of decline (STS).

With these distinctions in mind, I will review some experiments and arguments that appear in the literature. In the light of the distinctions, I believe that the work has a different meaning than first appears.

First, I will go over the proactive interference interpretation of the Peterson and Peterson (1959) findings (e.g., Keppel & Underwood, 1962). According to this interpretation, nothing new is involved in short-term memory. The constructs used for rote learning should, therefore, apply equally well to short-term memory.

There is an element of truth in this claim. Since the short-term memory situation will ordinarily give rise to output both from LTS and STS, factors that affect LTS will play a role. Therefore, factors involved in rote learning will have an effect. This does not mean, as stated above, that nothing new is involved in short-term memory. All that it means is that something old, i.e., familiar, is also involved.

This point and other related points become clear in considering the proactive interference interpretation of the Peterson and Peterson data in Fig. 16. According to this interpretation, proactive interference is what is demonstrated in that figure. Proactive interference increases as a function of two factors: the amount of material learned previously and the amount of time that elapses between study of an item and its test. Therefore, the Peterson and

Peterson curves should appear only after some number of items have already been learned.

This argument and data in support have been presented by Keppel and Underwood (1962) and Loess (1964). The results of Keppel and Underwood's Experiment 2 are shown in Fig. 23. The three curves represent the proportion correct over three delay periods when data for a first, second, and third test are separated.

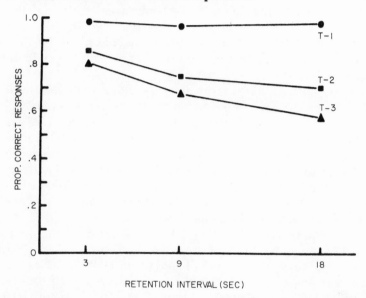

Fig. 23. Proportion of trigrams recalled as a function of delay periods and the number of the trial on which testing occurred: trial 1 (T-1), trial 2 (T-2); or trial 3 (T-3). (After Keppel & Underwood, 1962, by permission of Academic Press, Inc., New York.)

It is clear that the usual distractor task curves start to appear after the first test. The curves form a family, each curve going to a different asymptote. The total number of items affects the asymptote. The effect of number of items on the asymptotes, on the LTS component, is, however, clear in the case of free recall, in the relation between list length and asymptote (Murdock, 1962) discussed earlier. If the asymptote differs, then the appearance of the forgetting curve will differ. It is, for example, impossible to demonstrate a loss when the asymptote is at or near 1.00 as in the case of the top curve in Fig. 23.

The data do not, however, settle any issue. In terms of the multiple-store approach, the Keppel and Underwood experiments show an effect on LTS similar to the effect shown with other experimental arrangements. Indeed, there are not one but two relevant LTS effects that have been demonstrated in free recall, probed recall, and ordered recall. One is the length of list effect. The other is the beginning peak — the so-called primacy effect. Either or both of these could play a role in the decline of information registered in LTS with succeeding trials in the distractor task.

The results of the Keppel and Underwood experiments do not change the picture of two storage mechanisms. In fact they fit in rather nicely with the pattern of results discussed to this point. Figure 23 is parallel to Fig. 4 above. The results lead to the next weak generalization.

*Most effects on short-term memory, upon examination, will be found to be effects on LTS.* This is simply a result of the large number of variables that affect LTS.

Most of the literature on short-term memory does not separate LTS and STS output. The reports either do not contain or do not present information on the effects of delay. Ordinarily, the amount recalled under various conditions with either a fixed delay or no delay is reported. These studies confound LTS and STS effects. There is no way to separate one from the other.

Even in cases in which delay information is available, the data are often not interpreted properly. There are, for example, data that demonstrate that information load, or task difficulty, affect LTS solely. The point is, however, not made in the report of the study.

Two series of experiments (Posner & Konick, 1966; Posner & Rossman, 1965) have demonstrated such effects with a variant form of distractor task. The curves for the Posner and Rossman data that involve variation of time of delay are shown in Fig. 24. The curves have been replotted in terms of proportion correct instead of proportion incorrect in order to make them comparable to the other distractor task curves shown here. One major effect of the variation of information load is on the asymptote, the LTS component. The difference between the record and backward counting conditions supports this statement. Whether there is also an effect on STS beyond the effect on LTS is not demonstrated. There are not sufficient data. There is nothing in the paper that would lend support to the idea that lesser amounts are held in STS with increased difficulty of delay task.

The results here do give insight, however, into the details of the processing involved in transfer from STS to LTS and how this transfer occurs in various memory tasks. I noted earlier in the

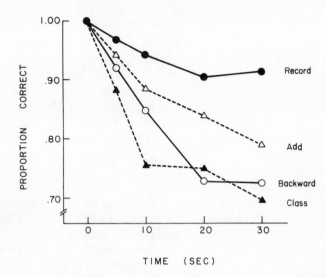

Fig. 24. Proportion of digits recalled as a function of delay task difficulty and length of delay period. (After Posner & Rossman, 1965, by permission of the American Psychological Association, Washington, D.C.)

discussion of the experiments by Glanzer *et al.* (1969) that changes in information load or difficulty of the delay task have no effect on the amount held in either STS or LTS. The results of that experiment on free recall have to be brought in line with those of Posner and Rossman. First it is important to note that there are three ways in which an additional task may affect storage of information: (*a*) it may change the rate of removal of items from STS; (*b*) it may block transfer of items from STS to LTS; (*c*) it may remove items already in LTS.

The data from free recall experiments show that (*a*) is not correct. The end peaks do not decline at different rates with different types of delay task (see Fig. 9). The same data show that alternative (*c*) is not correct. The overall asymptote of the serial position curve does not change with the several types of the delay task.

The one remaining possibility is that variation of the load of the delay task affects the probability of transfer of items from STS to LTS. If that were so then there should be a limited effect on free recall and a strong effect on distractor tasks. There would be a limited effect in free recall, because only the last few items would be affected. Specifically, these would be items that are still in STS and not yet transferred to LTS when the load is imposed. Early list items will already have cleared STS, being either forgotten or registered in

LTS. In this respect free recall differs from the distractor tasks. In distractor tasks, every item is followed closely by the delay task, and there is effective blocking of transfer to LTS for every item. It is possible even within the distractor task to show that the difficulty of the delay task has its greatest effect on that part of the item that most closely precedes the delay task. Posner and Rossman (1965) showed this in their Experiment IV.

From this it follows that in the distractor task every item should be affected. It also follows that in the free recall task with a relatively long series of items, the blocking of transfer would show only at the very end of the list. The specific way in which it would show in both tasks would be in the lowering of the LTS asymptote. Figure 9 does not indicate any strong basis for assuming that anything other than the asymptote has been affected.

The effect of the blocking can be looked at in the free recall curves such as those in Fig. 9. The last position in each curve can be plotted as in Fig. 25. The probability of recall at the last position is plotted for each delay task at each delay duration. Here I have taken

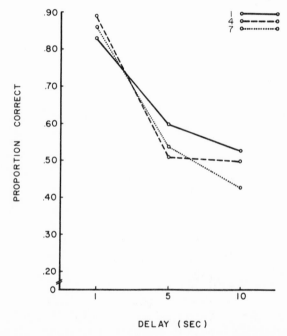

Fig. 25. The effect of delay with different load upon the proportion of recall of the last list item in free recall. (After Glanzer *et al.*, 1969, by permission of Academic Press, Inc., New York.)

the data from the first experiment mentioned earlier that made use of the variables of delay and information load (Glanzer *et al.,* 1969). The pattern of results in Fig. 25 is very much like that of Posner and Rossman's in Fig. 24. The curve for the adding 1 task goes to a higher asymptote than the other two tasks. Similar although less clear plots are obtained for the next to last and second from the last positions. This would follow from the effect of distance discussed above and verified in Posner and Rossman's Experiment IV.

Difficulty of the delay task then, according to the argument here, has no effect on the removal of items from STS. Its effect is to block the transfer of information from STS to LTS.

To support this analysis it would be good to have some further data. Fortunately, there are such relevant data in experiments by Baddeley, Scott, Drynan, and Smith (1969), Bartz and Salehi (1970), Murdock (1965), and Silverstein and Glanzer (1971). Murdock varied the load on *S*s during free recall with a secondary card sorting task. Baddeley *et al.* and Bartz *et al.* used the Murdock arrangement with both postlist delay and no-delay conditions. Silverstein and Glanzer ran an experiment similar to the Baddeley *et al.* and Bartz *et al.* experiments. Since I have the full serial position functions for that experiment I will present them here. I will only note that all the experiments indicate essentially the same results — that imposed load during the list presentation affects the amount held in LTS not STS. In Murdock's experiment, this can be seen in the fact that load interacts with the serial position function. The early part of the serial position curves are separate one from the other. The later sections merge. In the Baddeley *et al.* experiment, this interaction results in a slight separation of the recall averages with no delay but a much more pronounced separation in the delay condition. In the Bartz and Salehi experiments, load affects the early part of the list only, while delay affects the end of the list. Bartz and Salehi also note that their data show no effect of load on the final list positions in the delay conditions. They state that this does not fit a simple dual storage model. Since this discrepancy does not appear in the Silverstein and Glanzer experiment, I will not consider it further here.

The experiment by Silverstein and Glanzer used a delay and no-delay condition. Instead of sorting cards during the list presentations, the *S*s added a pair of numbers, e.g., 23 + 4, during the interval between words. The addends were varied, being either 1's, 4's, or 7's, with the larger addend giving the more difficult task. It was expected that the load would have an effect only on LTS and not on STS. Since the load had been applied while every item was present in STS, the blocking effect would be spread over the entire list, not just in the final positions. Both no-delay and delay conditions were used to permit the separation of the LTS and STS. During the delay condition, which was 4 seconds long, the S read six words. The results are shown in Figs. 26, 27, and 28.

Figure 26 displays the serial position curve for free recall without delay under three levels of concurrent task difficulty. The results replicate Murdock's. There is an interaction of task difficulty with serial position. All but the last few positions are lowered as difficulty

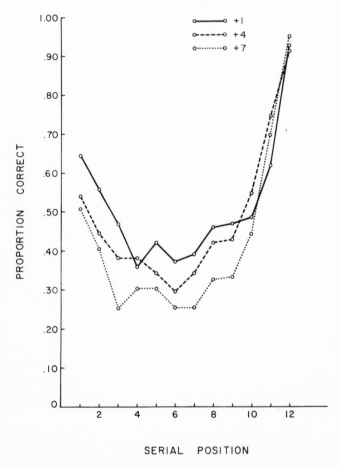

Fig. 26. Serial position curves for three levels of concurrent task difficulty. (After Silverstein & Glanzer, 1971, by permission.)

increases. Figure 27 displays the serial position curve for the delay conditions. Although the separation of the curves is not as clean as that in the curves of Fig. 26, it is clear that the overall effect of the delay task is in line with expectations. There is no evidence of interaction between serial position and task difficulty under

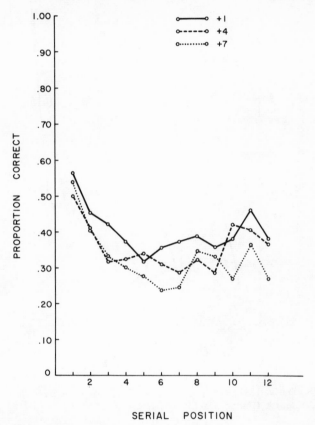

Fig. 27. Serial position curves for three levels of concurrent task difficulty, with a postlist delay. (After Silverstein & Glanzer, 1971, by permission.)

statistical test. Figure 28 displays the estimate of STS based on Eq. (3) given earlier. Statistical tests of these data indicate that only serial position is a significant factor. The curves for the three levels of task difficulty do not differ.

Most of the points that I have made above have already been made by Baddeley *et al.* (1969). Murdock notes, moreover, that the task load effects could also be attributed to effects of total presentation

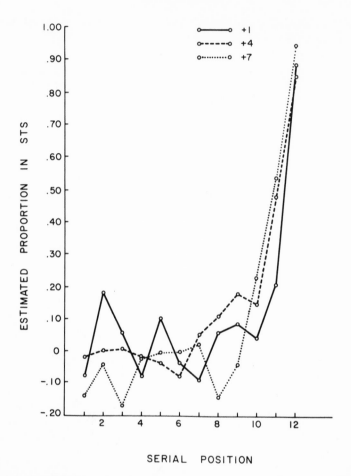

Fig. 28. Derived STS curves for three levels of concurrent task difficulty. (After Silverstein & Glanzer, 1971, by permission.)

time. It can be argued that difficult tasks take more time. In this sense, the results here all follow from the results on rate of presentation. The less available time the S has between successive words the lower the LTS level. The STS remains unaffected (Raymond, 1969).

The experiment above rules out, however, a number of possible theoretical alternatives with respect to information load. It shows that task difficulty or information has the same effect on LTS as rate of presentation. It also has the same effect on STS as rate of presentation — none. If there is something special that information load does beyond rate of presentation or amount of available time, it does not appear here.

A few remarks should be added on this matter of rate of the delay task. Fast rates in a secondary task or a delay task block registration in LTS. If a level asymptote in the serial position curve for a delay condition is desired, it is necessary to set the rate of the delay task processing close to the presentation rate of the main list items. If the rate is too slow, then that part of the asymptote that has not yet been fixed will end up at a higher level giving a slight end peak. If the rate is too fast, then there will be a dip in the end positions. This can be seen in some of the figures presented earlier. The effects of rate of the delay task can be seen in two studies using distractor tasks. The experimenters (Conrad & Hull, 1966; Kulp, 1967) varied the rate of the processing of items in a distractor task. The effect of rate of the delay task is clearly displayed in Fig. 2 of the paper by Kulp. The figure shows that the delay curves for the two rates of delay task go to different asymptotes.

It follows from the arguments above that a delay period filled with several difficult and several easy tasks would have a different effect depending on the order of the tasks. If the difficult tasks came first, then it would have its effect while a large amount of the list information remains in STS. The difficult task would not only remove the items in STS, it would also block their transfer to LTS more completely until they were removed. If the easy delay tasks came first, they would remove the items from STS. They would not, however, be as effective in blocking the transfer of the items to LTS before the items were removed. By the time that the difficult delay task is imposed, the list items have all cleared STS. There is no transfer for the task to block. This deduction is supported in three experiments by Dillon and Reid (1969) using a distractor task.

Now that the differentiation between effects on LTS or asymptote and effects on STS or rate of decline has been gone over, I can turn to some other cases in the literature. In these cases my interpretation is different than the author's because of the differentiation.

There is the general issue of the role of acoustic confusion on STM. Here the reference is to the recall of strings of items that bear some phonetic relation to each other. The most popular form of this task is one in which letter names that share a vowel in pronunciation are presented. This material was first used by Conrad (1964) in an important experiment establishing the role of acoustic factors in memory. In this material a highly similar string would be drawn from the set BCDGPTVZ or from the set FLMNSX. An example of a highly similar string is BGDV. An example of a dissimilar string is FBJQ.

Although there are a large number of studies that show that this type of similarity has an effect on recall, there is little evidence that its effect is on STS. The data are collected in situations with no variation of delay or with no determination of serial position effects. When there is no delay, overall recall scores are a composite of output from STS and LTS. When there is a delay but it is fixed, the recall scores reflect LTS components primarily.

An example of a study using a fixed delay is one by Wickens, Born, and Allen (1963). In this study, the investigators showed that changing the material to be recalled from letters to numbers or numbers to letters in a sequence of distractor trials resulted in a rise in performance. Since the data were obtained with a fixed-delay task the effects are most likely assignable solely to LTS. Whether STS is also involved cannot be determined.

Although the literature on the effects of acoustic similarity on short-term memory is massive, it settles nothing with respect to a key issue: the effect of similarity on STS, and whether that effect is different from the effect on LTS. The relatively few published studies that contain information that separates LTS and STS effects give results that disagree. In particular, the results do not agree with popular generalization that acoustic similarity affects STS, and semantic similarity affects LTS. This generalization is incorrect or at best oversimplified.

Bruce and Crowley (1970) gave free recall lists to Ss with sequences of acoustically similar (gain, cane, vain, reign) or semantically similar words (bean, carrot, corn, potato) embedded in the list. They imposed a delay after each list to remove items in STS. Both types of similarity had an effect on LTS, increasing the total amount held. Craik and Levy (1970) carried out a similar free recall study but used only no-delay conditions and estimated STS for acoustically and semantically similar words. Their findings on LTS agree with those of Bruce and Crowley (1970) — both forms of similarity increase the total amount held in LTS. Their estimates of the amount held in STS showed that acoustic similarity did not have a significant effect on the amount. Semantic similarity did, however, decrease the amount held in STS.

Results in line with the acoustic–STS, semantic–LTS generalization are, however, found in two studies using the probe technique. Levy and Murdock (1968) in their Experiment II, gave 10 word lists to Ss. The lists consisted of either acoustically similar (nest, vest, pest, rest, etc.) or acoustically dissimilar words. They found an interaction of similarity with serial position, with the end peak lower for similar words. Acoustic similarity reduces the amount held in STS.

Kintsch and Buschke (1969) carried out a similar study in which they compared probe recall of lists made up of homophone pairs with lists made up of unrelated words. The results agree with Levy and Murdock's (1968). Recall was poorer at the end of the list for the homophones. They use the serial position curves to isolate the STS and LTS components.

In a parallel experiment, Kintsch and Buschke show an effect of synonym pairs on the recall of items from the early serial positions. They identify this as an effect of semantic similarity specific to LTS. They show that STS is unaffected. This study is a complete demonstration of the acoustic-STS, semantic-LTS pairing that has been argued for by Baddeley and Dale (1966). All that seems necessary at this point is to iron out the differences with the free recall data cited above. Since there are obvious differences between free recall and probe procedure, it might seem easy to reconcile the two sets of results.

Unfortunately, this is not so. There are also results from distractor studies that do not agree.

Posner and Konick (1966) in their Experiments III and IV gave a distractor task, varying the confusability of the letters making up the trigrams to be recalled. The delay task, adding or classifying numbers, was continued by the $S$ for 0, 5, 10, or 20 seconds. The results lend clear support to the idea that there is an effect of similarity on the LTS component. The delay curves go to different asymptotes for high and low similarity conditions. The results do not, however, indicate any clear effect on STS. This would have to appear here as an effect on the rate of approach to the different asymptotes. These results may, of course, merely indicate a difference between free recall and distractor results on the one hand and probe results on the other. Unfortunately, this distinction is not likely to be useful. The probe studies themselves do not agree.

Bruce and Murdock (1968) used a paired-associates probe technique with both acoustically similar and dissimilar words. The serial position curves show a clear effect of similarity on the LTS component and no effect on the STS component (see their Fig. 2). Their data further indicate that the similarity effect on LTS is proactive rather than retroactive, but that point is not important here.

In summary, the effects of similarity on LTS and STS are not established. Most of the work cited on this effect does not differentiate LTS and STS effects. The few studies that do permit the differentiation give conflicting results.

Many of the results on short-term memory are interpreted differently in light of the STS-LTS distinction. One example is found in a study of free recall by Tulving and Patterson (1968). In that study sequences of related words, e.g., father-mother-son-daughter, were embedded in lists. In two of the experimental conditions, the block of successive related words was placed either in the four final list positions, Condition E, or in four middle list positions, Condition M. Tulving and Patterson note a striking pattern of results (see Fig. 29). They claim that these results do not fit a two-storage model (p. 246). An examination of the results in the light of LTS and STS shows, however, a very good fit. The argument that I will make here has also been made by Craik and Levy (1970).

It is clear that the grouping of related words gives them an advantage in their registration in LTS. This has been discussed earlier in relation to distance effects. The LTS asymptote will be different for the blocked related words. The study therefore involves two

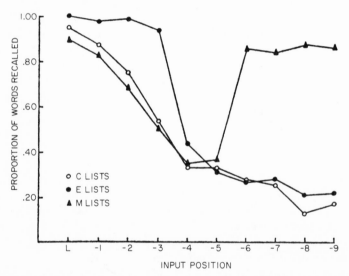

Fig. 29. Serial position curves for control lists condition (C) and for the lists with blocks of four semantically related words in either the middle (M) or end (E) list positions. The curves are plotted backward with the last list position first. Only the last ten positions are given. (After Tulving & Patterson, 1968, by permission of the American Psychological Association, Washington, D.C.)

levels of LTS. $LTS_1$ is the storage level for the unblocked, unrelated words; $LTS_2$ is the storage level for the grouped, related words. $LTS_1$ can be estimated from the middle sections of the curve for the control condition, C, since the STS should not be present there. Similarly, $LTS_2$ can be estimated from the middle section of the $M$ curve. The last few positions are, as usual, a composite of STS and LTS. In the case of curve $M$

$$P_i(R) = P(LTS_1) + P_i(STS) - P(LTS_1) \cdot P_i(STS)$$

In the case of curve $E$

$$P_i(R) = P(LTS_2) + P_i(STS) - P(LTS_2) \cdot P_i(STS)$$

It is possible therefore to use any two of the curves in Fig. 29 to reconstruct the third. By making use of the equations above and the data given on the $C$ and $M$ curves, the following values are obtained: $P(LTS_1) = .21$, from positions 6 through 9 of the $C$ curve; $P(LTS_2) = .86$, from the same positions in the $M$ curve.

$P(LTS_1)$ is used to estimate $P_i(STS)$ for the last four list positions in the $C$ curve. Starting with the last position, $P_i(STS)$ is estimated, according to Eq. (3), as .934, .836, .689, and .415. Combining these estimates with $P(LTS_2)$ the following values are computed for the last four positions of the $E$ curve: .991, .978, .957, and .920. These may be compared with the empirical values read from Fig. 29 — 1.000, .986, .990, and .943. The estimate can be improved by taking account of the fact that the $C$ curve does not actually give the best estimate for $P(LTS_1)$. It is, however, good enough to show that the curves in Fig. 29 can be interpreted in terms of LTS and STS.

## X. General Characteristics of STS

Up to this point, I have shown that the STS is a highly buffered system in a limited sense. It is buffered in the sense that very few experimental variables affect it. In the considerable number of variables that I have considered, only two seem to have any strong effect on STS — the number of items entered and the appearance of an exact repetition. It is not clear at this point whether similarity of items has any effect on STS. And the effect of repetition may also be specific to some characteristic of the experimental situation.

There are two ways to rationalize this considerable robustness of the STS. One way is in terms of the system qua memory system. If the STS is one of a set of processors arranged in series, then it would be desirable to have it responsive to as few disturbances as possible.

Its main job is to hold a block of recent items available for further processing. If it does anything other than hold the items, then information is lost to the rest of the system. This is an oversimplified statement. It also may not be the most fruitful way to view the STS. I will present one that I think has certain advantages over this one.

Before I do this I want to emphasize the generality of the LTS-STS distinction and the robustness of STS. In particular, I want to argue that STS is independent of: (a) age; (b) intelligence; (c) mnemonic skill.

## A. INDEPENDENCE OF AGE

Craik (1968) has compared adult Ss ages 22 and 65 on free recall tasks. He has separated the STS and LTS components by the method used above and by another analytic formula. He finds that the amount registered in LTS decreases with age, but that the amount in STS is constant.

There also have been several probe-recall studies comparing children of different ages. The results of these studies are, however, unclear. I will turn to a study carried out by Thurm and Glanzer (1971) comparing the performance of 5- and 6-year-old children in free recall. The items used in presentation were pictures of objects whose names were familiar to the children, e.g., apple, clock, lion, star. The children called out the names of these as they were shown at a 3-second rate. They were shown series of items that were systematically varied in length from two to seven items. After each list they were asked to recall as many names as they could. The results are shown in Fig. 30. The curves show two systematic effects. One is the effect of list length that had been noted earlier in the Murdock (1962) data. The other was the effect of age. The five-year-olds clearly do worse than the six-year-olds on list lengths 4, 5, 6, and 7. They do not do worse, however, in the last few positions. The STS holds up across the age levels.

A full examination of the assertion that STS is independent of age must, of course, include a much broader range of ages than I have mustered up here. What has been presented, however, is in line with the assertion.

## B. INDEPENDENCE OF INTELLIGENCE

Ellis (1970) has compared the recall performance of retardates with college students of approximately the same age. The Ss were

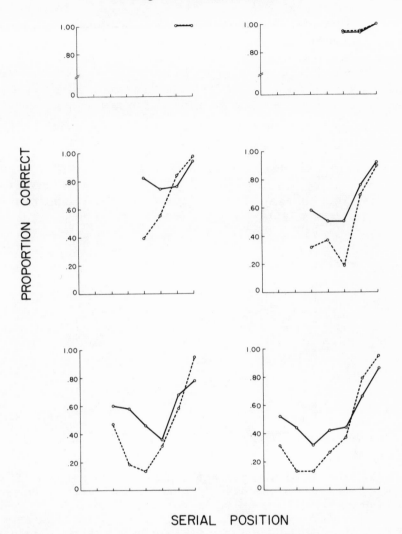

PROPORTION CORRECT

SERIAL POSITION

Fig. 30. Serial position curves for five-year-old (broken line) and six-year-old (solid line) children with lists of length 2, 3, 4, 5, 6, and 7 words. (After Thurm & Glanzer, 1971, by permission.)

given a nine-item position probe task with both fast and slow presentation rates. The serial position curves obtained (see their Fig. 3) show the expected interaction of mental age with serial position. The curves are widely separated across all serial positions except the last few where they merge.

There is another interesting aspect of the results. The data for the normal Ss show the interaction between presentation rate and serial position discussed earlier (see Fig. 2). The data for the retardates, however, do not show this interaction. The serial position curves for both fast and slow presentation are almost identical. The retardates evidently do not make use of the additional time available in slow presentation to improve the registration of information in LTS.

## C. INDEPENDENCE OF MNEMONIC SKILL

Raymond (1968) separated the data of Ss who scored high and those who scored low in free recall. The serial position curves for these two groups of Ss are shown in Fig. 31. The standard interaction

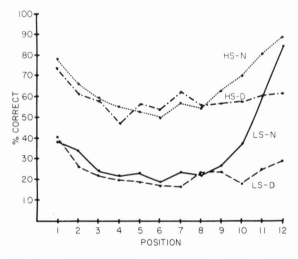

Fig. 31. Serial position curves for high scoring (HS) and low scoring (LS) Ss on delay (D) and no-delay (N) free recall. (After Raymond, 1968, by permission of the author.)

effect of the no-delay curves for the two groups is clear. Raymond applied Eq. (3) to derive two serial position curves for STS — one for the high scoring and one for the low scoring Ss. When this was done, she obtained two nearly identical curves (see Fig. 32).

I wish to emphasize the generality of the LTS-STS distinction and the robustness of STS to prepare for its further identification. In line with this emphasis, a recent study by Baddeley and Warrington (1970) is of interest. Following up earlier clinical observations of effects of brain damage that are specific to LTS, they demonstrate that, in free recall, their amnesic Ss have normal STS but defective LTS.

## XI. Relation of STS to Language Processing

I will consider here the idea that the system I have been discussing is intimately involved in the processing of language. A more extreme statement would identify the STS and LTS components with stages in the processing of speech. If this idea is correct, then full understanding of the mechanisms and processes considered would depend on viewing their relation to language processing. Furthermore, this idea would suggest the examination of special aspects of the functioning of STS and LTS.

The close relation of memory to language has been pointed out previously. Usually this is done in discussions of the distinctions

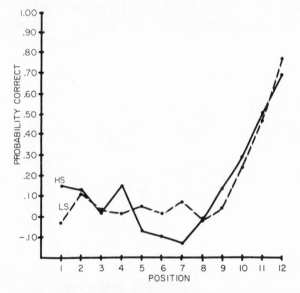

Fig. 32. Derived STS curves for high scoring (HS) and low scoring (LS) $S$s. (After Raymond, 1968, by permission of the author.)

between linguistic competence and performance. In those discussions, the role of memory is simply mentioned in a vague and general fashion. Yngve (1960) was the first to examine constructively and in some detail the role of STS in language processing. He identifies STS with the first stage of language processing.[5] It is interesting that he assumed, in his examination, that STS was governed by simple displacement. Yngve went into the details of the computation necessary to process a sentence. On the basis of the

---

[5] Yngve separates an operating register from the STS in his outline of language processing. I have not done this.

capacity limitations of STS he tried to derive or rationalize some of the special structural characteristics found in natural language, e.g., discontinuous constituents.

Another investigator to consider the relation of memory to language processing is Neisser (1967). He notes the importance of rhythmic pattern in memory and argues that the synthesis of these patterns involves the same mechanisms as the synthesis of speech (p. 235). The role of grouping factors is, I agree, of great importance in the understanding of both language processing and memory. I will expand on this point below.

There are two types of evidence that I will draw on to support the relation or identification of speech processors and memory mechanisms. One is evidence on the special role of auditory as opposed to visual presentation. The other is the role of grouping factors in recall. Both of these types of evidence lend at best indirect support.

## A. AUDITORY *VERSUS* VISUAL PRESENTATION

The initial stage of the memory system handles auditory information most efficiently. This can be seen in the fact that when the same list is given with auditory and visual presentation, there is better recall of the auditory list. Examination of the serial position function shows that this advantage is, under ordinary conditions, limited to the last few positions, the positions associated with STS. Murdock and Walker (1969) have presented such curves. Murdock and others have carried out a number of investigations of this effect. A number of proposals have been offered as to the specific characteristics of storage as indicated by various findings. I will not go into these proposals here. It is sufficient that I underline the advantage of auditory material. The system is set up to handle auditory input.

The term auditory might be understood as implying that STS is primitive in the sense that it is restricted to processing of input at a phonemic level. This implication, I believe, is incorrect. I will present some evidence that indicates a rather complex function for STS.

## B. GROUPING EFFECTS

The grouping effects noted by Neisser (1967) play a pervasive role in both the production and understanding of speech. They are even strong in the restricted verbal performance permitted in the laboratory. Ebbinghaus (1885) noted that he could not avoid grouping syllables in the reading of his lists. He coped with the effect by imposing a standard intonation pattern on his reading.

When Ss read a list of words out loud, they will produce a recognizable intonation pattern for any regular characteristic of the list that permits grouping. The ubiquity of grouping intonation effects has also been noted by investigators of speech. Lieberman (1967) has, for example, argued for "breath group" as a physiologically based universal of human speech that plays an important role in the segmenting of speech.

At this point there is no basis for distinguishing the effects of intonation pattern from the effects of other types of grouping. As I indicated above, the Ss' intonation patterns are omnipresent and will reflect whatever grouping cues are available. I will handle the two terms, for the present, as roughly equivalent.

A recent study by Gianutsos (1970) sheds light on the differential effect of grouping in LTS and STS. She presented 18-word lists to Ss in which the successive words were temporally grouped by threes or ungrouped, i.e., presented at a steady rate. A number of factors were varied including the presentation rate. One of the striking findings, demonstrated in several of the experiments, is that, in free recall, grouping has a beneficial effect solely on STS. Figure 33 demonstrates this effect.

This pattern is characteristic of several sets of data reported by Gianutsos. They all indicate that grouping facilitates the recall of the last one or two groups.[6] The grouped items were not only recalled better, they were recalled in different order. In the grouped conditions, the final two groups tended to be recalled first and in forward order. In ungrouped lists, although S tends to recall items from the end of the list first, he tends to recall those items in reversed order (Deese & Kaufman, 1957).

There is another clear finding that should be mentioned. The grouping effect is heightened as the overall presentation rate increases. The pattern seen in Fig. 33 is more marked if the 18-word list is given in 18 seconds than if it is given in 36 seconds. Gianutsos notes that this effect may hold the explanation of some of the conflicting results on the effect of rate on short-term memory. An increase in rate, as pointed out earlier, decreases the amount registered in LTS. An increase in rate, however, also facilitates

---

[6] Gianutsos also demonstrated an effect of grouping on LTS. The effect, restricted to the beginning peak, is not relevant to the present discussion.

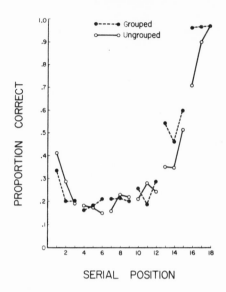

Fig. 33. Serial position curves for grouped and ungrouped presentation. (After Gianutsos, 1970, by permission of the author.)

grouping and thus increases the amount held in STS. The relative size of these opposed effects will determine the overall effect of rate.

The grouping effect found here is a striking one. One aspect of the effect that requires further examination is the role that grouping plays in registration in LTS over repeated trials. It is clear that grouping is, in that case, advantageous (Müller & Schumann, 1894).[7] The way in which an STS advantage is converted to an LTS advantage has, however, not been analyzed.

In the early sections of the paper, a number of variables were considered, all of which had an effect on LTS but not on STS. It might have seemed that nothing other than other items could affect STS. Indeed, I offered a generalization based on that thought. It now appears that there are two other factors with an effect specific to STS: the modality of the presentation and grouping. Both factors are likely to be important if the STS plays a key role in language processing, like that outlined for it by Yngve.

I will now fit the processing of speech into the flow chart presented in Fig. 1. I will consider only the reception of speech.

[7] Müller and Schumann (1894) also point out that the specific intonation pattern, i.e., trochee *versus* iamb, is important in determining the amount their Ss learned. This implies the role of a factor beyond simple grouping. They also mention the role of breath groups during learning.

Yngve's (1960) analysis was concerned only with the production of speech.

An input sequence goes through initial sensory processing and then appears in STS. The temporal length of the sequence is variable. While the sequence is in STS, a computation is carried out that determines the interpretation of the sequence. The results of the computation are then registered in LTS. The results of the computation are an interpretation of the sequence. An initial determination of the sequence to be analyzed is probably obtained from grouping cues.

Two processes are involved in the computation. One is the checking of tentatively defined units with the Ss' lexicon, a listing of possible units with related information. The other process is the application of the grammar to the sequence. Both these processes, the lexical and the grammatical, probably take place repeatedly and cyclically until a solution that is acceptable on both bases is reached. The processing in STS involves, therefore, repeated exchanges with LTS for both the lexical and grammatical processing.

A question of importance is the size of the unit that is held in STS. The evidence at hand indicates that the unit is at least a word or a morpheme. This is implied by Craik's (1968) finding that the length of the list words did not affect the total number of words held in STS. The evidence at hand also implies that the unit may be less than a newly generated sentence. This inference may be drawn from the fact that even when the $S$ can put a pair of words into mnemonic combination, he still holds individual words in STS (Glanzer & Schwartz, 1971). The answer might be then that the unit in STS is a word or morpheme. I would like, however, to consider another possibility. This is that the unit that STS holds is any item that is in the $S$'s lexicon. This would include units smaller than a word but also, possibly, units larger than a word — phrases, sentences. The phrases and sentences would be set units, not sequences that the $S$ has to construct *de novo* solely on the basis of the input and the stored lexicon and grammar. Computations of sentences that are not already in the $S$'s lexicon will, according to this, be handled as multiple unit sequences in STS.

The possibility that STS holds long sequences as units is particularly interesting for two reasons. One is for the insight it gives into the processing in the system. The other is for the corrective value it has. I noted earlier that the tendency has been to look at STS as a primitive processor handling relatively simple units. I am now considering the possibility that it may handle very large units, if those units are already set in the $S$'s lexicon.

In order to test this idea an experiment was set up,[8] using proverbs as the material for free recall lists. Proverbs are sentences or phrases that are part of $S$'s lexicon. If what I have said above is correct, these should be held in STS much the same way that individual words are held. In particular, it should be possible to generate a serial position curve of the standard form with an end peak. It should also be possible to lower that end peak with a delay task.

To test these assertions, lists of familiar proverbs were assembled, and set up in 15-proverb lists. Each list was read to $S$s at the rate of one proverb every four seconds. The $S$s then gave immediate recall at the end of half of the lists and delayed recall after the other half. Delayed recall consisted of having the $S$ repeat a sequence of four words before recalling the list proverbs. The experiment was run in two languages with Hebrew speaking $S$s given Hebrew proverbs and English speaking $S$s given English proverbs. Since the results were the same in both groups, I will present the overall data for the combined groups (see Fig. 34).

There are two important characteristics of the curves. One is that the no-delay condition shows an end peak comparable to the end peaks seen in preceding figures. There is little reason to doubt that the end peak would shift to later positions if the list were lengthened. The material in STS, however, consists not of several words but of several sentences with a mean length of 4 to 4.5 words each.

If there is any doubt about identifying the end peak with STS, the delay curve is of interest. It is clear there that the STS component is vulnerable here to subsequent items as in the case of words. It is also clear that sequences involving a number of morphemes may function as a single unit in STS.

## XII. Closing Statement

I have started from a simple free recall task and some simple results. On the basis of the results I have built a detailed picture of some aspects of the recall process. I have, of course, omitted many important aspects of the process. There are many investigators who are actively working on these aspects.

[8] This experiment was carried out with the assistance of Micha Razel and Tova Meryn Zaltz.

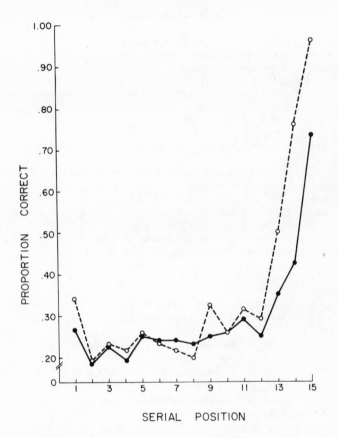

Fig. 34. Serial position curves for free recall of proverbs under delay (solid line) and no-delay (broken line) conditions.

In the course of the examination of recall, I have drawn a picture of the STS as a limited store that holds input for processing. I have claimed that it responds solely to the number of items that enter the overall system, with three exceptions. It handles repetitions of an item currently in STS as if the two representations were one. It responds to intonation grouping. It is particularly responsive to auditory material. I have argued further that the STS is an important part of the system for the processing of language and that a full understanding of either the language processing system or memory system involves an understanding of the overlap or identity of the two systems.

## REFERENCES

Atkinson, R. C., & Shiffrin, R. M. Human memory: A proposed system and its control processes. In K. W. Spence & J. T. Spence (Eds.), *The psychology of learning and motivation: Advances in research and theory.* Vol. 2. New York: Academic Press, 1968. Pp. 89–195.

Baddeley, A. D., & Dale, H. C. A. The effect of semantic similarity on retroactive interference in long- and short-term memory. *Journal of Verbal Learning and Verbal Behavior,* 1966, 5, 417–420.

Baddeley, A. D., Scott, D., Drynan, R., & Smith, J. C. Short-term memory and the limited capacity hypothesis. *British Journal of Psychology,* 1969, 60, 51–55.

Baddeley, A. D., & Warrington, E. K. Amnesia and the distinction between long- and short-term memory. *Journal of Verbal Learning and Verbal Behavior,* 1970, 9, 176–189.

Bartz, W. H., & Salehi, M. Interference in short- and long-term memory. *Journal of Experimental Psychology,* 1970, 84, 380–382.

Brown, J. Some tests of the decay theory of immediate memory. *Quarterly Journal of Experimental Psychology,* 1958, 10, 12–21.

Bruce, D., & Crowley, J. J. Acoustic similarity effects on retrieval from secondary memory. *Journal of Verbal Learning and Verbal Behavior,* 1970, 9, 190–196.

Bruce, D., & Murdock, B. B., Jr. Acoustic similarity effects on memory for paired associates. *Journal of Verbal Learning and Verbal Behavior,* 1968, 7, 627–631.

Conrad, R. Acoustic confusions in immediate memory. *British Journal of Psychology,* 1964, 55, 75–84.

Conrad, R., & Hull, A. J. The role of the interpolated task in short-term retention. *Quarterly Journal of Experimental Psychology,* 1966, 18, 266–269.

Craik, F. I. M. Two components in free recall. *Journal of Verbal Learning and Verbal Behavior,* 1968, 7, 996–1004.

Craik, F. I. M. The fate of primary memory items in free recall. *Journal of Verbal Learning and Verbal Behavior,* 1970, 9, 143–148.

Craik, F. I. M., & Levy, B. A. Semantic and acoustic information in primary memory. *Journal of Experimental Psychology,* 1970, 86, 77–82.

Crowder, R. G., & Morton, J. Precategorical acoustic storage (PAS). *Perception & Psychophysics,* 1969, 5, 365–373.

Dallett, K. M. Number of categories and category information in free recall. *Journal of Experimental Psychology,* 1964, 68, 1–12.

Deese, J. Serial organization in the recall of disconnected items. *Psychological Reports,* 1957, 3, 577–582.

Deese, J., & Kaufman, R. A. Serial effects in recall of unorganized and sequentially organized verbal material. *Journal of Experimental Psychology,* 1957, 54, 180–187.

Dillon, R. F., & Reid, L. S. Short-term memory as a function of information processing during the retention interval. *Journal of Experimental Psychology,* 1969, 81, 261–269.

Ebbinghaus, H. *Uber das Gedächtnis: Untersuchungen zur experimentellen Psychologie.* Leipzig: Duncker & Humbolt, 1885. Translation by H. A. Ruger

& C. E. Bussenius, *Memory: A contribution to experimental psychology.* New York: Teachers College, Columbia University, Bureau of Publications, 1913.

Ellis, N. R. Memory processes in retardates and normals: Theoretical and empirical considerations. In N. Ellis (Ed.), *International review of research in mental retardation.* Vol. 4. New York: Academic Press, 1970. Pp. 1–32.

Gianutsos, R. Free recall of grouped words. Unpublished doctoral dissertation, New York University, 1970.

Glanzer, M. Distance between related words in free recall: Trace of the STS. *Journal of Verbal Learning and Verbal Behavior,* 1969, **8,** 105–111.

Glanzer, M., & Cunitz, A. R. Two storage mechanisms in free recall. *Journal of Verbal Learning and Verbal Behavior,* 1966, **5,** 351–360.

Glanzer, M., Gianutsos, R., & Dubin, S. The removal of items from short-term storage. *Journal of Verbal Learning and Verbal Behavior,* 1969, **8,** 435–447.

Glanzer, M., Koppenaal, L., & Nelson, R. Effects of relations between words on short-term storage and long-term storage. In preparation.

Glanzer, M., & Meinzer, A. The effects of intralist activity on free recall. *Journal of Verbal Learning and Verbal Behavior,* 1967, **6,** 928–935.

Glanzer, M., & Schwartz, A. Mnemonic structure in free recall: Differential effects on STS and LTS. *Journal of Verbal Learning and Verbal Behavior,* 1971, **10,** 194–198.

Greeno, J. G. Paired-associate learning with massed and distributed repetitions of items. *Journal of Experimental Psychology,* 1964, **67,** 286–295.

Hellyer, S. Supplementary report: Frequency of stimulus presentation and short-term decrement in recall. *Journal of Experimental Psychology,* 1962, **64,** 650.

Jahnke, J. C. Serial position effects in immediate serial recall. *Journal of Verbal Learning and Verbal Behavior,* 1963, **2,** 284–287.

Jahnke, J. C. Supplementary report: Primacy and recency effects in serial-position curves of immediate recall. *Journal of Experimental Psychology,* 1965, **70,** 130–132.

Jahnke, J. C. Delayed recall and the serial-position effect of short-term memory. *Journal of Experimental Psychology,* 1968, **76,** 618–622. (a)

Jahnke, J. C. Presentation rate and the serial-position effect of immediate serial recall. *Journal of Verbal Learning and Verbal Behavior,* 1968, **7,** 608–612. (b)

Keppel, G., & Underwood, B. J. Proactive inhibition in short-term retention of single items. *Journal of Verbal Learning and Verbal Behavior,* 1962, **1,** 153–161.

Kintsch, W., & Buschke, H. Homophones and synonyms in short-term memory. *Journal of Experimental Psychology,* 1969, **80,** 403–407.

Kulp, R. A. Effects of amount of interpolated activity in short-term memory. *Psychological Reports,* 1967, **21,** 393–399.

Levy, B. A., & Murdock, B. B., Jr. The effects of delayed auditory feedback and intralist similarity in short-term memory. *Journal of Verbal Learning and Verbal Behavior,* 1968, **7,** 887–894.

Lieberman, P. *Intonation, perception, and language.* Cambridge, Mass.: MIT Press, 1967.

Loess, H. Proactive inhibition in short-term memory. *Journal of Verbal Learning and Verbal Behavior,* 1964, **3,** 362–368.

Madigan, S. W. Intraserial repetition and coding processes in free recall. *Journal of Verbal Learning and Verbal Behavior,* 1969, **8,** 828–835.

Melton, A. W. Repetition and retrieval from memory. *Science,* 1967, **158**, 532.

Melton, A. W., & von Lackum, W. J. Retroactive and proactive inhibition in retention: Evidence for a two-factor theory of retroactive inhibition. *American Journal of Psychology,* 1941, **54**, 157-173.

Müller, G., & Schumann, F. Experimentelle Beiträge zur Untersuchung des Gedächtnisses. *Zeitschrift für Psychologie und Physiologie der Sinnesorgane,* 1894, **6**, 81-190, 257-339.

Murdock, B. B., Jr. The serial position effect of free recall. *Journal of Experimental Psychology,* 1962, **64**, 482-488.

Murdock, B. B., Jr. Short-term memory and paired-associate learning. *Journal of Verbal Learning and Verbal Behavior,* 1963, **2**, 320-328.

Murdock, B. B., Jr. Effects of a subsidiary task on short-term memory. *British Journal of Psychology,* 1965, **56**, 413-419.

Murdock, B. B., Jr. Recent developments in short-term memory. *British Journal of Psychology,* 1967, **58**, 421-433.

Murdock, B. B., Jr., & Walker, K. D. Modality effects in free recall. *Journal of Verbal Learning and Verbal Behavior,* 1969, **8**, 665-676.

Neisser, U. *Cognitive psychology.* New York: Appleton-Century-Crofts, 1967.

Peterson, L. R. Immediate memory: Data and theory. In C. N. Cofer and B. S. Musgrave (Eds.), *Verbal behavior and learning: Problems and processes.* New York: McGraw-Hill, 1963. Pp. 336-353.

Peterson, L. R. Short-term verbal memory and learning. *Psychological Review,* 1966, **73**, 193-207.

Peterson, L. R., & Peterson, M. Short-term retention of individual verbal items. *Journal of Experimental Psychology,* 1959, **58**, 193-198.

Peterson, L. R., Wampler, R., Kirkpatrick, M., & Saltzman, D. Effect of spacing presentations on retention of a paired associate over short intervals. *Journal of Experimental Psychology,* 1963, **66**, 206-209.

Phillips, J. L., Shiffrin, R. M., & Atkinson, R. C. Effects of list length on short-term memory. *Journal of Verbal Learning and Verbal Behavior,* 1967, **6**, 303-311.

Pollatsek, A. Rehearsal, interference, and spacing of practice in short-term memory. Technical Report No. 16. Human Performance Center, University of Michigan, 1969.

Posner, M. I., & Konick, A. F. On the role of interference in short-term retention. *Journal of Experimental Psychology,* 1966, **72**, 221-231.

Posner, M. I., & Rossman, E. Effect of size and location of informational transforms upon short-term retention. *Journal of Experimental Psychology,* 1965, **70**, 496-505.

Postman, L., & Phillips, L. W. Short-term temporal changes in free recall. *Quarterly Journal of Experimental Psychology,* 1965, **17**, 132-138.

Puff, C. R. Clustering as a function of the sequential organization of stimulus word lists. *Journal of Verbal Learning and Verbal Behavior,* 1966, **5**, 503-506.

Raymond, B. Factors affecting long-term and short-term storage in free recall. Unpublished doctoral dissertation, New York University, 1968.

Raymond, B. Short-term and long-term storage in free recall. *Journal of Verbal Learning and Verbal Behavior,* 1969, **8**, 567-574.

Rundus, D., & Atkinson, R. C. Rehearsal processes in free recall; A procedure for direct observation. *Journal of Verbal Learning and Verbal Behavior,* 1970, **9**, 99-105.

Silverstein, C., & Glanzer, M. Difficulty of a concurrent task in free recall: Differential effects on STS and LTS. *Psychonomic Science,* 1971, **22,** 367–368.

Sperling, G. The information available in brief visual presentations. *Psychological Monographs,* 1960, 74 (Whole No. 498).

Sumby, W. H. Word frequency and serial position effects. *Journal of Verbal Learning and Verbal Behavior,* 1963, 1, 443–450.

Thurm, A. T., & Glanzer, M. Free recall in children: Long-term store versus short-term store. *Psychonomic Science,* 1971, 23, 175–176.

Tulving, E., & Arbuckle, J. Y. Sources of intratrial interference in immediate recall of paired associates. *Journal of Verbal Learning and Verbal Behavior,* 1963, 1, 321–334.

Tulving, E., & Patterson, R. D. Functional units and retrieval process in free recall. *Journal of Experimental Psychology,* 1968, 77, 239–248.

Underwood, B. Some correlates of item repetition in free-recall learning. *Journal of Verbal Learning and Verbal Behavior,* 1969, 8, 83–94.

Waugh, N. C. Immediate memory as a function of repetition. *Journal of Verbal Learning and Verbal Behavior,* 1963, 2, 107–112.

Waugh, N. C. Presentation time and free recall. *Journal of Experimental Psychology,* 1967, 73, 39–44.

Waugh, N. C., & Norman, D. A. Primary memory. *Psychological Review,* 1965, 72, 89–104.

Weingartner, H. The free recall of sets of associatively related words. *Journal of Verbal Learning and Verbal Behavior,* 1964, 3, 6–10.

Wickelgren, W. A. Acoustic similarity and retroactive interference in short-term memory. *Journal of Verbal Learning and Verbal Behavior.* 1965, 4, 53–61.

Wickens, D. D., Born, D. G., & Allen, C. K. Proactive inhibition and item similarity in short-term memory. *Journal of Verbal Learning and Verbal Behavior,* 1963, 2, 440–445.

Yngve, V. A model and an hypothesis for language structure. *Proceedings of the American Philosophical Society,* 1960, 104, 444–466.

# BY-PRODUCTS OF DISCRIMINATION LEARNING[1]

## H. S. Terrace

COLUMBIA UNIVERSITY, NEW YORK, NEW YORK

## I. Introduction

When an organism learns a discrimination, the discriminative stimuli may acquire functions other than their basic function of occasioning differential responding. In addition, the discriminative

[1] This work was supported in part by NSF grant GB-8111X and by NIH grant HD-00930.

stimulus correlated with extinction, or with a relatively poor schedule of reinforcement, may acquire aversive, inhibitory, and emotional functions. Discrimination learning may also result in an increase in the excitatory potential of the stimulus correlated with the richer schedule of reinforcement.

The nondiscriminative functions of discriminative stimuli that are by-products of the formation of a discrimination can be illustrated by the following example. Consider a simple successive discrimination between a yellow (580 nm) and a green light (550 nm). During discrimination training, a hungry pigeon's responses to yellow (S+) are reinforced on an intermittent schedule. His responses to green (S—) are never reinforced. Once differential responding to yellow and to green has been established, one may also observe the following phenomena:

1. Emotional responses occur following the onset of S— (Terrace, 1966c).

2. If a suitable target such as a second pigeon is present, aggressive behavior toward the second pigeon would occur following the onset of S— (Azrin, Hutchinson, & Hake, 1966).

3. The pigeon could be trained to escape from S— where the sole consequence of the escape response is the removal of S—. That is, the escape response does not result in a concomitant increase in the frequency of reinforcement in S+ (Terrace, 1971b).

4. During a generalization test, in which test stimuli of other wavelengths were presented, the maximum frequency of responding does not occur at S+ (580 nm) but is instead shifted away from S—. Thus, the peak of a postdiscrimination generalization gradient would occur at 590 nm rather than at S+ (Hanson, 1959).

5. It can be shown that S— can reduce responding in a way that cannot be attributed to a mere loss of excitation (Brown & Jenkins, 1967). In this sense, S— functions as an inhibitory stimulus. S— also exerts inhibitory stimulus control in the sense that, during a generalization test, the frequency of responding to test stimuli *increases* as the distance between the test stimulus and S— increases (Jenkins & Harrison, 1962).

6. The rate of responding to S+ is considerably higher than the rate of responding that would occur during equivalent non-differential training (Reynolds, 1961a). Similar results could be obtained from a discrete trial procedure in which only one response could occur during each trial. Under this condition, the latency of responding to S+ would be shorter following discrimination training than following a comparable number of reinforcements earned under a nondifferential reinforcement procedure (Jenkins, 1961).

These by-products of discrimination learning are neither universal nor permanent characteristics of discrimination learning (Terrace, 1966a). Under certain conditions the phenomena listed above do not occur at all. If, for example, a discrimination is trained so that responses to S— (errors) do not occur, none of the by-products of discrimination learning described above are observed (Terrace, 1963a, 1963b, 1964, 1966c, 1971b). When these phenomena occur following discrimination learning with errors, they gradually disappear with extended training.

The discussion of by-products of discrimination learning which follows in this chapter will be influenced strongly by their failure to occur under certain conditions and by their nonpermanent nature. Each phenomenon will at first be discussed separately. However, once we can specify the conditions under which a discriminative stimulus can acquire aversive, inhibitory, emotional, and excitatory functions we will consider the extent to which these functions co-vary as a function of the same variables.

## II. Discrimination Learning with and without Errors — Training Methods

Our inquiry into what factors are responsible for the establishment of nondiscriminative functions of discriminative stimuli will make repeated references to discrimination learning with and without errors. It will, therefore, be advantageous to precede our discussion of by-products of discrimination learning with a brief summary of the training procedures that have been used in each case.

### A. GENERAL CONSIDERATIONS

By definition, all procedures for training a discrimination employ some form of differential reinforcement. Since excellent summaries of providing differential reinforcement procedures are available elsewhere (e.g., Blough, 1971; Nevin, 1971), we will restrict our discussion here to the barest possible characterization of those training procedures that have been used in experiments concerned with by-products of discrimination learning.

Most of the experiments we will consider have used the successive discrimination procedure (Nevin, 1971) which allows only one discriminative stimulus to be presented at any given time. In the typical case, reinforcement is available for responding to one stimulus (S+), but not for responding to a second stimulus (S—). In some experiments, however, responding to both discriminative stimuli is reinforced on different schedules of reinforcement.

In experiments in which S+ is alternated with S−, an error may occur during either type of trial. An error is defined as the failure to respond to S+ or the occurrence of a response to S−. In a *noncorrection* procedure, the sequence of discriminative stimuli and the duration of each stimulus is unaffected by the occurrence of errors. In a *correction* procedure, however, the occurrence of an error results in either the prolongation or the repetition of the discriminative stimulus in the presence of which the error occurred. Thus, S+ or S− is prolonged or repeated until a predetermined interval of time has elapsed during which no errors have occurred. Since, in actual practice, errors on positive trials are exceedingly rare, the net effect of the correction procedure is the prolongation of S− until responding to S− has ceased. Accordingly, our subsequent use of the term "error" will refer exclusively to responses to S−.

## B. Procedures for Training a Discrimination without Errors

Let us consider first a relatively easy problem for a pigeon: respond if red, don't respond if green. The red and green stimuli are alternated, in an irregular sequence, on a response key in a standard experimental chamber for a pigeon (Ferster & Skinner, 1957). When the key is red, key-pecks are reinforced on a variable interval *(VI)* schedule (cf. Ferster & Skinner, 1957) by allowing the pigeon to eat grain from the food-hopper for three seconds. When the key is green, key-pecks are never reinforced.

A typical pigeon who starts on the red-green discrimination problem after 21 days of nondifferential training for responding to red will make more than a thousand responses to green during the first few sessions of discrimination training. Afterward, the number of errors declines abruptly and stabilizes at a near-zero level.

The same discrimination can be trained with zero or a near-zero number of errors by changing two features of the above procedure. Instead of starting discrimination training after three weeks of nondifferential reinforcement for responding to red, discrimination training begins during the first experimental session, immediately after the key-peck is conditioned. This practice is rarely followed in experiments on discrimination learning since the Experimenter is often interested in establishing a baseline rate of responding to the stimulus correlated with reinforcement (S+), and also because the *E* wants to establish a strong response to S+ that will not be disrupted when the stimulus correlated with nonreinforcement (S—) is introduced.

The second procedural difference between the standard discrimination training procedure and the procedure used to produce errorless discrimination learning stems from the original values of the discriminative stimuli. In the standard procedure, S+ and S— are always of the same intensity and duration and differ only with respect to wavelength. In the errorless training procedure the first presentation of S— is very brief (one second as compared to a duration of 30 seconds for S+), and the intensity of S— is so low that a human observer cannot see any light through the translucent response key. The initial values and the changes that are made in the intensity and the duration of S— during the first session are shown schematically in Fig. 1. The changes in stimulus value are made

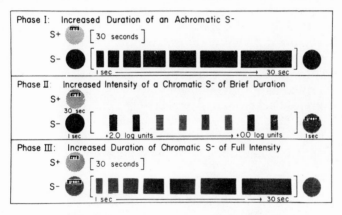

Fig. 1. Schematic representation of a procedure for training a red–green discrimination without errors. See text for additional details.

between successive presentations of S—. Thus, after each presentation of S—, either the duration or the intensity of S— is increased.

During Phase I, the intensity of S— is held constant, at its minimal level, and the duration of S— is increased progressively until the duration of S— equals the duration of S+ (30 seconds). During Phase II, the duration of S— is reduced to 1 second and held constant at this value while the intensity of S— is increased gradually until it is equal to the intensity of S+. During Phase III, the duration of the fully intense S— is increased progressively until the duration of S— equals the duration of S+. During the next two sessions the durations of S+ and S— are increased progressively until they each have a duration of 3 minutes.

Pigeons trained on the procedure shown in Fig. 1 made zero or, in some instances, only a few errors. As we shall see later, the performance of those Ss who make a small number of errors (on the order of 25 or less) resembles the performance of those Ss who make zero errors but differs markedly from those Ss who make many errors. For this reason, we shall refer to both the Ss who make zero errors and to the Ss who make only a few errors as errorless Ss.

Discriminations more difficult than the red-green discrimination can be trained without errors by appropriate variations of the above procedure (cf. Terrace, 1963b). Consider, for example, a discrimination between a vertical (S+) and a horizontal line (S—). When trained in the usual manner, pigeons typically make more errors in acquiring a vertical-horizontal discrimination than in acquiring a discrimination between lights of different wavelengths. Figure 2 describes the procedure that was used to train the vertical-horizontal discrimination without errors. Discrimination training begins with the red-green problem. This discrimination is trained without errors by using the procedure described above (Phase I). The vertical and horizontal lines are then superimposed upon the red and green backgrounds, respectively (Phase II). The stimuli are presented in this manner for five sessions. During the following session (Phase III), the intensities of the red and green backgrounds are progressively diminished until the vertical and the horizontal lines

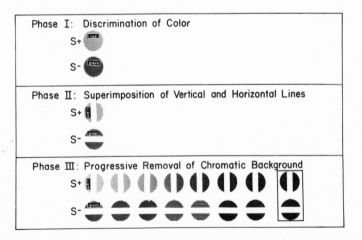

Fig. 2. Procedure for transferring from a red–green to a vertical–horizontal discrimination without errors. See text for additional details.

appear on achromatic (black) backgrounds. In this manner the vertical-horizontal discrimination can be trained without any errors.

### III. Overt Emotional Reactions to S—

The first characteristic of discrimination performance we will consider is an overt emotional reaction following the onset of S—. Each of the photographs shown in Fig. 3 was taken within 5

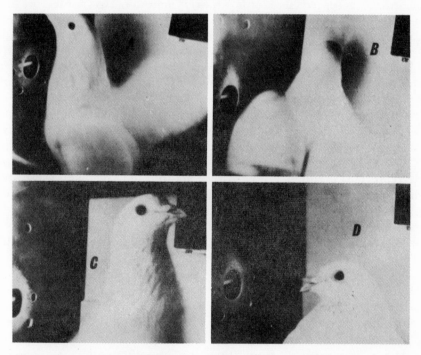

Fig. 3. Photographs of reactions to S—. Each photograph was taken 5 seconds after the onset of S—. Pigeons A, B, and C learned the discrimination with errors. Pigeon D learned without errors. (Terrace, 1966c, by permission of Appleton-Century-Crofts, New York.)

seconds of the onset of S— during the fifth session of vertical-horizontal discrimination training (Terrace, 1966c). The pigeons shown in Panels A, B, and C learned the vertical-horizontal discrimination with errors; the pigeon shown in Panel D learned the same discrimination without errors. It is clear that the reactions to S— of those pigeons who learned the discrimination with errors are different from the reactions of the pigeon who learned the discrimination without errors. Typical reactions of the pigeons who learned with errors include agitated wing flapping (Panel A), striking the key with a wing (Panel B), or turning 180 degrees away from the key (Panel C). These reactions should be compared with the behavior of a pigeon who learned the same discrimination without errors (Panel D). Pigeons who learn without errors typically settle down quietly in front of the key and remain this way until S+ is again presented.

The reactions shown in Panels A, B, and C of Fig. 3 certainly seem to satisfy accepted standards of overt emotional responses. In all instances these pigeons appear to be aroused by the onset of S−. Informal observations over an extended period of time revealed the following characteristics of the overt emotional responses shown in Fig. 3. Such responses are usually confined to the initial portion of the S− interval. Typically, these responses appear at irregular intervals during the initial presentations of S−. As responding to S− declines, the frequency of emotional reactions following the onset of S− increases. By the third or fourth discrimination session, such reactions regularly follow the presentation of S−.

Overt emotional responses such as those shown in Fig. 3 tend to decrease in frequency by the end of the second week of discrimination training. The occurrence of these reactions at the onset of S−, and their gradual disappearance following extended exposure to S−, during which little nonreinforced responding occurs, are consistent with the notion that these reactions are emotional. While a more precise account of these reactions would be desirable (e.g., minute-by-minute observations by a group of independent observers), it seems safe to conclude that emotional reactions to S− occur only after discrimination learning with errors, and that these reactions are not a permanent characteristic of discrimination performance.

Other observations supporting the hypothesis that S− elicits emotional reactions following discrimination learning with errors can be found in experiments on simple extinction. Miller and Stevenson (1936), for example, have described the agitated behavior of rats during the extinction of a bar-press response. Similar observations have been reported by Skinner (1938) and by many undergraduate students in introductory laboratory courses. It is important to note than in both the Miller and Stevenson and the Skinner experiments, the frequency of "agitated" behavior (biting of bar and increased activity) was observed mainly at the start of extinction and thereafter declined in frequency.

The results of an experiment by Wagner (1963) on the agumentation of a startle response also supports the hypothesis that S— functions as an emotional stimulus. One group of rats was trained by a successive discrimination procedure in a U-shaped runway. S— was a white noise combined with a flashing light. A second group of rats, which was trained in the same apparatus on a nondifferential schedule, received the same amount of exposure to the white noise-flashing light combination. This was accomplished by placing each subject in a neutral cage in which food was never presented. During the second phase of the experiment, both groups were placed in a stabilemeter. At irregular intervals, the white noise-flashing light combination was presented for three seconds prior to the presentation of a sudden loud 1000-Hz tone.

Figure 4 shows the magnitude of the mean startle response for each group during two consecutive blocks of 10 trials. The Ss who were given discrimination training showed a stronger startle response than did the Ss of the control group. During the second block of trials, the differences between the groups was negligible. Wagner concluded that "the more vigorous reaction of experimental Ss to the startle tone is consistent with the view that the CS produced a relative increase in emotionality for those Ss for which it had previously been paired with frustrative non-reward [Wagner, 1963, p. 146. Copyright 1963, by the American Psychological Association, Inc.]."

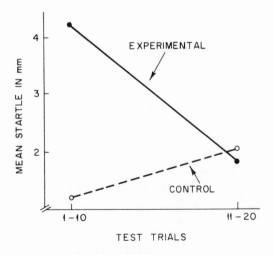

Fig. 4. Amplitude of startle response during first and last half of test series. (Wagner, 1963.) Copyright 1963, by the American Psychological Association, Inc.

Wagner's experiment was performed to study one of the predictions of Amsel's theory of frustrative nonreward (Amsel, 1958, 1962). According to Amsel, nonreinforcement produces an emotional frustrative reaction ($r_f$) which becomes conditioned to the stimuli associated with nonreinforcement ($s_f$). While Amsel's theory is, of course, consistent with our hypothesis that S— elicits emotional responses following discrimination learning with errors (i.e., nonreinforced responses to S—), the experimental tests of this theory performed by Amsel and by his students were not concerned with direct observations of the $r_f$ in the presence of S—. Instead, they studied the presumed effect of frustration on the subsequent response to S+. We will therefore postpone our discussion of Amsel's experiments until we consider behavioral contrast, a phenomenon which is more analogous to Amsel's observations than is the occurrence of an emotional response in the presence of S—.

## IV. Behavioral Contrast

By definition, a discrimination is said to have been established once the frequency of responding to S1 differs from the frequency of responding to S2. In most experiments on discrimination learning, the focus of interest is on the elimination of responding to S—. One might, however, also observe whether the strength of the response to S+ has been influenced by discrimination training. It turns out that the strength of the response to S+ almost always changes during discrimination training. In most instances, one of two possible types of interaction between responding to S+ and S— is observed. Either the strength of the response to S+ increases or it decreases as compared to its baseline value. Since the schedule of reinforcement in effect during S+ remains constant, we must look elsewhere in trying to account for the changes in the strength of the response to S+. In this section we will first discuss in a general way the nature of interactions between responding to S+ and to S—. Our initial purpose will be more to conceptualize these interactions than to summarize the results of experiments which have studied them. After the basic types have been described we will focus our attention on those interactions which have recently been the subject of much study and which are also relevant to the differences in performance that distinguishes discrimination learning with errors from discrimination learning without errors.

A decrease in the strength of the response to S+ following the start of discrimination training could be attributed to the generalization of inhibition from S— to S+ (Hull, 1943, 1952; Spence, 1936, 1937). While such decreases in the strength of the response to S+ have occasionally been reported (e.g., Amsel, 1971; Gynther, 1957; Skinner, 1938, Ch. V) they do not appear to be a reliable phenomenon. Strange as it may seem, the more typical finding is an increase in the strength of the response to S+. In this section we will be concerned mostly with the second type of interaction. It should be noted, however, that our emphasis of the second type of interaction should not be construed as an attempt to minimize the importance of the first type. It is rather the case that this emphasis reflects the much larger body of experiments which have studied the increase in the strength of the response to S+.

Like many other psychological phenomena, the increase in the strength of the response to S+ that has been observed following the start of discrimination training has been given different names by different psychologists. Our first task in this section will be to identify some examples of this interaction and to describe the conditions under which they have been observed. At the same time, we will not assume that all of these interactions are manifestations of the same underlying processes. Indeed, it soon becomes apparent, as one sifts through examples of interactions between responding to S+ and to S—, that much work remains before one can decide that all such interactions are analogous.

## A. POSITIVE CONTRAST

Pavlov (1927, p. 188) referred to an increase in the magnitude of the response to S+ following the start of discrimination training as "positive induction" — a term he attributed to Herring and to Sherrington. The basic example of positive induction cited by Pavlov in his observation that a dog salivates more on an S+ trial preceded by an S— trial than on an S+ trial preceded by another S+ trial (Pavlov, 1927, p. 186). This is shown in Fig. 5 where the open bars represent the amount of salivation obtained on S+ trials preceded by S— trials, and the filled bars represent the amount of salivation obtained on S+ trials preceded by another S+ trial.

In Skinner's discussion of Pavlov's observations (Skinner, 1938, p. 175), he referred to the increase in the frequency of the response to S+ as "positive contrast" to call attention to the divergence in the rates of responding to S+ and to S—. The term "induction" was used by Skinner as a synonym for "generalization" to refer to a *decrease*

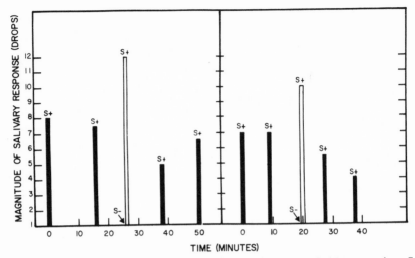

Fig. 5. Magnitude of salivary response on S+ trials preceded by a previous S+ trial (filled bars) and on S+ trials preceded by an S— trial (open bars). (Pavlov, 1927, reprinted from "Conditioned Reflexes," by permission of the Clarendon Press, Oxford.)

in the rate of responding to S+ that accompanied a decrease in the rate of responding to S—. While Skinner accepted Pavlov's data on the occurrence of an increase in the rate of response to S+ following the start of discrimination training, he felt that contrast was not an important characteristic of discrimination performance: "Little is at present known except that contrast is usually a temporary phenomenon appearing at only one stage of a discrimination ... It is doubtful whether contrast is a genuine process comparable with induction [Skinner, 1938, p. 175]."

Whatever grounds Skinner may have had for questioning the genuineness of contrast were eliminated by Reynolds' extensive experiments in which he showed that an increase in the frequency of responding to S+, following the start of discrimination training, was a reliable phenomenon that can be obtained under a wide variety of conditions (e.g., Reynolds, 1961a, 1961b). Reynolds referred to this increase as "positive behavioral contrast." An example of positive behavioral contrast from an experiment by Reynolds (1961a) is shown in Fig. 6 which shows the rate of responding to red (S+) during discrimination training (center panel) in which responding to red was reinforced on a *VI* schedule and responding to green was extinguished. The rate of responding to red shown in the center panel should be compared with the rate of responding to red during

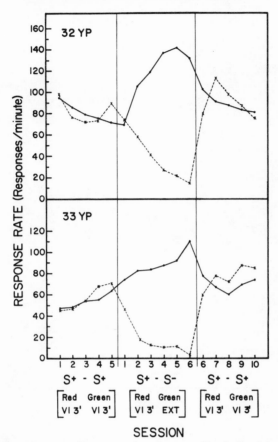

Fig. 6. Rate of responding to red and green discriminative stimuli during nondifferential reinforcement (left- and right-hand panels) and during differential reinforcement (center panel). *Key:* Red ●——●; green x- - - -x. (From Reynolds, 1961a.) Copyright 1961, by the Society for the Experimental Analysis of Behavior, Inc.

the preceding and the subsequent phases of the experiment during which responding to both red and green were reinforced on identical *VI* schedules of reinforcement. We see that the average rate of responding to S+ during each of the discrimination sessions is greater than the rate of responding to S+ during the nondifferential reinforcement sessions.

The "frustration effect," a term introduced by Amsel, is yet another way in which psychologists have referred to an increase in the strength of the response to one discriminative stimulus following a change in the reinforcement schedule associated with the second discriminative stimulus. In Amsel's experiments (e.g., Amsel & Roussel, 1952), the dependent variable is typically running speed in the second compartment of a two-part linear runway. During baseline training, reinforcement is available in both goal boxes. Subsequently, reinforcement is omitted from the first goal box on half the trials. The frustration effect refers to a relative increase in running speed in the second compartment. This can be seen in Fig. 7

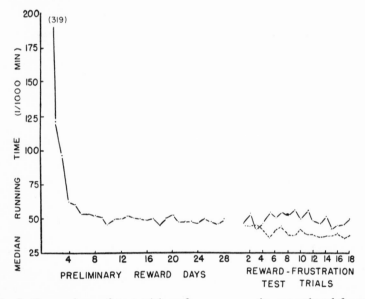

Fig. 7. Comparison of test trial performance on the reward and frustration conditions. *Key:* Reward——·; frustration  — — —· (Amsel & Roussel, 1952.) Copyright 1952, by the American Psychological Association, Inc.

which shows the baseline running speed in the second compartment and the running speeds in the second compartment following those trials in which reinforcement was and was not provided in the first goal box. Since the two parts of the runway are discriminably different, and running is consistently reinforced only in the presence of one of the discriminative stimuli, the frustration effect appears to be analogous to the previously discussed increases in response strength following the start of discrimination training.

The "Crespi effect" is yet another phenomenon that appears to resemble the interactions we have discussed previously. The Crespi effect (which has also been referred to as "positive contrast" and "elation") refers to a higher asymptotic level of running speed following a switch from a small to a large reinforcement than would have been obtained had training consisted entirely of large reinforcement trials (Crespi, 1944). Similarly, the asymptotic level following a shift from a high to a low magnitude of reinforcement is lower than would have been the case had training consisted entirely of trials on which a small magnitude had been obtained. (This latter effect has been referred to as "negative contrast" and "depression.")

The Crespi effect differs from behavioral contrast and the frustration effect in two important ways. Typically, the Crespi effect has been observed only when the switch from one magnitude of reinforcement to another has to be made between sessions. Secondly, this shift occurs without the use of a differential reinforcement procedure. Those experiments in which a differential reinforcement procedure has been used have generally failed to obtain an elation effect, and only some of these experiments have succeeded in obtaining a depression effect (cf. review by Dunham, 1968). In the absence of procedures which can establish immediate shifts in the rate of responding to one discriminative stimulus following a change in the magnitude of reinforcement for responding to a second discriminative stimulus, it seems premature to group the Crespi effect together with behavioral contrast and the frustration effect.

## B. NEGATIVE CONTRAST

After a discrimination is trained, it can be abolished by reinforcing responding to each discriminative stimulus on identical schedules of reinforcement. When this is done an interaction between responding to S+ and what was formerly S− is often observed. Again, two types of interaction are possible. The first, which derives from the Spence-Hull model, would hold that the strength of the response to S+ should increase because of the generalization of excitation generated by reinforced responding in the presence of what used to be S−. The second type of interaction is a decrease in the strength of the response to S+ following reinforcement in the presence of S−. Our concern in this section will be exclusively with the second type of interaction that is possible following the abolition of a discrimination. As we shall see, this type of interaction is conceptually similar to positive behavioral contrast in the sense that the change in the strength of the response to S+ is opposite in direction from what one would expect from the Spence-Hull model.

Reynolds' 1961 experiment provides a good example of the second type of interaction. We will follow Reynolds' usage and refer to this type of interaction as *negative contrast*. Following discrimination training in which S1 was correlated with a *VI* schedule and S2 was correlated with extinction, the schedule in S2 was changed either to *VI* or to variable ratio *(VR)*. In both instances a *decrease* in the rate of responding to S1 was observed. This decrease was not as large as the increase that was observed previously following a shift from *MULT VI VI* to *MULT VI EXT*.

In the previous section we have noted that the phenomenon referred to as positive behavioral contrast shares certain characteristics with what Pavlov referred to as positive induction. The relationship between negative behavioral contrast and negative induction is less clear. Pavlov's experiments on negative induction did in fact attempt to transform a negative into a positive discriminative stimulus (Pavlov, 1927, pp. 188-203). Pavlov compared two ways in which this might be accomplished. In the first, the positive stimulus was alternated in an irregular series with the second stimulus which used to function as S--. Each presentation of S1 and S2 is followed by food. The second method was to simply present S2 by itself. Food was provided during each S2 trial. Only the second method was successful in reversing the function of S2 from a negative to a positive stimulus. Pavlov attributed the failure of the first method to an intensification of the inhibitory effect of S2 which was presumed to be a consequence of reinforcement presented in S1. Until such aftereffects could be eliminated, the inhibitory effect of S2 (based upon the prior extinction of responding to S2) could not be abolished even when S2 was followed by reinforcement.

From these examples we can see that negative induction and negative contrast both refer to situations in which a stimulus which was previously correlated with extinction is now correlated with reinforcement. For Pavlov, however, the dependent variable was the ease with which a formerly negative discriminative stimulus could be converted into a positive discriminative stimulus. For Reynolds, however, the dependent variable was the rate of responding to the positive stimulus.

While our discussion of interactions between responding to S+ and to S− has by no means been exhaustive, we have seen that they can be observed under a wide variety of conditions, and that much work remains to be done to establish to what extent such interactions are conceptually analogous. Space limitations, however, dictate a more modest goal. Rather than attempt to derive a relationship between all of the different types of interactions that occur during the acquisition and the abolition of a discrimination by appealing to what in many cases would amount to fragmentary data, we will restrict the scope of our discussion of interactions and concentrate instead on defining some of the boundary conditions of the two most widely studied interactions. These are positive behavioral contrast and the frustration effect.

## C. VARIABLES EFFECTING POSITIVE BEHAVIORAL CONTRAST

We have seen that Reynolds has used the term "positive behavioral contrast" to refer to an increase in the rate of responding to S+ following the start of discrimination training (cf. Fig. 6, p. 207). This intriguing finding which, at first glance, seems contrary to the Spence-Hull model of an algebraic combination of gradients of excitation and inhibition, poses two related questions: What aspect of discrimination learning is responsible for the occurrence of contrast, and how are we to define contrast? We will discuss the first of these questions in the following section. A consideration of the second question will have to be postponed until Section VIII at which time we will be able to make use of our discussion of inhibitory stimulus control.

### 1. Relative Rate of Reinforcement versus Relative Rate of Responding?

The importance of the first question becomes apparent when one considers that discrimination learning typically entails both a reduction in the rate of responding to S— and a reduction in the relative frequency of reinforcement in S—. Figure 6, for example, shows not only that the rate of responding to green is reduced, but that the relative frequency of reinforcement decreases from .5 to 0 at the start of discrimination training. As we shall see, however, not all reductions in the rate of responding to S2 result in contrast. Likewise, not all instances of a reduction in relative reinforcement result in contrast. From these considerations alone we can see that until the first question can be answered we cannot provide a rigorous definition of contrast. Our first problem then is to summarize the conditions under which contrast does and does not occur.

Reynolds (1961a) formulated the following relativistic specification of the conditions for contrast:

> Contrast ... depend(s) upon a relation among the schedules of reinforcement currently controlling an organism's behavior ... The frequency of reinforcement in the presence of a given stimulus,

*relative to the frequency during all of the stimuli that successively
control an organism's behavior,* in part determines the rate of
responding that a given stimulus controls [Reynolds, 1961a, p. 70,
italics in original. Copyright 1961, by the Society for the Experimental Analysis of Behavior, Inc.]

A wide variety of studies support Reynolds specification of the rate
of responding to S1 as proportional to the relative frequency of
reinforcement in S1. These include Reynolds' 1961b study in which
the relative frequency of reinforcement in S2 is varied by changiing
the value of *VI* and *VR* schedules, Nevin's 1968 study in which the
relative frequency of reinforcement in S2 was determined by the
value of a *DRO* schedule, Bloomfield's 1967 study which varied
relative frequency of reinforcement with *drl* and *FR* schedules, and
Catania's 1963 study which demonstrated that the relativistic
specification of response rate to S1 holds for concurrent schedules of
reinforcement. Data from three of these experiments (Bloomfield,
1967; Nevin, 1968; Reynolds, 1961b) are shown in Fig. 8. Over a
wide range of relative reinforcement frequency (.1-1.0) the rate of
responding to S1 appears to be directly proportional to the relative
reinforcement frequency in S1.

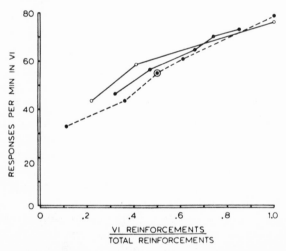

Fig. 8. Response rate in a constant variable interval *(VI)* component of a
multiple schedule, as a function of the proportion of reinforcement obtained in
the *VI* component when the reinforcement schedule in the other component is
varied. The function for *MULT VI drl* is from Bloomfield (1967). The function
for *MULT VI FR* is from Reynolds (1961b). The function for *MULT VI drl* is
from Nevin (1968). *Key: MULT VI drl* ●——●; *MULT VI FR* ○——○; *MULT VI
DRO* ●– – –●. Copyright 1966, 1968, by the Society for the Experimental
Analysis of Behavior, Inc.

Exceptions to the generalization that the rate of responding to S1 is proportional to the relative frequency of reinforcement occurring in S1 may be derived from a variety of studies. Terrace (1963a, 1963b, 1966c), for example, has shown that behavioral contrast does not occur after errorless discrimination learning. Since the relative frequency of reinforcement in a *MULT VI EXT* schedule is the same in both discrimination learning with and without errors, one cannot appeal to this variable in accounting for the contrast that is observed after discrimination learning with errors.

The absence of contrast following discrimination learning without errors prompted this writer to suggest that contrast resulted from a reduction in the rate of responding to S2. Normally, the rate of responding to a discriminative stimulus varies directly with the frequency of reinforcement. We have seen previously (cf. Fig. 8), however, that a reduction in the rate of reinforcement in S2 is confounded with a reduction in the rate of responding to S2. A number of studies have demonstrated that it is possible to reduce the rate of responding to a discriminative stimulus without reducing the frequency of reinforcement in S2. This has been done by using a *drl* schedule (Terrace, 1968, Experiment III), by punishing responding to S2 with a mild electric shock (Terrace, 1968, Experiment II), by providing an external clock on *drl* (Reynolds & Limpo, 1968), on *FI* (Brownstein & Newsom, 1970), and on *VI* (Brownstein & Hughes, 1970) schedules of reinforcement, and by varying the antecedent training conditions as in the transition *VI 5 VI 5 → VI 1 VI 5* (Terrace, 1968, Experiment I). In all of these experiments, contrast occurred only if the rate of responding to S2 was reduced.

Having seen that contrast can occur when the reinforcement frequencies in S1 and S2 are equal, it is instructive to reconsider those studies which have demonstrated a relativistic relationship between rate of responding in S1 and the relative frequency of reinforcement in S1. Our concern in doing so is to inquire to what extent a reduction in the rate of responding to S2 per se contributed to the increase in the rate of responding to S1. While a linear relationship between rate of responding to S1 and the relative frequency of reinforcement in S1 supports Reynolds' relativistic specifications of contrast, it by no means demonstrates that relative reinforcement frequency is the sole determinant of contrast. Let us consider, for example, the individual data presented Nevin's 1968 study (Table II) in which subjects were trained on a *MULT VI 1 DRO 1 min* schedule. An examination of these data reveals that contrast occurred in two out of five cases, even though at least twice as many reinforcements were earned in S2 than in S1 and in a third instance in which the reinforcement densities in S1 and S2 were essentially the same. In this and in related studies, it seems as if contrast occurs when the rate of responding to S2 is decreased even when the frequency of reinforcement in S1 and S2 is the same. In all instances in which response rate was reduced by the *DRO* schedule in which contrast did not occur, more reinforcements were earned in S2 than in S1. It therefore appears that, in these instances, the effects of rate reduction in S2 were offset by the increase in the reinforcement frequency in S2.

Whereas the rate of responding to S1 is often proportional to the relative frequency of reinforcement in S1, it is also clear that this factor does not act independently of a reduction in the rate of responding to S2 which results from the reduction of the relative frequency of reinforcement in S2. When the relative frequencies of reinforcement in S1 and S2 are equal, a reduction in the rate of responding to S2 will nevertheless result in an increase in the rate of responding to S1. It is, unfortunately, also possible to show that a reduction in the rate of responding to S2 is not a sufficient condition for the occurrence of contrast. We cannot, therefore, conclude that a reduction in the rate of responding to one of two alternating discriminative stimuli is sufficient for the occurrence of contrast.

That a reduction in the rate of responding to S2 is not a sufficient condition for the occurrence of contrast can be shown on both empirical and hypothetical grounds. Wilkie (1970) has shown that when S2 is correlated with a schedule which provides reinforcement at variable intervals, independently of whether or not a response occurs, the rate of responding is reduced below the level that is maintained when the S2 is correlated with a normal *VI* schedule. During discrimination training in which S1 is correlated with a normal *VI* schedule, and S2 was correlated with a similar "free" *VI* schedule, the rate of responding to S2 was reduced without a reduction in the relative frequency of reinforcement in S2. There was, however, no increase in the rate of responding to S1.

Wilkie's procedure can be distinguished from other multiple schedules in that the frequency of reinforcement in S2 is not effected by whether or not the S responds. Thus, there is no contingency which favors a reduced rate of responding. This procedure may be interpreted in one sense as one which does not result in the inhibition of responding to S2, i.e., there is no reason for the S to "hold back" his responding or to engage in behavior antagonistic to the key-peck.

Another way of reducing the rate of responding in the presence of some discriminative stimulus that does require the suppression or inhibition of responding is to satiate the $S$. While this may prove difficult within the confines of the short intercomponent interval employed in the typical multiple schedule, it may be possible to reduce the rate of responding to S2 by satiation if the interval between S1 and S2 was sufficiently long or if different reinforcers were used in S1 and in S2 (cf. Premack, 1969). At present we can only hypothesize the results of such an experiment, but it would seem unlikely that satiation during the presentation of S2 would result in an increase in the rate of responding to S1. A reduction in response rate due to satiation would seem to be analogous to a reduction in response rate resulting from the free reinforcement procedure in that inhibition does not seem responsible for either type of reduction of response rate. As we shall see in Section VIII, it seems reasonable to hypothesize that a reduction in the rate of responding to S2 which does not result from inhibition of the response to S2 will not produce contrast.

## 2. Long-Term versus Transient Contrast Effects

Positive behavioral contrast can be characterized by a number of measures. While it is true that in the free operant situation the term "contrast" refers to an increase in the overall rate of responding to S+ that results from discrimination training, this increase can be specified in a number of different ways. One can examine as Pavlov did, whether the response strength in S+ components preceded by one or more S— components (S+|S—) is greater than the response strength in S+ components preceded by one or more S+ components (S+|S+). Terrace (1966c, pp. 319-322) has shown that the rate of responding in S+|S— components was higher than the rate of responding to S+|S+ components. The difference between the S+|S— and the S+|S+ rates of responding was not, however, sufficiently large to account for the overall increase in the rate of responding to S+ from its prediscrimination baseline level.

Another aspect of the overall increase in rate of responding to S+ that has been studied is the constancy of the rate of responding to S+ within a particular component. A number of experiments (e.g., Boneau & Axelrod, 1962; Catania & Gill, 1964; Nevin & Shettleworth, 1966) have shown that, following an S— component, the rate of responding to S+ is highest at the onset of S+, after which the rate of responding to S+ gradually decreases. This effect has been called a positive transient contrast. Conversely, following an S+ component, the rate of responding to S+ is lowest at the onset of S+, after which it gradually increases. This effect has been referred to as a negative transient contrast.

Even when one considers only the overall session rate of responding to S+ in describing a contrast effect, the pattern of the rate increase is not always as shown in Fig. 6. The gradual increase in the rate of responding to S+ shown in Fig. 6 occurs typically in experiments in which the duration of each presentation of S— is constant. If, however, a "correction procedure" is used, which prolongs S— until $t$ seconds without a response has elapsed, a different contrast function is obtained (cf. Bloomfield, 1966).

The left-hand panel of Fig. 9 shows contrast functions obtained during discrimination training in which a correction procedure was used. We see a sharp rise to a relatively high peak rate of responding to S+. This peak is usually maintained for only a few sessions after which the rate of responding decreases to a stable level which is considerably higher than the prediscrimination baseline. The right-hand panel of Fig. 9 shows rate functions obtained from Ss who were trained on the same discrimination problem with a noncorrection procedure. Under this condition, the rate of responding to S+ tended to increase at at slower rate until it stabilized at an asymptotic level slightly below the rate of peak responding to S+.

### 3. On the Permanence of Contrast

If training in which a correction procedure is used is extended for a sufficiently long period of time, the rate of responding to S+ eventually decreases to its prediscrimination baseline level. Terrace (1966a), for example, has shown that after two months of daily discrimination training, in which a correction procedure was used, the rate of responding to S+ decreased to its prediscrimination level. No information is available as to whether or not contrast gradually disappears after discrimination training with a noncorrection procedure.

It has also been shown that sequential and transient contrast effects also disappear with extended training (Nevin, 1968; Terrace, 1966c). It should be noted, however, that sequential and transient contrast effects disappear more rapidly with extended discrimination training than does the overall increase in the rate of responding to S+. Why these phenomena show different time courses is presently not known.

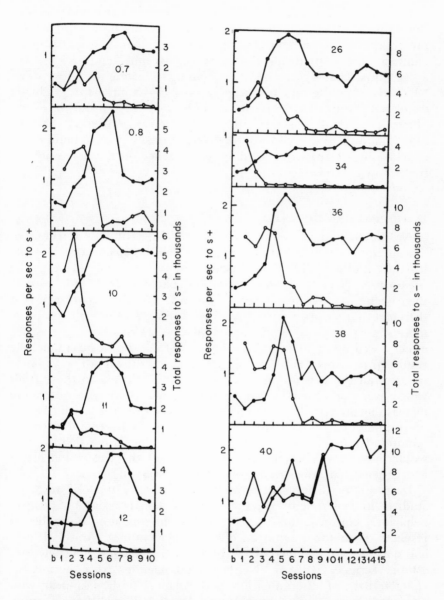

Fig. 9. Rate of the responding to S+ (filled circles) and to S− (open circles) during the acquisition of a discrimination under a correction (left-hand panel) and a noncorrection (right-hand panel) training procedure. (Bloomfield, 1966.) Copyright 1966, by the Society for the Experimental Analysis of Behavior, Inc.

One obviously important parameter of contrast that has not been the subject of systematic study is the interval between stimulus presentations. Bloomfield (1968) has shown that transient positive contrast can be obtained if the interval between S– and S+ is as large as 24 hours. That is, the rate of responding following the onset of S+, 24 hours after the end of the preceding S– component, gradually decreased during the S+ component. Bloomfield did not, however, obtain an overall contrast effect. It is clear, however, that the interstimulus value needs to be systematically varied before any conclusions are reached regarding its influence on the magnitude of the contrast effect.

### D. THE FRUSTRATION EFFECT

An understanding of the effect of the interstimulus effect is of crucial importance in relating positive behavioral contrast and the frustration effect. This is true because the type of study in which the frustration effect is obtained typically spaces its trials more widely than is the practice in studies of positive behavioral contrast. It is therefore not surprising that the frustration effect has proven to be more similar to positive transient contrast than to a positive contrast effect based upon an overall session rate. Consider, for example, the results of the Amsel and Roussel (1952) study shown in Fig. 7. There we see that the frustration effect is confined entirely to those trials which were preceded by nonreinforcement. There was no overall increase in the speed of running on S+ trials over the baseline speed of running. These data were obtained with trials separated by 20 minutes. It would be interesting to see whether a massing of trials would have any effect on the magnitude of the frustration effect and, in particular, the speed of running on S+|S– trials.

Despite the difference in procedure and the type of response studied in experiments on the frustration effect and on positive behavioral contrast, these phenomena seem similar in a number of respects. Both the frustration effect (MacKinnon & Amsel, 1964), and contrast are maximal at the onset of S+ (Nevin & Shettleworth, 1966; Terrace, 1966c). Neither phenomenon is a permanent characteristic of discrimination performance; both disappear with extended discrimination training (cf. Amsel & Ward, 1965; Terrace, 1966a).

Recent studies using a two-chain schedule (e.g., Davenport, Flaherty, & Dryud, 1966; Davenport & Thompson, 1965; Staddon & Innis, 1966) show promise of allowing more direct comparisons between the frustration effect and contrast than has been possible with the double alley apparatus. In particular, they allow the $E$ to manipulate the stimulus conditions associated with nonreinforcement, the schedule of reinforcement and the intertrial interval, in a manner that is more analogous to free-operant studies.

Further work along the lines suggested by the two-chain schedules cited above would help determine the validity of Amsel's recent assertion that ". . . there is no very good evidence that the positive induction-contrast phenomena, as studied under both the Pavlovian and Skinnerian experimental arrangements, depend for their demonstration on differential conditioning or discrimination learning [Amsel, 1971, p. 234]." Amsel formulated this conclusion after considering the results of an experiment performed by Scull, Davies, and Amsel (1971). The experiment compared the rates of responding to S1 following training on a *MULT FI 30" EXT* schedule and on a *MIX FI 30" EXT* schedule. In the *MIX FI 30" EXT* schedule there are no discriminative stimuli correlated with either the *FI 30"* or the extinction components. Despite the absence of discriminative stimuli during *MIX FI 30" EXT* training, the increase in this group's rate of responding following an *EXT* component was as great as the comparable increase in the rate of responding of the *MULT FI EXT* group.

It can easily be argued, however, that the equivalent effect of nonreinforcement on both the multiple and mixed schedule groups of the Scull, Davies, and Amsel experiment does not warrant the conclusion that contrast can be obtained without discrimination training. Rats and pigeons have been shown to discriminate between intervals of time of different length (cf. Catania, 1970; Reynolds & Catania, 1962). It would therefore seem reasonable to argue that the passage of 30 seconds without a reinforcement is a sufficiently potent cue to indicate to the $S$ that he is in the extinction component of the *MIX FI EXT* schedule. The results of the Scull, Davies, and Amsel experiment seem to simply indicate that exteroceptive discriminative stimuli such as key lights, tones, etc., are not needed to train a discrimination. The mere passage of time or the occurrence of reinforcement itself (cf. Jenkins, 1965) may suffice to indicate to the $S$ what schedule of reinforcement is in effect. Just the same, the question raised by Amsel regarding the necessity of discrimination training in the usual sense should not obscure the basic similarity between contrast and the frustration effect. Both appear to result from the nonreinforcement of a response that has been reinforced in a different stimulus condition.

## V. Aversive Properties of S—

We have alluded on a number of occasions to the presumed aversive properties of S— which result from the nonreinforcement of responding to S—. Amsel (1962) for example refers to frustration generated by nonreinforcement as a negative drive. The drive of conditioned frustration is held to be functionally similar to other primary negative drives in that the organism will seek to diminish the intensity of the conditioned frustration drive. We have seen earlier, however, that Amsel's experiments could not be considered as direct demonstrations of frustration. In order to determine whether or not S— actually functions as an aversive stimulus, it is necessary to employ other paradigms.

Ferster's (1958) experiments on time-out *(TO)* from positive reinforcement provides an instructive example of an attempt to demonstrate that nonreinforcement is aversive. Chimpanzees were first trained to pull a lever on a *VI 3 min* schedule. After 45 seconds during which food was available on the *VI 3 min* schedule, a *3 min* *TO* period followed during which no food was available. The onset of *TO* could, however, be postponed for as much as 10 minutes by responding on a second lever. Ferster concluded that responding on the second lever was reinforced by the avoidance of *TO* from reward. It is equally plausible, however, if not more parsimonious, to argue that Ferster's chimpanzees were simply trying to maximize the amount of time during which S+ was in effect. Accordingly, the results of this and many other studies (e.g., Kaufman & Baron, 1966; Morse & Herrnstein, 1956; see also Leitenberg, 1965; Wagner, 1969, for other examples) which purport to show that a S will learn to avoid the onset of S— or *TO* can be accounted for by the more parsimonious interpretation that the S was attempting to maximize positive reinforcement.

Direct proof that S— is an aversive stimulus requires the demonstration that S— affects behavior in a manner similar to the way in which a primary negative reinforcer affects behavior. Can one, for example, condition and maintain a response whose consequence is the removal or the postponement of S—?

The strategy required to demonstrate that S— functions as an aversive stimulus in experiments on discrimination learning differs slightly from the strategy which has been followed in experiments in which primary negative reinforcers are used. The most important difference stems from the necessity of showing that whatever behavior is strengthened by removing S— cannot increase the frequency of positive reinforcement. If the response that removes S— also increases the frequency of positive reinforcement, one could not claim unequivocally that the removal of S— maintained the response in question. We must conclude, therefore, that an avoidance paradigm is not suitable for demonstrating the aversiveness of S—. Fortunately, an escape response is free from the above criticism. However, as we shall see shortly, other factors must be controlled before we can assert that S— functions as an aversive stimulus.

An experiment by Adelman and Maatsch (1956) sought to demonstrate that frustrative nonreward could establish an escape response. The dependent variable in this study was the strength of a new response whereby Ss could escape from the goal box (by jumping) in which food was not presented. Even though Adelman and Maatsch reported a reliable increase in jumping, these results cannot be accepted as unequivocal evidence that the goal box was aversive for two reasons. The first is procedural. The Es reported that some of the Ss were aided by the E in making their initial jump response. The second is that even if the help provided by the Es was not a decisive factor, the greater frequency of jumping in those Ss that experienced nonreinforcement in the goal box may simply be a manifestation of an increase in activity resulting from nonreinforcement.

In a subsequent study by Wagner (1963), two groups of rats were first trained to run to a goal box in which food was placed on half of the trials. For one group (frustration condition), an intermittent light and noise cue was provided as the subjects approached the goal box on nonrewarded trials. For the second group (nonfrustration), the same cue was presented while the rat was in the start box. In a later stage, the rats could escape from the intermittent light and noise cue by jumping over a hurdle from one side of a two-way shuttle box to the other. Toward the end of this test, Wagner observed that the frustration group responded more rapidly than did the nonfrustration group. This difference, however, was not the result of an increase in the speed of hurdle jumping during escape training. Rather, it resulted from a decrease in the speed of the nonfrustration group. Thus, if one assumes a higher state of nonstimulus specific arousal in the case of the frustration group, these results can be accounted for without appealing to an aversive function of S—.

Recent experiments by Daly (1969) and by Rilling, Askew, Ahlskog, and Kramer (1969) have overcome some of the objections raised to earlier studies purporting to show that S— functions as an aversive stimulus. Daly's statistical analysis of hurdle jumping speed in an experiment similar to Wagner's showed evidence that the speed of hurdle jumping did increase with continued escape training, but it was not clear to what extent this effect was obtained in individual Ss. There also remains the question of whether, in both the Wagner and the Daly experiments, the tendency of the frustrated subjects to jump across a hurdle was not simply a manifestation of an overall increase in activity elicited by the cues correlated with nonreward. This same problem arises in Rilling's study which showed that pigeons would learn a new response whose consequence was the temporary removal of S−. While Rilling *et al.* showed this effect in all of his Ss during original discrimination training and during reversal training, the tendency to emit the new response may have resulted from an overall increase in activity resulting from nonreinforced responding. Yet another interpretation of the Rilling study stems from the report that it is possible to strengthen a response whose consequence is mere stimulus change. This phenomenon, which has been shown in rats (Kiernan, 1964; Lockard, 1963), might account for the tendency of Rilling's subjects to turn off S− for short periods of time.

An experiment by this author (Terrace, 1969, 1971a) demonstrated that pigeons could be trained to escape from S−, and that the presumed escape response could not be attributed to either an increase in frustration-produced activity or to the reinforcing properties of stimulus change *per se*. This experiment also demonstrated that the escape response could be maintained on a fixed-ratio schedule, and that the extinction of the escape response resulted in an abrupt decrement in escape responding.

In the first part of this experiment, four groups of pigeons were trained on a successive vertical-horizontal discrimination. Three of the groups learned the discrimination with errors by a method similar to the "late-constant" procedures described earlier. Group IV was trained to acquire the same discrimination without errors by the "early-progressive" and the "superimposition and fading" procedures described earlier.

A second key was made available during the first experimental session immediately after the key-peck was conditioned. The second key remained available throughout the course of the experiment, both when S+ and S− were presented. For Groups I (discrimination learning with errors) and IV (discrimination learning without errors), a response to the left key turned off S− for five seconds. During this time the houselight and the light on the left key remained on. Thus, following a response to the left key, S− was removed and the S was confronted with a visible blank key. Technically speaking, the blank key is a second S—. In this experiment, however, as in many other similar experiments (e.g., Brown & Jenkins, 1967; Terrace, 1966c), the blank key occasioned virtually no responding. Groups II and III served as "displacement" and "stimulus change" control groups, respectively. For Group II (the displacement control group), responding to the second key had no effect. For Group III (a stimulus change control), responding to the left key turned off the white light behind the *left* key for 5 seconds. Responding to the left key, however, had no effect on the stimulus presented on the right key.

The range and the mean number of responses to the left key of each group is shown in Fig. 10. Responding to the left key during the

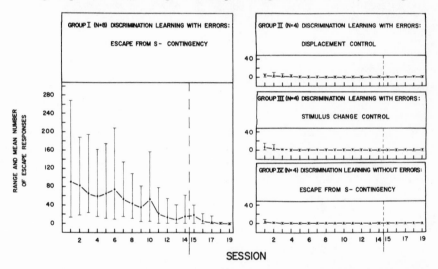

Fig. 10. The range and mean number of responses to the left key emitted by the Ss of the four experimental groups during each discrimination session. See text for additional details. (Terrace, 1971b, by permission of Academic Press, Inc., New York.)

last five sessions (extinction of left key responding) is shown to the right of the dashed vertical line.

During the first discrimination training session, the Ss of Group I responded to the left key an average of 91 times. The range of responses to the left key was 14-268. Throughout the course of discrimination training, the average number of escape responses declined steadily until it reached a minimum value of eight responses during the thirteenth discrimination training session.

None of the Ss of the other groups (II, III, IV) responded very much to the left key. In no instance did the maximum amount of responding to the left key of any of these groups overlap with the minimum amount of responding to the left key that was observed in Group I.

This experiment demonstrated that a pigeon will learn a new response whose sole consequence is the removal of S—. Escape from S—, however, was only observed following discrimination training with errors. It was also shown that responding to the left key could not be attributed to an increase in emotionality or activity resulting

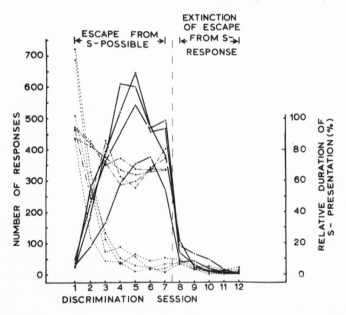

Fig. 11. The number of responses to the left key (heavy functions), the number of responses to S— (short-dashed functions) and the proportion of the programmed time that S— was actually presented (short-long dashed functions) of each S during each discrimination training. See text for additional details.

| Number of escape responses | Subject number | Number of responses to S— | Relative duration of S— presentations |
|---|---|---|---|
| o———o | G-183 | o- - - - - - -o | o— · —o |
| ●———● | G-224 | ●- - - - - - -● | ●— · —● |
| x———x | G-225 | x- - - - - - -x | x— · —x |
| ▲———▲ | G-233 | ▲- - - - - - -▲ | ▲— · —▲ |

Terrace, 1971b, by permission of Academic Press, Inc., New York.

from nonreinforced responding to S—, nor to a tendency to change the value of a discriminative stimulus *per se.*

A second experiment demonstrated that the escape response could be maintained by a schedule which required five responses *(FR5)* for each offset of S—. The results of this experiment are shown in Fig. 11. These functions show the number of escape responses emitted by each subject during each discrimination. It is clear that escape responding could be maintained on the *FR5* schedule and that the main effect of the ratio requirement was to raise the level of escape responding. Figure 11 also shows that the effect of eliminating the escape contingency or responding to the left key (sessions 8-12) was an abrupt decline in the frequency of escape responding. In each case, the frequency of escape responding reached zero by the end of the twelfth session.

Both experiments have demonstrated that S— can function as s secondary negative reinforcer following discrimination training with errors. They also showed that the occurrence of nonreinforced responding is the crucial factor in rendering S— aversive. A major theoretical implication of these results is that a secondary negative reinforcer can be established without recourse to a primary negative reinforcer. We are thus able to equate functionally the operation of presenting a primary negative reinforcer with the operation of withholding a primary positive reinforcer. This is possible because the effect of pairing a stimulus with nonreinforced responding was shown to be similar to the effect of either presenting a negative reinforcer, or pairing a stimulus with a primary negative reinforcer. All of these situations are conducive to the establishment and maintenance of escape behavior. It must be noted, however, that the aversiveness of S— does not appear to be as strong or as permanent as the aversiveness of a primary negative reinforcer.


## VI. The Peak-Shift

In 1956, Guttman and Kalish demonstrated that reliable generalization gradients could be obtained from individual Ss if the generalization test was preceded by training on a schedule which established a strong resistance to extinction. Hanson (1959) used this procedure to obtain generalization gradients following successive discrimination training. In Hanson's experiment, pigeons were first reinforced for responding to 550 nm on a *VI 1 min* schedule. They were then divided into four groups and each group was trained to

discriminate between 550 nm (S+) and one of four different S−'s
(555, 560, 580 or 590 nm). Figure 12 shows the gradients obtained
from each group (dashed functions) and, as a reference, the gradient
obtained by Guttman and Kalish (1956) after nondifferential
training to 550 nm (solid function).

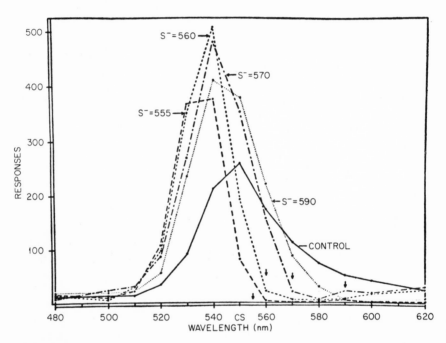

Fig. 12. Postdiscrimination generalization gradients (dashed functions) and
gradients obtained following nondifferential training (solid function). See text
for additional details. (Hanson, 1959.) Copyright 1959, by the American Psychological
Association, Inc.

The gradients obtained from each of the discrimination groups
differed from the control gradient obtained from the Guttman and
Kalish study in two major respects. The location of the peak was not
at S+ (550 nm) but was instead shifted away from S− (to 540 nm).
A second distinguishing characteristic of the postdiscrimination
gradients was that their peaks were higher than the peak of the
control gradient. Our concern at this point will be restricted to the
first difference which Hanson referred to as the "peak-shift." The
second difference, the relatively higher peak, appears to be a
manifestation of positive behavioral contrast (cf. Section IV).

## A. A NEGATIVE PEAK-SHIFT

In Hanson's study, and in most subsequent work on generalization following successive discrimination training, the rate of responding to S— was reduced to a zero or to a near-zero level prior to the generalization test. Thus, as shown in Fig. 12, the frequency of responding to S—, as well as to the test stimuli adjacent to S—, is essentially zero. It is possible, however, to obtain a postdiscrimination generalization gradient before the rate of responding to S— declines to zero. For example, Guttman (1965) trained pigeons to discriminate between 550 nm and 560 nm following nondifferential training in which responding to stimuli of 19 different wavelengths (510-600 nm) was maintained on a *VI* schedule. For some *Ss* ($N$ = 4) S+ was 550 nm and S— was 560 nm. For the remaining *Ss* ($N$ = 2) S+ was 560 and S— was 550. Discrimination training was terminated after an *S* was responding to S+ at least three times more frequently than it was responding to S—. Each *S* was then given a generalization test of wavelength. The average generalization gradient is shown in Fig. 13. Two clear effects of discrimination training can be seen. Those test stimuli located beyond S+ and away from S— occasioned the largest frequency of responding. This is analogous to the peak-shift reported by Hanson. Figure 13 also shows, however, that the three stimuli beyond S—, away from S+, occasioned the lowest

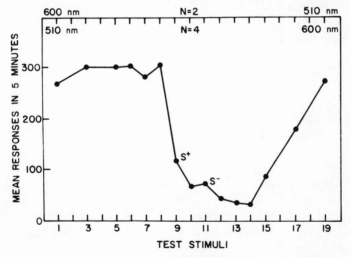

Fig. 13. Mean total responses for various wavelengths in generalization testing following discrimination training in which the rate of responding to S— was not reduced to zero. (Guttman, 1965, by permission of Stanford University Press, Stanford, California.)

frequency of responding. Guttman referred to the reduction in responding away from S— as a "negative peak-shift."

A similar finding was reported by Stevenson (1966). In Stevenson's experiment discrimination training was carried out to the same criteria of no responding used by Hanson. For one group, however, only test stimuli immediately above and below S— were presented during the generalization test. These test stimuli did not include S+. The gradient obtained from these Ss is similar in form to the negative peak-shift portion of the gradient shown in Fig. 13. Less responding occurred at stimuli beyond S—, away from S+, than occurred at S—.

From a logical point of view, the negative peak-shift appears to have the same significance as the positive peak-shift reported by Hanson. The negative peak-shift has, however, received little attention in research on postdiscrimination generalization gradients. Undoubtedly, the main reason for the absence of interest in the negative peak-shift is the practice of most researchers to reduce responding to a near-zero level prior to testing for generalization.

## B. The Generality of the Peak-Shift

While the subject of most studies of the peak-shift has been the pigeon, and the stimulus continuum from which the discriminative and test stimuli have been selected has been wavelength, there have been some heartening exceptions. La Berge (1961) obtained a peak-shift from human Ss along the dimension of verticality. A peak-shift has been obtained from pigeons on the line-orientation continuum (Bloomfield, 1969; Hearst, 1968) and on the dimension of auditory frequency (Jenkins, personal communication). Pierrel and Sherman (1960, 1962) have obtained a peak-shift from rats along the auditory intensity continuum. It appears, therefore, that peak-shifts can be obtained on both prothetic and on metathetic continua (cf. Stevens, 1957). In attempting to obtain a peak-shift on prothetic continua, it is necessary to control for stimulus intensity dynamism (cf. Hull, 1949). Pierrel and Sherman (1960) for example, tested for generalization in different groups, both when S— was less intense and when it was more intense than S+. Since a peak-shift was obtained from both groups, stimulus intensity dynamism does not appear to be responsible for the shift in the location of the peak of the generalization gradient. Peak shifts have also been obtained in studies in which the conditioned response was established by classical conditioning. Examples include Cowan's (1968) study which obtained a peak-shift from rabbits in which the conditioned response was an eyeblink and Ramsey's (1969) report of a peak-shift in monkeys where the conditioned response was heart rate.

Peak-shifts have been obtained under a variety of testing procedures. In addition to Hanson's method in which the test stimuli (including S+ and S−) were presented in extinction, peak-shifts have been obtained in studies in which S− was omitted from the test stimuli presented during the generalization test (Stevenson, 1966) and where responding to S+ was reinforced during the generalization test (Blough, 1961; Pierrel & Sherman, 1960, 1962). Peak-shifts can be obtained both when a warm-up period precedes the generalization test (Thomas, Ost, & Thomas, 1960) and when a warm-up period has been omitted (e.g., Hanson, 1959). During the warm-up period, S+ and S− are alternated as during discrimination training and responding to S+ is reinforced. The generalization test, however, is carried out in extinction. It is also interesting to note that peak-shifts have been obtained when as much as 21 days intervened between the last day of discrimination training and the generalization test (Thomas *et al.,* 1960).

## C. DISCRIMINATIVE TRAINING CONDITIONS WHICH RESULT IN A PEAK-SHIFT

It was noted previously that the peak-shift does not occur following errorless discrimination learning. This was shown by Terrace (1964) in an experiment in which a discrimination between 580 nm (S+) and 540 nm (S−) was trained with and without errors. Errorless discrimination learning was accomplished by the fading procedure described earlier. A third group was given nondifferential training to 580 nm before the generalization test. The results are shown in Fig. 14. The peaks of the gradients obtained from the nondifferential group (left-hand column) and from the errorless group (middle column) occurred at 580 nm, the value of the stimulus correlated with reinforcement. The peak of the gradients obtained from the group who learned without errors was shifted away from S− and was located at 590 nm. The absence of a peak-shift following errorless discrimination learning has been confirmed in an experiment performed by Grusec (1968).

An important extension of Hanson's experiment by Guttman (1959) demonstrated that a peak-shift can be obtained following differential reinforcement in which both discriminative stimuli were correlated with reinforcement. In Guttman's experiment, S1 (550 nm) was correlated with a *VI 1 min* and S2 (570 nm) was correlated

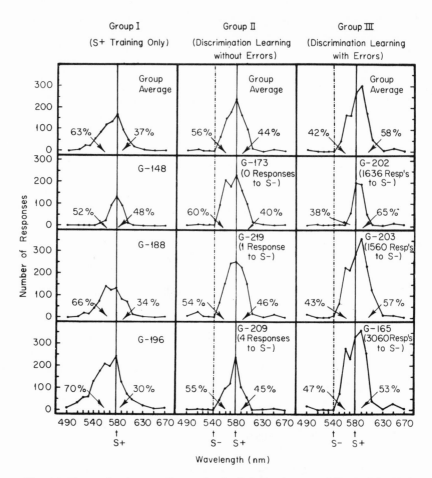

Fig. 14. Generalization gradients obtained following nondifferential training, and following discrimination learning with and without errors. (Terrace, 1964.) Copyright 1964, by the American Association for the Advancement of Science.

with a *VI 5 min* schedule. The peak of a postdiscrimination generalization gradient was located at 540nm, a shift away from S2. As Hanson's data show, the same result would have been obtained had S1 and S2 been correlated with a *VI 1 min* schedule and with extinction, respectively.

A replication of Guttman's procedure by Terrace (1966c, 1968) confirmed the occurrence of a peak-shift following differential reinforcement based on *VI 1 min* and *VI 5 min* schedules. However, these studies also showed that a peak-shift was not a necessary consequence of *MULT VI 1 VI 5* training. If *MULT VI 1 VI 5* discrimination training is preceded by nondifferential training in which S1 and S2 are each correlated with identical *VI 1 min* schedules, a peak-shift will occur following after *MULT VI 1 VI 5* training. If, however, *MULT VI l VI 5* training is preceded by nondifferential training in which S1 and S2 are each correlated with identical *VI 5 min* schedules, a peak-shift will not be obtained. These results suggest that a reduction in the frequency of reinforcement *and/or* the rate of responding in the presence of S2 is responsible for the peak-shift following *VI 1 VI 5* training.

Other experiments by Terrace (1968) have indicated that the critical antecedent condition for the occurrence of the peak-shift was a reduction in the rate of responding to S2. In one experiment (Terrace, 1968, Experiment II), responding to two monochromatic stimuli (S1 = 561 nm; S2 = 586 nm) was maintained at equal rates by identical *VI 1 min* schedules. Responding to S2 was then reduced to an above zero level by punishing each response with electric shock. The rate of responding to S2 was sufficient, however, to produce all of the reinforcements set up by the *VI 1 min* schedule. In each case (*N*=3), a peak shift away from S2 was obtained. In another experiment, S1 was correlated with a differential reinforcement of a *drl* schedule. All responses on the *drl* schedule were reinforced so long as they were separated from one another by *t* seconds. The value of *t* in this experiment ranged between 6 and 8 seconds. In all cases, at least as many reinforcements were obtained on the *drl* schedule as were obtained on the *VI* schedule. A peak-shift was obtained from all of those *S*s whose rate of responding to S2 decreased during *MULT V I drl* training.

Further evidence that a sufficient condition for the occurrence of the peak-shift is a reduction in the rate of responding to one of two discriminative stimuli during prior differential reinforcement comes from an experiment performed by Yarczower, Dickson, and Gollub (1966). These *E*s were able to vary the rate of responding to S2 and the probability of reinforcement in S2 independently of one another by using different tandem variable interval − *drl (TAND VI drl)* schedules in the presence of S1 and S2 respectively. A *TAND VI drl* schedule is one in which two conditions must be met for reinforcement to occur. After a particular interval of time has elapsed (whose average value is specified by the value of the *VI* schedule), the next response is reinforced so long as it is separated from the previous response by at least *t* second. The value of *t* is defined by the value of the *drl* schedule. Since no exteroceptive stimulus is provided to indicate that a particular interval on the variable interval schedule has elapsed, the effect of the added *drl* requirement is to place an upper bound on response rate. This maintains responding at a lower rate than the rate that would have been obtained on a similar *VI* schedule which was not in tandem with a *drl* schedule.

By adjusting the values of the different *TAND VI drl* schedules in the presence of S1 and S2, Yarczower *et al.* could either vary the rate of responding to a particular discriminative stimulus without altering the frequency of reinforcement or vary the frequency of reinforcement without altering the rate of responding. Yarczower *et al.* found that a peak-shift was obtained after differential reinforcement in which the rate of responding to S2 was reduced to a value lower than that prevailing in S1 even though the frequencies of reinforcement earned in S1 and S2 were equal. No peak-shift was obtained, however, following differential reinforcement in which the rates of responding to·S1 and to S2 were maintained at equal values but where the frequency of reinforcement to S2 was lower than the frequency of reinforcement to S1.

The experiments we have considered thus far, in which a peak-shift has been observed, have all used training procedures in which the frequency of positive reinforcement in S1 and S2 differed, or where the schedules of positive reinforcement in S1 and S2 required different rates of responding to S1 and to S2. It is also possible, however, to produce a peak-shift by merely pairing a stimulus with a negative reinforcer. This was demonstrated by Grusec (1968) who first trained a wavelength discrimination with and without errors. The peaks of the initial gradient obtained from these Ss were located at S+. The Ss were then given additional discrimination training in which half of the Ss received brief shocks in the presence of S−. These shocks, which could neither be avoided nor escaped from, did not disrupt errorless performance. The peaks of a second generalization gradient obtained from those Ss who experienced shock in the presence of S− were shifted away from S−. The peaks of the gradients obtained from the errorless Ss who did not receive shock were located at S+.

Analogous results were obtained from a second group of Ss who learned the same discrimination with errors. The initial peaks of the first generalization gradients obtained from these Ss were shifted away from S−. After the first generalization test, half of the Ss who learned with errors were given addition discrimination training in which S2 was paired with noncontingent shock. No shock was administered during the subsequent discrimination training of the remaining Ss. The magnitude of the peak-shifts obtained on the second generalization gradients of those Ss who received noncontingent shock was larger than on the first test. There was, however, no increase in displacement away from S— in the peaks of those Ss who did not experience shock in the presence of S2 between the first and the second generalization tests. These results, which are shown in Fig. 15, indicate clearly that a negative reinforcer and a

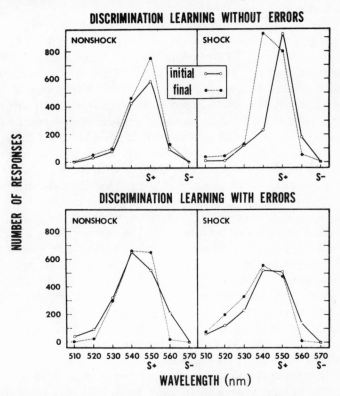

Fig. 15. Generalization gradients obtained following discrimination learning with and without errors. In each case half of the Ss were given noncontingent shock in the presence of S— following the first generalization test. See text for additional details. (Grusec, 1968.) Copyright 1968, by the Society for the Experimental Analysis of Behavior, Inc.

reduction of the rate of responding in the presence of S2 have a similar effect. It should be recalled that Experiment II of Terrace's 1968 study yielded similar conclusions regarding the functional equivalence of a stimulus associated with the presentation of a negative reinforcer and the absence of positive reinforcement.

The data summarized above indicated that those training

conditions which produce contrast also produce a peak-shift and vice versa. Some exceptions, however, have been reported to the general rule that contrast and the peak-shift co-vary as a function of the same training conditions. It would therefore appear worthwhile to consider the results of two studies which purport to show that a peak-shift can occur following discrimination training in which contrast had not occurred.

The first of these studies was performed by Yarczower *et al.* (1966). In this experiment pigeons were trained on a *MULT tand VI 30 sec drl 4 sec — EXT* schedule. Contrast did not occur during discrimination training. However, a peak-shift was obtained during a subsequent generalization test. Unfortunately, Yarczower, *et al.* did not determine what would happen if the *drl* requirement, which was in tandem with the *VI 30 sec* schedule, was removed from the first component of the multiple schedule. If it turns out that the absence of contrast during this type of differential reinforcement was simply the result of the *drl* contingency in tandem with the *VI* schedule, this exception to the generalization that the peak-shift and contrast tend to occur under the same conditions appears to be trivial.

Friedman and Guttman (1965) have argued that the results of one of their experiments can be interpreted as evidence that a peak-shift can be obtained in a postdiscrimination generalization gradient even though contrast had not occurred during discrimination training. In this experiment, discrimination training was carried out in two phases. During the first phase, S+ was a 550 nm homogeneous patch of monochromatic light, while S— was a 550 nm patch of monochromatic light upon which a white cross was superimposed. During the second phase of discrimination training, the value of S— was changed from the 550 nm-white cross combination to a 570 nm patch of monochromatic light. A subsequent generalization test of wavelength showed a peak-shift away from 570 nm. Friedman and Guttman considering this finding to be significant since contrast did not occur during the second phase of discrimination training, the phase in which the 570 nm S— was introduced. At best, however, this experiment shows that a peak-shift can be obtained when the S— used during the generalization test was not the same S— which was alternated with S+ when contrast occurred. But given that both discriminations were trained in the same apparatus, and that little responding to S— occurred during the second phase of discrimination training, it is not too surprising that contrast did not occur during this phase. It should also be noted that the absence of contrast during the second phase may simply reflect an asymptotic level of responding to S+ that was achieved during the first phase of discrimination training. For these reasons the results reported by Friedman and Guttman do not appear to jeopardize the generalization that contrast and the peak-shift co-vary as a function of similar training conditions.

## D. Training Procedures Which Do Not Produce a Peak-Shift

We have seen previously that a peak-shift is not obtained following discrimination learning in which unreinforced responses to S— do not occur (Terrace, 1964). However, a peak-shift will also not occur after differential reinforcement in which nonreinforced responding occurred to S— if (a) training in S— is "massed" or (b) the generalization test is conducted after an extended period of discrimination training.

Honig, Thomas, and Guttman (1959) demonstrated that no peak-shift is obtained if the test for generalization follows a single presentation of S—. In this experiment, different groups of Ss were extinguished in the presence of S— for either 20 or 40 minutes following baseline training to S+. S+ was presented again prior to the generalization test. No peak-shift was obtained following either duration of massed extinction. The procedure of massing a S's exposure to S— should be compared with the "method of contrasts" in which S+ and S— are typically alternated in some irregular series. We have seen previously that peak-shifts are obtained in generalization tests given after discrimination learning with errors. The method of contrasts was used in all of these experiments.

A study by Friedman and Guttman (1965) explored further the conditions under which massed extinction will not produce a peak-shift. In one of these experiments, differential reinforcement, administered via the method of contrasts, was used to train a discrimination between a circular patch of monochromatic light whose value was 550 nm (S+) and a circular patch of monochromatic light of 550 nm upon which a white cross was superimposed (S—). After this discrimination was mastered, massed extinction in the presence of 570 nm was administered. During a subsequent generalization test, a peak-shift was obtained. In a second experiment, Friedman and Guttman first trained a discrimination between 550 nm (S+) and a *TO* condition during which both the key light and the house light of the pigeon chamber were extinguished (S—). The key-peck was subsequently extinguished in the presence of 570 nm for a period of 20 minutes. A peak-shift was not obtained during a subsequent generalization test.

The obvious difference between the two procedures used by Friedman and Guttman is that in their first experiment, nonreinforced responding occurred to an S— which was alternated with S+. In the second experiment, no responding occurred during *TO*, a finding which is consistent with the results of many other experiments on *TO* behavior in the pigeon. These results suggest that nonreinforced responding to an S—, which at some point alternates with S+, is a critical factor in determining whether or not a peak-shift will occur following the massed extinction procedure.

Preliminary data from this author's laboratory (Rosen & Terrace, 1971) indicate that a peak-shift does occur following massed extinction if five minutes of S+ follows massed extinction. A peak-shift occurs during a subsequent generalization test whether or not responding to S+ is reinforced during the 5-minute interval which follows massed extinction. Yet, another interesting result of this experiment is the finding that free food (presented at the rate at which they would have been earned on a *VI* schedule) in the presence of a blank key will also suffice to produce a peak-shift. The significance of these findings will be discussed in Section VII,E where analogous data concerning inhibitory stimulus control following massed extinction are discussed.

We have seen previously that emotional responses to S—, the aversive function of S—, and behavioral contrast were not permanent characteristics of discrimination performance. This is also true of the peak-shift. Terrace (1966a) has shown that a peak-shift is not obtained if a generalization test is given after 60 sessions of discrimination training *(MULT VI EXT)*. It was also shown in the same experiment that, when the generalization tests were given following blocks of 15 discrimination sessions, the magnitude of the peak-shift was greatest during the early portion of discrimination training, after which the peak gradually reverted back to S+.

## VII. The Inhibitory Function of S—

Conditioned inhibition, a concept formulated by Pavlov (1927), has played a prominent role in the theoretical models of discrimination learning developed by Spence (1936, 1937) and by Hull (1943, 1952). Until recently, however, the concept of inhibition has received little attention in empirical and theoretical studies of discrimination learning. This lack of interest appears to have resulted both from the failure of the Spence-Hull model of discrimination learning to specify how inhibition might be measured and manipulated in experimental studies and from the unanswered criticisms of the concept of inhibition by Loucks and by Skinner.

Loucks (1933) noted that Pavlov had not made a strong case for the usefulness of the concept of inhibition at the behavioral level, and that from a physiological point of view, Pavlov's model of conditioned inhibition contained numerous inconsistencies. Skinner (1938) argued that the mere decrease in response frequency, as observed during simple extinction or during the formation of a discrimination, does not require the concept of inhibition. Either of these phenomena could be accounted for more parsimoniously by appealing to a reduction in the level of excitation.

During the last decade, three major theoretical analyses, by Jenkins (1965), Rescorla (1969), and Hearst, Besley, and Farthing (1970), along with numerous experiments, have restored interest in the behavioral analysis of inhibition. While there is still no general agreement as to just how inhibition should be measured, there remains little doubt that inhibition can be measured, and that it is a useful concept in describing the formation of a discrimination. In this section, we will first discuss briefly three methods for measuring conditioned inhibition and then turn to the question of how these measures may be related among themselves and to the by-products of discrimination learning we have discussed earlier.

## A. INHIBITORY STIMULUS CONTROL

The first measure of conditioned inhibition that we will consider was formulated by Jenkins (1965; see also Honig, Boneau, Burstein, & Pennypacker, 1963; Jenkins & Harrison, 1962). In this incisive analysis of the concept of inhibition, Jenkins (1965) suggested how the Pavlovian model of *conditioned inhibition* could be interpreted in a way that neutralized Skinner's criticism and which also allowed one to study empirically the gradients of inhibition postulated by the Spence-Hull model. Jenkins noted that one characteristic of an inhibitory stimulus, as postulated by Pavlov, was its control of not-responding. According to this point of view, S— came to control a response antagonistic to the response to S+. Jenkins suggested that the control of S— over not responding might be measured in much the same way in which we measure the control of responding exerted by S+.

We have noted earlier that the Guttman and Kalish procedure allows us to demonstrate stimulus control with respect to S+ by showing that the tendency to respond to a test stimulus decreased as the distance between the test stimulus and S+ increased. A demonstration that S— controlled not-responding would require a similar decrease in not-responding as the distance between S— and the test stimulus increased. That is, there should be an increase in *responding* to a test stimulus as one increased the distance between the test stimulus and S—. Accordingly, a U-shaped gradient, with a minimum at S—, would be evidence that S— controlled not-responding.

Jenkins also noted that this type of generalization test presupposes discrimination learning in which S+ and S— are on orthogonal continua, e.g. line orientation *versus* wavelength. If S+ and S— were on the same continuum, the amount of responding to a particular test stimulus could be accounted for either by the distance between S+ and the test stimulus *or* between S— and the test stimulus. If, however, S+ and S— were selected from continua along which test stimuli could be varied independently of one another, it would seem more reasonable to argue that the frequency of responding to a particular test stimulus was determined by the distance between that test stimulus and the training stimulus on that continuum. Suppose, for example, that S+ was a vertical white line, and S— was a homogeneous field of light of a particular wavelength. If responding to test stimuli along the wavelength dimension increased as the distance between the test stimulus and S— increased, it would be hard to account for this change in responding by the differences between the test stimuli and S+. As noted previously, this type of gradient is considered evidence of inhibitory stimulus control.

Experiments by Jenkins and Harrison (1962) and by Honig *et al.* (1963) have shown that gradients with minima at S— are obtained following discrimination training between stimuli from orthogonal continua. Figure 16 shows the gradients obtained by Jenkins and Harrison following discrimination training between white noise (S+) and a tone whose frequency was 1000 Hz (S—). We see that response frequency is lowest at S—, and that response frequency increases progressively as the distance between S— and the test stimuli increases.

A subsequent experiment performed by Terrace (1966b) showed that U-shaped gradients along the S— continuum could be obtained only after discrimination learning with errors. As we shall see, however, one feature of the design of that experiment prevents one from arguing that inhibitory stimulus control occurs only after discrimination learning with errors. The discriminative stimuli were a

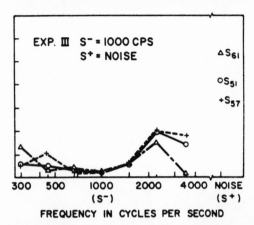

Fig. 16. Gradients of inhibition. See text for additional details. (Jenkins & Harrison, 1962.) Copyright 1962, by the Society for the Experimental Analysis of Behavior, Inc.

white vertical line on a black background (S+) and a monochromatic field (S−). For some Ss, the wavelength of S− was 580 nm; for others, it was 550 nm. In this experiment, some of the Ss acquired the discrimination without errors and without the aid of any special training techniques. Generalization gradients obtained from those Ss who learned with errors were U-shaped functions centered at S−. The generalization gradients obtained from the Ss who learned without errors were flat functions which indicated essentially no responding to any of the test stimuli.

How is the flat gradient representing no responding along the wavelength continuum to be interpreted? Terrace (1966b, 1967) argued that these results indicated an absence of inhibitory stimulus control. He also concluded that S− functioned as a neutral stimulus. This interpretation has been criticized on a number of grounds. Deutsch (1967) asserted that the flat, zero-level gradient was evidence of inhibition at all values along the continuum and thus concluded that there was a greater amount of inhibitory stimulus control following discrimination learning without errors than following discrimination learning with errors. Terrace (1967) replied that this conclusion was not valid. Not only was Deutsch falling back upon the discredited assumption that the mere absence of responding indicated the presence of inhibition, but he was also ignoring the widely accepted convention that a flat generalization gradient indicated a lack of stimulus control with respect to the dimension along which the gradient was obtained.

In a more cogent criticism of Terrace's 1966 experiment,

Bernheim (1968) noted that the *post hoc* method of selecting errorless Ss prevented one from concluding that S— does not function as an inhibitory stimulus following errorless discrimination learning. Bernheim argued that these Ss may represent a subpopulation of pigeons who do not respond readily to any wavelength stimuli. This argument does not rule out the interpretation that S— has no inhibitory function following errorless discrimination learning. It simply poses an alternative account of Terrace's (1966c) results which could not be easily dismissed.

Two subsequent experiments, one by Terrace (1971a) and one by Lyons (1969), have, however, indicated that an aversion for wavelength stimuli by some pigeons does not make for a plausible account of Terrace's (1966b) results.

In Terrace's (1971a) experiment, the discriminative stimuli were a homogeneous field of white light (S+) and a homogeneous field of monochromatic light, whose dominant wavelength was 550 nm. A fading procedure was necessary to train this discrimination without errors. This rules out the possibility that a flat generalization gradient based upon the absence of responding along the wavelength continuum could be attributed to an aversion to wavelength stimuli. As shown in Fig. 17, the gradients obtained from the errorless group

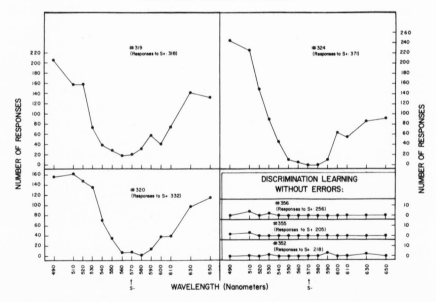

Fig 17. Gradients of inhibition following discrimination learning with and without errors. See text for additional details. (Terrace, 1971a, by permission.)

were flat. On the other hand, gradients with a minimum at S— were obtained from all of the Ss of the group who learned this discrimination with errors. Since the argument that the flat gradients of wavelength generalization obtained from the errorless group resulted from an aversion to wavelength stimuli does not apply in this case, it seems reasonable to conclude that the flat gradients do reflect the absence of inhibitory stimulus control.

Lyons' (1969) experiment employed a different procedure for training a discrimination without errors. Each time it appeared to the E that a pigeon was about to respond to S—, the E turned off S— and the houselight for 2 seconds. While this procedure did not completely prevent the occurrence of errors, the Ss who were trained in this manner responded to S— much less frequently than did those Ss who learned the same discrimination in the conventional manner. It should be noted, however, that the Ss of Lyons' "errorless" group made hundreds of responses to S—. Even though the behavior of these Ss may be functionally equivalent to the Ss who had learned the same discrimination with few or no errors, it may be premature to gloss over the substantial amount of responding to S— by Lyons' "errorless" Ss.

In Lyons' study, S+ was a circular field of monochromatic light (550 nm), and S— was a white vertical line on a black background. Following discrimination training with and "without" errors, the two groups were given a generalization test in extinction during which the angle of rotation of the white line was varied. For half of the Ss of each group the white line was presented on a 555 nm background (S+). Lyons' purpose in superimposing the test stimuli on S+ during the generalization test was to raise the level of responding to the test stimuli. The results obtained by Lyons are shown in Figs. 18 and 19. Figure 18 shows the gradients of those Ss who were tested with different line orientations on a black background. Figure 19 shows the results of those Ss for whom the test stimuli were presented on a monochromatic background (S+). The results shown in Fig. 18 confirmed Terrace's previous observation that discrimination training with errors results in a U-shaped gradient with a minimum at S—, and that errorless discrimination training results in a flat gradient.

The results shown in Fig. 19 appear to require a different interpretation. When the test stimuli were superimposed on the monochromatic background (S+), *peaks* at S— were obtained both from the groups which learned with and without errors. Why these peaks occurred at S— does not at present seem well understood. Lyons (1969) offered the following explanation of the peak at S— obtained by the errorless group: "... During errorless training the

**H. S. Terrace**

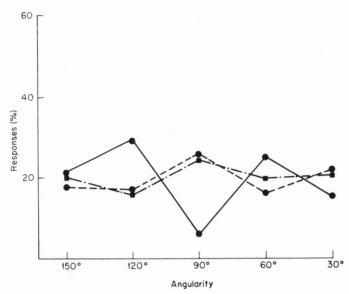

Fig. 18. Generalization gradients based upon the mean percentage of total responses to each angle for the three groups tested in the presence of line orientation alone. *Key:* Error ●——●; errorless ●— — —●; control ■— · —■. See text for additional details. (Lyons, 1969.) Copyright 1969, by the American Association for the Advancement of Science.

bird became familiar with the negative stimulus, which somehow became a positive stimulus in the context of the generalization with the positive stimulus present [p. 491. Copyright 1969, by the American Association for the Advancement of Science]." This explanation, however, appears to hold equally well for the gradients obtained from the group which learned with errors and therefore seems to be no explanation at all.

While Lyons' procedure of superimposing S+ on all of the test stimuli along the S— continuum during generalization testing has promise as a valuable tool for the study of inhibition, the findings of his 1969 study fall short of fulfilling that promise. The superimposition procedure increased responding for only half of the Ss (Lyons, personal communication). A similarly nonuniform effect of superimposing S+ on the test stimuli was reported by Yarczower (1970). Indeed, at this stage it appears that the only effect of the superimposition procedures may be an increase in the variability of the generalization gradients. Hopefully, further work can refine this procedure so that the uniformity of the results it produces are comparable to those obtained by other procedures.

While our knowledge of the sufficient conditions for the

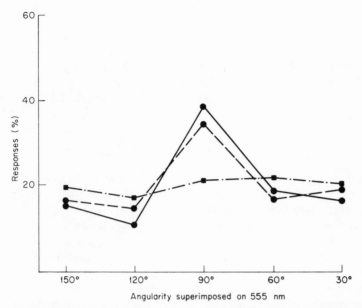

Fig. 19. Generalization gradients based upon the mean percentage of total responses during generalization testing to each angle for the three groups tested on the line orientation dimension with the positive stimulus present. *Key:* Error ●——●; errorless ●— — —●; control ■— · — · —■. See text for additional details. (Lyons, 1969.) Copyright 1969, by the American Association for the Advancement of Science.

establishment of inhibitory stimulus control is not as extensive as it is in the case of contrast or the peak-shift, the data on hand indicate that those conditions which produce a peak-shift and contrast also produce inhibitory stimulus control. We have mentioned previously that inhibitory stimulus control does not occur following errorless discrimination learning. Neither does contrast nor the peak-shift. Conversely, discrimination learning with errors results in contrast, the peak-shift and inhibitory stimulus control. Parallels between the conditions which produce contrast, the peak-shift and inhibitory stimulus control have also been obtained in experiments in which discriminations were trained by differential reinforcement procedures other than *MULT VI EXT*. In an experiment on the effect of *MULT VI DRO* training Nevin (1968) found that inhibitory stimulus control did not occur if contrast had not occurred during discrimination training. Weissman (1969) has reported that *MULT VI 1 VI 5* training and *MULT VI 1 drl* training produced both contrast and inhibitory stimulus control.

In an extension of the Honig, Thomas, and Guttman experiment on the peak-shift described earlier, Rosen and Terrace (1971) studied the effects of massed extinction on inhibitory stimulus control. Their results mirrored precisely the findings reported earlier concerning the conditions which were sufficient to produce the peak-shift. In this experiment, each $S$ received 2 hours of massed extinction in the presence of 570 nm following 20 sessions of $VI$ training in the presence of a white vertical line. Inhibitory stimulus control was not obtained if a generalization test followed directly the 2-hour interval of massed extinction. Inhibitory stimulus control was obtained if any of the following conditions intervened between massed extinction and the generalization test: $(a)$ 3 minutes of S+ during which responding was reinforced on a $VI$ $1$ $min$ schedule; $(b)$ 3 minutes of S+ during which responding was not reinforced; $(c)$ 3 minutes of noncontingent reinforcement provided by a $VI$ $1$ tape in the presence of a blank key. Similar findings have been reported by Weissman (1969).

In his recent review of the status of inhibition Hearst $et$ $al.$ (1970) concluded that the demonstration of dimensional control along the S— continuum does not in itself indicate that a stimulus is inhibitory. Hearst $et$ $al.$ argues that the minimum point of such a gradient (whose value is usually zero) may simply reflect a neutral point on an excitatory-inhibitory continuum (see also Wilton & Godbout, 1970). According to this point of view, extinction in the presence of S— simply eliminates the excitation that has built up during acquisition. The gradient of inhibitory stimulus control (so-called) is presumed to result from a generalization of extinction. That is to say, the effect of reducing excitation at S— spreads to the test stimuli in some proportion of their distance from S—.

It is mainly the above argument which led Hearst $et$ $al.$ to conclude that a gradient of inhibition is not an adequate demonstration of an inhibitory effect. Following Rescorla's (1969) treatment of conditioned inhibition in Pavlovian conditioning, Hearst $et$ $al.$ proposed the criterion of a stimulus-induced reduction of excitation as the only "unambiguous" evidence of inhibition. We will postpone discussion of this criterion until after we have considered some examples at the end of the following section. It should, however, be noted at this point that the gains in parsimony that result in postulating a generalization of the *absence* of excitation as an alternative explanation of an inhibitory gradient seem vanishingly small. Just how the absence of excitation generalizes from S— to the other test stimuli is not stated. While an appeal to the absence of excitation might account for the absence of responding to S−, it is not clear how this type of explanation could be extended to the generalization gradients obtained along the S− continuum.

## B. INHIBITION AS A STIMULUS-PRODUCED DECREMENT IN RESPONDING

In the previous section we have considered the generalization gradient along the S− continuum as a measure of inhibitory stimulus control. A greater than zero slope was considered evidence of inhibitory stimulus control, just as a greater than zero slope along the S+ continuum might be considered evidence of excitatory stimulus control. There remains the problem, however, of other interpretations of a gradient of zero slope along the S− continuum. One might argue that even when such problems as the *ad hoc* method of subject selection in Terrace's (1966b) study are avoided, a gradient of zero slope does not necessarily indicate the absence of inhibitory stimulus control (cf. Farthing & Hearst, 1968; Hearst *et al.*, 1970). One argument against such an interpretation is that the conclusion that inhibitory stimulus control is absent is valid only for the continuum under study. There remains the possibility that inhibitory stimulus control can be obtained by varying S− along other dimensions. Gradients of zero slope may have been obtained because the Ss simply did not attend to the continuum along which S− was varied. This problem does not appear to effect the conclusion of Terrace's (1971a) study since there is no *a priori* reason to presume that the errorless subjects were not attending to wavelength stimuli. However, this factor may be important in interpreting the results of other studies which obtained flat gradients but which did not use a comparison group such as the group who learned the same discrimination without errors.

Yet another difficulty in interpreting a flat gradient arises when the gradient represents a uniform level of zero responding. If following discrimination learning without errors, the S had learned to respond to S+ and not to its absence, one would exepct a flat gradient along the S− continuum. We have seen, however, that a flat gradient based on a zero level of responding might not necessarily mean that S− is neutral. By superimposing S+ on each test stimulus from the S− continuum, it may be possible to elevate responding along the S− continuum. If, as Lyons' study suggests, a flat gradient is not obtained following a generalization test in which S+ is superimposed on the test trials, the conclusion that S− functions as a neutral stimulus following discrimination learning without errors would have to be rejected on the grounds that a gradient based on no responding, albeit at zero slope, is not sensitive enough to reveal an inhibitory (or, as Lyons suggests, an excitatory?) function of S−. It should be noted, however, that the results of studies which have tested for inhibitory stimulus control with the test stimulus from the S− continuum superimposed on S+ are far from consistent. As mentioned previously, the gradients obtained by Yarczower (1970) did not show a uniform effect of superimposition.

The above considerations nevertheless suggest that it may be possible to demonstrate an inhibitory function of a stimulus on the absence of inhibitory stimulus control. Farthing and Hearst (1968) and Hearst et al. (1970) have argued that "an inhibitory stimulus . . . (may be distinguished) from inhibitory dimensional control in an analogous fashion to the manner in which one might distinguish between an excitatory stimulus and excitatory dimensional control [Hearst et al. (1970), p. 376. Copyright 1970, by the Society for the Experimental Analysis of Behavior, Inc.]." While a flat gradient obtained along one of the dimensions which define S+ demonstrates that no excitatory control exists with respect to that dimension (cf. Terrace, 1966b), a flat gradient cannot be accepted as evidence that S+ does not have an excitatory effect. If independent tests show that S+ can increase the frequency of responding above the level that would be obtained when that stimulus is absent S+ is, by definition, an excitatory stimulus. Likewise, Rescorla (1969), Hearst et al. (1970) and Hearst (1968) have argued that a stimulus has an inhibitory function if, as a result of conditioning, it can decrease the frequency of responding below the level that would have been obtained when the stimulus was absent. In his analysis of conditioned inhibition in classical conditioning paradigms Rescorla states that: "A conditioned inhibitor has been defined as a stimulus which through learning comes to control a tendency opposite to that of a conditioned excitor [Rescorla, 1969, p. 79. Copyright 1969, by the American Psychological Association, Inc.]." Hearst proposed a similar definition of conditioned inhibition based upon the operant conditioning paradigm: "An inhibitory stimulus is a stimulus that develops during conditioning the capacity to decrease response strength below the level occuring when that stimulus is absent [Hearst et al., 1970, p. 376. Copyright 1970, by the Society for the Experimental Analysis of Behavior, Inc.].

An experiment by Brown and Jenkins (1967) illustrates how one can measure the reduction in responding that follows the presentation of a conditioned inhibitor. This experiment was conducted in three phases. During the first phase a red-green discrimination was trained. Responding to the right half of a split key was reinforced when both halves were red. When both halves of the split key were green, responding to the left key was reinforced. During the second phase a discrimination was trained between the presence (S–) and the absence (S+) of a tone. Throughout this phase of the experiment each side of the key was red. Responding to the right half was reinforced only in the absence of the tone. The last phase began after it was shown that the original discrimination (red: peck right; green: peck left) was still intact. The last phase tested the inhibitory function of the tone by determining to what extent its presence reduced responding to the left side of the key when both sides of the key were green. This test was conducted in extinction. Brown and Jenkins observed that the presence of the tone sharply reduced the frequency of responses to the left key when the key was green. In the absence of the tone, differential control by red and green over right and left responding was maintained. Responding to green by a control group which had no experience with the tone prior to the extinction test was unaffected by the presence of the tone. These results indicate that the tone had become a conditioned inhibitor by virtue of the differential reinforcement procedure which was in effect during Phase II and that the decrement in responding that followed the presentation of the tone could not be attributed to a "generalization decrement" (cf. Skinner's 1938 analysis of Pavlov's results) or to "external inhibition" (cf. Pavlov, 1927).

Both inhibitory stimulus control and the stimulus-produced decrement in responding discussed in this section seem to have one important feature in common. In both cases it appears that S– occasions responding antagonistic to the response to S+. Jenkins (1965) has noted that the absence of responding to S– can be classified into two mutually exclusive categories responses which are antagonistic to the response to S+ and "other behavior." Jenkins argued that other behavior, e.g. pecking at the floor, grooming, is not under the control of S–. What S– does control is behavior which is incompatible with the response to S+. Thus when one changes the value of the test stimuli on the S– continuum the tendency not to respond decreases and accordingly more responding occurs as the distance between S– and the test stimuli increases. Likewise, when S– is combined with S+ as in the Brown and Jenkins experiment, the tendency to respond to S+ is reduced since S– is occasioning responding which is incompatible with responding to S+. An obvious experiment which has yet to be performed is to vary the value of S– in the Brown and Jenkins procedure. The results of such an experiment should prove helpful in integrating the dimensional measure of inhibition discussed in the previous section with the measure advocated by Hearst *et al.* The expected finding would of course be a decrease in the suppression of responding as the distance between the frequency of the tone and its original value is increased.

## C. Resistance to Reinforcement

In his discussion of conditioned inhibition, Pavlov noted that stimuli associated with extinction were more difficult to establish as excitatory stimuli than stimuli which had never been paired with extinction. Pavlov referred to this phenomenon as "extinction beyond zero" (Pavlov, 1927).

An attempt by Hearst *et al.* to study the inhibitory effect of a stimulus in an operant paradigm by measuring the relative difficulty of converting that stimulus to a reinforcing stimulus suggests that this method may provide a valuable complement of the methods discussed above. Hearst's procedure consists of two phases. During the first phase a discrimination between two stimuli from orthogonal continua is trained to a given criterion from this continuum. Subsequently, a generalization test is given in which a series of test stimuli from the S— continuum are presented. Unlike the Guttman and Kalish procedure, however, responding to each of the test stimuli is *reinforced* during the generalization test which was carried out on successive days. Responding to each stimulus was reinforced on a *VI 30"* schedule. The focus of interest in this experiment was the number of responses to each test stimulus during each generalization test. The results are shown in Fig. 20. During the first test we see that responding occurred to all of the test stimuli but there was relatively little responding to the stimulus that was formerly S—. During subsequent testing, the frequency of responding to S— increased to a level which at first was equal to the frequency of responding to the other test stimuli but which subsequently exceeded the frequency of responding to some of these stimuli. While the significance of the ultimate "inversion" of the gradient obtained along the S— continuum cannot be understood without further experimentation the results of Hearst's study show that (*a*) a generalization test in which responding to the test stimuli is reinforced will yield gradients comparable in shape to gradients of inhibition obtained during generalization tests conducted in extinction, and (*b*) that one can obtain inhibitory gradients in which responding to S— occurs at a greater than zero frequency.

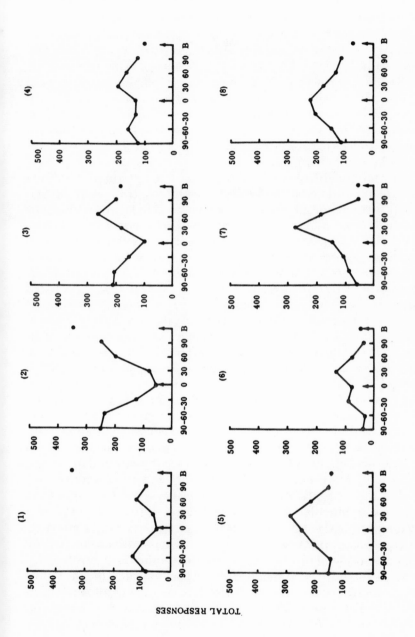

DEGREES OF LINE TILT

Fig. 20. Line-tilt gradients for one *S* over eight successive daily generalization tests with intermittent reinforcement at all stimulus values. During training S— was zero degrees. See text for additional details. (Hearst *et al.*, 1970.) Copyright 1970, by the Society for the Experimental Analysis of Behavior, Inc.

D. The Effects of Extended Training on Inhibition

We have seen previously that emotional responses (Terrace, 1966c), the aversive function of S— (Terrace, 1971a), contrast (Terrace, 1966a), the frustration effect (Amsel & Ward, 1965) and the peak-shift (Terrace, 1966a) are not permanent characteristics of discrimination performance. Each of these phenomena disappear with extended training. Little evidence is available at present regarding the three measures of inhibition we have discussed above. Unfortunately, the small amount of data on hand do not allow for any simple conclusion regarding the permanence of inhibitory effects in discrimination performance.

In the only published study which sought to determine the effect of extended training on inhibitory stimulus control, Farthing and Hearst (1968) reported that the slope of a relative gradient of inhibition *increased* during the first 16 sessions of discrimination training. If one assumes that the degree of inhibitory stimulus control is proportional to the slope of the gradient (cf. the argument that the slope of a gradient of excitation reveals the amount of excitatory stimulus control), it would appear that extended discrimination training increases inhibitory stimulus control. It should be noted, however, that 16 sessions is a relatively short amount of discrimination training, and one would want to see what happens to inhibitory stimulus control after extended discrimination training before attempting to conclude whether or not inhibitory control is permanent.

Selekman (1971) in an unpublished dissertation has reported that the slope of a *relative* gradient of inhibition remains essentially the same throughout 60 sessions of discrimination training. In Selekman's study, however, contrast was also present after 70 sessions of discrimination training. It appears therefore, that, in this study as well, more training is required before any conclusions are reached about the performance of inhibitory stimulus control. In view of the frequently observed relationship between contrast and inhibition (Terrace, 1966b) one would want to extend discrimination training beyond the point at which contrast disappears before deciding about the performance of inhibitory stimulus control.

A somewhat different picture of the permanence of inhibitory stimulus control emerges from absolute gradients of inhibition obtained by Yarczower (1970). In this study, gradients of inhibition were obtained either early in discrimination training when contrast was still present or late in discrimination training after contrast had disappeared. Inhibitory stimulus control was obtained only from those Ss who still showed contrast prior to the generalization test.

At present, there is no information as to whether the stimulus-induced decrement described by Brown and Jenkins (1967) or the resistance to reinforcement effect described by Hearst *et al.* (1970) vary in their magnitude with extended training. It seems unlikely, however, that the Brown and Jenkins stimulus-produced effect would decrease with extended training. Just as one would expect S- to occasion the absence of responding indefinitely in a simple *MULT VI EXT* schedule, one would also expect the S— of the Brown and Jenkins experiment to have its effect indefinitely. However, as we shall see in Section VIII, it may turn out that the inhibitory effect described by Brown and Jenkins continues after S— has lost its aversive function or its ability to elicit emotional responses. On the other hand, inhibitory stimulus control may disappear as the emotional or aversive function of S— dissipates. What seems clear at present is that much experimentation is required to clarify just how the three measures we have discussed are related to one another.

## VIII. A Theory Regarding By-Products of Discrimination Learning

Our overview of the conditions under which one can obtain the by-products of discrimination learning described in this chapter has revealed two major ways in which they are related. None of them occurs following discrimination learning without errors. It is also the case that gross emotional responses, the aversiveness of S—, contrast, the frustration effect, and the peak shift tend to disappear with extended discrimination training. While not consistent, the little evidence available thus far on the permanence of inhibitory stimulus control indicates that, under certain conditions, inhibitory stimulus control also disappears with extended discrimination training. Our concern in this section will be to integrate these and other generalizations about by-products of discrimination learning into a theoretical framework, capable of specifying the conditions under which these by-products occur.

One of the first constraints we must consider in attempting to derive such a theoretical framework is the transitory nature of these by-products. What is required is a model of the acquisition of a discrimination rather than a "steady-state" model of discrimination performance. At present, however, we have neither an adequate model of the acquisition of a discrimination which can account for the by-products we have considered nor a steady-state model of discrimination performance which addresses itself to transitions from one steady-state to another. Accordingly, it seems prudent at this time to limit our goal to formulating a framework capable of integrating the available information on the acquisition of a discrimination.

It is worth noting that one possible benefit of a model of what takes place during the acquisition of a discrimination is that, if nothing more, it would stimulate the production of other models of acquisition. Recent attempts to create models of operantly-conditioned behavior have been almost entirely concerned with steady-state behavior, i.e. behavior which is free of the very transient characteristics of concern to the theorist interested in the acquisition of such behavior. Herrnstein (1970), for example, has recently proposed a set of equations which describes the rate of responding produced by certain multiple and concurrent schedules of reinforcement. Among the predictions which Herrnstein's model is capable of making is the rate of responding on various multiple schedules such as *MULT VI VI* or *MULT VI EXT*. While it is true that these equations can describe the results of a wide variety of experiments, they presently contain no provision for predicting the different rates of responding to S+ on a *MULT VI EXT* schedule following discrimination learning with and without errors. Nor can such equations predict the time course of behavioral contrast when it does occur. While one could cite additional findings that cannot be presently derived from Herrnstein's equations, the above examples should suffice to indicate that such steady-state equations cannot describe the transitory character of the by-products we have considered in this chapter.

Yet another problem with the equations of the type formulated by Herrnstein and others (e.g., Catania & Reynolds, 1968) for predicting the rate of responding on a multiple schedule is that the relative rate of reinforcement is the primary independent variable. While this variable can predict the rate of responding on a wide variety of multiple and concurrent schedules, there are some notable exceptions. Aside from errorless discrimination learning, which entails the same relative rate of reinforcement as discrimination learning with errors but which does not result in contrast, we have seen other examples of contrast developing under training conditions in which the relative frequencies of reinforcement correlated with different discriminative stimuli were the same (cf. Section IV, C, 1).

One experiment, not elaborated previously, is of special relevance in demonstrating that the rate of responding in a multiple schedule cannot always be specified by the relative frequency of reinforcement. In this experiment (Terrace, 1968, Experiment III), pigeons were trained on a *MULT VI drl* schedule following baseline training on a *VI* schedule. During the initial presentation of S2 some of the Ss responded at a low rate, most likely because of the change from the 580 nm stimulus correlated with the *VI* component to the 550 nm stimulus correlated with the *drl* component. These Ss continued to respond at a low rate throughout *MULT VI drl* training. The initial rate of responding in the *drl* component of the remaining Ss was much higher. With continued training, the *drl* rate of these Ss decreased to values comparable to the rate of those Ss who started responding in the *drl* component at a lower rate. In both cases the value of the *drl* was adjusted to insure that the frequency of reinforcement in S2 was at least as great as in S1. Contrast, however, occurred only in those instances in which the rate of responding in the *drl* component decreased from an initially high value to a stable low value. This experiment demonstrates that when reinforcement frequencies in S1 and S2 are maintained at an equal value, contrast occurs only when the rate of responding to S2 decreases. It appears, therefore, that relative reinforcement frequency will not suffice as an independent variable in a model of the acquisition of discrimination learning that is concerned with contrast.

At the same time we have also seen that a reduction in the rate of responding to a discriminative stimulus is not a sufficient condition for the occurrence of contrast. Reducing the rate of responding by administering free food does not necessarily produce contrast (cf. Wilkie, 1970). We are therefore left with the question of how reductions in the rate of responding that are generated by extinction (as in discrimination learning with errors), a *drl* schedule (as in a *MULT VI drl* schedule) or by punishment *(MULT VI VI + shock)* differ from a reduction in the rate of responding that results from free food administered in the presence of a discriminative stimulus. The most obvious difference would appear to be that in the first set of examples responding at a lower rate is required by the schedule in effect, and that the reduction in response rate is accompanied by an emotional reaction to S2. In the first set of examples it appears as if there is an *active holding back* of responding and that, in the second example, response suppression is absent. The organism presumably avoids making a response in the first set of examples in order to avoid the emotional consequences of nonreinforcement.

Two distinctly different types of experiments indicate that the effects of nonreinforced responding share certain properties of negative reinforcement. As described in Section VI, Grusec (1968) has reported that nonreinforced responding to S— and noncontingent electric shock delivered in the presence of an S— to which no responses were made had the equivalent effect of producing a peak-shift away from S—. As described in Section V, Terrace (1971b) has shown that, following discrimination learning with errors, S— functions as an aversive stimulus by demonstrating that responding which allows an S to escape from S— can be maintained at a high rate.

The available evidence concerning the aversiveness of responding on a *drl* schedule is also consistent with the evidence on the aversiveness of nonreinforced responding. Fantino (1968) has demonstrated that pigeons prefer a *VI* schedule (which does not require a low rate of responding) to a *drl* schedule. Subsequently, Weissman (1969) has shown that inhibitory stimulus control, with respect to the stimulus correlated with a *drl* schedule, is obtained following training on a *MULT VI drl* schedule.

The principle that emerges from these experiments is that discrimination training which uses contingencies resulting in the suppression of behavior in the presence of a discriminative stimulus establishes that stimulus as an inhibitory stimulus. In the previous section, we have seen that there appears to be a number of ways in which the inhibitory function of a stimulus can be measured. At this writing there are no data available which would allow us to consolidate these measures. Accordingly, the discussion which follows will emphasize initially inhibitory stimulus control. It is this measure which has been the most widely studied measure of inhibition in operant studies of discrimination learning.

In most of the examples we have considered thus far it seems that contingencies which result in a decrease in response rate also produce emotional responses. At present there is no way of arguing that emotional responses are a necessary condition for the establishment of inhibitory stimulus control. The evidence on hand, however, points to the suppression of responding as a basic characteristic of discrimination learning which results in the by-products we have described in this chapter. This observation provides a basis for distinguishing between two types of discrimination learning. Both types of discrimination learning share the characteristic that responding to two or more discriminative stimuli occurs at different rates. In one case, however, the S learns to respond to S+ and not to respond to S−. Not-responding is presumed to consist of responses which are *antagonistic* to the response to S+. This can be demonstrated by obtaining gradients of excitation centered around S+, and gradients of inhibition centered around S− (cf. Jenkins, 1965; Terrace, 1966b). In the second case, the S learns to respond to S+ but does not learn to make a response antagonistic to the response to S+ in the presence of S−. Not-responding following discrimination with errors is presumed to be of the second variety of not-responding postulated by Jenkins (1965). Examples of this type of not-responding includes pecking at objects in the experimental chamber, grooming, and so on.

Citing inhibitory stimulus control as the essential characteristic of the first type of discrimination learning is obviously consistent with the observations made in Section VI regarding the conditions under which the peak-shift occurs (cf. Hearst, 1968). Another interesting implication of our attempt to relate the by-products we have discussed to the establishment of inhibitory stimulus control is that it provides a basis for defining contrast without appealing to either the rate of responding or frequency of reinforcement in S2. Contrast could be defined simply as an increase in the strength of the response to S+ that results from alternating S+ with an inhibitory stimulus. This definition is of course similar to Pavlov's concept of positive induction. It is also consistent with Premack's observation that ". . . inhibition and contrast are two sides of the same coin [Premack, 1969, p. 130]." While much research would be required to establish the validity of this definition it does hold the promise of focusing interest on certain variables in the study of contrast which have yet to receive systematic study. For example, one wonders what would happen if S+ is alternated with a noncontingent primary or a secondary negative reinforcer. Such stimuli, whose inhibitory function could be demonstrated in other contexts, could be presented to a pigeon in the presence of a blank key. As noted previously, a blank key functions for a pigeon as an S− which occasions little or no responding. It does not seem unreasonable to expect an increase in the rate of responding to S+ of those Ss for whom S+ alternates with the inhibitory stimulus and no change in the rate of responding to S+ of those Ss for whom S+ was simply alternated with a blank key. This type of experiment could also be done following errorless discrimination training between S+ and a conventional S−. The results of a similar experiment on the peak-shift (Grusec, 1968) suggest that one would expect to obtain contrast only when an inhibitory stimulus is combined with an "errorless" S—.

Another important experiment which follows from the notion that contrast results when S+ is alternated with an inhibitory stimulus would examine the relationship between contrast and the interstimulus interval between components of a multiple schedule. As noted in Section V, this interval is usually of short duration. If one assumes, however, that the inhibitory effect of S— dissipates during a prolonged interstimulus interval, one would expect less contrast as the duration of the interstimulus intervals increases. It would also be interesting to determine whether or not the peak-shift is influenced by the value of the interstimulus interval in effect during discrimination training and during the generalization test.

While one can continue to suggest many other ways in which the concept of inhibitory stimulus control can be used to account for the occurrence of other by-products of discrimination learning, a number of problems must be solved before one can feel secure in citing inhibitory stimulus control as a necessary condition for the occurrence of such by-products. These have to do with the permanence of inhibitory stimulus control and the relationship between inhibitory stimulus control and other measures of inhibition. If contrast, the peak-shift, and the aversive function of S— are not permanent characteristics of discrimination performance, and if one assumes that inhibitory stimulus control is a necessary precursor of these phenomena, one would hope that inhibitory stimulus control also disappeared with extended discrimination training. The evidence we have considered on this matter has been inconclusive. Two studies (Farthing & Hearst, 1968; Selekman, 1970) failed to obtain a change in the shape of relative gradients of inhibition during extended discrimination training. However, another study (Yarczower, 1970) found that the value of the slope of absolute gradients of inhibition declined to zero with extended training. It should be noted that in both the Farthing and Hearst and in the Selekman studies, contrast was also maintained throughout discrimination training. In Yarczower's study, however, which failed to obtain inhibitory stimulus control after extended discrimination training, contrast had disappeared prior to the test for inhibitory stimulus control. Thus, all of these studies showed a consistent relationship between the occurrence of contrast and the occurrence of inhibitory stimulus control.

Even if it is shown that inhibitory stimulus control does disappear with extended discrimination training, there remains the question of how inhibitory stimulus control is related to the stimulus-induced decrement in excitation which Hearst *et al.* (1970) have cited as the least ambiguous evidence of inhibition. While no evidence is available concerning the permanence of this phenomenon, we have noted previously that there is little reason to believe that the inhibitory effect demonstrated by the Brown and Jenkins experiment would disappear during extended discrimination training. Just as one does not expect to see a restoration of responding to S— in a simple *MULT VI EXT* schedule as discrimination training continues, one would not expect the inhibitory effect of the tone used in the Brown and Jenkins experiment to decrease with extended discrimination training. If we assume that inhibition is a necessary condition for the occurrence of contrast as well as of the peak-shift and the aversive function of S—, how can we reconcile the presumed permanence of one measure of inhibition with the impermanence of contrast and other by-products of discrimination learning?

The best answer to this question would appear to derive from Jenkins' analysis of the two types of not-responding in the presence of S—: responses which are antagonistic to the response to S+ and "other behavior." At the start of discrimination training with errors, or more generally, discrimination training in which some contingency produces a reduction in the rate of responding to S2, the subject presumably learns to make a response antagonistic to the response to S+. At this point, one would expect to see both inhibitory stimulus control and an increment in responding to S+ when S2 is alternated with S+. Learning specifically not to respond to S2 is presumed to be a consequence of an emotional response that was evoked by nonreinforcement. Since this emotional response declines in strength with increased exposure to S2 (during which nonreinforced responding occurs less frequently), one would expect fewer nonresponses of the antagonistic variety in the presence of S2 as discrimination training continues. The decline of nonresponding of the antagonistic variety does not, of course, mean that responding to S2 increases with further exposure to S2. It is rather the case that one would expect an increase in the second type of nonresponding, i.e. not-responding which consists of grooming, pecking at particles of food on the floor, and so on. Since it is assumed that only the antagonistic type of nonresponding is under the stimulus control of S2, one would expect inhibitory stimulus control to disappear with extended training. However, since S2 continues to occasion the second type of not-responding, one would expect to obtain a decrement in excitation whenever S2 is combined with S+.

The above analysis assumes that not-responding of the antagonistic variety is under stimulus control, whereas the second type of nonresponding is not. Ultimately, this question must be put to experimental test. An obvious place to start would be to vary the frequency of the inhibitory tone in the Brown and Jenkins paradigm at different stages of discrimination training. This experiment would seek to determine whether frequencies other than the training frequency will inhibit responding. A U-shaped gradient obtained after extended discrimination training from such an experiment should not, however, be regarded as a refutation of the present analysis which assumes that the two types of not-responding hypothesized by Jenkins can be used to distinguish initial and terminal *performance*. It may prove necessary to devise more sensitive techniques for distinguishing between the two types of not-responding proposed by Jenkins. One interesting possibility would be an experiment which measured electromyographically what happens in the presence of S−. If antagonistic responses do in fact define one category of not-responding, electromyographic recordings may provide a basis for distinguishing this type of not-responding from the second category described above.

An important conclusion to be derived from the present analysis is that terminal performance following discrimination learning with errors is identical to the initial performance following discrimination learning without errors. Because nonreinforced responding did not occur in the presence of S−, it is assumed that antagonistic not-responding in the presence of S− do not develop. Not-responding to S− could be accounted for entirely by the second type of not-responding. As a result, one would not expect to see any evidence of inhibitory stimulus control. In this sense S− is neutral. S− does, however, occasion the second type of not-responding. Thus, when S− is combined with S+, one may obtain a decrement in responding. This is exactly the state of affairs one would expect after extended discrimination training following discrimination learning with errors.

## IX. Conclusions

Learning to make a response antagonistic to the response to S+ in the presence of a discriminative stimulus appears to be a sufficient condition for the establishment of contrast, the aversive function of S−, and the peak-shift. It appears that an S may learn not to respond to S− in order to avoid aversive emotional responses that follow nonreinforced responding. As a result, S− becomes a signal for making a response antagonistic to the response to S+. This tendency can be demonstrated when S+ and S− are on orthogonal continua by varying the value of test stimuli and showing that, as the distance between S− and the test stimulus increases, there is less of a tendency not to respond to the test stimulus, i.e., more responding occurs to the test stimulus as the distance between S− and that test stimulus increases.

An immediate consequence of the acquisition of stimulus control over not responding by S− is an increase in the strength of the response to S+. This effect is presumed to be an aftereffect of witholding responses to S−. In this sense, our conclusion regarding the relationship between contrast and inhibition is similar to Premack's observation that ". . . inhibition and contrast are two sides of the same coin [Premack, 1969, p. 130]."

Inhibitory stimulus control can be related to the peak-shift through the combination of relative gradients of excitation and inhibition. Hearst (1968) using the same approach followed by Spence and his analysis of transposition, has shown that the peak-shift can be derived from a combination of relative excitatory gradient and a relative inhibitory gradient.

Since it is assumed that inhibitory stimulus control results from the emotional response of frustration, which occurs in the presence of S−, one would expect inhibitory stimulus control, the aversive function of S−, contrast, and the peak-shift to disappear following extended discrimination training during which nonreinforced responding no longer occurred. The evidence on contrast, the peak-shift, and the aversive function of S− indicate that these phenomena are not permanent characteristics of discrimination performance. The little evidence available on the permanence of inhibitory stimulus control is inconclusive.

Of equal interest in understanding the dependence of the other by-products of discrimination learning we have considered on inhibition is the relationship between inhibitory stimulus control and other measures of inhibition (cf. Hearst *et al.*, 1970). It is hoped that such information will soon provide a basis for determining the validity of the hypothesis concerning the two different types of discrimination learning that has been presented in this chapter. Both types of discrimination learning result in differential responding to two or more discriminative stimuli. It is assumed, however, that inhibitory stimulus control is established only in the first type of discrimination learning, and that inhibitory stimulus control is a sufficient condition for the occurrence of the aversive function of S−, contrast, and the peak-shift.

## REFERENCES

Adelman, H. M., & Maatsch, J. L. Learning and extinction based upon frustration, food reward and exploratory tendency. *Journal of Experimental Psychology*, 1956, 52, 311–315.

Amsel, A. The role of frustrative non-reward in noncontinuous reward situations. *Psychological Bulletin*, 1958, 55, 102–119.

Amsel, A. Frustrative non-reward in partial reinforcement and discrimination learning; Some recent history and a theoretical extension. *Psychological Review*, 1962, 69, 306–328.

Amsel, A. Positive induction, behavioral contrast, and generalization of inhibition in discrimination learning. In H. H. Kendler, & J. T. Spence (Eds.), *Essays in neobehaviorism: A memorial volume for Kenneth W. Spence.* New York: Appleton-Century-Crofts, 1971.

Amsel, A., & Roussel, J. Motivational properties of frustration: I. Effect on a running response of the addition of frustration to the motivational complex. *Journal of Experimental Psychology*, 1952, 43, 363–368.

Amsel, A., & Ward, J. S. Frustration and persistence: Resistance to discrimination following prior experience with the discriminanda. *Psychological Monographs*, 1965, 79 (4, Whole No. 597).

Azrin, N. H., Hutchinson, R. R., & Hake, D. F. Extinction-induced aggression. *Journal of the Experimental Analysis of Behavior*, 1966, 9, 191–204.

Bernheim, J. W. Comment. *Psychonomic Science*, 1968, 11, 327.

Bloomfield, T. M. Two types of behavioral contrast in discrimination learning. *Journal of the Experimental Analysis of Behavior*, 1966, 9, 155–161.

Bloomfield, T. M. Behavioral contrast and relative reinforcement frequency in two multiple schedules. *Journal of the Experimental Analysis of Behavior*, 1967, 10, 151–158.

Bloomfield, T. M. Discrimination learning in animals; an analysis through side-effects. *Nature (London)*, 1968, 217, 929–930.

Bloomfield, T. M., Behavioral contrast and the peak-shift. In R. M. Gilbert & N. S. Sutherland (Eds.), *Animal discrimination learning.* New York: Academic Press, 1969.

Blough, D. S. The shape of some wavelength generalization gradients. *Journal of the Experimental Analysis of Behavior*, 1961, 4, 31–40.

Blough, D. S. Discrimination learning. In R. S. Woodworth and H. Schlosberg (Eds.), *Experimental psychology.* New York: Holt, Rinehart & Winston, 1971, in press.

Boneau, C. A., & Axelrod, S. Work decrement and reminiscence in pigeon operant responding. *Journal of Experimental Psychology*, 1962, 64, 352–354.

Brown, P. L., & Jenkins, H. M. Conditioned inhibition and excitation in operant discrimination learning. *Journal of Experimental Psychology*, 1967, 75, 255–266.

Brown, P. L., & Jenkins, H. M. Auto-shaping of the pigeon's key-peck. *Journal of the Experimental Analysis of Behavior*, 1968, 11, 1-8.

Brownstein, A. J., & Hughes, R. G. The role of response suppression in behavioral contrast: Signaled reinforcement. *Psychonomic Science*, 1970, 18, 50-52.

Brownstein, A. J., & Newsom, C. Behavioral contrast in multiple schedules with equal reinforcement rates. *Psychonomic Science*, 1970, 18, 25-26.

Catania, A. C. Concurrent performances: reinforcement interaction and response independence. *Journal of the Experimental Analysis of Behavior*, 1963, 6, 253-263.

Catania, A. C. Reinforcement schedules and psychophysical judgments. In W. N. Schoenfeld (Ed.), *The theory of reinforcement schedules*. New York: Appleton-Century-Crofts, 1970.

Catania, A. C., & Gill, C. A. Inhibition and behavioral contrast. *Psychonomic Science*, 1964, 1, 257-258.

Catania, A. C., & Reynolds, G. S. A quantitative analysis of the responding maintained by interval schedules of reinforcement. *Journal of the Experimental Analysis of Behavior*, 1968, 11, 327-383.

Cowan, R. E. Peak-shift following classical conditioning. Unpublished master's thesis, University of Missouri, 1968.

Crespi, L. P. Amount of reinforcement and the level of performance. *Psychological Review*, 1944, 51, 341-357.

Daly, H. B. Learning of a hurdle-jump response to escape cues paired with reduced reward or frustrative non-reward. *Journal of the Experimental Analysis of Behavior*, 1969, 12, 146-157.

Davenport, J. W., Flaherty, C. F., & Dryud, J. P. Temporal persistence of frustration effects in monkeys and rats. *Psychonomic Science*, 1966, 6, 411-412.

Davenport, J. W., & Thompson, C. I. The Amsel frustration effect in monkeys. *Psychonomic Science*, 1965, 3, 481-482.

Deutsch, J. Discrimination learning and inhibition. *Science*, 1967, 156, 988.

Dunham, P. J. Contrasted conditions of reinforcement: a selective critique. *Psychological Bulletin*, 1968, 69, 295-315.

Fantino, E. Effect of required rates of responding upon choice. *Journal of the Experimental Analysis of Behavior*, 1968, 11, 15-22.

Farthing, G. W., & Hearst, E. Generalization gradients of inhibition after different amounts of training. *Journal of the Experimental Analysis of Behavior*, 1968, 11, 743-752.

Ferster, C. B. Control of behavior in chimpanzees and pigeons by time out from positive reinforcement. *Psychological Monographs*, 1958, 72(8, Whole No. 461).

Ferster, C. B., & Skinner, B. F. *Schedules of reinforcement*. New York: Appleton-Century-Crofts, 1957.

Friedman, H., & Guttman, N. Further analysis of the various effects of discrimination training on stimulus generalization gradients. In D. I. Mostofsky (Ed.), *Stimulus generalization*. Stanford, Calif.: Stanford University Press, 1965.

Grusec, T. The peak-shift in stimulus generalization: Equivalent effects of errors and non-contingent shock. *Journal of the Experimental Analysis of Behavior*, 1968, 11, 39-49.

Guttman, N. Generalization gradients around stimuli associated with different reinforcement schedules. *Journal of Experimental Psychology,* 1959, **58,** 335-340.

Guttman, N. Effects of discrimination formation on generalization measured from a positive-rate baseline. In D. I. Mostofsky (Ed.), *Stimulus generalization.* Stanford, Calif.: Stanford University Press, 1965.

Guttman, N., & Kalish, H. I. Discriminability and stimulus generalization. *Journal of Experimental Psychology,* 1956, **51,** 79-88.

Gynther, M. D. Differential eyelid conditioning as a function of stimulus similarity and strength of response to the CS. *Journal of Experimental Psychology,* 1957, **53,** 408-416.

Hanson, H. M. Effects of discrimination training on stimulus generalization. *Journal of Experimental Psychology,* 1959, **58,** 321-334.

Hearst, E. Discrimination learning as the summation of excitation and inhibition. *Science,* 1968, **162,** 1303-1306.

Hearst, E., Besley, S., & Farthing, G. W. Inhibition and the stimulus control of operant behavior. *Journal of the Experimental Analysis of Behavior,* 1970, 14 (Suppl.).

Herrnstein, R. J. On the law of effect. *Journal of the Experimental Analysis of Behavior,* 1970, 13, 243-266.

Honig, W. K., Boneau, C. A., Burstein, K. R., & Pennypacker, H. S. Positive and negative generalization gradients obtained after equivalent training conditions. *Journal of Comparative Psychological Psychology,* 1963, **56,** 111-116.

Honig, W. K., Thomas, D. R., & Guttman, N. Differential effects of massed extinction and discrimination training on the generalization gradient. *Journal of Experimental Psychology,* 1959, **58,** 145-152.

Hull, C. L. *Principles of behavior.* New York: Appleton-Century-Crofts, 1943.

Hull, C. L. Stimulus intensity Dynamism (V) and stimulus generalization. *Psychological Review,* 1949, **56,** 67-76.

Hull, C. L. *A behavior system: An introduction to behavior theory concerning the individual organism.* New Haven, Conn.: Yale University Press, 1952.

Jenkins, H. M. The effect of discrimination training on extinction. *Journal of Experimental Psychology,* 1961, **61,** 111-121.

Jenkins, H. M. Generalization gradients and the concept of inhibition. In D. I. Mostofsky (Ed.), *Stimulus generalization.* Stanford, Calif.: Stanford University Press, 1965.

Jenkins, H. M., & Harrison, R. H. Generalization gradients of inhibition following auditory discrimination learning. *Journal of the Experimental Analysis of Behavior,* 1962, 5, 435-441.

Kaufman, A., & Baron, A. Use of withdrawal of reinforcement with the escape-avoidance paradigm. *Psychological Reports,* 1966, 19, 959-965.

Kiernan, C. C. Positive reinforcement by light: Comments on Lockard's article. *Psychological Bulletin,* 1964, **62,** 351-357.

La Berge, D. Generalization gradients in a discrimination situation. *Journal of Experimental Psychology,* 1961, 1, 88-94.

Leitenberg, H. Is time-out from positive reinforcement an aversive event? A review of experimental evidence. *Psychological Bulletin,* 1965, **65,** 428-441.

Lockard, R. B. Some effects of light upon the behavior of rodents. *Psychological Bulletin,* 1963, **60,** 509-529.

Loucks, R. B. An appraisal of Pavlov's systematization of behavior from the experimental standpoint. *Journal of Comparative Psychology*, 1933, **15**, 1-47.

Lyons, J. Stimulus generalization as a function of discrimination learning with and without errors. *Science*, 1969, 163, 490-491.

MacKinnon, J. R., & Amsel, A. Magnitude of the frustration effect as a function of confinement and detention in the frustrating situation. *Journal of Experimental Psychology*, 1964, 67, 468-474.

Miller, N. E., & Stevenson, S. S. Agitated behavior of rats during experimental extinction and a curve of spontaneous recovery. *Journal of Comparative Psychology*, 1936, 21, 205-231.

Morse, W. H., & Herrnstein, R. J. The maintenance of avoidance behavior using the removal of a conditioned positive reinforcer as the aversive stimulus. *American Psychologist*, 1956, 11, 430. (Abstract)

Nevin, J. A. Differential reinforcement and stimulus control of not-responding. *Journal of the Experimental Analysis of Behavior*, 1968, 11, 715-726.

Nevin, J. A. Stimulus control. In J. A. Nevin (Ed.), *Contemporary experimental psychology*. Chicago: Scott-Foresman, 1971, in press.

Nevin, J. A., & Shettleworth, S. J. An analysis of contrast effects in multiple schedules. *Journal of the Experimental Analysis of Behavior*, 1966, **9**, 305-315.

Pavlov, I. P. *Conditioned reflexes*. (Transl. by G. V. Anrep) London: The Clarendon Press, 1927.

Pierrel, R., & Sherman, J. G. Generalization of auditory intensity following discrimination training. *Journal of the Experimental Analysis of Behavior*, 1960, 3, 313-322.

Pierrel, R., & Sherman, J. G. Generalization and discrimination as a function of the $S^D-S^\Delta$ intensity difference. *Journal of the Experimental Analysis of Behavior*, 1962, 5, 67-71.

Premack, D. On some boundary conditions of contrast. In J. Tapp (Ed.), *Reinforcement and behavior*. New York: Academic Press, 1969, 136.

Premack, D. A functional analysis of language. *Journal of the Experimental Analysis of Behavior*, 1970, 14, 107-125.

Ramsey, D. A. Cardiac activity in the rhesus monkey under several classical conditioning procedures and operant avoidance. Unpublished doctoral dissertation, Columbia University, 1969.

Rescorla, R. A. Pavlovian conditioned inhibition. *Psychological Bulletin*, 1969, 72, 77-94.

Reynolds, G. S. Behavioral contrast. *Journal of the Experimental Analysis of Behavior*, 1961, 4, 57-71. (a)

Reynolds, G. S. Relativity of response rate and reinforcement frequency in a multiple schedule. *Journal of the Experimental Analysis of Behavior*, 1961, 4, 179-184. (b)

Reynolds, G. S., & Catania, A. C. Temporal discrimination in pigeons. *Science*, 1962, 4, 387-391.

Reynolds, G. S., & Limpo, A. J. On some causes of behavioral contrast. *Journal of the Experimental Analysis of Behavior*, 1968, 11, 543-547.

Rilling, M., Askew, H. R., Ahlskog, J. E., & Kramer, T. J. Aversive properties of the negative stimulus in a successive discrimination. *Journal of the*

*Experimental Analysis of Behavior,* 1969, 12, 917-932.

Rosen, A., & Terrace, H. S. Excitatory and inhibitory stimulus control following massed extinction. 1971, in preparation.

Scull, J., Davies, D., & Amsel, A. Behavioral contrast and frustration effect in multiple fixed interval schedules. *Journal of Comparative and Physiological Psychology,* 1971, in press.

Selekman, W. Gradients of preference and post-discrimination gradients along the wavelength continuum following training to a white light. Unpublished doctoral dissertation, Columbia University, 1970.

Skinner, B. F. *The behavior of organisms; an experimental analysis.* New York: Appleton-Century, 1938.

Spence, K. W. The nature of discrimination learning in animals. *Psychological Review,* 1936, 43, 427-449.

Spence, K. W. The differential response in animals to stimuli varying within a single dimension. *Psychological Review,* 1937, 44, 430-444.

Staddon, J., & Innis, N. An effect analogous to frustration on variable reinforcement schedules. *Psychonomic Science,* 1966, 4, 287-288.

Stevens, S. S. On the psychophysical law. *Psychological Review,* 1957, 64, 153-181.

Stevenson, J. G. Stimulus generalization: The ordering and spacing of test stimuli. *Journal of the Experimental Analysis of Behavior,* 1966, 9, 457-468.

Terrace, H. S. Discrimination learning with and without errors. *Journal of the Experimental Analysis of Behavior,* 1963, 6, 1-27. (a)

Terrace, H. S. Errorless transfer of a discrimination across two continua. *Journal of the Experimental Analysis of Behavior,* 1963, 6, 223-232. (b)

Terrace, H. S. Wavelength generalization after discrimination learning with and without errors. *Science,* 1964, 144, 78-80.

Terrace, H. S. Behavioral contrast and the peak-shift. *Journal of the Experimental Analysis of Behavior,* 1966, 9, 613-317. (a)

Terrace, H. S. Discrimination learning and inhibition. *Science,* 1966, 154, 1677-1680. (b)

Terrace, H. S. Stimulus control. In W. K. Honig (Ed.), *Operant behavior: Areas of research and application.* New York: Appleton-Century-Crofts, 1966. (c)

Terrace, H. S. Discrimination learning and inhibition (reply to Deutsch). *Science,* 1967, 156, 988-989.

Terrace, H. S. Discrimination learning, the peak-shift, and behavioral contrast. *Journal of the Experimental Analysis of Behavior,* 1968, 11, 727-741.

Terrace, H. S. Aversive properties of S−. In N. S. Sutherland (Chm.) Discrimination learning. Symposium presented at the XIX International Congress of Psychology, London, 1969.

Terrace, H. S. Discrimination learning and the concept of inhibition. Paper presented at Symposium on Inhibition, University of Sussex, Brighton, Great Britain, 1971. (a)

Terrace, H. S. Escape from S−. *Learning and Motivation,* 1971, 2, in press. (b)

Thomas, D. R., Ost, J., & Thomas, D. Stimulus generalization as a function of the time between training and testing procedures. *Journal of the Experimental Analysis of Behavior,* 1960, 3, 9-14.

Wagner, A. R. Conditioned frustration as a learned drive. *Journal of Experimental Psychology,* 1963, 66, 142-148.

Wagner, A. R. Frustrative non-reward: A variety of punishment. In B. A. Campbell & R. M. Church (Eds.), *Punishment and aversive behavior.* New York: Appleton-Century-Crofts, 1969.

Weissman, R. G. Some determinants of inhibitory stimulus control. *Journal of the Experimental Analysis of Behavior,* 1969, 12, 443–450.

Wilkie, D. M. On some determinants of behavioral contrast. Unpublished doctoral dissertation, University of Manitoba, 1970.

Wilton, R. N., & Godbout, R. C. Stimulus control in discrimination learning. *British Journal of Psychology,* 1970, 61, 109–114.

Yarczower, M. Behavioral contrast and inhibitive stimulus control. *Psychonomic Science,* 1970, 18, 1–3.

Yarczower, M., Dickson, J. F., & Gollub, L. R. Some effects on generalization gradients of tandem schedules. *Journal of the Experimental Analysis of Behavior,* 1966, 9, 631–639.

# SERIAL LEARNING AND DIMENSIONAL ORGANIZATION

*Sheldon M. Ebenholtz*

UNIVERSITY OF WISCONSIN, MADISON, WISCONSIN[1]

## I. Introduction

The vocal mechanisms of the larynx so constrain the output of speech sounds that linguistic utterances must be produced in temporal succession rather than simultaneously. It follows that the proper reception of speech sounds and their decoding into meaningful linguistic units, such as words and phrases, is critically dependent upon order information. In a general sense the processing of auditory information produces temporally extended units such as melodies and linguistic sound patterns. Thus, even though one may have multiple simultaneous inputs to the auditory apparatus, as in the case of a large orchestra, perception is rarely that of the instruments sounding simultaneously over some short cross-section of time. Rather it is characteristically that of events extended in the temporal domain, organized according to sound quality, beat, etc. Even this brief analysis of auditory input and verbal output may

[1] Present address: Dalhousie University, Halifax, N.S., Canada.

suffice as an illustration of the importance of temporal-order information in such basic activities as speaking and listening. One should not be surprised to find, therefore, that psychologists have long believed temporal-order information to be crucial to an adequate understanding of verbal learning.

The experimental study of serial learning began with the creative insights of Hermann Ebbinghaus (1885). Simply put, Ebbinghaus was able to transform the doctrine of philosophical associationism into the empirically founded discipline known today as verbal learning. Although this task required considerable independence of thought, Ebbinghaus was not able to free himself of the dominant conception of associationism, i.e., the principle that the order in which ideas recur reflects the order of the original experience. Accordingly, Ebbinghaus assumed that the ability to recall a string of words in some constant sequence was attributable to the presence of associative bonds between each word and its immediately succeeding neighbor. Furthermore, these bonds were assumed to exist between nonadjacent terms as well. Thus, Ebbinghaus wrote:

> ... the associative threads, which hold together a remembered series, are spun not merely between each member and its immediate successor, but beyond intervening members to every member which stands to it in any close temporal relation. The strength of the threads varies with the distance of the members, but even the weaker of them must be considered as relatively of considerable significance [p.94].

It is now apparent that Ebbinghaus' connectionist views have been extraordinarily influential in shaping the explanations offered by modern psychologists for many of the phenomena of verbal learning.

The present chapter explores alternative conceptions to those of Ebbinghaus concerning serial learning with particular emphasis on the role of organizational processes.

## II. The Information Available after Serial Learning

Consider a set of 10 consonant—vowel—consonant (CVC) nonsense syllables to have been learned by the method of anticipation to a criterion of one perfect recitation of the entire list. What information has the $S$ acquired? He has, of course, learned to output the items in a constant order and hence some information, such as the items themselves, is entailed by the learning of the sequence. Other information such as the position of an item is not logically entailed by sequence learning, for it is perfectly possible to recall in order without knowing the list positions of the component terms except for each succeeding item relative to the preceding one. The present section serves to identify several types of information obtained as a result of learning a serial list.

## A. Item Learning and Contextual Associations

Early in learning, even before a substantial number of correct responses are made, Ss show evidence of having learned the individual items by yielding a combination of intralist intrusions (ILIs) and correct responses. The former tend to be distributed as a bowed function of serial position (Deese & Kresse, 1952; Harcum & Coppage, 1969), with middle positions showing greater numbers of ILIs than end positions, but also providing the source of the ILIs, i.e., ILIs tend both to occur at central serial positions and to come from these same locations. On the other hand, correct responses occur early in learning primarily at the beginning and end positions and tend *not* to be given as intrusions elsewhere in the list. It is readily established then that the capability of recalling items (i.e., response availability) occurs rapidly in serial learning. Of course, after reaching final criterion, free recall tests clearly indicate that the items are available for recall outside of the serial anticipation procedure (Postman & Rau, 1957). It is also the case that items whose availability may not be in question, such as common nouns, come very quickly to form a circumscribed response set such that the S restricts his response output exclusively to those items composing the serial list. Presumably, the establishment of contextual associations (e.g., McGovern, 1964) may underlie both response availability and the formation of a retrieval context (i.e., a selector mechanism, Underwood & Schulz, 1960) in which recall is restricted to the relevant response set. The concept of "contextual association" is, of course, in need of greater elaboration than is now available. For example, it is by no means clear that a contextual association has properties equivalent to an interitem association. This problem, however, is not as critical to the present discussion as to the problem of free recall (e.g., Asch & Ebenholtz, 1962a; Tulving, 1968).

## B. Item Location and Interitem Associations

In 1920, Woodworth and Poffenberger described serial learning as entailing two types of associations. They observed,

Evidently the first member of the list is associated with the first position, so that the effort to begin the list calls up the first member. Were it not for this association with position, there would apparently be nothing to recall the first member. The last member can also be shown to be associated with its position, for it is often rightly recalled when the preceding member is wrong. Hence it is probably that the advantage of the very first and last members is largely due to association with their positions. The middle terms do not become strongly associated with their position for the reasons that the positions are themselves vague and not sharply perceived. The associations which operate to recall the middle terms are mostly sequential connections of the terms one with another [Woodworth & Poffenberger, 1920, p.72].

We have here one of the earliest statements of a dual process model of serial learning although attempts to evaluate experimentally a dual process model did not occur until quite recently (Ebenholtz, 1963a; Young, 1962, 1968). It would appear that the assumption that Ss use position cues in serial learning was not as attractive to researchers as the association models in the Ebbinghaus tradition (e.g., Bugelski, 1950).

It is perhaps worth noting that the notion of association with temporal and spatial position was not newly formulated with Woodworth and Poffenberger but occurred earlier in the works of G. E. Müller and his students (e.g., Gamble & Wilson, 1916; Müller & Schumann, 1894). In more recent times prior to 1960, position associations in a serial list had been acknowledged, although infrequently, as playing a minor role in serial learning. For example, Irion (1946) showed Retroactive Inhibition (RI) in the serial learning of original and interpolated lists composed of the identical sets of adjectives but in different serial orders, and Melton and Irwin (1940), in their widely cited study of RI, recognized the role of position identity as a mediator of interlist intrusions. This study, based upon the successive learning of two *serial* lists, was most influential in developing the notion of unlearning as an explanatory device in accounts of RI, although this concept as applied in contemporary research refers almost exclusively to paired-associate paradigms. An additional exemplary study is that of Schulz (1955). Based upon a suggestion of Underwood that generalization may occur among serial positions, Schulz designed a study which investigated the ability of Ss to indicate the ordinal number of the serial position of items taken in random order from a recently learned serial list. This study clearly showed that position information was present as a result of serial learning, but that severe limits to the accuracy of position naming also existed. There were, thus, various hints throughout the history of verbal learning that position information was available to Ss, and that position functioned as a stimulus, at least to some extent. It was not until the 1960s, however, that the role of position cues in serial learning was actively investigated, many times with strikingly similar paradigms, yet in widely separated laboratories.

The search for evidence concerning the role of position cues in serial learning has been based largely, though not exclusively, on the use of transfer paradigms (e.g., Ebenholtz, 1963b; Keppel & Saufley, 1964; Young, 1962). In Young's study, Ss learned two serial lists in succession with the second list containing the identical items as the first. Half of these items retained their first-list positions, the remaining items being redistributed into new positions on a random basis. Also included was a control condition in which the second serial list contained all new items relative to the first. Young found that although items whose positions remained unchanged were learned with greater percentages of correct responses than were items at rearranged positions, the control condition, having no repeated items, was learned in fewer trials than the experimental condition. This finding was also shown by Keppel and Saufley (1964). Thus, it would appear that position identity is a condition of negative transfer, a conclusion that can hardly be used in support of the contention that position cues facilitate serial learning.

A similar transfer paradigm was used by Ebenholtz (1963b), in which the transfer list for Group I contained items half of which were matinained at their old serial positions. However, in contrast with the transfer lists of Young (1962) and Keppel and Saufley (1964), the remaining positions of the transfer list were filled with new items, not having appeared at all in the first list. A control group, learning a completely new second list, was also included and, in addition, a mediation control group was provided.[1a] In this latter condition every other item on the transfer list was repeated from the first list, but their serial positions were at least four steps displaced. However, the relative order of these displaced items was preserved on the two serial lists. For all three groups, the first list may be represented by the sequence A-B-C-D-E-F-G-H-I-J-A. The second list of Group I maintained the position identity of every other item, and these alternated with new items. The latter are indicated by the letter

---

[1a] The full description of this group was omitted from a frequently cited review by Jensen and Rohwer (1965). These authors then proceeded to indicate (correctly) the shortcomings of a study lacking just such a control condition!

K in the sequence $K_1$-B-$K_2$-D-$K_3$-F-$K_4$-H-$K_5$-J-$K_1$. The second list of the mediation control group (Group II) contained the identical sequence as the first group, but the repeated items were at least four positions removed from their original list 1 locations, e.g., F-$K_4$-H-$K_5$J-$K_1$-B-$K_2$-D-$K_3$-F. Note that in order to match the sequences of Groups I and II each list had to be constituted of a closed "chain." This was accomplished by repeating the initial item at the end of each list. Both Groups I and II represent a condition in which the repeated items of the second list may be mediated, as suggested by Young (1962), by the occurrence of the appropriate nonrepeated stimulus from the first list, e.g., H on List 2 may produce, implicitly or otherwise, its List 1 response, I, which in turn might facilitate the List 2 response, J. If such mediation were in fact responsible for the increased levels of learning of repeated items, one should expect Groups I and II to learn the repeated items at equivalent rates. This outcome would constitute evidence for mediation and against the positive role of position identity. Comparisons with a control group (Group III), in which the second list contained no repeated List 1 items, permitted an estimate of the positive or negative direction of transfer.

The results clearly showed that only those repeated items that occurred in the same position on both lists (Group I) were learned at a faster rate than corresponding control items (Group III), i.e., repeated items that occurred at displaced positions (Group II) were learned at rates equivalent to that of nonrepeated items (Group III). Thus, the study provided no evidence for mediation, but demonstrated the positive role of position identity. Furthermore, relative to Group III, the repeated syllables of Group I showed positive transfer, and this stands in contrast with the overall negative transfer found by Keppel and Saufley (1964) and Young (1962). Assuming that these studies also showed negative transfer for the subset of items repeated in position, then the most obvious reason for the different results is the use of new items by Ebenholtz, rather than repeated List 1 items at displaced or scrambled List-2 positions. Because of the change in position information, repeating an item at a displaced position may be a condition of negative transfer, hence designs that include such items together with items that maintain the same serial position across lists, actually represent a net positive and negative effect. Add to this the presence of associative interference due to the recombining of some first-list interitem associations in List 2 (i.e., A-B, A-$B_r$), and the final outcome of overall negative transfer is at least not surprising. It is true that the recombining of some first-list associations should lead to associative interference in Ebenholtz's experiment as well, but in this case the A-B, A-D paradigm is applicable and this generally produces less interference than A-B, A-B$_r$. The serial-to-serial transfer paradigms are thus not without some interpretative difficulty; nevertheless, they do lend support to the assumption that position information plays a positive role in serial learning.

A second paradigm, or variants of it, also has been used to investigate the role of position cues in serial learning. The logic rests on the assumption that position, of necessity a relational concept, is defined in terms of the boundaries, i.e., the beginning and end of the series. It follows that position information would be rendered useless if not totally eliminated by beginning the series with a different term on each trial.[2] In a sense, this approach is similar to that discussed above, in that the trial-to-trial transfer of position information in principle could not take place in the absence of constant position cues. The various experimenters who have employed this paradigm uniformly have shown a slower rate of learning with the varied starting syllable method in comparison with the conventional method (e.g., Bowman & Thurlow, 1963; Ebenholtz, 1963b; Lippman & Denny, 1964; Saufley, 1967; Winnick & Dornbush, 1963). The interesting question as to whether S organizes the sequence by establishing his own beginning and perhaps end syllable as well remains unanswered ( K. Breckenridge, Hakes, & Young, 1965; Keppel, 1965).

That S has formed direct interitem associations as a result of serial learning was assumed by Ebbinghaus (1885), although he did not offer a direct test of this proposition. It was, rather, the notion of remote associations that appeared to require experimental verification and indeed many investigators since Ebbinghaus have turned to this task (Slamecka, 1964). One technique for investigating remote associations has been termed the Association Method (McGeoch & Irion, 1952), for it requires S to associate, i.e., to respond with an item, when presented with each term chosen randomly from a recently learned serial list. When Ss respond to the stimulus term with items from nonadjacent positions in the serial list, they are said to have produced evidence of remote associations. Since the degree of separation between a stimulus term and its associate

---

[2] In order to avoid gaps this procedure requires that the series begin and end with a common term, e.g., on Trial 1 the series would be represented as A-B-C-D-E-A, whereas on Trial 2 S might learn the sequence C-D-E-A-B-C.

was assumed to correlate with associative strength, i.e., the greater the degree of remoteness, the weaker the associative strength, the frequency of remote associates was expected to diminish with degree of remoteness (e.g., McGeoch, 1936).

There are problems with the interpretation of remote association studies, not the least of which stems from the fact that the adjacent, i.e., correct associate should always have an associative strength greater than any remote associate. Hence, the very occurrence of remote associations is itself anomalous without additional conceptions such as response oscillation, etc. In the present context, it may be noted that the Association Method yields correct (viz., zero degree remote) associates as well as errors (viz., remote associates), and this former category can be offered as evidence that as a result of serial learning Ss have formed some binary associative units. Indeed, recent studies by Heslip and Epstein (1969) and Voss (1969) have shown large numbers of correct associates on a modified association test taken at different stages of learning, but also that the frequency of such correct responses was insufficient to account for performance during the most recent serial anticipation trials.

Further evidence that at least binary associative units, to some extent, are formed during serial learning is provided by transfer paradigms in which Ss learn a paired associate (PA) list composed of items taken from adjacent positions on a previously learned serial list (SL) (e.g., Horowitz & Izawa, 1963; Postman & Stark, 1967; Young, 1961). Thus given a serial list of items A-B-C-D-E-F, etc., the PA list might be composed of pairs such as A-B, C-D, E-F, for a single function PA list or A-B, B-C, C-D, D-E, E-F, for a double function list. Negative transfer paradigms are also possible, e.g., A-D, D-B, B-E, E-C, C-F, and both positive and negative transfer has been reported (R. L. Breckenridge & Dixon, 1970). Unfortunately, an unambiguous interpretation of positive transfer from SL to PA is not possible because of the potential mediating effects of position information associated with the stimulus terms used in PA learning (Postman & Stark, 1967, p. 350). Thus, if the stimulus term of a PA pair contained information about its position in the previously learned SL, this information could be used to retrieve the proper PA response as being the term occupying the succeeding serial position.[3] Even if position information was nonspecific so that only the general locus in the SL was represented, the response selection process might

[3] This process would facilitate learning in positive transfer paradigms and be a source of interference in negative transfer designs.

nevertheless profit from such a cue by narrowing the pool of responses that might serve as appropriate associates to the stimulus.

The Association Method and the analysis of SL to PA transfer both fail to offer a pure test of the question of whether binary associates, unmediated by knowledge of positions, are formed in SL. However, the studies by Heslip and Epstein (1969) and Voss (1969) suggest an answer. In the former experiment Ss received different numbers of trials at serial learning and were then tested either for knowledge of item position or for the next succeeding item in the SL. Position information was measured by having the S locate each item, one at a time, in a spatial array corresponding to the temporal positions of the items during the serial anticipation trials. The association test was administered with S instructed ". . . to try to guess what word in the list followed each item that was presented." Results indicated that as the level of serial learning increased, correct responses on the association test increased at a faster rate than correct position responses, although the magnitude of the position error continued to decrease with learning. It is appropriate to conclude that since position information cannot account for the relatively high levels of performance on the association test, some interitem associations are formed in serial learning.

## C. List Length

Does the S know the number of items comprising the serial list he has just mastered? Heslip and Epstein (1969) noted, "If Ss used ordinal numbers as cues in acquisition, they would, of course, know how many items there were in the list [p. 66]." Of approximately 130 Ss in their study only one guessed correctly that he had learned a 13-item SL. There are relatively few studies (e.g., Asch, Hay, & Diamond, 1960, p. 178; Lippman & Denny, 1964, p. 496) to have raised this interesting question and while the answer would, from the results of Heslip and Epstein, appear to be negative, other related questions may be posed. It is possible that even though the S may not have encoded the exact number of serial units, he may have apprehended some less precise features of list length so that Ss may in fact reliably guess quite different numbers after having been exposed to a 13-item list in comparison with an 8- or 24-unit series. It is also conceivable that Ss encode, not the ordinal number of the item, but the distance into the list relative to the beginning and end of the series. Thus, if stopped at some point in a trial, S may have some representation of the number of items from the beginning or end to the item in question but may not know list length as such (e.g., $S$ may know the item is third from the end, but he may not know how far it is from the beginning). In any event, the question of list length information would appear to be potentially fruitful.

After mastering a serial list, we may now conclude, the $S$ has learned the individual items and their sequence, he has some knowledge of the positions of the items in the series, and, if given an association test or an appropriately designed transfer task, he gives some evidence of having formed interitem associations between adjacent terms. $Ss$ may have some knowledge of list length as well. Given these various aspects of the overall serial learning process, it is not unreasonable to expect that explanatory accounts of SL will emphasize one or more of these subprocesses.

The following section deals with the phenomenon known as the serial position effect (SPE), a phenomenon that characteristically accompanies learning by serial anticipation. The explanatory account developed for the SPE will emphasize the utilization of position information in serial learning.

## III. The Independence of Sequence Learning and the Serial Position Effect (SPE)

The study of serial learning entails two related, but quite distinct, problems. First is the very problem of serial order itself (Lashley, 1951) as it relates to behavior at, for example, the point of list mastery. At this point the $S$ recites, in perfect order, a set of terms whose preexperimental sequence was unknown, or totally different from that prescribed by the experimental context. Thus, the order of emission of terms can be learned, and one problem facing researchers in verbal learning is to develop a theoretical account of the learning process such that the sequential behavior can be deduced. Naturally one is interested in explaining precriterial performance as well, but the goal remains that of accounting for the fact that the items eventually do come to be emitted in the proper order.

The second problem stems from the fact that the order in which individual items are acquired during learning is not identical with the order produced at the criterial trial. It is rather the case that items at the beginning and end of the list are recalled correctly prior to items occupying central positions, and this order of learning is accomplished with considerable regularity among $Ss$ (Jensen, 1962a). Thus, Jensen (1962a) has suggested that the order of learning a

10-unit list in terms of their positions, would be 1, 2, 10, 3, 9, 4, 8, 5, 7, and finally 6. This peculiar order of learning gives rise to the frequently encountered SPE, the second major problem associated with serial learning.

Given the distinction between the problems of serial order on the one hand and the SPE on the other, the question arises as to the potential fruitfulness of a single learning model from which to deduce both aspects of serial learning. If one proceeds, for example, in the Ebbinghaus tradition, with an account of serial order in terms of the processes of adjacent and remote associations and derivatives of these such as the notion of associative interference or competition, then these processes must be made to account for the SPE as well (Bugelski, 1950; Hull, Hovland, Ross, Hall, Perkins & Fitch, 1940). In general, it is consistent with the single process approach to assume that those variables affecting the learning of serial order should likewise have some influence on the SPE. Such attempts, however, have not been successful, for the shape of the distribution of percentages of errors at each position, representing the SPE, has been shown to be invariant over variables that have affected the rate of learning. Summarizing this state of affairs, which derives mainly from the work of Braun and Heymann (1958) and McCrary and Hunter (1953), Murdock (1960) has stated

> Thus, the shape of the serial position curve is essentially constant despite variations in the distribution of practice, rate of presentation, familiarity of the items, individual differences, meaningfulness of material, interitem interval, and intertrial interval. Yet we know that every one of these variables has a consistent effect on learning as measured, say, by number of trials to criterion. Since these variables influence learning but do not affect the shape of the serial position curve, it would almost seem that the shape of the serial position curve has nothing whatever to do with learning [p. 24].

It is consistent with these observations to advance the proposition that the learning of serial order and the SPE are independent processes, but that both are *learning processes* nevertheless. Consider, now, two logical domains, one consisting of the set of instances of serial order, i.e., instances of the various ways of learning a sequence, and the other representing the set of instances of the SPE. In Fig. 1, these sets are represented in a familiar Venn diagram with partially overlapping domains. The overlapping area representing the intersection of the two sets contains instances common to both the learning of serial order and the occurrence of the SPE. The

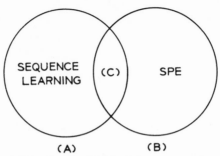

Fig. 1. (A) The conditions under which Ss learn to produce a set of items in a fixed sequence. (B) The set of conditions productive of a serial position effect (SPE). (C) The intersection of A and B representing conditions productive both of sequence learning and the SPE.

conventional serial anticipation procedure would be a member of the intersection as would be other serial recall procedures in which the SPE accompanies recall of the required sequence.[4] The remaining areas of the two domains represent instances of procedures (or processes) that lead either to sequence learning or to the SPE, but not to both. The following sections examine the various members of these sets.

## A. SEQUENCE LEARNING IN THE ABSENCE OF AN SPE

Several examples of the learning of serial order in the absence of an SPE are available. In one case, a cumulative method of serial learning was investigated by Jung (1964). The cumulative method (CM) is in some sense a part-whole technique in which on the first "trial" the S is shown the first item only. The second item is then shown together with the first on the second trial, a three-unit list is presented on the third trial, etc. In Jung's experiment, Ss were presented with nine bigrams. A complete presentation of the entire list took nine trials. Immediately after the first complete presentation, Ss were instructed to recall the items in their correct order and to record them in writing in a column containing nine spaces. Jung compared performance under CM with the standard

---

[4] SPEs have been reported to characterize the distribution of errors in word spelling tasks (Jensen, 1962c) as well as the distribution of errors in the recall of tachistoscopically presented stimuli (e.g., Crovitz & Schiffman, 1965). To the extent to which the latter task entails a set either to report out or to encode in sequence as from left to right, it qualifies as a member of the intersecting set along with word spelling.

method (SM) of serial anticipation in which the nine items were presented for five trials. In this fashion both groups received 45 presentations of the individual items, and hence total presentation time was equated. His study showed recall to be at about five items for both groups with no significant differences between SM and CM, even when the total number of responses, regardless of correct position, were tallied. Similar results have been found recently by Mandler and Dean (1969) in a multitrial free recall experiment, and by Jung (1964) and Mandler (1970) for PA learning with the cumulative method. Of special interest in the present context is the finding by Jung (1964) of a typical SPE under SM, but ". . . for CM no such bowed curve was obtained. Rather the earlier an item appeared in the list, the more often it was correctly recalled. Thus, the items in the middle of the list were more often recalled than those appearing toward the end of the list [p. 298]." The tendency to learn the items in the order in which they are presented was also observed by Mandler and Dean (1969) and may therefore be a characteristic of the cumulative method. This represents an interesting contrast with the method of anticipation for the CM would seem to be more appropriate to the Ebbinghaus chaining conception of serial learning than the SM. One might anticipate finding greater transfer effects in CM to PA than presently available SL to PA tests of the chaining hypothesis have yielded (e.g., Young & Casey, 1964).

A second example of sequence learning in the absence of a SPE is provided by a study by Epstein (1962) of the effects of grammatical structure on learning. Epstein compared grammatical with nongrammatical (anomalous) sequences over nonsense and meaningful words, respectively. An example of the grammatically ordered nonsense sequence is: "The glers un cligs wur vasing un seping a rad moovly." The corresponding nongrammatical sequence was: "cligs seping a wur rad un moovly glers the un vasing." Ss were shown the sequence arranged from left to right by the method of whole presentation for a period of seven seconds. They were then given 30 seconds to fill in a set of horizontally arranged dashes, corresponding to the number of items in the previously exposed sentence. The exposure–recall procedure continued until all words were reproduced in correct order. A second experiment explored the same question but presented the items one at a time on a memory drum at a two-second presentation rate and used the method of anticipation to one correct recitation. In the first experiment, Epstein's results showed that grammatically structured sequences were learned significantly more rapidly than matched nongrammatical sequences and this held for meaningful as well as nonsense words. However, no comparable significant differences occurred in the second experiment which utilized the method of anticipation. It is of interest that for both structured and unstructured sets the error distributions of the second experiment did yield the SPE, whereas in the first experiment the order of learning tended to be from left to right. It seems likely that the left-right order of learning is more compatible with the organizational processes implied by the grammatically structured series than is the order of learning which occurs under serial anticipation procedures. Indeed, the data of the second experiment suggest an interaction effect of learning method with type of sequence (i.e., whole presentation-serial anticipation *vs.* grammatical-nongrammatical), for the structured categories of materials actually showed more trials and errors to criterion than their nonstructured counterparts when learning was by the method of anticipation. This suggests a negative transfer effect of incompatible organizations on learning.

There are perhaps two additional methods that qualify as instances of sequence learning without the accompanying bowed SPE. In one case, *S*s learned a sequence of items by the method of anticipation but with the starting term systematically varied on successive trials. Ebenholtz (1963b) has shown such a method to require more trials and to produce responses misplaced at positions further removed from their correct position than in the case of serial learning with a constant starting position. Both findings are consistent with the assumption that position information is attenuated with the varied starting position method. The more rapid rate of learning under the conventional method has also been demonstrated by Bowman and Thurlow (1963), Keppel (1964), Lippman and Denny (1964), Winnick and Dornbush (1963). The question whether an SPE is generated when learning occurs by varying the starting item cannot be answered without some qualification, for there are several ways of identifying serial order by this method. When plotted with respect to the serial order of items on the very first trial, Keppel (1964) showed no significant variation of percentage errors across the serial positions. A similar plot of correct responses by Lippman and Denny (1964, Fig. 4) likewise bears little resemblance to the conventional SPE. The latter authors also plotted the mean number of correct anticipations per trial against an order derived from the item most frequently given correctly by a given *S*. This item was arbitrarily designated as "one" with the next succeeding item as "two," etc.

Thus, each $S$ contributed a potentially idiosyncratic order. However, even when plotted in this fashion, thereby insuring a primacy component to the curve, with the exception of the last two items, the order of learning tended to be from the first (i.e., the most frequently correct item) to the last. The best available evidence, therefore, is that the varied starting position method qualifies as a technique of sequence learning without an SPE. An additional candidate for membership in this class is the double-function method of learning PAs (Primoff, 1938; Young, 1959). This technique requires each term to serve both as a stimulus and a response. Thus a typical set of pairs might be represented as follows: A-B, B-C, C-D, D-E, E-F, F-G, G-A. The actual order of pair presentation, however, would not, except for special purposes, be the order as presented above, but rather some random or systematic rearrangement. This procedure is, after all, an instance of sequence learning, for when learning is complete each term leads associatively to the next in a closed cycle. On the face of it one might argue that there is no beginning or end to this sequence, and hence an SPE cannot logically be computed. However, from an empirical point of view, plotting mean number correct against serial position, with the latter defined essentially arbitrarily as far as serial order was concerned, showed no advantage for one position relative to any other (Shuell & Keppel, 1967, Fig. 1, Cond. C-S). Of course, when there are some single function pairs in the list these tend to be learned more rapidly than the other double-function pairs and produce an SPE (R. L. Breckenridge & Dixon, 1970; Postman & Stark, 1967). This result is probably due to the decrease in interfering backward associations leading to an enhanced rate of learning of the pairs at the termini of the association sequence, i.e., the pairs A-B and F-G in the sequence A-B, B-C, C-D, D-E, E-F, F-G.

Some instances of sequence learning in the absence of the typical SPE have been adduced. No doubt other examples exist or will be uncovered as studies of the serial aspects of verbal learning proceed.[5] It may be concluded that an SPE is not an inevitable consequence of sequence learning. In the next section, instances of the SPE unaccompanied by sequence learning will be presented and consideration will be given to those common processes which might underlie the SPE.

[5] The serial recall procedure, investigated by Battig and his colleagues (see, e.g., Battig, 1969), would also seem to qualify as a condition productive of sequence learning, but without a typical SPE, i.e., end items fail to show a drop in errors.

## B. The "Ubiquity" of the SPE

In serial learning the SPE is defined by the number of errors (or correct responses) associated with each item in the series. A typical plot of the SPE represents the positions of these items at equally spaced intervals and in an order from left to right along the abscissa, corresponding to the temporal order of presentation within a given trial. It is significant that the characteristic SPE of serial learning would be quite different were some nonconventional order chosen for the graphical representation of the positions, yet any such plot would represent equally well the relationship between, e.g., mean number of errors and serial position. What rational purpose might be served by plotting the SPE with the positions arranged in their temporal order? One answer is that the SPE obtained under these conditions turns out to have a shape that is relatively simple and hence easy to describe. But perhaps a more useful answer is that the fact that the values of the abscissa can be ordered, e.g., as from least to most, without ambiguity, i.e., that there is an ordinal relation among the $x$ values, permits the statement of a unique *function rule*. Such a rule yields a description of the relation between the members of the set of $x$ values and the corresponding set of $y$ values as, e.g., the simple rule that "as serial position increases from beginning to end, errors first increase and then decrease." Were temporal position to have merely a nominal status, one could succeed in representing the relation between any given serial position and the errors associated with it, as in the case of a bar graph, but no single function rule could be offered that would hold true over some specified domain of serial positions. It is apparent, then, that the potential value of descriptive generalizations would be lost by treating each position independently, i.e., nominally, as though the dimensional aspect of temporal position were absent. Only when position is regarded as an ordered dimension can there be an unambiguous specification of the SPE.

In the following studies, the SPE is shown to occur in the absence of fixed temporal orders of presentation. In all of these cases, however, there remains an ordinal relation among the members of the sets of items used in learning with reference to which the SPE is defined.

Among the earliest to report an SPE with a PA paradigm was Phillips (1958). As part of a larger study of mediated verbal similarity, she had Ss associate five Turkish words with five different Munsell grays in a modified paired-associate procedure. The five pairs were learned bidirectionally so that on each trial either $S$ was shown a color patch and attempted to recall the associated word or a word was shown with $S$ required to point to the appropriate color. In each case $S$'s failures to respond were corrected by $E$. The gray samples were never displayed in the order of their Munsell values, and their temporal orders of presentation were varied from trial to trial. The particular word–color pairings were also varied from $S$ to $S$. Phillips did not present a figure of the results of this part of her study; however, she reported a significant ($p <.01$) F value associated with the mean trials to criterion at each Munsell scale position. Furthermore, the two colors representing the termini of the series were learned significantly more rapidly than the colors corresponding to the three central positions. Clearly, if mean trials had been plotted against colors with the latter arranged in serial order, an SPE would have been made apparent.

A very similar procedure was used by Ebenholtz (1965) in a transfer study. In this experimnt, $S$s learned eight paired associates by the method of anticipation (i.e., A, A-B presentation). Stimuli were either horizontal line lengths ranging from .5 to $4\frac{5}{8}$ inches, or .5-inch diameter patches of Munsell grays ranging in value from 1 through 9. Response terms were CVCs and varied in Glaze association value from 80 to 100%. Particular care was taken to insure that the various PA-presentation orders never matched the ordinal sequence of either set of stimuli. In both cases, when errors were plotted against the ordinal numbers of the stimuli and arranged in serial order, an SPE emerged, i.e., pairs containing stimuli from the extremes of the dimension produced fewer errors than the remaining pairs.

An SPE also has been demonstrated in the case of PA learning with positions within a vertical array of rectangles as stimuli and high association-value CVCs as responses (Ebenholtz, 1963a). Items associated with top and bottom locations were learned with fewer errors than items associated with central locations. The same pattern of errors was demonstrated by Jensen (1962d) in two tasks, both of which also depended on spatial discriminations. In one experiment, $S$s were required to reconstruct an array of nine simple geometric objects arranged in a horizontal pattern. After viewing the objects, $S$s were presented with a haphazard arrangement, and they then proceeded to attempt to reconstruct the original order. Learning and reconstruction trials alternated until the $S$ reproduced the series in correct spatial order. The second task required the $S$ to learn to associate a particular geometric pattern with one of nine response buttons arranged in a horizontal array. The geometric patterns were projected on a nearby screen one at a time in an approximately random order. Correct button presses were signalled by a "bong," but correction of errors was not permitted. In both tasks, the greatest relative difficulty in learning was associated with central spatial locations, end positions being learned with least difficulty.

Clearly, having to associate a unique response to each of the members of a series of neutral colors, line lengths, or spatial locations is productive of an SPE. It also appears to be the case that having to select the correct response position from among a horizontal array likewise is productive of the SPE. The SPE, however, is not limited to these dimensions. Murdock (1960) has shown that a SPE can be produced with such widely varying stimulus dimensions as tonal intensity, area, and weight, thus extending the number of instances of the SPE in the absence of a constant temporal order of presentation. Furthermore, it would appear that nonsensory continua are capable of yielding an SPE as well. DeSoto and Bosley (1962) presented Ss with 16 names, one at a time on cards, and required them to associate one of the class labels, Freshman, Sophomore, Junior, and Senior, with each. The same response was correct for four different names, but in other respects a paired-associate procedure was followed in which Ss were given immediate correction after each response. The numbers of intrusion errors ("no responses" were not permitted) were least for the Freshman and Senior labels, most for Sophomore and Junior. Thus, an SPE emerged with respect to the learned dimension of college matriculation categories.

The same modified PA procedure in which several stimuli share a given response has been used by Pollio (1966), Pollio and Draper (1966), and Pollio, Deitchman, and Richards (1969). In the first study cited, the terms "beautiful, pretty, fair, homely, and ugly" comprised the response set with three nonsense-syllable stimuli per response. The second study used the numbers 1, 2, 3, 4, and 5 as responses, and the third study investigated the effects of the response set "cold, cool, mild, warm, and hot." In each instance, an SPE occurred in which responses at the boundaries of the series were learned more rapidly than terms representing the center of the series. In the latter study, however, a deviation from this pattern emerged when the time of year in which Ss were run was analyzed. When learning took place in June and July, mean trials to criterion for the "cold" response failed to drop. Thus, the responses appeared to be learned in order with "hot" being easiest and "cold" the most difficult.

A similar departure from the typical SPE occurred in a standard PA study by Ebenholtz (1966a) in which the numbers 1 through 8 were responses with high association-value nonsense syllables as stimuli. In this case, pairs having lower numbers were learned with fewer errors than pairs containing higher numbers. These two instances of failure to obtain an SPE both occurred when the ordered set served as response terms rather than as stimuli. It is possible, therefore, that whatever factors eventually turn out to be responsible for these failures may themselves interact with the stimulus or response function of the ordered set. Some support for this conclusion stems from the fact that in the same study, Ebenholtz found the typical SPE when numbers 1 through 8 or 1 through 10 were used as stimuli in a PA task. Indeed this result has been reported for the numbers 1 through 9 as well (Young, Hakes, & Hicks, 1967).

A final example demonstrating that the SPE extends to learned or conceptual as well as to sensory dimensions was provided by two transfer studies from serial learning to paired associates (Ebenholtz, 1966a, 1966b). Subjects first learned an SL of high-association value syllables to a criterion of one errorless trial. A PA task followed in which the items of the previously learned SL served as stimuli with relatively common disyllabic nouns as response terms. In both studies, pairs containing stimuli from terminal SL positions were learned with fewer errors than pairs having stimuli that derived from central SL positions. That the SPE was not due to the differential numbers of correct anticipations associated with the end items during serial learning was evaluated by having a control group learn the same items by the method of free recall (FR) with presentation order varied over trials. Such items would not be expected to contain order information when used as stimuli on the subsequent PA task, although they could vary in frequency of correct recalls and hence could influence PA learning. However, the correlation between frequency of correct responses in FR and in the PA task for corresponding pairs was close to zero. On the other hand, SL performance did correlate highly and significantly with PA learning, indicating that it was the position of the stimulus item during SL, and not the degree of stimulus recall that determined the relative ease of PA learning. Further implications of this particular SL to PA paradigm will be discussed below.

It may be concluded that the SPE is a rather robust phenomenon, and certainly not restricted to learning tasks requiring the maintenance of a constant temporal order. In light of the evidence discussed in Section A above, the assumption of the independence of sequence learning and the SPE, as represented in Fig. 1, would appear to be justified, viz., neither phenomenon is predicated upon the other for its occurrence.

## C. AN INDUCTIVE GENERALIZATION

Whenever the same phenomenon appears in widely varying contexts, it is appropriate to attempt to formulate a generalization which might explicate the conditions common to all the occurrences of the phenomenon. In the survey of instances of the SPE, the items, or a stimulus or response subset, were capable of being ordered, e.g., from least to most, left to right, etc., along the dimension represented by the items. Since the single factor common to all instances of the SPE was that of dimensionality, the rule to be formulated must be one that expresses the way in which $S$s encode or otherwise respond to this dimensional aspect of the material. It is proposed that $S$s respond first by noting the boundaries of the series, and then by locating each item in a position defined relative to either one or both of the series extremes. It is further assumed that location by dimensional position is a source of information that becomes a property of an item strictly by virtue of its inclusion in an ordered series, i.e., it is a series property such as beginning, middle, and end, which is shared by the items that constitute the series. Because item location so defined is a property of series in general and not of the unique sensory or semantic aspect of any particular dimension, it may be inferred that position information is *transdimensional,* i.e., the position property of an item acquired in the context of one dimension will produce positive transfer when used in association with the appropriate position in any other dimension.

A number of studies support this conclusion. For example, Ebenholtz (1965) investigated transfer between two PA tasks having a common set of eight nonsense syllable responses. The stimuli for one task were eight horizontal line lengths, and for the other were composed of a set of eight gray patches varying from white to black. Both sets of stimuli have been described in greater detail above. For the positive transfer group the syllable paired with the shortest line length was also paired with the lightest gray, the next shortest line shared its response with the next lightest gray, etc. The negative transfer group learned the same pairs, but there was only a random correspondence between a response term and the series position of the associated stimulus terms on the two dimensions. Two groups transferred from line lengths to grays and two groups transferred in the reverse direction. In all conditions learning was by the method of anticipation and in no case did the sequence of pair presentation correspond to that of the stimuli arranged in order of stimulus magnitude.

If one considers the associations to have been formed between the sensory or nominal aspect of each stimulus and its respective response terms, then the transfer paradigms are all of one type, i.e., A-B, C-B, for line lengths and reflectance are surely quite dissimilar as stimuli. On the other hand, assuming that $S$s utilize position information and that such information is transdimensional, the positive transfer group represents an A-B, A-B paradigm, the negative transfer condition that of A-B, A-B$_r$. For both directions of transfer, maintaining the response terms at common (dimensional) positions on both tasks led to substantial facilitation in the rate of learning relative to the random arrangement. These results clearly permitted the rejection of the A-B, C-B interpretation and acceptance of the A-B, A-B, and A-B, A-B$_r$ paradigms respectively.

Further evidence for the transdimensional aspect of position learning derives from studies of transfer from PA to SL and from SL to PA. In one experiment (Ebenholtz, 1963a), the PA task consisted of learning to associate nonsense syllables with spatial positions in a vertical array of rectangles. The logic was similar to that described above, i.e., for one group the syllable associated with the top window was also the first item of the SL, the syllable second from top occurred in the second serial position, etc. Of course, the temporal order of presentation of the PA list was varied from trial to trial and never corresponded with the temporal order of the SL. Rather, the spatial locations of the syllables in PA were in correspondence with their temporal locations in SL. A second group learned the same tasks, but the items occurred at disparate spatial and temporal locations, and a third group maintained the relative positions of items across the two tasks, i.e., items in temporal succession in the SL were made to appear at spatially contiguous locations in the PA, but they appeared at disparate positions nevertheless. This study again showed transfer to be facilitated when mediated by position information common to both the initial and transfer tasks while the two groups with items at disparate locations performed at approximately equivalent levels.[6]

Position-mediated transfer across nominally dissimilar stimulus dimensions also has been investigated in SL to PA transfer studies (Mueller, 1970; Young *et al.*, 1967) in which the PA responses were composed of the SL items and the stimuli were numbers corresponding to the serial positions of these items. Young *et al.* (1967) described the purposes of their experiments IA and IB as follows:

> Following learning of a serial list, say, of adjectives, Ss are transferred to a PA list in which the responses are the serial-list adjectives and the stimuli, ordinal position numbers. Appropriate number-adjective pairing should, according to the absolute position hypothesis, facilitate PA learning since the appropriate paradigm is A-B, A-B. Furthermore, re-pairing the position numbers and adjectives randomly should constitute the A-B, A-B$_r$ paradigm of negative transfer [p. 429].

These deductions are equivalent to those discussed above in the context of line length–reflectance and spatial position–SL transfer studies. It is necessary to emphasize that reasoning from the concept of dimensional organization, the use of numbers represents no more or less of a test of the use of position information in SL than does the use of any other dimensionally organized set of terms. A positive outcome in such tests, therefore, does not warrant the conclusion that the S uses numbers as mediators in SL any more than the conclusion that line lengths or reflectances are used as mediators. What can be inferred, however, is that some general representation of position or dimension location does indeed mediate learning in *both* the SL and the transfer tasks employed in the test.

The interpretation of the transfer tasks in terms of A-B, A-B and A-B, A-B$_r$ paradigms rests on the assumption that the A terms are positions, and the B terms, in the case of Young *et al.*, are adjectives previously learned in serial order. However, one can also reason on

---

[6] Jensen and Rohwer (1965) failed to find overall positive transfer in a similar SL to PA study. It is, of course, difficult to evaluate negative evidence of this sort, but it is possible that the use of a 2:2 second rate of PA presentation compared with a 3:3 rate in the study described contributed to increasing the difficulty of the transfer task and thereby decreasing the likelihood of obtaining positive transfer. Furthermore, the authors distributed 12 positions horizontally across the face of a memory drum without any space intervening between frames. Ebenholtz (1963a) used 10 positions distributed over a vertical distance of about 11¾ inches. Thus, the two spatial arrays could have varied in position discriminability, a factor serving to limit the utilization of position information.

the assumption that, to some extent, sequential associations are formed in SL. From this view, if A-B represents the interitem associations in SL, and C represents the number stimuli in PA learning, the appropriate paradigm is A-B, C-B.[7] Assuming response learning to be relatively high for adjectives, this is a negative transfer paradigm based upon interference from the first list backward association (B-A) with the transfer list backward association (B-C). The expected overall transfer, taking into account the contributions of both position and specific interitem association, is, therefore, a net effect of positive and negative transfer. Young *et al.* (1967) evaluated their experimental conditions relative to a control group that learned number–adjective pairs, none of which adjectives were in common with those appearing in SL. Their results indicated no overall transfer in either the positive or negative paradigm; however, where position cues led one to expect positive transfer ". . . there was positive transfer from the ends of the serial list and negative transfer from the middle [p. 432]." The condition for which negative transfer was inferred showed "negative transfer from the ends of the list [p. 432]." A second experiment was carried out in which "Subsequent to serial learning one group learned a PA list of number–adjective pairs formed from the ends of the serial list [i.e., numbers 1–4 and 13–16] while a second group learned a list whose pairs were formed from the middle of the serial list [i.e., numbers 5–12] [p. 49]." Control groups learned serial lists unrelated to their number–adjective pairs, and two additional experimental groups received instructions concerning the relationship between the serial and PA lists. The results showed that the end positions tended to produce positive transfer, middle positions negative transfer, though primarily for the instructed groups. This outcome, although in the proper direction, does not, however, constitute strong support for the utilization of position information in SL.

A similar SL to PA study was conducted by Mueller (1970) in which the PA list was composed of number–CVC pairs or CVC–number pairs. Mueller also included an additional condition in which the PA task was constituted as a double-function list. The

---

[7] If one assumes that the transferred SL items were stimuli rather than responses, then the SL associates can be represented as A-B and the PA pairs as C-A. This too is a negative transfer paradigm based upon interference from the first list forward association (A-B) with the PA list backward association (A-C). This inference that the assumption of sequential associations in SL leads to negative transfer is contrary to the conclusion of Young *et al.* that zero transfer should be expected under these conditions.

numbers (actually adjectives such as first, second, etc., were used) were assigned according to the position of the CVC in SL or were distributed randomly, similar to Groups IA and IB of Young *et al.*; however, no control condition receiving an unrelated SL was included. Generally, the results supported the assumption of position-mediated transfer for both the stimulus and response function of the position adjective. In addition, the largest differences between the positive and negative transfer paradigms tended to occur at end positions, a finding which is consistent with the results of Young *et al.*

Also consistent with the above are the results of a study by Winnick and Dornbush (1968) which examined transfer of number-syllable PA pairs to a SL composed of the PA response terms. As in the above studies, positive and negative transfer paradigms were examined by appropriate pairing of the PA numbers (i.e., 1–12) with the position of the response term in the (subsequently learned) SL. A third group used the numbers 9–20 as their PA stimuli, and a control group had words as stimuli in their PA task. Winnick and Dornbush found SL to be highly facilitated when the PA number stimuli corresponded with the SL position of the associated responses. Less positive transfer was shown for the group using the numbers 9–20 in place of 1–12, and the negative transfer group did not differ from the level of the control condition. From the point of view of dimensional organization, the numbers (presented as words to S) 9–20 qualify as an instance of an ordered set of stimuli, and hence the associated response terms should benefit from PA learning as much as those having had stimuli 1–12. The deciding factor concerns S's apprehension of the dimensional aspect of the stimuli. It is possible that Ss simply did not fully utilize the position information under this condition, but rather responded primarily to the nominal attributes of the stimuli. Obviously, an independent test of the saliency of the dimensional aspects of certain ordered dimensions over others is necessary. In this respect, it would have been useful to know whether the three PA conditions involving number-words as stimuli all produced an SPE. The relatively poor transfer for the condition using numbers 9–20 would be consistent with an attenuated SPE in the corresponding PA task.

Overall, there is positive evidence for the transdimensional aspect of position information, with the strongest evidence provided by Winnick and Dornbush (1968) in their study of PA to SL transfer. The other studies tended to show relatively small differences (e.g., Young *et al.*, 1967), or where differences were more apparent a "neutral" or "unrelated," control list was not included as part of the design (Ebenholtz, 1963a, 1965; Mueller, 1970) so that comparisons between positive and negative transfer paradigms constituted the major source of evidence. Finally, it may be noted that a test of the transdimensional hypothesis has not yet been carried out with the type of dimension or paradigm investigated by DeSoto and Bosley (1962) and by Pollio and his associates (e.g., Pollio, 1966; Pollio & Draper, 1966; Pollio et al., 1969). One should expect from the present view, that having learned, for example, to associate properly the responses, hot, warm, mild, cool, and cold, each with its own set of stimuli, the same stimuli, when appropriately paired with another set of responses such as 1, 2, 3, 4, 5, or beautiful, pretty, fair, homely, and ugly (or perhaps Monday, Tuesday, Wednesday, Thursday, and Friday) should produce positive and negative transfer as in the previously discussed paradigms.

In summary, the conditions under which the SPE occurs together with the evidence for the transdimensionality of dimension location permit the conclusion that when the $S$ is faced with a learning task requiring that he discriminate among items varying along some dimension, the $S$ will make his discrimination not merely in terms of the available sensory or semantic differences, but on the basis of positions in the series occupied by the item as well. The generalization may then be drawn that *whenever discrimination occurs on the basis of dimensional location, the SPE will result*. The bowed curves of serial learning as well as those produced in the PA paradigms reviewed previously are thus seen to arise out of a failure to discriminate properly among positions and not items, although item distinctiveness can be an important variable. In emphasizing the importance of series location rather than some characteristic of the items, the present view differs from the model proposed by Murdock (1960) in which distinctiveness is based upon the logarithm of the energy values of the items comprising the series. In other respects, the present views are compatible with Murdock's model, for organization according to dimensional position is possible in all instances to which the model applies.

It is of interest to note that the process of dimensional organization can account for the general shape of the SPE, but not for more specific characteristics such as the degree of skewness. It is likely that the skewed functions found typically in SL are due simply to the attempt by naive $S$s to learn the series in order from beginning to end. This attempt is, of course, only partially successful, but enough so as to yield the preponderance of errors just beyond the central positions. Evidence for this subject strategy in the diminishing frequencies of extralist intrusions (from first to last positions) has been offered recently by Harcum and Coppage (1969). The particular skew or magnitude of kurtosis associated with the SPE in paradigms other than SL can best be interpreted in terms of the conditions specific to each paradigm, e.g., degree of stimulus similarity, or an instructional set to organize the items in a fashion different from that required by dimensional organization, etc.

The principal assumption of the present approach has been that when the S is exposed to items that have an ordinal aspect to them, he organizes the material by learning the locations of the items relative to the boundaries of the series. Position thereby comes to be an added attribute of an item which that item might otherwise not have, except in association with the series. In the case of the standard anticipation method of serial learning, the application of these assumptions permits the inference that the items come to acquire a positional attribute according to location in the temporal series. Insofar as series location represents a rather broad category containing many items in the center of the list, one should not expect position to be much of an aid to anticipation learning at that locus. As indicated in an earlier reference to Woodworth and Poffenberger (1920), this reasoning represents the basis for the postulation of item-to-item associations between the central items of a series, and hence to the formulation of a dual-process model (Ebenholtz, 1966b; Young et al., 1967) of serial learning. Thus, the anticipation of a correct sequence of central items requires the formation of direct interitem associations, whereas at the ends of the list, retrieval may be mediated primarily by the use of list location as a cue.

A testable implication of this approach follows from the observation that in learning a previously learned SL, but in reverse order (Young, Patterson, & Benson, 1963) position identity is most severely disrupted at the ends of the series. Assuming that position cues are of little value at central list positions, it follows that list location cannot mediate positive transfer at this locus. However, interitem associations between centrally located items can be a source of positive transfer in backward learning, on the assumption of associative symmetry (Asch & Ebenholtz, 1962b). The results of Young et al. (1963) support this dual process interpretation by showing positive transfer for central items, although the authors construed this outcome ". . . as favorable to an hypothesis which assumes that the functional stimulus in serial learning is the position the item holds in the list [p. 338]." This conclusion is consistent with the fact that the positions of the central items are least disrupted on the reversed list, but it is inconsistent with the data showing relatively poor utilization of position information for these very items (Heslip & Epstein, 1969; Hicks, Hakes, & Young, 1966; Schulz, 1955; Voss, 1969).

Perhaps the most significant inference from the present view, however, is that the very process whereby items are organized according to list location, i.e., position learning, is presumed to be responsible for the SPE on the grounds that terminal positions are more discriminable than central ones. Since the role of interitem associations in the explanation of the bowed curve is thereby minimized, it is to be expected that variables which are known either to facilitate or inhibit such association formation should have little or no influence upon the SPE unless they also affect position learning in similar ways. The invariance of the SPE as demonstrated by Braun and Heymann (1958) and McCrary and Hunter (1953) over variables which do affect the rate of list learning is consistent with the view that the SPE is based upon processes which are independent of either item learning or the formation of interitem associations.

It is important to stress that position or dimension location is a learned attribute of an item, for this permits an explanation of the occurrence of the SPE in circumstances where it would not otherwise be expected. Thus, in the case of PA learning of numbers and syllables, there can be little doubt that the characters 1 through 10, for example, are quite discriminable, that one does not mistake a 5 for a 6 or a 6 for a 7. Yet PA learning has been shown to be rather poor for pairs containing these terms (Ebenholtz, 1966a). The assumption that Ss respond not to the form character but to the positional attribute of the number relative to the boundaries of the number series (viz., 1 and 10) permits the deduction of the SPE in this case. It is also worth noting that, for the reasons just indicated, presentation of the numeral indicative of ordinal position together with the item in a serial learning task (Jensen & Blank, 1962) will not alter the SPE. A further implication here is that however dimensional position is represented in the S, it need not entail mediation by the number series, for the explicit use of numbers neither reduces the errors in serial learning nor eliminates the SPE. There would thus be no gain in the storage and retrieval of position information when transformed into the number code.

A second example of the SPE based upon acquired positional properties can be deduced in the case of the SL to PA transfer paradigms. Such experiments (e.g., Young, 1961) have explored the possibility of the transfer of specific interitem associations from SL to PA as evidence for the presence of such associations during intial SL. Consider an SL composed of items A-B-C-D-E-F-G. Then the appropriate (positive) PA transfer list would be represented as either A-B, C-D, E-F, in a single-function paradigm, or A-B, B-C, C-D, D-E, E-F, F-G, in a double-function list. Actually the latter list contains two pairs (viz., A-B and F-G) having one member each (A and G) used in a single function only. Since pairs containing single function terms are likely to be learned relatively easily, a bowed SPE in PA learning would be expected on this account (Postman & Stark, 1967; Shuell & Keppel, 1967). In order to avoid this artifact, only complete double function transfer lists (e.g., Shuell & Keppel, 1967) or single function lists (e.g., Horton & Turnage, 1970; Jensen, 1963) will be analyzed. Using a complete double function design based upon a prior SL in which the initial and final items were identical, Shuell & Keppel (1967) obtained an SPE in PA learning. Similarly, both Jensen (1963) and Horton & Turnage (1970) produced an SPE in PA learning of single function transfer pairs. Jensen interpreted this outcome in terms of the transfer of specific associations and noted ". . . by the end of serial learning the items differ in associative strength according to serial position with the earliest learned items being the most overlearned and consequently having the greatest associative strength [p. 273]."

From the present view, the obtained SPE in the PA task follows from the assumption that as a result of serial learning, the items have acquired the properties of relative position, perhaps in the same way that numbers, being initially neutral, themselves come to represent relative position within a series. In order to test the assumption that position is an acquired attribute, Ebenholtz (1966a, 1966b) designed a transfer task in which previously learned SL items were used as stimuli and new common nouns as responses. Such a design represents an A-B, A-D paradigm on the assumption of the transfer of specific interitem associations, and one should therefore expect an inverted SPE, i.e., highly overlearned pairs from the extremes of the SL should cause the greatest interference. To the contrary, however, the several experiments examining this paradigm produced a typical SPE with more rapid learning of pairs containing stimuli taken from terminal serial positions than from central locations. There was also some indication of a departure from the SPE for pairs containing stimuli taken from the middle of the SL, suggesting the presence of associative interference at this locus. These results support the interpretation of the SPE in PA transfer studies in terms of the assumption that Ss respond to the PA stimuli according to their positional properties, acquired during the learning of the SL. The SPE may be said to occur in PA transfer for the same reason that it occurs in serial learning, namely because of organization by series location. The presence of the SPE in PA transfer studies thus lends credence to its interpretation in terms of the mediating role of position information (Postman & Stark, 1967).

The assumption that SL leads to the acquisition of positional attributes has been tested in a different paradigm by Woodward (1966). In this study, Ss each learned two 10-item serial lists by the conventional method of anticipation, but by alternating practice between the two series on successive trials.[8] The criterion was reached when Ss were capable of one perfect recitation on each list, though not necessarily in succession. A PA task then followed in which a positive (P) transfer group learned pairs composed of items that had previously occupied *identical* serial positions, one pair member from each SL respectively. A negative (N) transfer group learned pairs composed of stimuli from one list and responses from the other list but randomly constituted from different locations on each list, and a third control (C) group learned irrelevant SLs followed by the PA task. Counterbalancing was such that all three groups learned the same SLs, though not the same pairs of lists, and the same PA lists as well. The usual procedure of varying the presentation order of pairs from trial to trial was, of course, followed.

It was assumed that position identity would mediate overall positive transfer for Group P, whereas for Group N, stimulus- and response-position incompatibility might produce some negative transfer early in learning and perhaps simply no overall transfer at all. It was also expected, for Group P, that an SPE would be evident in PA learning on the assumption that the position property would be a most effective mediator for pairs composed of items from terminal serial positions, and least salient for pairs chosen from central serial positions. A contrasting outcome can be derived from the assumption that SL entails the formation of sequential associations and the allied implication that the bowed curve of SL represents the overlearning or strengthening of associations between terminal items relative to those more centrally located. Consider the SLs A-B-C-D-E-F and G-H-I-J-K-L. Since Woodward's experiment

[8] A similar technique has been used by Dey (1970) to provide evidence for the role of position identity in mediating interlist intrusions.

required Ss in Group P to learn pairs A-G, B-H, C-I, D-J, E-K, and F-L, associative interference should have occurred since, on the sequential association hypothesis, the SL to PA transfer represented an A-B, A-D paradigm.[9] Furthermore, the greater the strength of A-B, the more likely is A-D learning to be retarded; consequently, pairs containing items from terminal serial positions should exhibit *more* interference than those from central positions. Thus, the inferences drawn from the assumptions of position learning and sequential associations respectively are contradictory with respect to the shape of the error distribution associated with the PA task. The two views also lead to different predictions in the case of overall transfer, since the assumption of sequential associations does not distinguish between Groups P and N, i.e., both represent negative transfer conditions.

The three groups did not differ in the learning of either of the two SLs. The mean trials to a criterion of one perfect recitation on the PA task were 6.25, 9.05, and 7.80 for Groups P, N, and C, respectively, $F(2,57) = 3.25$, $p < .05$. Individual comparisons showed significant differences for Group P *vs.* Group N only, $F(1,38) = 7.25$, $p < .05$. This outcome is consistent with the role of position as a mediator in PA learning, although the failure to find a significant difference between Groups P and C does not permit the conclusion that overall positive transfer occurred.

Figure 2 represents the distribution of PA errors according to the position of the stimulus member in prior SL. In the case of Group N, two curves are recorded depending upon whether the abscissa represents the position of the stimulus (S) or response (R) member of the pair (in Group P both S and R represented the same position). The curve for Group C was generated by plotting each pair according to the position its stimulus would have had had it been learned in Group P. The shape of the curve for Group P shows a relative

---

[9] The true paradigm is somewhat more complicated than indicated. Consider the two SLs to be composed of pairs such as A-B, B-C, C-D, D-E, E-F, and G-H, H-I, I-J, J-K, K-L, respectively. The derivative or transfer pairs (for Group P, for example) are A-G, B-H, C-I, D-J, E-K, and F-L. Such a transfer task represents not one but a variety of interference paradigms. For example, the SL pair A-B and the PA pair A-G represent in contemporary notation an A-B, A-D paradigm. On the other hand, the pairs G-H, A-G represent the A-B, D-A relation. The pairs A-B, B-H represent an A-B, B-D type, whereas the pairs G-H, B-H conform to an A-B, D-B paradigm. Thus the specification of the paradigm depends upon the particular SL in which the pair is identified and upon the stimulus or response function the item assumes in its SL. In all cases, however, an interference paradigm results.

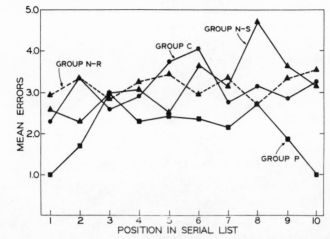

Fig. 2. Mean errors in paired-associate (PA) learning for the negative (N), positive (P), and control (C) conditions as a function of the position of the stimulus (S) or response (R) member in prior serial learning. Data from Woodward (1966).

facilitation for end pairs, and this is consistent with the assumed role of position information. The dip at central positions relative to positions 3 and 8 is somewhat unusual, but it is similar to the SPE obtained by Ebenholtz (1966b) in a PA transfer task in which the pairs contained stimuli from a previously learned SL. The central section may, conceivably, represent differential negative transfer and hence may be interpreted as a portion of the inverted SPE to be expected from the assumed role of sequential associations at these positions.

Analysis of variance of errors on Groups P, N(R), and C was performed between the two end positions (1 and 10) and the central positions (2–9), the latter corrected for differential numbers of items. Results showed significant effects of groups $F(2,57) = 5.28$, $p < .01$, positions, $F(1,57) = 6.19$, $p < .05$, and their interaction, $F(2,57) = 3.63$, $p < .05$. The corresponding analysis for Groups P, N(S) and C indicated significant effects of groups, $F(2,57) = 4.52$, $p < .05$, and positions, $F(1,57) = 6.35$, $p < .05$. Analysis of individual groups showed, as suggested in Fig. 2, that only for Group P was there a significant difference in errors, $t(19) = 3.63$, $p < .01$, with end positions substantially lower than central positions. It may be concluded that position identity mediates the formation of individual pairs of stimulus and response members and that such mediation effects are most likely to occur when the mediators represent end rather than central locations. Woodward's study thus represents further evidence of the relation between the availability of position information and the SPE. Whether pair formation mediated by position information is in some theoretically significant fashion different from pair formation mediated primarily by stimulus and response contiguity remains a question, i.e., should one consider there to be an *association* between the pair members in both instances?

## D. DIMENSIONAL *VS.* HIERARCHICAL ORGANIZATION

In noting the effects of spatial configurations on serial learning, Asch *et al.* (1960) commented:

> The learners' *knowledge* of the ends of the series constitutes one condition of the serial gradient. It seems necessary to conclude that the gradient requires, as one condition, a particular cognitive operation, namely, the identification of the beginning and end of the series, and the location of items with respect to these boundaries. ... it follows that the gradient is not exclusively the product of associative operations; it rather presupposes a particular organization of the data to be learned [p. 196].

From my point of view, these organizational processes are possible whenever an ordinal relation exists among the members of a set of items. Dimensional organization represents an organization of items arranged according to location on a dimension, with location defined relative to the boundaries of the series.

In serial learning, for example, it is proposed that each item acquires a position tag, though not necessarily a different one, containing information such as beginning, middle, and end, which specifies location relative either to both or only one of the boundaries of the temporal series. To some extent (Heslip & Epstein, 1969; Schulz, 1955) these positions can be resolved as learning proceeds, so that fewer items share the identical tag than when learning began. For example, with some practice, the clusters of items sharing the "beginning" and "end" tags, respectively, may be reduced by the assignment of additional tags such as "first" and "last," with perhaps the "middle" tag also being assigned to slightly fewer items than early in learning. The studies of Schulz (1955), Heslip and Epstein (1969), and Voss (1969), however, do indicate that this process appears to asymptote quite early and generally fails to reach the point where each item in the list has its own unique position tag.

It is appropriate to note the possible relation between the notion of dimensional position in the present context and Mandler's (1967) development of the concept of organization.[10] For this purpose, position may be regarded as a category containing at least one item at each of the termini of the series and many items at the center of the series, the exact number depending upon list length and degree of learning. Mandler has developed the notion that memory is facilitated by organization based upon the growth of categories having a limited storage capacity. Accordingly he has suggested that

> ... categories will be formed and 3-7 items assigned to them. Once these initial categories are filled up, new categories will be created to accommodate additional items. But in turn, there will be a limit of about 5 ± 2 categories at the first level of categorization. When all slots are taken up with first level categories, a second level of categories will be formed, each of which may contain up to about seven first-level categories, and so forth. In this manner, a hierarchical system of categories can be built up with increasing level of complexity and an exponential growth in the size of the system [p. 366].

By contrast, the present view suggests that the function of learning with dimensionally organized material is best served by emptying the position categories, in order to approach the level of one item per position, and not by filling them. This, of course, is the result of the necessity to recall items in a certain order in serial learning and in the PA paradigms with dimensionally organized stimuli or response sets. In these cases if more than one item is stored in a given category (position), a retrieval cue to that category (position) must cause all items in the category to be recalled, and hence the production of intrusion errors. Since correct performance is compatible with only one item per category, serial learning and the other PA paradigms already described are, from Mandler's approach, extremely inefficient since the limit of 5 ± 2 items per category is never approached. Perhaps new hybrid paradigms should be explored which permit more than one item per position category, but continue to require that categories be "accessed" in a fixed sequence.

It is possible, however, that the limit to the number of position categories does follow the principle suggested by Mandler, so that

---

[10] The proposed role of dimensional organization is an alternative to models based exclusively upon interitem associations. In this respect the present approach differs from that proposed by Lesgold and Bower (1970) where items within a chunk are associatively linked as are the chunks themselves, although the former more strongly than the latter.

one might expect a maximum of seven positions to be utilized in tasks involving dimensionally organized material. Now even if this capacity is assumed not to be seriously attenuated by the necessity to discriminate among highly similar categories (e.g., the central positions), there remains the serious problem of accounting for performance which exceeds that of mastery of a seven-item list. Mandler has suggested that memory may be expanded through the development of a hierarchically ordered system of categories. However, this approach cannot be effective in those cases where retrieval must follow a given order or be specific to a given stimulus as in PA learning.

There are perhaps two ways to extend the range of recall of dimensionally organized material without appeal to a hierarchical strategy. One is by rote association between the nonpositional (nominal) attributes of the items, e.g., interitem associations in serial learning. This possibility has already been discussed as a way of overcoming position confusion in the middle of a serial list. In this fashion, both position confusion and the problem of capacity being limited by the use of a maximum of seven position tags may in some degree be avoided. A second strategy, more consistent with the notion of dimensional organization, is also available. This approach requires the development of multiple, duplicate organizations at the same level in the memory system. In the context of dimensionally organized material, multiple organizations would develop when more than one set of boundaries were identified within the list. This procedure would then permit more categories to be available, i.e., in principle $5 \pm 2$ positions for each set of boundaries, hence facilitating the rate of learning by reducing position confusion.

The multiple bowing found by Asch *et al.* (1960) and by Wishner, Shipley, and Hurvich (1957) clearly reflects the effects of several sets of boundaries within one series. In the former study, serial learning was investigated in the context of various spatial patterns. For example, in one experiment the items appeared in succession in spaces around the perimeter of a triangular contour. In the latter study, Ss learned SLs that were divided into two or three parts by changing the color or type size used to prepare the memory drum tapes. Of special interest is the finding by Wishner *et al.* (1957) of evidence for systematic dips in the error curves of the control groups in which Ss learned homogeneous lists of 14 and 18 items. The authors referred to the possibility of intentional organization, which in the present context would appear to be a likely strategy when the S is faced with a relatively long or difficult SL. Since dimensional organization relies heavily upon the presence of boundaries relative to which position tags are assigned to items, it follows that whereas emphasis on boundaries facilitates learning and the SPE, the elimination of boundaries should operate to decrease the rate of learning and decrease the likelihood of obtaining an SPE. There is considerable support for this conclusion (e.g., Ebenholtz, 1963b; Glanzer & Peters, 1962; Keppel, 1964; Lippman & Denny, 1964; Saufley, 1967; Winnick & Dornbush, 1963).

## IV. Alternative Interpretations of the SPE

### A. Von Restorff Effect and End Anchoring

It is possible to develop an account of the SPE in serial learning based upon the assumption that the end items serve as anchors to which adjacent terms are gradually associated. End items may be regarded as anchors by virtue of their proximity to the intertrial interval which is assumed to endow these items with a status analogous to the isolated items of the Von Restorff effect. The assumption that learning proceeds outward from highly discriminable anchor points in an orderly fashion, together with some auxiliary mechanism to account for the skew in the SPE of serial learning, has been suggested by a number of authors (e.g., Glanzer & Peters, 1962; Jensen, 1962a; Lippman & Denny, 1964). While it is likely that isolation effects contribute somewhat to the relative advantage in learning of end items over the remaining items, there is considerable doubt that such facilitation spreads in decreasing strength to nearby items (Jensen, 1962b). Such a gradient should, of course, be a necessary outcome of the Von Restorff effect in order for it to serve as a basis from which to deduce the SPE. As a rule, however, such a gradient is not obtained, viz.,

> ... the organizing aid of the isolated item is quite specific to that item. The isolated item does not appear to serve as an anchor point around which new items are learned. No evidence was found to suggest that the isolated item divides the serial list into two parts, each learned serially. The data suggest that organizational aids are specific to the isolated term [Wallace, 1965, p. 421].

These restricted effects of isolation would seem to constitute a critical shortcoming of all approaches that rely on Von Restorff-type phenomena for an explanation of the SPE, and hence to require their rejection. It is also the case that these approaches do not appear to be general enough to account for much of the data described in the present essay.

## B. REMOTE ASSOCIATIONS AND EBBINGHAUS' DERIVED LISTS

The tendency to develop a theoretical account of both sequence learning and the SPE in terms of identical concepts has been mentioned earlier. The best examples of this approach are the studies of Bugelski (1950) and Hull *et al.* (1940). In the former case, remote associations presumed to occur during serial learning were also explicitly posited as the basis for the SPE. From the present view, however, the SPE of serial learning is merely one instance of a large class of SPEs, of which only a few are accompanied by a constant temporal order of presentation as in serial learning. Since remote associations are defined in terms of the degree of *temporal* contiguity, it follows that they are as such irrelevant to a general explanation of the SPE.

An interpretation of remote associations, i.e., intralist intrusions, consistent with the notion of dimensional organization, requires their redefinition, as Slamecka (1964) has suggested, as errors of location. Accordingly, adjacency and remoteness should be understood in terms of the particular dimension exhibiting the SPE and certainly not exclusively in temporal terms. Given the assumption that adjacent positions are most confusable, and that $S$s tend to restrict their responses to one area or locus of the dimension (according to the position tag of the stimulus), it follows that low orders of "remote associations" are more probable than higher orders. Hence, a "remote association" gradient should be found in all instances of dimensional organization, including, of course, serial learning.

Figure 3A represents the gradient of remote associations compiled by Bugelski (1950). Since the numbers of theoretically possible remote associations diminish with increasing degrees of remoteness, the obtained totals were weighted in inverse proportion to their theoretical frequencies. The gradient clearly shows a diminishing frequency with increasing degrees of remoteness, and this outcome is consistent with those formulations which assume that strength of associations (and hence their frequency of occurrence) varies with degree of temporal contiguity. That this interpretation is not a necessary one is demonstrated by the presence of similar gradients obtained from intralist intrusion errors resulting from PA learning. In these paradigms, the presentation order was either random or perfectly balanced over items, thereby precluding the presence of a

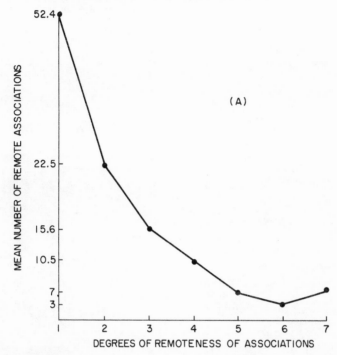

Fig. 3A. The remote association gradient obtained with an eight-item serial list. From Bugelski, 1950, with permission from the American Psychological Association, Washington, D.C.

temporal gradient. Figures 3B and C were derived from studies of dimensional organization described previously, in which an SPE was shown in the context of a PA paradigm.[11] In each case, the correct response was designated as zero-degrees remote, the response that would have been correct had it been given to the adjacent stimulus on the dimension was defined as a first-degree remote association, etc. The obtained frequencies were corrected for unequal opportunity of occurrence. It is apparent that the gradients are remarkably similar to those obtained in serial learning.

Figure 3D was derived from the published data of the studies of Pollio (1966) and Pollio and Draper (1966), also described earlier, in which the response terms were dimensionally organized. The frequencies of remote associations were corrected for unequal

[11] The two studies investigated transfer tasks, but the data on which the gradients were based derived from the initial tasks only.

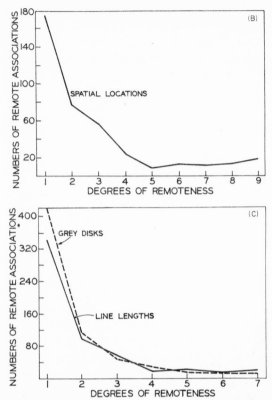

Figs. 3B and C. The frequency of remote associations (misplaced responses) as a function of degree of remoteness, i.e., positions removed from the correct location. The gradients were obtained with lists of eight paired associates. Data from Ebenholtz, 1963a(B), 1965(C).

opportunities,[12] and the degrees of remoteness were defined in terms of the five positions represented in the response dimension, e.g., beautiful, pretty, fair, homely, and ugly. Thus, for example, a one-degree remote error would occur when "pretty" was given but where "beautiful" was a correct response. The two studies are consistent with those reported above in that a diminishing frequency of remote associations occurs as degree of remoteness increases. However, the shape of the gradients in Fig. 3D is not the same as those represented in Figs. 3A, B, and C. There are two possible sources of this discrepancy, one being the small numbers of

[12] Pollio and Draper (1966) performed a similar analysis, but it appears that they did not correct for the unequal opportunities of occurrence of the various degrees of remote associations, although they did correct for guessing tendencies and error frequency at each position.

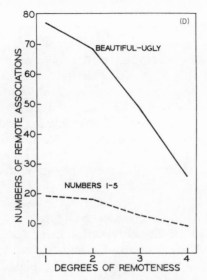

Fig. 3D. Remote association gradients derived from a "many into one" paired-associate (PA) procedure. Beautiful-ugly data from Pollio, H. R. *Psychological Reports*, 1966, 19, 643-647. Reprinted with permission of author and publisher; numbers 1-5 data from Pollio and Draper, 1966.

dimension locations (i.e., five) represented in the two studies, and the second being the PA procedure in which the same response term must be associated with several different stimuli (DeSoto & Bosley, 1962). Despite the variation in shape, however, all five studies exhibit a diminishing remote association gradient. They are consistent, therefore, with the interpretation of intralist intrusions (i.e., remote associations) in terms of errors of location. It may be concluded, then, that both the SPE and the gradient of remote associations arise from the conditions of dimensional organization.

A second source of evidence is also available to evaluate the hypothesized relation between dimensional organization and the remote-association gradient. The negative effects on serial learning that occur when the starting position is varied from trial to trial have already been described. If this procedure is interpreted as one in which the role of dimension location is reduced, if not eliminated, relative to the SM then the distribution of intralist errors should be less constrained in the varied position (VP) method than in the constant position (CP) procedure. Ideally, if position cues were totally absent under Condition VP, a given intrusion would be just as likely to occur in adjacent as in remote serial positions. Ebenholtz

(1963b) compared the number of errors no more than one position removed from their correct location (i.e., adjacent or A-errors) with the number of errors at least two positions removed (i.e., remote or R-errors). He found that there were more Ss showing greater numbers of R over A errors under Condition VP than under Condition CP. On the other hand, more Ss showed a preponderance of A errors under Condition CP than under Condition VP. Thus, adjacent intrusions were more likely under standard SL, remote intrusions were more likely under the varied starting position method.

This finding has been replicated in an unpublished study using 11-item serial lists in which for both conditions the first and last items were identical. Under Condition VP, the starting syllable was shifted by three positions on succeeding trials. The results again indicated more rapid acquisition for Condition CP. Furthermore, of 12 Ss in Group VP, eight showed a higher frequency of R over A errors, two showed a tie, and two yielded a higher frequency of A errors. For the 12 Ss in Group CP, the corresponding values were two, two, and eight. The Ss showing tied scores were dropped from the analysis, and a Fisher Exact Probability Test showed the distributions of Ss in the two categories (i.e., $R < A$ and $A < R$) to vary significantly ($p < .02$) between the two groups. The hypothesis that position information is attenuated under Condition VP and that such information is responsible for the relatively high frequency of occurrence of first-degree remote (i.e., Type A) associations under standard SL conditions is confirmed by these data.

This essay on serial learning began with an observation of Ebbinghaus', and perhaps it is appropriate to close with a further note on Ebbinghaus' contribution following the analysis of Shebilske and Ebenholtz (1971).

Ebbinghaus devised the method of derived lists in order to test the notion of remote associations. The method entailed the learning of an SL and then after 24 hours, learning a list derived from the first by skipping various numbers of items. For example, if the first list were represented as A-B-C-D-E-F-G-H, a first-order derived list would be represented as A-C-E-G-B-D-F-H. Second- and third-order derived lists were produced by skipping two and three items, respectively, in analogous fashion. In these experiments, Ebbinghaus learned first, second, third, and seventh-order derived lists composed of 16 items each. In any one condition, six different lists were constructed. These were always learned in succession on one day, and then 24 hours later their respective derived lists were learned. The procedure used in developing the seventh-order derived lists departed somewhat from that already described in that they contained pairs of items from all six lists, e.g., Items 1 and 9 from Lists I, II, III, IV, V, and VI, plus Items 2 and 10 from Lists I and II. These lists nevertheless contained eight pairs of items, each pair being composed by skipping seven intervening syllables.

Ebbinghaus (1885) commented on the possible outcome of learning the first-order list as follows:

> Every member of the transformed series was, in the original series, separated from its present immediate neighbor by an intervening member . . . If these intervening members are actual obstructions to the associative connection, then the transformed series are as good as entirely unknown. . . . no savings in work should be expected in the repetition of the transformed series [p. 96].

It is of some importance to note that Ebbinghaus did not entertain the possibility of interference or negative transfer, for he believed that the missing intervening members could do no more than render the derived lists equivalent to unrelated transfer lists. Ebbinghaus then went on to state the more familiar deduction from his assumption of remote associations, viz., that ". . . syllables now in succession have already been bound together secretly with threads of a certain strength. In the learning of such a series it will be revealed that noticeably less work is required than for the learning of an altogether new series [p. 96]."

The problem of the proper control condition was then considered, and it is much to his credit to note that Ebbinghaus was quite aware of the need to control for differential item familiarity. He wrote,

> By means of the first learning they are impressed not merely in their definite order but also purely as individual syllables; with repetition they become to some extent familiar, at least more familiar than other syllables, which had not been learned just before. Moreover, the new series have in part the same initial and final members as the old. Therefore, if they are learned in somewhat less time than the first series required, it is not to be wondered at. The basis of this does not necessarily lie in the artificial and systematic change of the arrangement, but it possibly rests merely on the identity of the syllables. If these were repeated on the second day in a new arrangement made entirely by chance they would probably show equally a saving in work [p. 98].

The implication here is that Ebbinghaus' control condition was a random-order derived list (Hakes & Young, 1966),[13] but this was *not* in fact the case. For the control condition, the "... initial and final syllables of the original series were left in their places. The remaining 84 syllables,[14] intermediates, were shaken up together and then, after chance drawing, were employed in the construction of new series between the original initial and final series[15] [p. 99.]."

Ebbinghaus found that it took less time to learn the derived lists than the original series, and that this savings diminished as the order of remoteness increased. Ebbinghaus replicated this outcome under conditions designed to obscure knowledge of the relation between original and derived lists, hence it would appear that his results were quite reliable. Recently, however, Hakes and Young (1966) have suggested that Ebbinghaus' control lists should be regarded as random-order conditions and hence as productive of negative transfer. The results with the various orders of derived lists could then be interpreted in terms of differential levels of negative transfer. It has already been noted, however, that Ebbinghaus' control condition does not correspond to a random-order list. There is, however, yet another objection to this interpretation. Ebbinghaus was, to understate the matter, a rather sophisticated subject. As noted, he learned six lists in succession, and in the first derived-list study he repeated this procedure 11 times for each derived-list condition. It would appear, therefore, not an unlikely assumption to conclude that Ebbinghaus could benefit but little from nonspecific transfer (Postman, 1968).

It follows that an ideal "neutral" second list would have to be learned at the same rate as the first list, i.e., with zero savings. His actual performance in his control condition, i.e., 12 seconds savings in one study and −5 seconds in another, was not far from this ideal, and suggested that item familiarity was not an important factor in the learning of derived lists. On the grounds, then, that Ebbinghaus'

[13] Hakes and Young (1966) reported that Irion (1946) had shown a random-order condition to be one of negative transfer. The conclusion may be true (Keppel & Saufley, 1964) but Irion's study did not prove it, for the experiment contained no "neutral" or unrelated-list control group, and Irion drew his conclusion on the questionable basis of a count of overt errors. But in any event, the random-order list does not correspond with Ebbinghaus' control condition.

[14] It may be recalled that Ebbinghaus worked with six 16-item series at one sitting. This represented a pool of 96 items, 12 of which were taken up at the terminal positions of the derived control lists.

[15] The word "series" is probably in error. It would appear that "syllables" was intended.

nonspecific transfer function was already at asymptotic levels, it can be concluded that his control condition was nearly perfect, and certainly not productive of negative transfer. It must be concluded, therefore, that the problem of interpreting Ebbinghaus' positive findings for remote associations in the context of recent evidence for negative transfer in derived list paradigms (Hakes, James & Young, 1964; Young, Hakes, & Hicks, 1965) remains unresolved. There are too many sources of difference in modern studies, relative to Ebbinghaus' procedures, to conclude with reasonable certainty about these discrepant findings. For example, Ebbinghaus learned six lists at one sitting, the transfer lists were learned 24 hours after the initial list, the method of whole presentation and testing are different from contemporary procedures, the asymptotic level of nonspecific transfer probably has not been achieved in modern attempts at replication, etc.

Modern studies of derived lists have tended to show zero or negative transfer (e.g., Slamecka, 1964; Hakes *et al.*, 1964) the latter being consonant with the assumption of associative interference in the derived list. This outcome is also consonant with the possibility of position interference from items at displaced locations on the derived list relative to the original list, although such negative transfer should, from the point of view of dimensional organization, be restricted to end items. However, since these are learned rather rapidly, the contribution of position cues to negative transfer should be quite small. Furthermore, if one assumes that sequential associations are formed between items at the center of a list, then lengthening the list may increase the relative numbers of such associations and thereby enhance the likelihood of finding negative transfer. The negative transfer found by Young *et al.* (1965) for 12 and 16-item lists, but not for an eight-item list, is consistent with this implication.


## V. Conclusions

The present chapter has explored the concept of dimensional organization with particular emphasis on serial learning. It has been suggested that the processes that underlie learning to output a set of items in a constant order, i.e., sequence learning, are orthogonal to those that are responsible for the serial position effect (SPE). The occurrence of the SPE under conditions of serial learning was attributed to dimensional organization of the temporally ordered series, and the general proposition was offered that whenever items are discriminated (i.e., organized) on the basis of their respective dimension locations, the SPE will occur. It may be concluded that the ability of the $S$ to utilize the position information contained in item sets possessing ordinal characteristics represents a basic organizational process relevant to the storage and retrieval of a large and varied array of verbal and sensory data.

## ACKNOWLEDGMENTS

The author is grateful to William Epstein, Ken Paap, and Wayne Shebilske for their thoughtful comments on an earlier draft of this chapter. Appreciation is also expressed to the author's students who, through the years, have provided the occasion for the critical analysis of many of the conceptions of verbal learning theory. Special thanks are due to my wife Jean, for her patience and cooperation, for the chapter was written during the fall semester, 1970–1971, without the benefit of leave of absence.

The quotations on pp. 268 and 307 are reprinted by permission of the publisher from Ebbinghaus, H., *Über das Gedächtnis: Untersuchungen zur experimentellen Psychologie*. Leipzig: Duncker & Humblot, 1885. Translation by H. A. Ruger and C. E. Bussenius, *Memory: A Contribution to Experimental Psychology*. (New York: Teachers College Press; copyright 1913 by Teachers College, Columbia University.)

## REFERENCES

Asch, S. E., & Ebenholtz, S. M. The process of free recall: Evidence for nonassociative factors in acquisition and retention. *Journal of Psychology*, 1962, 54, 3–31. (a)

Asch, S. E., & Ebenholtz, S. M. The principle of associative symmetry. *Proceedings of the American Philosophical Society*, 1962, 106, 135–163. (b)

Asch, S. E., Hay, J., & Diamond, R. M. Perceptual organization in serial rote-learning. *American Journal of Psychology*, 1960, 73, 117–198.

Battig, W. F. Advantages of recall over anticipation methods in verbal learning. *Behavior Research Methods and Instrumentation*, 1969, 1, 217–220.

Bowman, R. E., & Thurlow, W. R. Determinants of the effect of position in serial learning. *American Journal of Psychology*, 1963, 76, 436–445.

Braun, H. W., & Heymann, S. P. Meaningfulness of material, distribution of practice, and serial-position curves. *Journal of Experimental Psychology*, 1958, 56, 146–150.

Breckenridge, K., Hakes, D. T., & Young, R. K. Serial learning in a continuous serial list. *Psychonomic Science*, 1965, 3, 139–140.

Breckenridge, R. L., & Dixon, T. R. Problem of the stimulus in serial learning. *Journal of Experimental Psychology*, 1970, 83, 126–130.

Bugelski, B. R. A remote association explanation of the relative difficulty of learning nonsense syllables in a serial list. *Journal of Experimental Psychology*, 1950, 40, 336–348.

Crovitz, H. R., & Schiffman, H. R. Visual field and the letter span. *Journal of Experimental Psychology*, 1965, 70, 218–223.

Deese, J., & Kresse, F. H. An experimental analysis of the errors in rote serial learning. *Journal of Experimental Psychology*, 1952, 43, 199–202.

DeSoto, C. B., & Bosley, J. J. The cognitive structure of a social structure. *Journal of Abnormal Social Psychology*, 1962, 64, 303–307.

Dey, M. K. Generalization of position association in rote serial learning. *American Journal of Psychology*, 1970, 83, 248–255.

Ebbinghaus, H. *Uber das Gedächtnis: Untersuchungen zur experimentellen Psychologie*. Leipzig: Duncker & Humblot, 1885. Translation by H. A. Ruger & C. E. Bussenius, *Memory: A contribution to experimental psychology*. New York: Teachers College, Columbia University, Bureau of Publications, 1913.

Ebenholtz, S. M. Position mediated transfer between serial learning and a spatial discrimination task. *Journal of Experimental Psychology*, 1963, 65, 603–608. (a)

Ebenholtz, S. M. Serial learning: Position learning and sequential associations. *Journal of Experimental Psychology*, 1963, 66, 353–362. (b)

Ebenholtz, S. M. Positional cues as mediators in discrimination learning. *Journal of Experimental Psychology*, 1965, 70, 176–181.

Ebenholtz, S. M. Serial-position effect of ordered stimulus dimensions in paired-associate learning. *Journal of Experimental Psychology*, 1966, 71, 132–137. (a)

Ebenholtz, S. M. Serial-list items as stimuli in paired-associate learning. *Journal of Experimental Psychology*, 1966, 72, 154–155. (b)

Epstein, W. A further study of the influence of syntactical structure on learning. *American Journal of Psychology*, 1962, 75, 121–126.

Gamble, E. A. McC., & Wilson, L. A study of spatial associations in learning and in recall. *Psychological Monographs*, 1916, 22, (4, Whole No. 96), 41–97.

Glanzer, M., & Peters, S. C. Re-examination of the serial position effect. *Journal of Experimental Psychology*, 1962, 64, 258–266.

Hakes, D. T., James, C. T., & Young, R. K. A re-examination of the Ebbinghaus derived-list paradigm. *Journal of Experimental Psychology*, 1964, 68, 508–514.

Hakes, D. T., & Young, R. K. On remote associations and the interpretation of derived-list experiments. *Psychological Review*, 1966, 73, 248–251.

Harcum, E. R., & Coppage, E. W. Explanation of serial learning errors within Deese-Kresse categories. *Journal of Experimental Psychology*, 1969, 81, 489–496.

Heslip, J. R., & Epstein, W. Effectiveness of serial position and preceding-item cues in serial learning. *Journal of Experimental Psychology*, 1969, 80, 64–68.

Hicks, R. Y., Hakes, D. T., & Young, R. K. Generalization of serial position in rote serial learning. *Journal of Experimental Psychology*, 1966, 71,916–917.

Horowitz, L. W., & Izawa, C. Comparison of serial and paired-associate learning. *Journal of Experimental Psychology*, 1963, 65, 352–361.

Horton, D. L., & Turnage, T. W. Serial to paired-associate learning: Utilization of serial information. *Journal of Experimental Psychology*, 1970, 84, 88–95.

Hull, C. L., Hovland, C. I. Ross, R. T., Hall, M., Perkins, D. T., & Fitch, F. B. *Mathematico-deductive theory of rote learning: A study in scientific methodology*. New Haven, Conn.: Yale University Press, 1940.

Irion, A. L. Retroactive inhibition as a function of the relative serial positions of the original and interpolated items. *Journal of Experimental Psychology*, 1946, 36, 262–270.

Jensen, A. R. An empirical theory of the serial-position effect. *Journal of Psychology*, 1962, 53, 127–142. (a)

Jensen, A. R. The Von Restorff isolation effect with minimal response learning. *Journal of Experimental Psychology*, 1962, **64**, 123-125. (b)

Jensen, A. R. Spelling errors and the serial-position effect. *Journal of Educational Psychology*, 1962, **53**, 105-109. (c)

Jensen, A. R. Temporal and spatial effects of serial position. *American Journal of Psychology*, 1962, **75**, 390-400. (d)

Jensen, A. R. Transfer between paired-associate and serial learning. *Journal of Verbal Learning and Verbal Behavior*, 1963, **1**, 269-280.

Jensen, A. R., & Blank, S. S. Association with serial position in serial rote learning. *Canadian Journal of Psychology*, 1962, **16**, 60-63.

Jensen, A. R., & Rohwer, W. D., Jr. What is learned in serial learning? *Journal of Verbal Learning and Verbal Behavior*, 1965, **4**, 62-72.

Jung, J. A cumulative method of paired-associate and serial learning. *Journal of Verbal Learning and Verbal Behavior*, 1964, **3**, 290-299.

Keppel, G. Retroactive inhibition of serial lists as a function of the presence or absence of positional cues. *Journal of Verbal Learning and Verbal Behavior*, 1964, **3**, 511-517.

Keppel, G. Comments on the hypothesis of implicit serial-position cues. *Psychonomic Science*, 1965, **3**, 471-472.

Keppel, G., & Saufley, W. H., Jr. Serial position as a stimulus in serial learning. *Journal of Verbal Learning and Verbal Behavior*, 1964, **3**, 335-343.

Lashley, K. S. The problem of serial order in behavior. In L. A. Jeffress (Ed.), *Cerebral mechanisms in behavior*. New York: Wiley, 1951. Pp. 112-136.

Lesgold, A. M., & Bower, G. H. Inefficiency of serial knowledge for associative responding. *Journal of Verbal Learning and Verbal Behavior*, 1970, **9**, 456-466.

Lippman, L. G., & Denny, M. R. Serial position effect as a function of intertrial interval. *Journal of Verbal Learning and Verbal Behavior*, 1964, **3**, 496-501.

Mandler, G. Organization and memory. In K. W. Spence & J. T. Spence (Eds.), *The psychology of learning and motivation: Advances in research and theory*. Vol. 1. New York: Academic Press, 1967. Pp. 327-372.

Mandler, G. Incremental acquisition of paired-associate lists. *Journal of Experimental Psychology*, 1970, **84**, 185-186.

Mandler, G., & Dean, P. J. Seriation: Development of serial order in free recall. *Journal of Experimental Psychology*, 1969, **81**, 207-215.

McCrary, J. W., & Hunter, W. S. Serial position curves in verbal learning. *Science*, 1953, **117**, 131-134.

McGeoch, J. A. The direction and extent of intra-serial associations at recall. *American Journal of Psychology*, 1936, **48**, 221-245.

McGeoch, J. A., & Irion, A. L. *The psychology of human learning*. (2nd ed.) New York: Longmans, Green, 1952.

McGovern, J. T. Extinction of associations in four transfer paradigms. *Psychological Monographs*, 1964, **78**,(16, Whole No. 593).

Melton, A. W., & Irwin, J. M. The influence of degree of interpolated learning o retroactive inhibition and the overt transfer of specific responses. *American Journal of Psychology*, 1940, **53**, 173-203.

Müller, G. E., & Schumann, F. Experimentelle Beiträge zur Untersuchung des Gedächtnisses. *Zeitschrift für Psychologie*, 1894, **6**, 81-190, 257-339.

Mueller, J. H. Response properties of the position indicant in serial learning. *Journal of Experimental Psychology*, 1970, **84**, 35-39.

Murdock, B. B., Jr. The distinctiveness of stimuli. *Psychological Review*, 1960, 67, 16-31.

Phillips, L. W. Mediated verbal similarity as a determinant of the generalization of a conditioned GSR. *Journal of Experimental Psychology*, 1958, 55, 56-62.

Pollio, H. R. Oppositional serial structures and paired-associate learning. *Psychological Reports*, 1966, 79, 643-647.

Pollio, H. R., Deitchman, R., & Richards, S. Law of contrast and oppositional word associates. *Journal of Experimental Psychology*, 1969, 79,203-212.

Pollio, H. R., & Draper, D. O. The effect of serial structure on paired-associate learning. *Journal of Verbal Learning and Verbal Behavior*, 1966, 5, 301-308.

Postman, L. Hermann Ebbinghaus. *American Psychologist*, 1968, 23, 149-157.

Postman, L., & Rau, L. Retention as a function of the method of measurement. *University of California Publications in Psychology*, 1957, 8, No. 3, 217-270.

Postman, L., & Stark, K. Studies of learning to learn: IV. Transfer from serial to paired-associate learning. *Journal of Verbal Learning and Verbal Behavior*, 1967, 6, 339-353.

Primoff, S. M. E. Backward and forward association as an organized act in serial and in paired associate learning. *Journal of Psychology*, 1938, 5, 375-396.

Saufley, W. H., Jr. An analysis of cues in serial learning. *Journal of Experimental Psychology*, 1967, 74, 414-419.

Schulz, R. W. Generalization of serial position in rote serial learning. *Journal of Experimental Psychology*, 1955, 49, 267-272.

Shebilske, W., & Ebenholtz, S. M. Ebbinghaus' derived-list experiments reconsidered. *Psychological Review*, 1971, in press.

Shuell, T. K., & Keppel, G. A further test of the chaining hypothesis of serial learning. *Journal of Verbal Learning and Verbal Behavior*, 1967, 6, 439-445.

Slamecka, N. J. An inquiry into the doctrine of remote associations. *Psychological Review*, 1964, 71, 61-76.

Tulving, E. Theoretical issues in free recall. In T. R. Dixon & D. L. Horton (Eds.), *Verbal behavior and general behavior theory*. Englewood Cliffs, N.J.: Prentice-Hall, 1968. Pp. 2-36.

Underwood, B. J., & Schulz, R. W. *Meaningfulness and verbal learning*. Philadelphia: Lippincott, 1960.

Voss, J. F. Serial acquisition as a function of stage of learning. *Journal of Experimental Psychology*, 1969, 79, 220-225.

Wallace, W. P. Review of the historical, empirical, and theoretical status of the Von Restorff phenomenon. *Psychological Bulletin*, 1965, 63, 410-424.

Winnick, W. A., & Dornbush, R. L. Role of positional cues in serial rote learning. *Journal of Experimental Psychology*, 1963, 66, 419-421.

Winnick, W. A., & Dornbush, R. L. Ordinal position in serial learning. *Journal of Experimental Psychology*, 1968, 78, 536-538.

Wishner, J., Shipley, T. E., Jr., & Hurvich, M. S. The serial-position curve as a function of organization. *American Journal of Psychology*, 1957, 70, 258-262.

Woodward, A. E., Jr. Transfer from serial learning to paired-associate learning as a function of positive and negative transfer paradigms. Unpublished master's thesis, Connecticut College, 1966.

Woodworth, R. S., & Poffenberger, A. T. *Textbook of experimental psychology*. (Mimeo. ed.) 1920, Columbia University Library.

Young, R. K. A comparison of two methods of learning serial associations. *American Journal of Psychology*, 1959, 72, 554-559.

Young, R. K. The stimulus in serial verbal learning. *American Journal of Psychology*. 1961, 74, 517-528.

Young, R. K. Tests of three hypotheses about the effective stimulus in serial learning. *Journal of Experimental Psychology*, 1962, 63, 307-313.

Young, R. K. Serial learning. In T. R. Dixon & D. L. Horton (Eds.), *Verbal behavior and general behavior theory*. Englewood Cliffs, N.J.: Prentice-Hall, 1968. Pp. 122-148.

Young, R. K., & Casey, M. Transfer from serial to paired associate learning. *Journal of Experimental Psychology*, 1964, 67, 594-595.

Young, R. K., Hakes, D. T., & Hicks, R. Y. Effects of list length in the Ebbinghaus derived-list paradigm. *Journal of Experimental Psychology*, 1965, 70, 338-341.

Young, R. K., Hakes, D. T., & Hicks, R. Y. Ordinal position number as a cue in serial learning. *Journal of Experimental Psychology*, 1967, 73, 427-438.

Young, R. K., Patterson, J., & Benson, W. M. Backward serial learning. *Journal of Verbal Learning and Verbal Behavior*, 1963, 1, 335-338.

# I. Introduction

The basic free recall experiment with which we will be concerned involves the presentation to a subject (S) of a list of words, one word at a time. After seeing all the words in the list, the S is asked to recall them in any order he chooses. The experimental paradigm derives its name from the fact that the S is not constrained to recall items in a particular order. The free recall paradigm has recently attracted much research interest because of evidence indicating the strong influence of various types of conceptual organization upon the S's recall. This evidence is of two sorts:

1. The experimenter (E) may choose sets of words with certain

[1] This research was supported by a grant, MH-13950-04, from the National Institutes of Mental Health to my research advisor, Gordon Bower. I am indebted to Professor Bower for his advice and assistance in the preparation of this paper.

organizational characteristics and note how that organization is reflected in recall. Bousfield (1953) reported that words which came from the same conceptual category (i.e., were instances of the same superordinate concept) tended to be recalled together. Bousfield and Cohen (1953) found that this clustering increased over trials, and Underwood (1964) found better recall for lists organized into a small number of conceptual categories. Jenkins and Russell (1952) examined free recall in a list that contained 24 pairs of words, each pair consisting of a stimulus word and its highest frequency associate. Although such associated pairs were not presented adjacently in study, there was a high probability for the items to be recalled together. Deese (1959a) found that sets of words which tend to elicit one another as free associates are more easily recalled than sets of words which are not interassociated.

2. Even when the E deliberately minimizes relationships among the list words, Ss apparently still impose their own idiosyncratic organization upon the word list. In their introspective reports subjects almost universally describe some sort of organizational strategy. Typical strategies include developing visual images in which the referents of the words interact, creating stories that involve the words as main actors, and finding some obscure property that applies to a number of words (e.g., "mother," "butter," and "cup" are all found in the kitchen). Subjects also claim to recall together the words they have grouped together during study rather than recalling words in a random order. It is as if the Ss created a small number of multiword units out of a long list of words and recalled these units rather than the words individually. If so, it is clear why categorized and highly interassociated lists are better recalled than those which are not. Such lists are more conducive to such a "unitization" strategy.

Alongside these introspective reports, there is evidence in the recall protocols themselves to indicate that Ss organize their recall even with "unrelated" words. By tabulating the frequency with which the same pairs of words are recalled adjacently across trials, it becomes clear that the order of recall shows much greater across-trial consistency or stereotypy than could be produced by randomly ordered recall (Bousfield, Puff, & Cohen, 1964; Tulving, 1962). Such stereotypy, occurring although the words are rerandomized on each presentation, is just what would be predicted if the Ss were recalling the words in groups or "subjective units."

This stereotypy of recall increases across trials on a list as does the number of words recalled. This correlation between stereotypy and amount recalled has led some theorists (e.g., Mandler, 1967; Tulving, 1968) to postulate that free recall learning is a consequence of progressive organization of the list into a small number of subjective units. This is called the "unitization hypothesis." Mandler and Pearlstone (1966) reported an experiment which offers impressive support for this hypothesis. Their Ss sorted 52 cards, each containing a word, into two to seven groups based on similarity of meaning. After sorting the cards once, the S was given the cards a second time in randomized order and instructed to resort them in the same way. This procedure was repeated until the S was able to sort the cards identically twice in a row. One group of Ss was told to study the words as they sorted them in order to be able to recall them later. The other Ss were not told that there would be a free recall test. In a subsequent free recall test both groups recalled equally well. From this result, Mandler and Pearlstone concluded that organization of a list of words into stable categories is a *sufficient* condition for a high level of recall. This is to be predicted from the unitization hypothesis which relates level of recall to the degree to which the list has been "chunked" into a small number of stable groups.

Despite this kind of evidence, we feel that the unitization hypothesis as it stands is inadequate as a theory of free recall. A first objection is that several experiments are now available indicating that measures of organization and of recall can vary independently (Cofer, 1967; Cofer, Bruce, & Reicher, 1966; Dallett, 1964; Puff, 1970; Rosner, 1970). Such failures of the general correlation indicate the need to make more explicit the structures and processes underlying the formation and retrieval of the "units." Once this is done, it might be possible to determine boundary conditions on the general prediction of "more organization, more recall."

A second objection to the unitization hypothesis arises from informal observations of ours when we have asked Ss to introspect on what they were doing as they studied and recalled a list of words. Consider the representative introspections, given in the Appendix, of one S as she studied a list of 40 words during a free recall trial. She had already studied and recalled this list once. At first glance she and most of her cohorts we have analyzed appear to do roughly what the unitization hypothesis claims, viz.; by using imagery, categorization, storytelling, etc., they try to organize words into groups during the input trial. Also Ss tend to recall the words in the groups they have created. However, there is a consistent sort of *instability* to the groupings which is totally alien to the spirit of the unitization hypothesis. Groups of words break into parts, which merge into new groups, which break apart again and remerge into old configurations. It would appear that Ss develop plans for retrieval that do not rely upon rigid subjective units. During the input trial, associations are established between individual words, but there is little effort to define stable units. A network of such interword associations constitutes a powerful retrieval system; if the S can recall just one word, he can recall all the words he has associated with that word, then in a second loop, all the words he has associated with those, and so on, recursively, until he has recalled every word he can reach by chaining through the associations he has developed during study. From this point of view it is not necessary that the S always aggregate the same words together during study, nor is it necessary that he trace out exactly the same search path through his associative network during recall. Indeed, anything that appears to be a unit is just a group of words which are highly interassociated and hence tend to occur together in the S's introspections during study and together in his output during recall.

In this paper we will be interested in developing a model of the processes underlying standard free recall. By "standard free recall" we mean to reference those experiments where the list to be studied is composed of common nouns chosen in a fairly random fashion. The words are presented one at a time at a constant rate. If it is a multitrial experiment, study and recall phases are alternated. It is our contention that, under these circumstances, most Ss spontaneously adopt an associative method for free recall similar to that outlined above. FRAN (Free Recall in an Associative Net) is a computer program that simulates this associative strategy for free recall. In Section II, we describe the hypothetical mental mechanisms which FRAN was constructed to simulate. In Section III, we describe how these mechanisms are used to effect the associative strategy. Section IV of this paper compares FRAN's performance with that of humans in several free recall and recognition experiments. The final section evaluates our theoretical positions and discusses possible theoretical extensions that would create a more powerful theory.

## II. The Mental Mechanisms

FRAN is a computer program implemented in LISP/360. We will not explain in detail the information processing occurring in the computer program itself. Rather we shall concentrate on describing the mental processes the program is simulating. In this section and the next, we will indicate what we think are the important characteristics of the mental structures and processes that underlie free recall.

## A. STRUCTURE OF LONG-TERM MEMORY

FRAN's memory is structurally divided into a sensory register, a short-term store (STS), and a long-term store (LTS), somewhat along the lines suggested by Norman (1968). LTS is the memory system that contains all the individual's knowledge about the world. Therefore, in deciding what the structural characteristics of LTS should be, we wanted a structure that would be adequate not only for simulation of free recall, but also adequate to encode any linguistic fact. Beginning with such general goals offers the possibility that phenomena of free recall will be integrated in the future with other phenomena in human verbal memory.

### 1. Information, Associations, and Labeled Associations

If verbal memory simply consisted of a set of symbolic units (e.g., words), it would contain no information about the world. Information takes the form of connections among the symbolic units. A simple type of connection is the traditional association which is, formally, just an ordered pair of symbolic units (e.g., "dog–cat," "jewel–diamond"). Perhaps because of their simplicity, such associations have historically received the greatest attention in theoretical reconstructions of the mind. However, it has been frequently argued (e.g., Deese, 1968; Kintsch, 1970) that such simple associations are inadequate for representing certain elementary facts about behavior. For instance, this representation in terms of ordered pairs does not explain how it is that we know that the relationship between "dog" and "cat" is one of coordinates, while the relationship between "jewel" and "diamond" is one of super-ordinate–subordinate. That is, what is lacking in an elementary dictionary of associated pairs is knowledge of the relationship exemplified by the pairs; this lack is a serious deficiency since people obviously can search for a word, B, that bears a specified relation, R, to a stimulus word, A.

The inadequacy noted above can be circumvented by replacing the ordered pair representation by ordered triples or *labeled* associations in which the third member of the triple is a symbol identifying (labeling) the relationship between the first two members of the triple which are single elements. So far as we can determine, there are no simple demonstrations of the inadequacies of labeled associations as there are for simple associations. We should point out, however, that for every ordered triple there exists an equivalent ordered pair of a special kind. That is, the ordered triple $<A\ B\ R>$ may be equivalently represented as the ordered pair $<<A\ B>\ R>$. Either notation is to be read as "A has relation R to B." Representation of such information in terms of ordered pairs is only possible, however, when we allow units in an association to include other associations (like the pair $<A\ B>$ above). This move clearly contradicts conventional stimulus-response analyses because it permits, as units of description, elements which do not have a one-to-one correspondence to stimuli or responses [see Bever, Fodor, and Garrett (1968) for arguments regarding the inadequacy inherent in this restriction on stimulus-response (S-R) theorizing]. Whichever of these representations one adopts, restricted ordered triples or generalized ordered pairs, one goes beyond traditional associative analysis with its simple listing of associated pairs.

We do not want to leave the impression that associations have been abandoned in our model. Quite the contrary, we believe the "data base" of a person's memory is a complex associative network and our model for free recall consists of operations for marking subgraphs of that associative network. Where we differ from the traditional association doctrine is that we consider association to be a generic name for a whole class of different types of relations between concepts, and we believe that the name of the relation has to be stored with each associated pair. With this emendation, then, our model for free recall falls in the tradition of associationistic explanations of learning. Frankly, we have a difficult time imagining any radically different alternative type of theory of free recall.

## 2. Semantic Markers?

Following their critical analysis, Deese (1966, 1968) and Kintsch (1970) rejected traditional associationism, but turned, not to a more powerful associative representation as we have, but rather to a representation in terms of semantic markers. In this choice, they were undoubtedly motivated by the desire to establish common theoretical ground with recent linguistic analysis (e.g., Bierwisch, 1967; Katz & Fodor, 1963). However, upon close inspection, it is clear that there is nothing to motivate their choice over our own. The claims made for such semantic marker theories are hardly noncontroversial in linguistics (e.g., Bolinger, 1965; Lyons, 1969; and Schank, 1970). Also is seems that many marker theories are structurally similar to associationist theories since, in the abstract, each concept is defined in terms of its pattern of "associations" to a base set of concepts, the alleged universal markers. Indeed, in Kintsch's analyses, it is not clear how he could encode his markers in a LISP memory structure efficiently and not adopt a representation essentially identical to that adopted for FRAN. Thus, it appears that the choice between the two conceptualizations may ultimately rest on heuristic considerations. We find the graph-theoretical representation, to which our associationist analysis leads us, much more congenial to our way of thinking (see also Quillian, 1969).

## 3. Free Association Norms?

The memory structure of FRAN, then, is a network of labeled associations between words. We think of the memory structure as representing what the $S$ knows when he enters the laboratory and not something that is built up during the experiment. We have resisted the temptation to assign strengths to the various associations. In FRAN's memory, an association either does or does not exist between a pair of words; it is an all-or-none affair. The immediate question is how are we to account for the fact that some associations appear much stronger than others in free association norms.

There are at least three answers to this challenge. The first is to question the assumption that a person in generating an association selects only from the words which are directly associated to the stimulus. It is possible that the individual may chain through a number of associations in his network before generating the response. If so, the structural characteristics of an all-or-none network may "conspire" to favor some words as responses over others. In fact, Kiss (1967) assumes just this in fitting his associative net models to normative association data. The second tact is to argue that the graduated character of free associations is a consequence of pooling across $S$s in the construction of associational statistics. Each $S$ has associations in an all-or-none manner, but only the strong associations are possessed by most $S$s. This analysis has the added utility of explaining in a natural way why weak associations are often bizarre — they represent the memory structure of only a few $S$s. The third response to the challenge is to question the relevance of free association norms to testing a theory concerning the structure of our knowledge of the world. Surely many responses appear in free association norms which have no semantic or conceptual relation to the stimulus word — included would be rhymes and all forms of "clang" associates. The point is that if we wished to find out whether people generally acknowledge a particular relation R between two words A and B, we would hardly set them the ill-defined and ambiguous task of freely associating to A in the hope that they might produce B. In any event, the force of these arguments is that the graduated character of free association norms need constitute no particular embarrassment to FRAN's network of all-or-none associations.

Another feature of FRAN's preexperimental associations is that they are symmetric; that is, if word B is an associate of word A, then A is an associate of B. The motivation for this decision is simply that if A has the relation R to B, then B has the inverse relation $(R^{-1})$ to A. For instance, if "cat" is a subordinate of "carnivore," then "carnivore" is a superordinate of "cat." In formal notation, if a person knows the relation $<<A\ B>R>$, he should also know the relation $<<B\ A>R^{-1}>$. To critics with a bent for parsimony, symmetric associations may appear as superfluous redundancies since one association could be inferred from the other. However, consider the problem of how a S could ever give the information contained in the association $<<A\ B>\ R>$ if he were asked "what do you know about B?" Without the symmetric association $<<B\ A>R^{-1}>$, that information would not be accessible from B. For such reasons, it was deemed necessary that FRAN have this symmetric property in her associations.

## 4. Details of FRAN's Memory

Having discussed the general properties of FRAN's memory, we will now state the details of the actual memory structure that was used in the simulations to be reported. First, it should be confessed that, despite our arguments for labeled associations, FRAN's associations are, in the present computer program, unlabeled. We made provision in the memory structure for labeling, and this provision will be utilized to good advantage in the process of list learning in free recall. We did not prelabel the associations because the information that would be contained in the labeling established prior to the experiment is not now used by FRAN in our free recall experiments. She simply finds and marks any associations she can between list words, being indifferent to the type of relation she finds bridging list words. We will argue in the next section that it is an empirical fact (although not *a priori* necessary) that the labelings are irrelevant to almost all predictions one would want to make in the standard free recall paradigm.

The memory structure chosen for FRAN in the simulation studies is less ambitious than our general theory in another way. Her vocabulary totals only 262 words, all nouns. The associations between words were chosen mainly by using dictionary definitions. Whenever a word was involved in the definition of another, two associations were created between the words, one in each direction. Additional associations were added whenever it was thought that a dictionary definition was deficient in some respect. We chose the words under the constraint that the associative network be connected; i.e., by chaining through associations it is possible to go from any word to any other word. Hobbes observed that "the mind can lead from anything to almost anything." In FRAN's connected memory, the qualification "almost" would not be necessary. An attempt was made to build in a number of superordinate concepts and their instances in order to facilitate simulation of free recall with categorized lists. In addition to the associations determined by these considerations, each word was given two random associations. This random component was an attempt to have FRAN's memory mimic some of the idiosyncratic information each S knows about the world.

Individual words are associated with as few as three or as many as 19 other words. The distribution of number of associations per word is given in Fig. 1. As can be seen, that distribution is quite negatively skewed; while most of the words have three, four, or five associations, the mean number of associations is 5.72. The words with a large number of associations are names of categories having many instances. This particular distribution is simply a consequence of the constraints under which the associations were chosen. It might seem that the particular associations chosen are irrelevant — that we might as well have used abstract symbols instead of words and imposed on these some artificial structure. However, we decided against such a move and we think for good reason. The functional consequences for free recall of various possible associative structures are not at all understood. In order to have a fair test of the model, it is necessary to begin with a graph structure that is as "humanlike" as possible. It is not unreasonable to suppose that the procedures just described did create a humanlike structure. It would be unreasonable to suppose this about an arbitrary associative network, since we do not understand the abstract structural characteristics of the

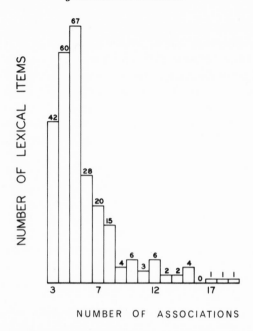

Fig. 1. Frequency of lexical items with each number of associations.

associative network that is human memory. Also use of actual words makes possible a comparison of the recall ordering FRAN gives to her words with the ordering human subjects give. Such comparisons would constitute an interesting test of our assumptions about the structure of human memory and the relation of that structure to free recall.

## B. THE SHORT-TERM STORE

The short-term store (STS) is an active subpart of the long-term store (LTS), the particular subpart varying from moment to moment. STS will denote that part of LTS which is currently in the focus of the subject's attention; i.e., it represents that part of his knowledge of which he is currently "conscious." As in Norman's model, the sensory features of the word presented activate and bring into STS the part of the associative structure corresponding to that word. It is assumed that STS has a small limited capacity of a few items. Therefore, once STS is filled, the act of entering a new item necessarily involves the loss of an old item from STS. The general rule for removing items from STS is that the item removed will be that one which has resided longest in the STS. Humans may be capable of more flexible control of their STS, and that is a potential area for future development of the model. Items in STS have two characteristics distinguishing them from the remaining items in memory. First, the S has immediate access to the items in STS. Other items in memory can only be accessed by chaining associatively from those items to which the S has immediate access. Second, it is assumed that the structural elaborations that underlie "learning" are made to any part of the associative network only while it is part of the STS. The nature of those elaborations will be detailed shortly.

FRAN has been given a STS of five words. The decision is somewhat arbitrary, but not unreasonable in light of the literature on short-term memory. What is meant by a STS of five words in FRAN is deliberately left somewhat vague. We occasionally want more than just five words to be active since FRAN attempts to tag some of the associations surrounding the word currently under study. This operation is crucial because FRAN's associative strategy requires that she be able to tag associative paths between the words in STS as well as to tag the words themselves.

We will now describe how FRAN's memory structure is modified during free recall learning. Any structural modification will necessitate the development of new associations. Associations in LTS express facts the person has learned about the world. Therefore, we assume that in free recall learning the structural modifications must be encodings of (reflections of) experiences of the S during the experiment. In particular, we shall assume that most of the associations developed during free recall record that individual words or individual associations between words were encountered during the experiment. The recording of such facts involves the development of two different types of associations: one type of association goes from an individual word to a hypothetical entry called the "LIST-$N$" marker, where $N = 1, 2, 3, \ldots$ indexes the ordinal number of the list being learned in the experiment; the second type of association goes from an associative pathway (between two words A and B) to the LIST-$N$ marker. This second type is an association that serves to label another association, and is the kind which traditionally S-R associationists have not used in their theorizing. But it is indispensible to FRAN's operation, since tagging associative pathways with LIST-$N$ is the only way FRAN has of directing her search of memory at recall.

LIST-$N$ is a hypothetical element introduced into LTS to index or stand for particular lists of words used in an experiment. The LIST-1, LIST-2, etc., entries may in fact be number words like "first," "second," or they may be different contextual cues that the person noticed or thought of during presentation of the separate lists. For brevity in the following, we will usually refer to the development of such indexical associations as "tagging" or "marking" the individual word or the associative pathway. It should be noted that tagging of a word establishes a one-way association *from* the word to the LIST-$N$ marker and not vice versa. The reverse association, from LIST-$N$ to a word, is rare, characterizing only those special words which serve as recall starters. These special words which are associated to the list marker are said to comprise the ENTRYSET, to be explained later.

Tagging with a list marker is assumed to be a stochastic process; specifically, the probability of successful tagging is exponentially related to the duration of the item in STS. The probability of success is described by the formula $1-a^T$, where $T$ is the time in seconds that the item is in STS and $a$ is a sort of "learning-rate" parameter that is allowed to vary from experiment to experiment. It may be that the processes underlying tagging are basically deterministic, but having no good ideas about them we will summarize the whole process with a probability.

The reader may proceed on the assumption that if a word is tagged, it very probably would be recognized as a list word from among a set of distractors on a later recognition test. Because of the necessity of handling false alarms or considering sophisticated guessing strategy, the actual model for recognition-test performance must be somewhat more complex than simply checking for presence or absence of an all-or-none list tag. This more sophisticated recognition model, developed along lines suggested by Bernbach (1967), will be discussed and used to interpret recognition results in Section IV, F of this paper.

### III. The Associative Strategy

#### A. A VARIETY OF POSSIBLE STRATEGIES

There are many conceivable strategies for doing free recall. While many Ss report using a strategy similar to that we have called associative, we have found a few Ss who reported very different strategies. Consider some of the spontaneous strategies that we have learned from postexperimental interviews with Ss:

(1) One S decided to study only every other word in an attempt to reduce memory load and focus attention on a subset of the list.

(2) Another *S* formed one image linking together the first three words he studied, another image linking the next three and so on. In recall he attempted to retrieve these images of triplets.

(3) A number of *S*s have attempted to do free recall (usually just the first trial) as a serial learning experiment, rehearsing serial linkages in STS.

(4) One *S* tried to organize his list alphabetically, associating each word with its first letter, then cueing recall by reciting the alphabet to himself.

(5) One *S* learned the list by paired-associate means, associating each word with a person he knew at Stanford by means of an image. Then, in recall, he "mentally walked along" a predetermined path through the campus and recalled the words as he met the people he had used as stimuli for the paired-associate task.

The last *S* is myself. My method is only a variant of the "method of loci" or method of mnemonic pegwords (see Bower, 1970). It is the optimal free recall strategy, far superior to the others mentioned including the associative strategy adopted by FRAN and by most of our *S*s. It would not be too difficult to reprogram FRAN so that she used the mnemonic pegword strategy. By so doing we would make her a more efficient free recall learner — roughly speaking, because the pegword strategy avoids the loss of access to associative clusters of words as does happen with the associative strategy. In any event, we have run FRAN on free recall with an associative strategy in the belief that this simulates how most of our *S*s are learning free recall lists most of the time.

In free recall learning, when presented with a word to study, most of our *S*s seem to just "let their mind wander" (their expression) or "free associate to the word." Inevitably, they associate a word they are studying to another word from the list. Our *S*s soon recognize that associating together words from the list is a powerful strategy in that a few words recalled from the list can serve as retrieval cues for recall of all the words associated to the first words, then all the words associated to these associates, and so on recursively. Once the value of this associative strategy is understood *S*s make more deliberate use of it. FRAN is a model that attempts to simulate the *S* when he has adopted the associative strategy unstintingly. Thus, comparison of her output to that of *S*s is only fully valid when the *S*s commit themselves to this free recall strategy from the outset of learning the list. One way to increase the chances that *S*s will start with such an associative strategy is to inform them prior to learning of the utility of this strategy, as we sometimes do with our *S*s. For

instance, in the experiment reported in Section IV,B we instructed
our Ss to use the associative strategy.

Note that it is a characteristic of the associative strategy that the
particular labels of the associations (i.e., the types of associative
relations) are unimportant. Therefore, the associations have not been
prelabeled in FRAN's current memory structure. Some plausible
alternative strategies for free recall would require the information
provided by labeled associations. For instance, if an S elected to only
associate list words with their superordinates, then he clearly needs
this relational information to guide his search. Such a strategy is
probably quite efficient when the list has been explicitly organized
into categories. Evidence presented in Section IV,E indicates that Ss
do deviate from the general associative strategy when the list has
been organized into categories.

It is our position that no matter what free recall strategy an S
adopts, (e.g., associative, pegword, superordinate category) it could
be implemented by the mental mechanisms described in Section II.
Different strategies correspond to different configurations of the
mechanisms. In this section we shall describe the organization of the
mental mechanisms underlying the strict associative strategy. At
present writing, FRAN is unlike people insofar as she always uses this
associative strategy for doing free recall. This is unobjectionable so
long as we are comparing FRAN's behavior to that of college student
Ss doing "standard free recall" with unrelated word lists, since it is
our conjecture that most of our Ss eventually stumble upon the
associative strategy for learning such lists. Where the strategy
variation becomes problematical is when we try to fit FRAN to
experiments deviating in certain ways from this standard testing
ground (e.g., use of categorized lists or hierarchically organized lists).
The unique manipulations of such experiments may lead Ss to
abandon the associative strategy in favor of others, like
superordination, which the current FRAN does not pretend to
simulate. A quaintly academic question is whether a model which
simulates learning under strategy A can be faulted for misfitting
results of experimental conditions that induce Ss to use alternative
strategies B, C, or D. For our own purposes, we have found FRAN's
behavior in such "nonstandard" experiments to provide a firm
anchor, standard, or reference point useful for giving contrastive
descriptions of the behavior of humans. By assessing FRAN's
deviations from the data, we may gain insights into limitations of the
associative strategy as well as noting what strategies people do adopt
in these situations.

## B. The Study Processes

During study, FRAN is occupied with three separate jobs in pursuing her associative strategy: these are the tagging of words, searching out and tagging of associative pathways between list words, and updating of good recall "starters" in ENTRYSET. We will elaborate on each of these processes.

### 1. Word Tagging

Whenever FRAN enters a word into STS an attempt will be made to tag that word as a word to be later recalled. FRAN will enter a word into STS if it has been presented for study or if it is found to be an associate of a word that has been presented for study and it is recognized as a member of the list under study. The probability of tagging a word that resides in STS for $T$ seconds is $1-a^T$. Since FRAN will attempt to tag any word entered into STS, she is restricted to only entering those words which are from the list. If she were to enter nonlist words into STS she might wrongly tag them as list members. Apparently human $S$s can enter nonlist words into their STS without tagging them, since this is what characterizes the superordination strategy which uses category labels as entry words for cueing recall even though these labels are not overtly recalled.

### 2. Association Tagging

The second process involves the examination of the associative surround of the word under study to see if there are any other list words to which it may be associated. It is difficult to determine how rapidly FRAN should examine associates of the word under study. One obvious assumption is that FRAN should study a constant $n$ associates for each second of study time. However, arguments may be given for the alternative assumption that FRAN should examine associates at a decreasing rate over time. For one thing, as FRAN exhausts the first-order associates to the word being studied and resorts to second-order (i.e., associates of associates of the target word) and higher-order associates, it should take longer to find them. Also, there should ideally be some "processing capacity" trade-off between the number of associates FRAN finds and tries to tag *versus* the rate at which she continues her search for new associates. The formula that has proven useful in our simulations is $N = 5 + T$, where $N$ is the number of associates examined in time $T$. Our interpretation of this formula is that within moments after exposure to the word, a rush of five associates comes to mind, but thereafter new associates are examined at the slower rate of one per second. This particular formula is highly dependent upon the fact that FRAN has only 262 words in her memory. We suspect that with a larger network, the search rate would have to be increased if FRAN is to maintain an accurate simulation of human recall results.

FRAN selects associates to examine in the following manner: she randomly selects one of the associates of the word she is currently studying. If she has already examined it (this is indicated by a temporary "check mark"), she randomly selects one of its associates. If that second-order associate has also been examined, she randomly selects one of its associates. This recursive process continues until a word is found which has not yet been examined. This random search may be viewed metaphorically as a blind excursion into the associative vicinity of the word being studied. That excursion is brought to a halt when something new (unchecked) is found. She will usually halt after one or two "steps" from the target word.

After finding a word that she has not previously examined during the current search, FRAN then checks to see if it is from the list she is studying. The word is identified as from the list if it satisfies at least one of the following three criteria: (a) it is currently in STS; or (b) it has been successfully tagged with an association to LIST-$N$; or (c) it is currently a member of "ENTRYSET." As will be detailed later, ENTRYSET is the subset of those list words which have become directly associated to the list marker.

If the word associate being examined fails all three of these criteria and therefore is not recognized, this examination ends with a failure, and FRAN returns to the target word being studied and commences another search out from this target. If the associate being examined is recognized, it is entered into STS. Consequently, another attempt is made to tag this associate. It may not have been previously tagged; FRAN could have recognized the word on the basis of its membership in ENTRYSET or STS. FRAN also attempts to tag the pathway she has found from the target word studied to the associate. Since FRAN's associative structure is symmetric, a path also exists from the associate to the studied word. An attempt is made to tag this backpath also. In the recall phase of the experiment, FRAN will use these marked associative paths to profitably guide her search for words in the list.

If the associative path FRAN has found between two list words involves several links, then she will try to tag each of these separate links. The tagging of each association is a probabilistic process independent of the tagging of every other association in the path. In the formula for tagging probability, $1\text{-}a^T$, $T$ will equal the time to study the presented word minus the time taken to find the associate. Even after finding and tagging a list associate, FRAN will continue looking for new associates for the word under study until she runs out of time or until the five slots in STS have been filled by the word under study and its associates.

We can make more understandable this process of searching the associative surround of a word for other list words by reference to Fig. 2. The word $A$ in that figure is under study for one second. According to the formula relating number of paths examined to study time, FRAN will examine $5 + T$ or six associates. The six panels of Fig. 2 each describe one of the six paths examined by

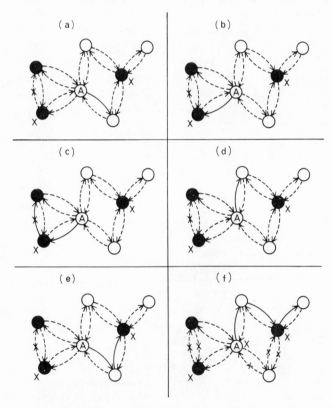

Fig. 2. A possible search of the memory structure surrounding Word A during study. See text for explanation.

FRAN, the path under examination being indicated by a solid line in the appropriate panel. FRAN randomly selects an associate of $A$ and examines it. If it has been examined [as in the case of panels (c), (e), and (f)] she randomly selects a second-order associate. In panel (f), that second-order associate had been previously examined in panel (e). Therefore, in panel (f) FRAN looks at a third-order associate. The solid nodes in the figures indicate words FRAN can recognize by one of her three criteria for word recognition. When she encounters such a word during search [as happens in panels (b), (c), and (e)] she would enter that word into STS, attempt to tag the word and the pathways in both directions between it and the target word, $A$. Such tags are indicated by $X$'s in Fig. 2. The $X$'s in panels (a) through (e) indicate paths and words tagged prior to this study trial on word $A$. The new $X$'s added by panel (f) indicate tags that were developed during the study of $A$. Since tagging is a probabilistic event, FRAN does not succeed in tagging all the words and paths she tries to tag.

For simplicity, it is assumed that FRAN will be busy tagging a target word, its associates, and the paths between them only when that word is under active study. As soon as a new word is presented for study, all this activity surrounding the previous target word ceases. However, the word and its associates may reside in STS for some time after a new word comes under study. Two reasons motivated this decision to restrict the tagging period. First, in recorded introspections, our $S$s appeared to stop thinking about the former word and its associates when a new word was presented. Thus, it seemed natural to assume no further modifications were being made to this part of LTS although it was still part of STS. Secondly, the computational task of determining the probability of tagging a word or associate is much reduced if the duration for which the tagging will be attempted is known at the outset of the tagging process. This duration can be determined only if it is known in advance when the tagging process for a given target word will terminate.

### 3. Selection of Entry Words

The third and final process in which FRAN is engaged during study is the creation of ENTRYSET. This involves the selection of a limited number of "entry words" into the network which can serve as initial words from which FRAN may chain associatively during recall. In the program, words in ENTRYSET are those which have an association from the LIST-$N$ marker. It is assumed that the number of words which can be associated in an experiment is very limited —

specifically three. It is also assumed that the ENTRYSET is composed initially of the first words seen. Thereafter, changes in ENTRYSET involves replacing present members by new members. A member of the ENTRYSET will be replaced under two conditions:

1. If an item appears that is perceptually more distinctive than any current member of the ENTRYSET, the distinctive item may be put on the ENTRYSET. While we thus acknowledge in theory a Von Restorff effect and effects of instructional emphases, the LISP funcions to simulate this feature are not implemented. FRAN is not a model of perceptual processing and has no way to determine if one word is perceptually more distinctive than another. This is another area for future development of the model.

2. FRAN has certain crude heuristics for determining during study which words are more central in the list; that is, for selecting those list words which lead associatively to the most other words from the list. Whenever a word is found which is more central than another in the ENTRYSET, the old one is deleted and the new one is added to ENTRYSET.

Thus, the three words in ENTRYSET constitute intuitively a very rough description of the entire list — its unique perceptual features and the major associative clusters in the list. Subjects commonly make remarks suggesting this ENTRYSET assumption. In rationalizing why they group words together, Ss often say something on this order: "I can only remember a few things at once. So I tried to reduce the number of things I had to remember." The concept of an ENTRYSET is one explication of what Ss mean by this remark. The principal motivation for introducing an ENTRYSET in the model was the belief that recall would be quite unstable and variable if the only way of accessing LTS was by random entry or with the words that happened to be in STS at the beginning of recall. It was felt that recall would proceed well only if FRAN had some way of directing her search to the relevant parts of LTS.

## C. THE RECALL PROCESSES

In recall FRAN is simultaneously engaged in two processes: recalling list words and studying the words she is recalling.

## 1. The Recall Algorithm

FRAN, is first of all, engaged in recalling the list words. FRAN always begins by recalling those words to which she has immediate access, viz., those in STS. Available evidence indicates that humans usually begin by recalling the current contents of STS. At the end of list input, the contents of STS are the last one to five items in the list and some of their associates (total sum is five). Postman and Keppel (1968) and Shuell and Keppel (1968) both report that Ss tend to recall first the last items studied. This output strategy accounts for the well-known recency effect, viz., that items presented in the last few input positions are better recalled than earlier items. Interfering tasks interpolated between study and recall eliminate this recency effect (Glanzer & Cunitz, 1966; Postman & Phillips, 1965). This effect is predicted by any model which assumes that the effect of such interfering tasks is to remove from STS the words filling it immediately at the end of the study trial.

FRAN uses these words from her STS and those from her ENTRYSET as retrieval cues or points at which to enter LTS. From these points she chains along the associative paths she has marked out during study. FRAN's memory may be represented by a symmetric connected graph like Fig. 3. As a consequence of study, certain words and associations have been tagged, and these are marked by X's in Fig. 3. In this way FRAN has marked out a subgraph as relevant for recall of this particular list. The subgraph

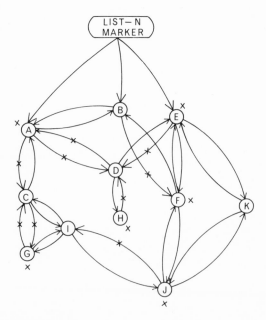

Fig. 3. A hypothetical memory structure that might exist after a study phase. See text for explanation.

marked out in this hypothetical case is given in Fig. 4. The subgraph need not be connected nor symmetric as was the original graph. Several entry points into the subgraph (i.e., words in ENTRYSET and the initial contents of STS) are available; in Figs. 3 and 4, arrows lead to these entry words. Any part of the subgraph that is not strongly connected (i.e., by arrows in the correct direction) to an entry point will not be recalled since FRAN will only examine that part of the subgraph which she can reach by following marked associative paths from the entry points. Therefore, although words H and J are marked in Fig. 4, they will not be recalled. FRAN also will not recall a word unless she can recognize it as from the list (she uses the same three criteria for word recognition as in study). Therefore, although the word C is part of the strongly connected subgraph, it will not be recalled. FRAN regards such words as mediators in an associative chain. In the case of C, it mediates recall of the marked word G.

We have defined which words FRAN will recall; we will now describe the order in which these words are recalled. FRAN searches the subgraph by randomly selecting one of her entry words and then searching that part of the subgraph that can be reached by following associations in a depth-first manner. Depth first means that FRAN will completely search a left-going branch of a node before searching any other branches that may lead from the node. It was trivial to

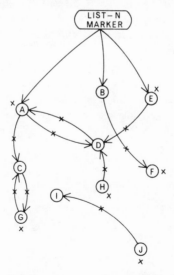

Fig. 4. The marked subgraph that is embedded in the memory structure of Fig. 3. See text for explanation.

define what was meant by "left-most" in FRAN's LISP memory structure. However, it is another matter to say what is meant by "left-most" in a human structure. Perhaps, it is the association that has the most distinctive tag.

FRAN leaves a temporary marking on every word encountered during her search. Occasional failure at temporary marking, something not possible in the current implementation of FRAN, would explain why some Ss repeat items during recall. After FRAN recalls all words she can by following associative paths from one entry word, another entry word is randomly chosen. This process continues until FRAN has recalled all the words that can be reached from her entry points. Thus, the order of recall is partly determined by the random selection of entry words and partly by the associative chains cued off by these words.

It might be thought that, having searched the part of her memory accessible from her entry words and still having more to recall, FRAN might set out and start randomly searching her memory for tagged words like H and J. The problem is that if FRAN is to have any reasonable chance of finding such lost words, she must be prepared to search a large portion of her memory. With a human, although not with the current implementation of FRAN, that would involve search of thousands of words. Moreover, associative memory is badly organized for an exhaustive search, and it seems certain that there would be a tremendous amount of looping in which the organization of memory would "conspire" to bring one back again and again to the same place without breaking out into new regions of memory. This difficulty is just what FRAN's memory strategies are directed against, i.e., these strategies constitute an attempt to build up a structure that will lead to the relevant parts of memory and avoid time-consuming random searches. It may well be that the human does recall an occasional word by something analogous to a random search, but we hold that, overall, this possibility is not important.

From this description of the associative retrieval process, only a small theoretical step is required to handle latencies and interresponse times (IRTs) in free recall protocols. The general characterization of the sequences of IRTs (cf. Pollio, 1968) is that there are "bursts" of two to seven items recalled with short IRTs followed by a longer IRT pause, then another burst of responses, another pause, etc. The items within a burst tend to be those which the S has grouped together in a "subjective unit." The pauses between successive recall bursts grow progressively longer as though Ss were exhausting the accessible units in memory.

To coordinate FRAN's retrieval concepts to this IRT description, a "burst of responses from a subjective group" corresponds to FRAN's recalling all items accessible from a given starter (taken either from the initial contents of STS or ENTRYSET). Assume that the retrieval-search process operates rapidly in this respect, following tagged associative pathways out from the starter word and from intermediate items recalled. By definition, the final word in such an associative recall chain is one from which *extensive* searching turns up no new tagged pathways or tagged items, so it is followed by a silent "deadtime." After such fruitless searching, FRAN then gives up on the final item of a given chain, and goes to fetch the next starter item from the initial STS or ENTRYSET, entering it into STS as the target for beginning another associative search. As a consequence of these several operations, FRAN would have relatively longer IRTs between "groups" that within groups of items. The fact that between-group IRTs grow progressively longer as the memory store is exhausted may be coordinated to the following facts about FRAN's operation: first, the items in STS may be recalled first with extreme rapidity, yielding short IRTs at the beginning of the protocol; second, the selection of a new starter either from ENTRYSET or earlier STS items may be governed by a "sampling-with-replacement" scheme (with editing and rejection of previously used starters). This means that the more entry words that have been used on a trial, the longer it will take the Executive to find another entry word it has not already used on this trial.

These several ideas about retrieval IRTs in free recall need further specification of details and implementation in the program. This is possibly a fruitful line for development of the model, since clearly the structural assumptions made above already suffice to explain the main features of free recall IRTs.

## 2. *Learning during Recall*

It is assumed that when FRAN recalls a word, she also studies it for a period of two seconds. Therefore, whenever FRAN recalls a word, at the same time she enters the word into STS and attempts to tag it, searches its associates for other list words, tries to mark the paths to and from these words, and tests to see whether she can place a more central item on ENTRYSET. Although a study time of two seconds was arbitrary, when a word is recalled the S clearly does have an opportunity to study it. The sole difference between seeing a word in study and seeing it in recall is the agent responsible for its presentation. There is no reason to assume that this difference should affect how the $S$ reacts to the word. The fact that FRAN is simultaneously studying while she is recalling implies that the subgraph to which she has access from her entry points (e.g., that in Fig. 4) does not remain constant during recall.

This concludes the description of the processes which occupy FRAN during recall. The study and recall processes may be repeated any number of times and in any order. Improvement in recall with repeated study and recall trials is due to two factors. First, with later repetitions FRAN has further opportunities to successfully tag words and their interassociations. Second, the composition of ENTRYSET becomes more and more optimal.

The reader will note that several parameters control the model's processes. All but one parameter are held constant in the simulations to be reported in the next section. The constant parameters are: the size of STS, equal to five words; the size of ENTRYSET, equal to three words; the formula $5 + T$, relating the number of associates examined to the time $T$ for study of a target word; and the study time for words recalled in the test phase, equal to two seconds. In addition, the associative structure of LTS constitutes a constant parameter of the simulations. The single variable parameter is $a$, the probability of not tagging a word in a second's worth of trying. Presumably, this parameter should also be constant from experiment to experiment for the same $S$s. However, because FRAN's memory structure is very much smaller than that of a human, we have let $a$ vary across experiments as a "slop factor" to take account of the possibility that the exact interaction between the experimental paradigm and memory structure may not be identical for FRAN and humans. By raising or lowering $a$ for a simulation, we only change the overall level of performance and we do not alter any of the within-experiment comparisons that we wish to make. Consequently, the fact that FRAN performs at about the same overall level in any experiment as do humans should not be taken as a significant result. The more discriminating test of the model is whether the within-experiment comparisons of human performance are reproduced in the simulations.

## IV. An Evaluation: FRAN *vs.* the Humans

### A. EVALUATION STRATEGY AND PRELIMINARY DETAILS

The test of our model is whether it can simulate, at least qualitatively, the effects of various experimental manipulations in free recall. Several such simulations are reported in this section. An unfortunate practical limitation on this research is that FRAN has become a very expensive $S$ from whom to gather data. For example, in compiled form, in a partition of the IBM System 360/67 that has 700,000 bytes of core, it requires about three seconds of CPU time to run one input-output cycle with one simulation $S$ on a list of 30 words. This long time is due to the inherent slowness of LISP and our extensive use of randomization functions (e.g., for simulating tagging probabilities). Although three seconds may appear brief to some readers, it in fact represents a tremendous amount of computing for a 360 machine; and the three seconds per $S$ per trial mounts rapidly as we simulate up to eight conditions in a given experiment, each condition with 10-20 $S$s who are run perhaps five trials.

To make very accurate statements about what our free recall model predicts for a particular experiment would require prohibitively long and expensive computer runs. Therefore, in the following experiments only a small number of simulation $S$s have been run for any condition. These artificial $S$s produce a recall data differing quite a bit from one $S$ to another; the variability is caused by list randomization, by random search activities, and by the stochastic tagging operations. Consequently, FRAN's data are subject to random fluctuation as are average data taken from a small number of $S$s.

Furthermore, simulation data have been obtained only for a single choice of parameters. It would be exorbitantly expensive to map out all possible parameter combinations and then to report that one yielding the best-fitting Monte Carlo data. For this reason, the following simulations give us a good idea of the character of the model's predictions, but the predictions can in no sense be construed as "theoretical best fits."

A few remarks are appropriate regarding our theoretical strategy. We take it for granted that a model like FRAN in its initial formulations will be wrong in some details. The strategy for scientific progress, then, is to try to pinpoint those inaccuracies. Hence, we tend to focus attention and discussion on FRAN's failures rather than her successes. By minimizing and by playing down those details which FRAN fails to match in human behavior, the model could have been presented in a more favorable light. However, our concern is not with propaganda but with understanding human performance. Because we understand FRAN's behavior, those aspects of human behavior which she matches are not so interesting as those aspects which she cannot match.

## B. STANDARD MULTITRIAL FREE RECALL

The following experiment was designed to obtain data to evaluate FRAN. Eighteen Stanford students participated for one hour in the experiment for a wage of $1.75. They were tested in groups of from one to seven. Three different lists of 32 words were used. They had been selected from FRAN's vocabulary randomly except that no two lists contained any words in common. The words were typed on slides and presented to the Ss by a slide projector at the rate of two seconds per word. Immediately after studying a list, the Ss had three minutes to recall the words they had just seen. Such study-recall cycles were repeated five times for a given list of words, with the word order being rerandomized on each study trial. Each S learned two of the three lists over the experimental session. With 18 Ss each studying two lists, there were 36 recall protocols in all.

The Ss had been informed ahead of time about the utility of an associative strategy like that adopted by FRAN and were instructed to restrict their recall efforts to such a strategy. That is, they were told that during study they should only look for conceptual relations between the words in the list and during recall they should use these relations to chain associatively through the list. As noted earlier, some Ss spontaneously adopt quite different strategies, and, while most Ss adopt strategies very similar to FRAN's, it is usually not until some point after the beginning of the experiment that they completely take up the associative strategy. We wanted data representing use of the associative strategy in a pure form over all trials of the experiment. In postexperimental interviews, our Ss unanimously reported that they had no difficulty using the associative strategy as instructed; they also thought it was very useful. While instructing Ss to use an associative strategy provides data less "contaminated" by random strategy variation, it complicates interpretation in a different way. To defend the assertion that FRAN is a plausible model of standard multitrial free recall, it is not enough to show that her behavior matches that of the humans in this experiment. It may be that, all our introspective reports to the contrary, the learning strategy spontaneously adopted by most Ss is not associative. Therefore, it should be shown that the data gathered from our Ss are similar to that gathered from Ss not instructed to use a particular learning strategy. We attempt to do this by accompanying our data with references to similar data in the literature.

From FRAN we also have 36 recall protocols. Each S's exact sequence of presentation of words was simulated in one of the 36 computer runs. The value of the parameter *a* was set at .55 for these simulations.

## 1. The Mean Learning Curve

A comparison of FRAN's learning curve with that of the humans is shown in Fig. 5. FRAN's increase in recall across trials very closely parallels that of the human *S*s. On each trial FRAN's recall is slightly

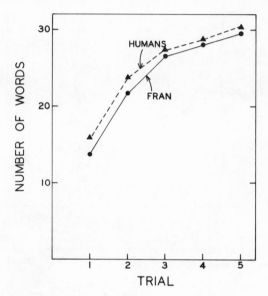

Fig. 5. FRAN and human *S*s compared with respect to mean number of words recalled as a function of trial.

less, but this discrepancy could be rectified by a lower value of the parameter a. In summarizing a considerable quantity of data, Murdock (1960) concluded that the free recall learning curve was exponential with an asymptote equal to the number of words in the list. This description characterizes the learning curves of both FRAN and the humans quite well.

## 2. Recall Conditional on Prior Recall or Nonrecall

The success of FRAN in matching the overall recall performance of *S*s hides one important difference that appears in Fig. 6. Figure 6 depicts, for FRAN and for our *S*s, their success in recalling a particular word conditional upon whether they had recalled that word (R) or not (N) on the previous trial. The points plotted for Trial 1 are just the unconditional probabilities of recall for that trial. The humans and FRAN are quite close for the curves labeled $P(R_n|R_{n-1})$, the probability of recall conditional on recall on the prior trial. FRAN is somewhat better, probably reflecting her greater efficiency in searching her marked subgraph. Human Ss may

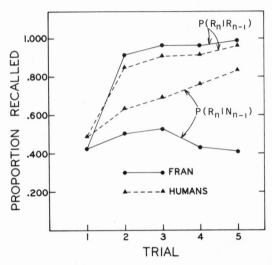

Fig. 6. FRAN and human Ss compared with respect to mean proportion of words recalled $(R_n)$ conditional on recall $(R_{n-1})$ or nonrecall $(N_{n-1})$ on the previous trial.

occasionally "forget" to check a word for associates leading from it, which is a failing that FRAN currently does not have. It would be trivial to introduce this into the program as random noise in retrieval. Therefore, the slight discrepancy in $P(R_n|R_{n-1})$ is not considered serious.

The much greater and theoretically more significant discrepancy is between the curves labeled $P(R_n|N_{n-1})$, the probability of recall of a word conditional on its nonrecall on the previous trial. Human Ss show a consistent increase across trials in their probability of recalling words missed on the previous trial; FRAN does not. The hardest words for FRAN to recall will be those that are "farthest away" from the rest of the words (where distance in the network is measured by the number of links intervening between two nodes). FRAN's study strategy, which mechanically allocates just two seconds study time to each word, will be inefficient in learning these "distant" words. Obviously these distant words constitute a larger proportion of nonrecalled words on later trials, and hence contribute more on later trials to the curve labeled $P(R_n | N_{n-1})$. Therefore, it is not too surprising that FRAN's recall of these words does not increase across trials. The reason that it does not show a monotonic decrease is that there are compensating factors such as (*a*) the greater probability that on later trials the words will have been tagged and hence recognized, and (*b*) the more efficient organization of the marked subgraph which makes possible the freeing of room in ENTRYSET for adding a new word which accesses new parts of memory. Since FRAN's memory is connected, even "distant" words will be eventually linked into the accessible subgraph and hence will be recalled.

For humans also, the curve, $P(R_n | N_{n-1})$ should have a greater proportion of difficult words as the experiment progresses. Why, then, do Ss show a monotonic increase in their ability to recall words previously not recalled? We think it is because human Ss adopt the strategy of giving special attention or special processing priority to these difficult words. This supposes, as seems plausible, that Ss can discriminate between easy (recalled) *versus* difficult (nonrecalled) items on a subsequent input trial. As one strategy, Ss could give extra time to studying the difficult words at the expense of temporally adjacent items that are already well learned. Another strategy would be for the S to keep the difficult word in STS from the time it is studied until the time recall is initiated and, then to output that word immediately.

If Ss were using this priority rating to replace items in STS, one would expect a greater than chance proportion of previously nonrecalled words to be recalled in the early part of the Ss' output. This priority effect has been found in several recall experiments (Battig, Allen, & Jensen, 1965; Battig & Slaybaugh, 1969). There was a similar tendency in our experiment for those words omitted on Trial 4 then recalled on Trial 5. Of those items that were not recalled on Trial 4, were presented in the first half of the input list on Trial 5 and were recalled on Trial 5, 62% were recalled in the first half of the output protocol. Of previously omitted words presented in the last half of the Trial 5 input and then recalled, 67% were recalled in the first half of the output protocol. The chance expectation for these percentages, given a randomly selected output order, is 50%, so the data show a tendency toward early recall of previously unrecalled items. On the other hand, FRAN shows just the opposite result, with corresponding figures of 17% and 40% for proportion of words recalled in the first half of the Trial 5 protocol given that they were not recalled on Trial 4 and were presented in the first *versus* second half of the Trial 5 input list.

The reason that FRAN's percentages are below chance is that recall of a previously unrecalled word often depends on use of a single entry word that was added during the just-prior study trial. Late in learning the marked subgraph will have become so interconnected that most words in the subgraph will be connected by marked pathways to most other words. Therefore, if any other entry words are used before the one leading to the few nonrecalled words, those other entry words will probably lead associatively to the recall of most of the list before the new item is recalled. With eight entry words (five from STS and three from ENTRYSET), the probability is .88 that the first entry word chosen is not the one that leads to the recall of the previously omitted word. As a consequence, recall of these newly appearing words tends to be postponed until a late position in the recall sequence.

### 3. Analysis of Complete Sequences

A more complete analysis of the changes in recall across trials is given in Table I which presents the frequencies of the 32 possible

TABLE I

Frequencies of the Various Combinations of Recall and
Nonrecall across Trials

| Events | FRAN | Human | Events | FRAN | Human |
|--------|------|-------|--------|------|-------|
| NNNNN  | 59   | 4     | RNNNN  | 8    | 1     |
| NNNNR  | 29   | 14    | RNNNR  | 1    | 1     |
| NNNRN  | 4    | 9     | RNNRN  | 0    | 0     |
| NNNRR  | 66   | 39    | RNNRR  | 4    | 24    |
| NNRNN  | 9    | 1     | RNRNN  | 2    | 2     |
| NNRNR  | 10   | 23    | RNRNR  | 0    | 5     |
| NNRRN  | 0    | 6     | RNRRN  | 0    | 2     |
| NNRRR  | 148  | 115   | RNRRR  | 22   | 46    |
| NRNNN  | 5    | 3     | RRNNN  | 1    | 2     |
| NRNNR  | 9    | 6     | RRNNR  | 0    | 3     |
| NRNRN  | 2    | 6     | RRNRN  | 0    | 3     |
| NRNRR  | 6    | 37    | RRNRR  | 3    | 21    |
| NRRNN  | 1    | 3     | RRRNN  | 0    | 4     |
| NRRNR  | 6    | 24    | RRRNR  | 4    | 17    |
| NRRRN  | 0    | 11    | RRRRN  | 0    | 5     |
| NRRRR  | 305  | 285   | RRRRR  | 448  | 430   |

recall sequences for a word over the five trials. In Table I, R stands for recall and N for nonrecall, so that RRRNR denotes recall on Trials 1, 2, 3, 5 and nonrecall on Trial 4. For both FRAN and human Ss, there were 1152 observations (32 words times 36 recall protocols).

Careful inspection of Table I reveals no glaring discrepancies between the two sets of data beyond those noted in conjunction with the $P(R_n|N_{n-1})$ curves in Fig. 6. The correlation between the frequencies of the various sequences for FRAN and for human Ss is .985. Therefore, if FRAN's frequencies had been used to predict the frequencies of the various events in the human data, FRAN would account for 97% of the variance. This "variance accounted for" is high despite the $P(R_n|N_{n-1})$ discrepancy because the latter statistic involves only a small percentage of the sequence data in Table I. Hence, one may justifiably point to the recall sequences in Table I as evidence that the major processes underlying free recall are being modeled, at least approximately, in FRAN. However, sufficient discrepancies exist to conclude that humans are capable of some complexities (e.g., giving priority to difficult items) which the current FRAN does not mimic.

### 4. Serial Position Curve

Another comparison of FRAN's performance with that of human Ss comes from examination of serial position curves, relating recall probability to the ordinal position of an item in the input list. Figure 7 illustrates a comparison between the serial position curves of FRAN and our Ss. The two sets of curves are quite similar to each other and to those reported in the literature (e.g., Murdock, 1962; Shuell & Keppel, 1968). Both the humans and FRAN show a primacy effect for the initial four words but only on the first trial. The primacy effect in FRAN is caused by the fact that ENTRYSET is composed initially from the first words seen in the experiment. As a consequence, these first words have a good chance of being in ENTRYSET or retrievable from another word in ENTRYSET at the time of recall.

Both FRAN and the humans show a recency effect on all trials for the last four words. FRAN's recency effect is more pronounced than that observed in this experiment. The recency effect in FRAN is due to the fact that, at the beginning of recall, STS is composed of the last few words and their associates, and these items are sure to be recalled. The magnitude of the predicted recency effect could be easily reduced by decreasing the size of STS from its current

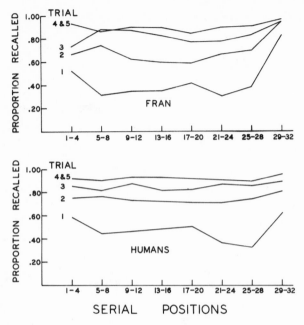

Fig. 7. FRAN and humans compared with respect to recall as a function of serial position of the word in the study sequence. Data for Trials 4 and 5 are pooled.

arbitrary size of five. Similarly, recency effects depend on a particular output strategy, of recalling items from STS before moving to those cued from ENTRYSET. Not all naive Ss use this output strategy initially, though they tend to adopt it as they become more practiced on free recall tasks. If this were true, then the average curve for humans, pooling across different output strategies, will show less of a recency effect than does FRAN which always uses the "last in, first out" recall strategy. For such reasons as these, we do not consider the differing magnitudes of recency for FRAN *vs.* our Ss to be a serious shortcoming of the model.

Except for the primacy effect on Trial 1, both the humans and FRAN show on all trials a stable level of recall for items preceding the last four recency items. While our assumptions regarding the use of STS and ENTRYSET can be seen intuitively to lead to a primacy effect on the first trial only and a recency effect on all trials, it might not seem obvious that FRAN would yield a constant level of recall for the remaining serial positions. All of these middle words have an equal probability of being tagged with a list marker; furthermore, it also appears that they would all have an equal probability of being tied into the accessible part of the subgraph and hence retrieved during recall. On Trial 1, words studied early in the list will have the advantage of being searched for from more words, while later words will have the advantage of there being more tagged words to search for when they are studied. These two factors manage to nicely balance out; it can be proven that the expected number of associative paths that will be tagged to and from a given word is the same for all serial positions.

## 5. Input-Output and Output-Output Correlations

The free recall phenomenon which FRAN was primarily designed to explain was the fact that the order of recall is not random but rather is highly structured. We examined the degree to which the order of output on Trial $n$ tended to maintain $(a)$ the order in which the words were studied on Trial $n$, and $(b)$ the order in which the words were recalled on Trial $n$ -1. Figure 8 illustrates a comparison between FRAN and our Ss with respect to these two types of recall stereotypy. For that figure the statistic, "proportion of repetitions," measures recall stereotypy and is defined as follows: for each $S$, let $j$ be the number of pairs of words that occurred adjacently in the study list (or in the prior trail's recall output) and which were recalled not necessarily adjacently on Trial $n$. Let $i$ be the number of these $j$ pairs that are recalled adjacently in the same order as they occurred in the study sequence (or in the prior recall). The statistic, proportion of repetitions, is defined as $\Sigma i/\Sigma j$, where $i$ and $j$ were summed over the 36 recall protocols for that trial. This statistic estimates the probability of recalling two words in the same adjacent order as they were studied (or recalled on the prior trial). If the recall order were random, the expected value of this statistic would be $\Sigma j/\Sigma k(k-1)$, where $k$ is the number of words recalled on Trial $n$. These expected values, shown as the lower lines in Fig. 8, are essentially identical for FRAN and our Ss.

As Fig. 8 shows, on all trials the obtained values were greater than those expected for both measures of correspondence, between order of input and output, and between order of prior output and current output. With respect to the proportion of repetitions of prior output pairs, FRAN appears much like human Ss. Both show an increase in this type of stereotypy across trials. Such an increase in output stereotypy has been reported by many investigators (e.g., Bousfield et al., 1964; Rosner, 1970; Tulving, 1962). Turning to the other comparison in Fig. 8, both FRAN and our Ss decrease across trials in

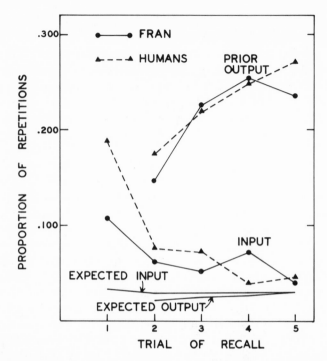

Fig. 8. FRAN and humans compared with respect to stereotypy of output order. Given in the figure are the probabilities with which adjacent pairs in the output of Trial $n$-1 are repeated in the output of Trial $n$ and the probabilities with which adjacent pairs in the input of Trial $n$ are repeated in the output of Trial $n$. See text for explanation of the statistic proportion of repetitions.

the frequency with which they recall word pairs in the same order as they were studied. For this measure FRAN fits the human data on Trials 2 through 5, but underpredicts considerably on Trial 1.

In trying to understand the discrepancy on Trial 1 it is well to understand why FRAN repeats input order with greater than chance frequency. Two factors operate to yield this latter result. First, the last few words in the input sequence are recalled immediately out of STS. Although they are recalled randomly from STS, they have a greater than chance probability of occurring adjacently, since the chance level is computed on the assumption that the words recalled are equally likely to come from any position in the list. Also the remaining words, because they cannot occur in the first five output positions, have as a consequence a slightly greater than chance probability of being recalled adjacently. The second factor yielding repetition of input adjacencies is particularly important on the first trial and it may be illustrated as follows: suppose FRAN, in searching out associates of a particular word A, comes upon the word B which had just preceded it in the study sequence. The word B is almost certain to still be in STS and therefore FRAN will recognize it as a list word; she will again attempt to tag word B (especially on the first trial, it may not yet be tagged), and she will attempt to tag the path leading from A to B, and the path from B to A. If she succeeds in tagging the path leading from B, she may use that path in recall to retrieve A from B. If she does, this will be one instance in which output order reflects input order. On the other hand, consider what would happen if FRAN, in searching out associates of A, came upon a list word C that had occurred much earlier in the study sequence. That word would probably not be in STS and, if it were not tagged, FRAN would not recognize it as a list word. Therefore, she would miss this opportunity to tag the associative path she had found from A to C. Comparing the A-B to the A-C case, it is seen that FRAN has a greater probability of marking associative paths between words which occur close together in the study sequence. Since this depends crucially on the fact that some words are not tagged, this tendency is especially strong on Trial 1 when many words are not yet tagged. In this way, FRAN tends to build a marked subgraph that reflects the input adjacencies. The results of the first trial shown in Fig. 8 indicate that these two factors are not enough because humans repeat input order more often than FRAN does.

There is another method for building a subgraph which would further emphasize input adjacencies and which a few Ss have mentioned in intensive postexperimental interviews that we have conducted in other free recall experiments. There is a tendency to deliberately seek out associative links between the word under study and the previous one. This search strategy would, of course, particularly favor the reproduction of input order in recall, and it might be contributing to the discrepancy between FRAN and our Ss on the first trial. FRAN currently only searches the associates of the word under study, but she could simulate this pair-wise searching method by doing a parallel search from both words, attempting to find an intersection. It seems likely that humans use some combination of these two methods.

It is interesting to consider whether FRAN would pass a Turing Test; i.e., whether we could successfully distinguish FRAN's recall protocols from those of humans. Ignoring irrelevant details like the format of output, it is clear that discrimination would not always be possible. Some protocols can easily be spotted as originating from a human. These are identifiable by such features as a tendency to give recall priority to previously omitted words and a tendency to preserve input adjacencies on the first recall trial. One could be fairly confident that such a protocol did not originate from FRAN. However, many of the human protocols are indistinguishable from FRAN's. The conclusion seems to be that, with respect to this standard multitrial free recall task, FRAN is like many humans, but that not all humans are identical. If this is so, it would be unrealistic to expect FRAN to give data identical to that averaged from 18 quite different individuals unless we want her to have a multiple personality.

## C. STUDY TIME AND RECALL

Waugh (1963, 1967) reported investigations relating study time to subsequent recall. A simple relationship between study time and recall was found, namely, that the number of words recalled from a list depended only on the total study time for the whole list. Variations in list length, presentation rate, and masses *vs.* distributed presentation times had no effect if study time was constant. Some of Waugh's conditions were simulated with FRAN to see to what extent FRAN could explain Waugh's results.

Waugh's two 1967 experiments will be of particular interest. In the first experiment, words were read to $S$s at the rate of one per second. There were nine experimental conditions consisting of 120, 60, 40, 30, or 24 words each appearing once within a list; or a basic set of 60, 40, 30, or 24 different words permuted two, three, four, and five times respectively, to yield a total of 120 words in all. Figure 9 shows Waugh's results, with each point based on 72 observations of free recall.

Seven of the nine conditions were simulated, each with the parameter $a$ equal to .65. To save money, the two lists with 40 words were omitted. Figures 10 and 11 compare the results of our simulations with those of Waugh's $S$s for these seven conditions. Since only 10 to 12 observations (simulation runs) contribute to any of FRAN's points, the predictions are not as stable as are Waugh's data. In these figures the arrows point from the value obtained in the simulation to Waugh's observed value. An X indicates essentially identical points. The straight lines in Figs. 9, 10, and 11 indicate the linear relationships in Waugh's data between study time per word and probability of recall of any word in the list.

Clearly, FRAN has managed to simulate the general relations

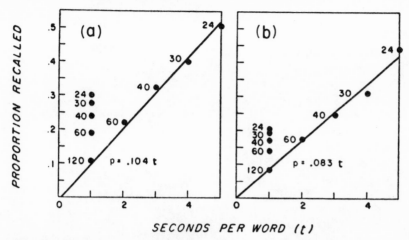

Fig. 9. Probability of recall for a given item as a function of its total presentation time. (The numbers denote the total numbers of items presented. The probabilities were estimated across all items in a list —Fig. 9a — or across items prior to the last seven — Fig. 9b.) The data are taken from Waugh (1967), by permission of the American Psychological Association, Inc.

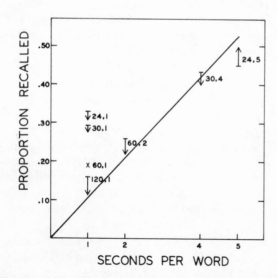

Fig. 10. FRAN and Waugh's Ss compared with respect to probability of recall of an item as a function of its total study time. Probabilities are pooled across all serial positions in the input list. The arrows point from the proportion recalled for FRAN to the proportion for the human Ss.

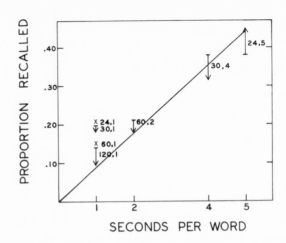

Fig. 11. FRAN and Waugh's *S*s compared with respect to probability of recall of an item as a function of its total study time. Only serial positions prior to the last seven items contribute to the estimate of probabilities. The arrows point from the proportion recalled for FRAN to the proportion for human *S*s.

among the observed points although her recall is somewhat higher overall. This could be rectified by a slightly lower value of the parameter *a*. The two most deviant predictions are for the list in which 120 words occurred once and for the list in which 24 words were presented five times. FRAN's excessive recall of the 120-item list may be related to the fact that 120 words is nearly half of FRAN's vocabulary, but is a trivial portion of an adult's vocabulary. Practically every word FRAN studied would have associates from the list. Her better-than-human performance may be due to the fact that retrieval becomes disproportionately easy in such circumstances.

In Fig. 12 we have replotted the data of Figs. 9 and 10 to show how total words recalled is related to the total study time. The point for 120 seconds is based on the average of the several points with this study time in Figs. 9 and 10. Murdock (1960) found a linear relationship between words recalled and study time, described by the equation $R_1 = 6.1 + .06t$, where $t$ was the time in seconds. That predicted relation is shown in Fig. 12. As can be seen, the values estimated from Murdock's equation are fairly close to the values obtained from FRAN and Waugh. However, the relation between study time and words recalled, either for FRAN or for Waugh's *S*s, is not linear although it is monotonically increasing. Deese (1960) also reports data in which this linear relationship was not upheld exactly.

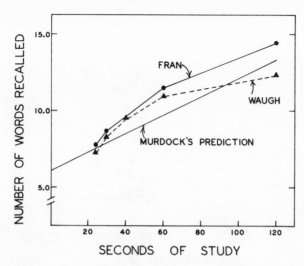

Fig. 12. FRAN and Waugh's Ss compared with respect to number of words recalled as a function of total study time. The predicted relation is taken from Murdock (1960).

In a second experiment, Waugh (1967) presented a list of 30 words for either one, two, three, four, or six seconds per word. In a massed condition, the word was presented for its total study time all at once. In a distributed condition, the words were presented only for a second at a time but appeared at several different positions in the input list. The results of her experiment are given in Fig. 13. The 100 observations contributing to each of her data points yield much more stable data than the 10 simulations (observations) that we have obtained from FRAN for each point. Only a subset of Waugh's conditions were simulated, those for one, two, four, and six seconds. FRAN and the humans are compared in Fig. 14 which is to be interpreted as were Figs. 10 and 11; i.e., the lines are taken from Waugh's data and the arrows point from our data to hers. Again, FRAN simulates the general relations in these data. Just how well FRAN does simulate the general relations can be seen in Fig. 15 which summarizes the data in Figs. 10, 11, and 14. It is a scatter plot in which each point corresponds to a single experimental condition. The value for a point on the ordinate is the proportion recalled by Waugh's Ss in that condition and the value on the abscissa is FRAN's proportion. If prediction were perfect all points would be on the diagonal line. Given that the proportions recalled are subject to random error, the result is very impressive.

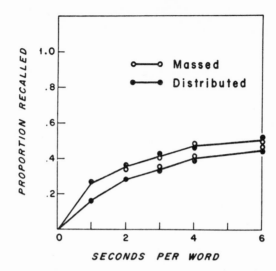

Fig. 13. Probability of recall for a given item as a function of its total presentation time, for all items in a list (upper function) or for items prior to the last seven (lower function). These data are taken from Waugh (1967), by permission of the American Psychological Association, Inc.

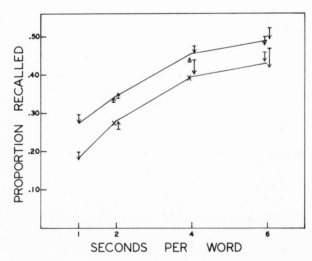

Fig. 14. FRAN and Waugh's Ss compared with respect to probability of recall of a word as a function of its total presentation time, for all items in a list (upper function) or for items prior to the last seven (lower function). The arrows point from the proportion recalled for FRAN to the proportion for human Ss. The data for the massed condition are given by the left arrow, for the distributed condition by the right arrow.

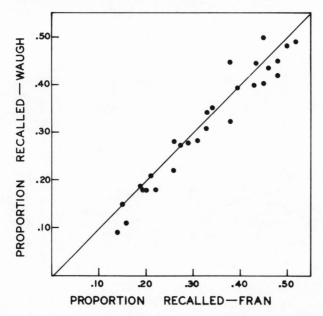

Fig. 15. Summary of data in Figs. 10, 11, and 14. Each point represents one list condition with the proportion either estimated from all items or just from the items prior to the last seven.

In an earlier study, Waugh (1963) examined free recall of 30 words presented at a one second rate, but with variation in the number of list words that were repeated. She described the procedure as follows:

> In order to control for serial position effects, we divided the 30-word lists into 14 early-late words, which occurred in positions 1-6 and 23-30 and 16 middle words, which occurred in positions 7-22.... We accordingly constructed five sorts of lists which differed in the number of repeated words that each contained. There were either 1, 2, 4, 6, or 8 words repeated in the middle group of 16. Each list represented an experimental condition, which I shall designate as Cond. 1, 2, 4, 6, or 8, according to the number of words that occurred twice in the middle segment of a list. In the early-late portion of the lists, the number of repeated words was always one less than the number repeated in the middle, so that the total number that occurred twice in a list was either 1, 3, 7, 11, or 15. In this last case, under Cond. 8, every word in the list occurred twice [Waugh, 1963, pp. 107–108, by permission of Academic Press, New York].

The results in this experiment are summarized in Fig. 16. Note that the total words recalled from the middle portion of the lists and from the early-late portion of the list are constant across conditions.

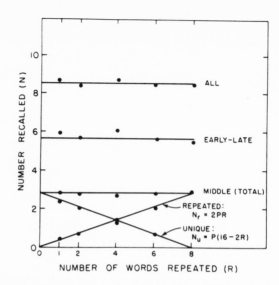

Fig. 16. Mean number of repeated and unique words recalled as a function of the number of words repeated within the middle 16 positions of a list. This figure is taken from Waugh (1963), by permission of Academic Press, New York.

Waugh's five experimental conditions were simulated with the value of $a = .65$. Figure 17 illustrates a comparison between the simulations and Waugh's results. As in previous figures, the arrows point from FRAN's prediction to Waugh's data. However, in contrast with previous figures, the straight lines are estimated from FRAN's data and not from Waugh's data. While each of her data points is based on over 300 observations, FRAN's rest on just 20 simulations, with correspondingly larger variances. While FRAN is recalling about the same number of early-late words as Waugh's Ss, FRAN's recall from the middle positions is about 25% lower. Except for this, the simulation data preserves the basic relations in Waugh's data. We probably could have matched recall both in the early-late portion and in the middle portion by simultaneously lowering the value of $a$ and decreasing the size of STS. The number of words recalled from the middle portion would then increase because $a$ (the probability of not tagging in a second) would be less. The increase in recall in the early-late portion due to the change in $a$ would be cancelled out by the reduction in the size of STS. We have already noted in Section IV,B, in discussing the serial position curve, that STS should have been smaller in FRAN.

Waugh was interested in the relation between recall of middle

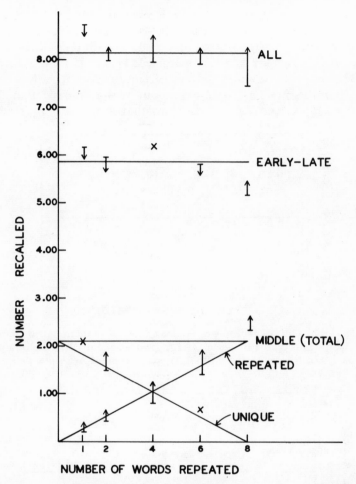

Fig. 17. FRAN and Waugh's $S$s compared with respect to mean number of repeated and unique words recalled. The arrows point from the proportion recalled for FRAN to the proportion for the human $S$s.

words that were repeated and those that were not. Letting P denote the probability of recalling a nonrepeated word, the issue was whether a repeated word would be recalled with probability $P + (1-P)P$ or with probability 2P. She was able to discriminate statistically in favor of the latter hypothesis. We did not have enough simulated data to make such a slight distinction, but the probability of FRAN's recall for the nonrepeated words was .135 and for the repeated words, .257 (averaged over the five conditions).

Waugh was also interested in whether recall would be affected by the lag between repeated words. The lag refers to the number of items intervening between the first and second presentation of a given word. Waugh's lag data for the middle 16 words are presented in Fig. 18. There is no apparent effect of lag upon recall, a fact which Waugh found surprising. There appears no reason to expect an effect of lag for FRAN, and Fig. 19 confirms that there was no systematic

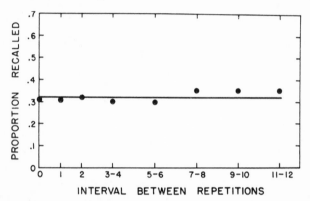

Fig. 18. Probability of recalling a repeated word as a function of the number of other words intervening between the first and second occurrences of a word. This figure is taken from Waugh (1963), by permission of Academic Press, New York.

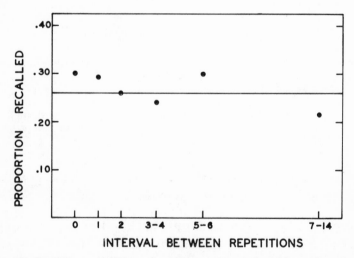

Fig. 19. FRAN's probability of recalling a repeated word as a function of the number of other words intervening between the first and second occurrences of the word.

effect for our simulations. In that figure, lags 7 through 14 were pooled because of small amounts of data for these positions.

It should be noted, in conclusion, that the experiments subsequent to Waugh's research (see Melton, 1970) have not always succeeded in replicating her findings that the effects of total study time are independent of variables such as massed vs. distributed presentation and the lag between repetition of items. These studies have involved various design differences such as rate of presentation. Whether FRAN will show similar departures from the simple relation between study time and recall when such experimental parameters are changed remains a question for further research.

## D. CUED RECALL

Slamecka (1968) reported six single-trial free recall experiments, each of which compared two groups of Ss given different conditions of recall. During testing, one group was given part of the list and was required to recall the remainder. The other group recalled the whole list that they had studied without such cues. Slamecka was concerned with recall on that portion of the list which both groups were required to recall. The consistent finding was that the control group, which had to recall all the list, did as well as or better than the experimental group which had been cued with part of the list. Cueing FRAN with words from the list should give her additional entry points into her subgraph at retrieval, and this should increase recall. The following discussion is concerned, first, with procedural factors that might have affected the cued vs. noncued recall difference in Slamecka's experiment, and, second, with the magnitude of increased recall that an associative model like FRAN predicts for the cued group.

### 1. Procedural Factors

Slamecka noted one possible reason why his cued Ss were often inferior to his noncued Ss. The cued S tended to spend about the first 10 to 20 seconds reading over the list of cue words which they had been given and which they were instructed not to recall. He conjectured that, in the time spent initially scanning the cue words, these Ss would lose access to the contents of STS from the prior study list. In an experiment in which the noncued group was given a comparably interfering task for the first 15 seconds, he found no difference in recall of the critical words by the cued and noncued groups.

This result suggested to us a reason why the cued group was not superior to the control group as FRAN would predict. The cued Ss have an additional task in recall which the control Ss do not have. Not only must they recall the words, but they must also check every word implicitly recalled against a list of words not to be recalled. Slamecka has shown that the second task may interfere with the first, but there is no reason to suppose that the interfering effects of the second task are limited to the first 15 seconds. What is clearly needed is an experimental design that equates the two groups with respect to this second task.

## 2. An Experiment

Thirty-two Ss had two study and recall tests on each of four lists of 40 common nouns. The words were presented on flashcards at a three second rate and Ss were given three minutes for recall. During the second recall test, all Ss were required to recall only a particular half of the list. That particular half was specified by the initial letters of the words to be recalled. For instance, a S might be asked to recall all the nouns that began with letters from A to M. The experimental manipulation was whether the S was given the list of words he did not have to recall on the second trial. By this procedure, all Ss would have to inhibit their recall of half of the list, but only one group would have the advantage of knowing what were the exact words on the inhibited half of the list. Comparison of the cued and noncued conditions was delayed until the second trial because it has been suggested that the list is not sufficiently organized on the first trial to take advantage of the cue words (although later data by Slamecka, 1969, dispute this point). Each of the 32 Ss recalled two lists under the cued condition and two lists under the noncued condition. They did not know in advance which lists would be tested with cueing. The variables of condition, list, and order of presentation were counter-balanced in a 4 x 4 greco-latin square. One greco-latin square was used with four blocks of four Ss and a different one with a second four blocks. In all there were 64 recall protocols for each condition.

On the first trial, when all Ss had to try to recall 40 words, 14.02 were recalled by those in the cued condition and 14.44 by those in the noncued condition. Under the cued condition, Ss recalled a mean of 10.33 words out of a possible 20 in the second recall; under the noncued condition, Ss recalled a mean of 9.63. Using as an error term the residual left when variance due to condition, subject, list, and greco-latin square is removed from the total variance, this difference is marginally significant at the .05 confidence level ($t$ test, 1 tail). Even if this difference is of marginal significance, it certainly is microscopic; cued Ss recalled only 7% of what could not be recalled without cueing.

Allen (1969) reported a cued-recall experiment that was specifically designed to augment the advantage of the cueing group. Closely associated pairs of words were input contiguously. It was hoped that this would induce the S to form associations between the pairs. After the Ss had recalled all the words they could without benefit of cues, half the Ss were presented with a set of cues consisting of one member from each pair. It was hoped that, if neither word in a pair had been recalled, cueing with one member would facilitate the recall of the other. Allen found that 15% of the words that could not be recalled without the aid of cueing were recalled with its aid. This is a significant difference, but not particularly impressive considering Allen's manipulations to obtain an effect.

## 3. Cueing of FRAN's Recall

Intuitively, one would think that an associative model like FRAN would yield a much larger advantage for cueing than was obtained in our experiment or Allen's. These intuitions were checked by running 32 simulations of the cued and of the control conditions of our experiment. The parameter $a$ was set at .65 for these simulations. In both the control and the cued conditions FRAN recalled only a specified half of the list as did our Ss. The cued condition was simulated by permitting FRAN to use as entry words the 20 cue words as well as the five from STS, and the three from ENTRYSET. This manipulation for the cued condition seemed reasonable given our intuitions that cueing a S with list words should give him extra points at which to access his memory.

In the control condition, after FRAN had recalled all the words she could, she studied those words she had recalled for an extra time. In studying these, she might succeed in finding paths to other list words and so recall them. The decision to let FRAN restudy the words she had recalled in the control condition was taken so that she would be engaging in some possibly beneficial activity to compensate for the time she was spending in the cued condition with the extra entry words. As it turned out, this was not a particularly rewarding additional activity; only three new words were recalled by means of this additional study in 32 simulations.

Turning to the results, 14.59 words were recalled on the first trial for simulations of the cued condition and 15.12 for the simulations of the noncued condition. This is slightly higher than the 14.02 and 14.44 reported above for the humans. On the second trial 14.59 of the 20 possible words were recalled in the cued condition and only 10.63 in the noncued condition, a difference of almost four words. Therefore, FRAN, with the aid of cueing, is able to recall 42% of the words she could not recall without the cues. This compares with the values of 7% in our experiment above and 15% in Allen's experiment. So, our intuitions were correct; an associative model predicts a much larger advantage of half-list cueing than is in fact found.

It would not have been difficult to have had FRAN behave differently in simulations of the half-list cueing task and thus reduce the difference predicted between the cued and the control conditions. The problem is to develop some independent motivation for such alternative assumptions. In the control condition, FRAN might be allowed to randomly search her memory looking for new words as another activity to compensate for the time spent with the extra cued words in the experimental condition. In a small memory like FRAN's, this would surely result in increased recall; but, as argued in Section III,C, it is doubtful whether this strategy is fruitful in a human-sized memory. Another assumption would be for FRAN to treat these half-list cue words with less careful consideration than is given to the other entry words. Perhaps, she would only look at a random subset of the associates of these words. It is not unreasonable to suppose that a human *S* when confronted with 20 cue words, most of which are of no help, may become somewhat negligent in his consideration of these words. While these two alternative assumptions have some plausibility, to our way of thinking, they are not as plausible as is FRAN's current behavior.

## E. RECALL OF CATEGORIZED LISTS

Much of the current interest in free recall surrounds research on the recall of categorized lists, i.e., lists composed of several instances from each of a set of categories. There has been considerable controversy as to the exact nature of the processes which underlie free recall of categorized lists. Shuell (1969) has outlined the three principal types of explanation that have been offered. First are explanations relying on Miller's (1956) notion of recoding. The general idea is that the words from a category are recoded into a single chunk, and that the $S$ recalls the chunk and not the individual words. This is a variant of the "unitization" hypothesis described in the Introduction. The basic difficulty with this explanation is that the details of how the instances are encoded into a chunk or how the chunk is decoded into its instances are left to the imagination. Because of this vagueness, it is not often contrasted with the other two theories about recall of categorized lists.

The second explanation of clustering is that offered by Bousfield (1953). His hypothesis was that the category name itself was implicitly recalled, and that recall of the category name facilitated recall of individual members. This is similar to the categorization strategy which we outlined in Section III,A. That strategy would consist of restricting search during study to those associative links of the subordinate-superordinate variety, trying to find superordinate concepts having several list items as instances. These superordinate concepts (whose names are usually not on the list) would probably form the members of ENTRYSET. Then at recall the $S$ could search for marked paths from these concepts to subordinates that were on the list.

The third interpretation is that free recall of both categorized and noncategorized lists is determined on the basis of word associations like those uncovered in free association tests. Associations of a categorial nature are not viewed as having special status. This approach is quite similar to FRAN's present associative strategy. According to this view, phenomena like clustering are to be explained by the fact that words from the same category tend to be highly interassociated. Support for this explanation comes from findings that recall and clustering are higher in lists composed of high-frequency associates of the category name (e.g., Cofer *et al.*, 1966). An opposing result was reported by Marshall (1967) who found that both recall and clustering were higher for pairs of words that were from the same category than for pairs of words that had equal associative strength but were not coordinates.

Both Cofer (1965) and Tulving (1968) have criticized attempts to distinguish experimentally between the categorization and the associative hypotheses. The general point of their argument is that these are but two of several possible ways to organize word lists, and that one should not expect a person always to use just one and the same basis for organization. Although the claim that $Ss$ use many strategies in free recall is undoubtedly correct, it leaves unresolved the empirical question of how much humans tend to use a categorization strategy as opposed to an associative strategy. One way to decide the issue is to compare FRAN's performance on categorized lists to that of humans. FRAN uses a pure associative strategy. So far, we have presented evidence largely consistent with the hypothesis that FRAN correctly models the main aspects of the associative strategy which Ss tend to adopt under standard free recall. If her performance on categorized lists deviates markedly from that of humans, we may have evidence that categorization strategies are quite prominent in such situations. We would also discover how characteristics of recall differ between the two strategies.

After searching the extensive literature on this topic, we decided to simulate an experiment by Dallett (1964) which manipulated two variables of interest in categorized recall, and which reported measures of overall recall as well as organization. Subjects in his Experiment IV studied lists of 24 words presented at a 1.4-second rate. The lists were composed either of two members from each of 12 categories, three members from eight, four members from six, or six members from four. Another variable was whether all the members of a category were presented contiguously (blocked presentation) or presented randomly scattered throughout the list (random presentation). There are eight combinations of the two methods of presentation and the four numbers of categories, and data were collected from 20 Ss in each condition. It is not possible to have FRAN study at time intervals like Dallett's 1.4 seconds that are not in discrete seconds. As a compromise, data were obtained for six simulations at a one second rate and six simulations at a two second rate. The parameter a was set at .5 for these simulations.

Figure 20a shows that the recall of FRAN and of the humans closely matches when instances of categories were presented in random order. Both show an increase in words recalled as the number of categories decreases. FRAN improves with fewer categories because she has to develop access to fewer "regions" of memory. Unfortunately, this result of higher recall with fewer categories is by no means universal. Bousfield and Cohen (1956), Cohen and Bousfield (1956), Mathews (1954), Tulving and Pearlstone (1966), and Dallett (1964, Experiment I) report divergent outcomes of this comparison. The observed effect of number of categories appears to depend on list length and also on the Ss sophistication with free recall.

The control data for FRAN represent recall of 24 randomly selected words. Ten simulations were run at both the one- and the

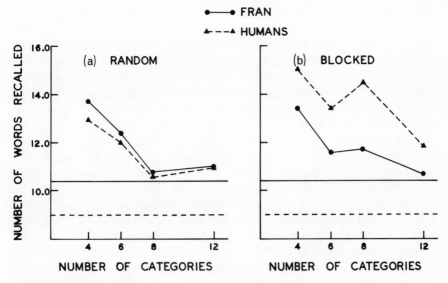

Fig. 20. FRAN and Dallett's $S$s compared with respect to number of words recalled out of 24 as a function of number of categories and mode of presentation (blocked $vs.$ random).

two-second input rates. Categorized recall was higher than the control recall for FRAN at all numbers of categories, a consistent result in the literature. The control recall reported by Dallett is not comparable because it was based on recall of lists composed of nouns, verbs, adjectives, and adverbs. With such control lists, it is none too surprising that his control recall was lower than FRAN's. Verbs, adjectives, and adverbs are generally more abstract than nouns, and abstract words are recalled less well.

Figure 20b illustrates a comparison between the data and the predictions when presentation was blocked. Although humans and FRAN both improve in recall with fewer categories, the humans are considerably superior to FRAN. The recall of the humans in the blocked condition was one to four words more than in the random condition, a result that has been replicated by Cofer, Bruce, and Reicher (1966). In contrast, FRAN recalled a mean of 11.94 words in the random condition, averaged across all numbers of categories, and a mean of 11.86 in the blocked condition.

In the blocked condition FRAN has a better chance than in the random condition of marking associations between words within a category. If FRAN finds an associative path between a word under study and a previous list word from the same category, in the blocked condition she will probably recognize the discovered word because it is likely to still be in STS. The word is still likely to be in STS in the blocked condition because it would have appeared only a few items earlier. If FRAN does recognize it, it will be re-entered into STS, and she will attempt to tag the paths to and from the word and attempt to tag the word itself. On the other hand, in the random condition, there is considerable chance that the discovered coordinate word will not be recognized. Failure of recognition is possible because the word is not likely to be in STS at the time and it may not have been tagged when originally studied. This increased probability of tagging paths between contiguous coordinate pairs should somewhat facilitate recall in the blocked condition.

This fact, that associative paths are more likely to be tagged between contiguous words, was also used in Section IV,B to explain why the input order was maintained to some degree in the output order. Glanzer (1969) has shown that related word pairs are more likely to be recalled if they are presented close together — a result which is to be predicted by this same factor within FRAN. In the simulations for the random condition, we examined recall of pairs of words from the same category which had occurred in positions 4 through 19 in the input sequence. The examination was restricted to these middle 16 positions to avoid any complications due to primacy and recency effects. The relevant data concern recall of the second member of a pair conditional upon the recall of the first member of the pair. When the lag between the two words was between zero and four words, the conditional probability of recall of the second member was 54%; for lags between 5 and 14, it was 49%. This result, like Glanzer's, is to be explained in terms of the fact that useable associative paths between two list words are more likely to be tagged the nearer the items appear to one another. However, the difference in our data is not very large, suggesting that extrinsic contiguity conferred relatively little advantage to the formation of associations.

A second, opposing factor apparently cancelled out this small contiguity advantage of the blocked condition. The disadvantage in the blocked condition is that the members of STS at recall are likely to come from fewer categories than in the random condition because the last words FRAN studies in the blocked condition are all from the same category. Therefore, FRAN will have access to fewer categorical clusters at recall through the contents of STS.

Why, then, do human Ss recall more with blocked than with random input? We suspect it is because under the blocked condition humans are likely to adopt the categorization strategy outlined previously. This strategy is effective with categorized lists, particularly where they are blocked. That humans were using this strategy can be inferred from Fig. 21 which reports clustering measures for FRAN and the human Ss. The measure used in this figure is the same as that Dallett reported, viz., deviation from expected clustering. This measure is calculated by counting the number of times one member follows another member of the same category in the output and substracting from that sum the expected number of such repetitions. The expected number is given by the formula: $(\Sigma m_i^2 / \Sigma m_i) - 1$, where $m_i$ is the number of items recalled from the $i$th category. For both the humans and FRAN, clustering

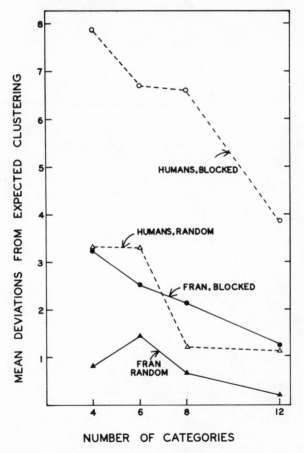

Fig. 21. FRAN and Dallett's Ss compared with respect to amount of category clustering. See text for explanation of clustering metric, mean deviations from expected clustering.

exceeds chance and the deviations from expectation increase as the number of categories decrease. Also, both humans and FRAN show much greater clustering with blocked presentation of the list. However, under all conditions, the humans show much more clustering than does FRAN, particularly in the blocked condition. Referring to the level of recall in Fig. 20b, it may be confirmed that the level of clustering shown by the humans under the blocked conditions was practically perfect. Such perfect clustering scores are to be expected, of course, if the human $S$s were using the categorization strategy as outlined. From their less than optimal clustering scores, $S$s in the random condition apparently were using some combination of the associative and the categorization strategy; or alternatively, some $S$s were using an associative strategy like FRAN and others, the categorization strategy.

## F. WORD RECOGNITION

Embedded within FRAN is a simple model of word recognition. In a word recognition test, there are three possible bases for FRAN to identify an item as a list member — membership in STS, membership in ENTRYSET, or an association between the item and the list marker. FRAN would be able to recognize any word meeting any of these three criteria. For any other word from the list and for all the distractors, FRAN would have to resort to some pure guessing strategy to determine which items (if any) to call list members. Essentially, then, FRAN can classify words into only two categories, those she remembers as coming from the list and those she cannot remember being in the list. However, humans can discriminate words into more than two categories as is shown by their ability to give ratings of their confidence that a test word was in the list. These confidence ratings bear a monotonic relationship to the probability that the word came from the studied list. As currently programmed, FRAN does not yield such multiconfidence ratings.

However, a simple and natural elaboration of the model will handle such confidence judgments in recognition. The requisite assumption presupposes an imperfect decision process that interprets associations to the list markers. In a forthcoming paper this recognition model will be described in detail. Essentially, it is a two-state recognition model like that of Bernbach (1967). In the terminology of signal-detectability theory, it is assumed that there is one normal distribution of values on the decision axis for tagged words and a different normal distribution for untagged words.

According to this model, a S will recognize a word whenever the word exceeds an adjustable criterion value on the decision axis. Therefore, it will occasionally happen that tagged words will not be recognized and untagged words will be recognized. With this brief elaboration of the recognition model in mind, we can now discuss some of the data from word recognition experiments.

The primacy effect in FRAN's free recall has been attributed to the fact that ENTRYSET in initially composed of the first words in the list, and the recency effect to the fact that, at the initiation of recall, STS is composed of the last words in the list and their associates. If recognition judgments take account of the contents of STS and ENTRYSET as we postulate, one would expect to find primacy and recency effects in recognition judgments. The data of Waugh and Norman (1968) confirm that this is the case. They also found that the recency effect is much more pronounced for those items that are presented for recognition judgment early in the test phase, a result consistent with FRAN's recognition component. If an item late in the study sequence is tested early, there is a high probability that it will still be in STS when tested and therefore recognized. As more items are tested before the late-studied word, the probability increases that the word will no longer be in STS.

Another interesting phenomena is the occurrence of intrusions in the free-recall output. In searching her memory, FRAN must decide whether each word she encounters is a list word or not. If the decision model described above were governing these judgments, FRAN would occasionally incorrectly identify as a list member one of the nonlist words she encountered in her search. FRAN, in her search at the time of recall, only examines words that are on marked associative pathways. Therefore, the only nonlist words considered are on associative pathways that have been marked out between list words. As a consequence, one would expect most intrusions to be strongly related to some of the words in the list. Deese (1959b) demonstrated that this is the case; he found a strong positive correlation between the frequency with which the words in the list evoked a particular word in free association and the frequency with which that word occurred as an intrusion in free recall.

While many variables such as presentation rate and serial position appear to have the same effect on recognition as on recall, a few variables affect the two testing methods differently. These differences are easily interpreted in terms of the processes underlying FRAN's performance. For instance, it is to be predicted that any manipulation that increases the organization of the list should facilitate the retrieval processes but not item recognition. Therefore, such manipulations should improve recall but leave word recognition unaffected. Cofer (1967) and Kintsch (1968) report data confirming this prediction.

Also, Ss should give better recall under intentional than incidental instructions because intentional Ss are likely to actively search out relationships and retrieval pathways amongst the list words. On the other hand, recognition performance depends only upon tagging of the word which, in turn, depends only upon the entry of the word into STS. Presumably, any incidental task that directs the S's attention to the word will insure that the word enters STS. Therefore, intentional learning instructions should not have any superiority over incidental if the method of test is recognition but will be superior on recall tests. Eagle and Leiter (1964) found that recall is better under intentional instructions, but recognition is actually better under incidental instructions. Both findings have been confirmed in other experiments (Dornbush & Winnich, 1967; Postman, Adams, & Phillips, 1955). Consistent with our interpretation of the facilitating effect of intentional instructions, Eagle and Leiter found that only those intentional Ss who reported using some recall strategy were superior to the incidental Ss. They also offered a plausible explanation of the unexpected superiority of the incidental group in recognition. Eagle and Leiter suggest that, under intentional instructions, Ss focus on particular words at the expense of others; in contrast, under incidental learning instructions, Ss distribute their time equally among the words. Focusing of attention may be useful in developing a successful system for retrieval, but the optimal strategy for recognition is to distribute an equal amount of time to each word. That recognition is optimal when S distributes his study time equally follows from FRAN's assumption that probability of tagging is exponentially related to the duration of time for which the word is studied.

# V. Concluding Remarks

Throughout Section IV, we confined ourselves to the tasks of comparing FRAN's performance with that of humans, of explaining FRAN's performance, and of conjecturing why humans deviated from FRAN's behavior when they did. The time is now come to evaluate the theoretical positions developed in Sections II and III in light of the results of Section IV. To summarize, three basic claims were made about free recall: (*a*) Most humans in conditions of standard free recall adopt the associative strategy of FRAN as described in Section III; (*b*) procedural deviations from the standard free recall paradigm may induce Ss to adopt strategies quite different from the associative; and (*c*) these different strategies could be implemented with the same mental mechanisms as outlined in Section II. The question now is, to what extent have these three claims been substantiated?

As for the claim that FRAN's associative strategy is the rule for standard free recall, the data presented in Sections IV,B,C, and F, as well as the introspective evidence referenced throughout this paper, provide positive support. The data in Section IV,D, the failure of humans to show substantial improvement when cued with list words, provide the only major source of embarrassment for this hypothesis. As noted, it would be easy to introduce minor alterations to FRAN's behavior that would reduce the difference she now shows between the cued and noncued conditions. However, these changes would be posthoc, and would only mitigate the embarrassment of the theory. Nonetheless, it would be mistaken to overemphasize the importance of this negative result. Both we and Allen have shown that cueing with list words has beneficial effects. Beyond this, the data of Tulving and Pearlstone (1966) and of Tulving and Osler (1968) showed that cueing with extralist words could have very beneficial effects. Therefore, Slamecka's original thesis about the complete independence of memory traces is quite probably wrong. The difficulty only concerns why the memory traces are not as dependent as our associative model would seem to predict.

If it is accepted that FRAN approximately models the associative strategy for standard free recall, it is fairly clear from Section IV,E that the associative strategy is not always the major strategy in all nonstandard free recall experiments. Dallett's data indicated that adoption of the alternative, categorization strategy increased as the categorized nature of the list was made explicit. Therefore, this is a stronger result than just that a different strategy was adopted when the paradigm was changed from standard free recall; rather, the nature of the strategy change was predictably related to the nature of the change in experimental parameters.

We have outlined how several different strategies could be implemented in terms of FRAN's mental mechanisms. The fact that these various strategies can be formulated in terms of FRAN's machinery supports the assertion that FRAN models the structures and processes underlying human memory in general. However, this fact alone is hardly sufficient. To mention a counter example, all these strategies can be implemented on any standard computer. This would hardly lead one to conclude that the structures and processes which underlie the computer have much relation to those in the human head. The reason why we can reject the raw computer as a model of human memory, independently of physiological considerations, is that it is possible to have the computer perform feats of memory of which the human is just not capable. The point is that anything which FRAN can do, humans must be able to do also. To substantiate our third theoretical contention will require stronger results than given in this paper. We must present data that would adequately substantiate that FRAN can simulate practically all memory strategies that people use; we must also show that we can instruct humans to adopt any strategy of which FRAN is capable.

We must address ourselves to one remaining question in this evaluation; viz., to what extent do the simulation results depend upon the particular parameters? Might we have produced simulations showing little benefit of cueing? Could we have obtained a difference between blocked and random presentation of lists? It is, of course, completely unfeasible to do the sort of parameter search that would determine an answer to these questions with certainty. Given that this is impractical, one must rest content with the type of informal answers provided in Section IV. Sometimes, as with the too-large recency effect, we pointed out it seemed clear that a change of parameters would eliminate this discrepancy in the simulation. In other circumstances, such as with the too-large cueing effect, the result seemed inevitable given the associative strategy, and there was no apparent way to avoid it by juggling the parameters.

Clearly, while some of the results are encouraging, FRAN is not a complete model of free recall. The model is not adequate even for all the details of standard free recall. Before FRAN would constitute an adequate "explanation" of free recall, we would have to augment the program so that she could adequately replicate all relevant relations found in all free recall experiments. This is clearly a tall order. Rather than attempting to achieve such a complete model, it will be more judicious to set our sights lower and seek a closer approximation of FRAN to the data.

There are a few theoretical changes that would transform FRAN into a more adequate model. One obvious improvement would be to give FRAN a larger memory. There is no technical reason why it could not be about 2000 concepts. Such a memory would at least be approaching the order of magnitude of a human's, and FRAN would be faced with some of the problems a human has when he must search for lost needles in a mnemonic haystack. Since FRAN's current memory is at least a hundred times less than that of a human, it is impossible to assign much psychological reality to some of her processes such as those selected to govern her search for and marking of associative paths. With a memory that approached human size, it would be possible to explore interesting questions about the exact manner in which the memory is searched. For instance, we might try to determine the rate at which associations are searched from a particular word. It will be remembered we used the crude formula $N = 5 + T$ to relate number of associations ($N$) to total study time ($T$). With a larger memory it would also be possible to have FRAN occasionally resort to a random search of her memory, as humans probably do, without being in danger of quickly exhausting the memory.

The other important direction in which FRAN should be improved is to permit her to adopt a variety of strategies and to give her some heuristic principles by which to select a particular strategy for a particular free recall task. This is much more easily said than done. Essentially, a meta-program is needed that is capable of writing a set of different programs, each program reflecting a different strategy. The program that we have developed for execution of the associative strategy would be just one of many strategy-implementing programs. Although there is some research in computer science on programs to write programs, nothing relevant to our complexities is at hand. Although the task of programming such a meta-program is beyond our current abilities and ideas, any fully adequate simulation program for human memory will have to take the form of such a meta-program.

## Appendix: An Introspective Report

The following is a transcription of the verbal introspective remarks offered by one student as she studied and recalled a set of 40 words presented at an eight-second rate. She had twice studied and recalled a previous list of 40 words. She had also studied and recalled this current list a previous time. In the first trial she had recalled in the following order the words tattoo, lieutenant, mercenary, destroyer, sideburns, skeleton, pumpkin, dignitary, city, pond, chestnut, mountain, kitchen, widow, wrist, student, and present.

*Study.* The word following each number indicates the word being studied.

Following it is a transcription of the *S*'s remarks. Each italicized word in the transcription is a word that was in the set of 40 to-be-recalled words:

1. garrison — *garrison, lieutenant, dignitary*
2. dignitary — *crown* queen, oh . . . *dignitary*
3. vulture — *vulture* . . . bird, there was a bird *present* . . . *vulture*, bird . . . *garrison*
4. disk — *disk* . . . *disk*, record, *disk*, can't remember statue
5. crown — *crown* queen, the *dignitary* visits the *crown* queen, the *lieutenant* is in the *garrison*
6. bowl — *bowl* . . . *bowl* of flowers . . . the *dignitary* visits the *crown* queen and gives her a *bowl* of flowers
7. present — I am *present*, I also am a *student*, I think . . . *student*
8. student — *student*, I am *present*, I also am a *student* . . . the *dignitary* is also a *student* philosopher
9. dragon — oh, I forgot all the fairy tales . . . *goose, dragon*, mother *goose* fairy tales
10. kitchen — *kitchen*, still the mother, the *widowed* mother
11. clergyman — *clergyman* . . . the *clergyman* visits the *widowed* mother who is in the *kitchen*
12. airport — *airport* . . . the *dignitary* arrives in a airplane in the *airport* to visit the *crown* queen with a *bowl* of flowers
13. lieutenant — *lieutenant* is in the *garrison* . . . and he is being attacked by a *vulture* who came through the window
14. pepper— *pepper* . . . the mother put the *pepper* on the food
15. chestnut — still the open fire, *chestnuts, pond*, next word is *pond*
16 pond — right . . . remember *garrison* and remember *dignitary*
17. wrist — *wrist*, still watch, *wrist* watch, *wrist* action, *wrist* watch
18. mountain — oh, instead of valley remember the *mountain* that created the valley
19. flashlight — you remembered *city* but you didn't remember *flashlight* and the reason you should remember *city* is because you have to use a *flashlight*
20. city — *city, flashlight* . . . *kitchen, dignitary, city, flashlight*
21. scorpion — *scorpion*, remember *vulture* with *scorpion*, the *garrison* is loaded with kooky animals
22. congregation — *congregation*, I am trying to remember a *congregation* of things, *congregation*
23. goose — *goose*, remember *dragon*, remember mother *goose* . . . a fairy tale . . . or you could remember happy times, *goose, dragon, pond, chestnuts*
24. cone — and an ice-cream *cone, goose, dragon, pond, chestnuts*, and an ice-cream *cone*
25. tub — *tub* . . . I still only remember bath and I'll never remember that and when you see *tub*, I remember rub-a-dub-*tub*, tune in *tub*, ah yes
26. pliers — *pliers*, they never will be remembered by me . . . oh, bicycle, to fix a bicycle you have to use some *pliers*
27. beard — *beard*, the *dignitary* had a *beard* and the *lieutenant* had the sideburns . . . Jesus
28. mercenary — the *lieutenant* was the *mercenary*, right

29. frontier — he is fighting on the *frontier*, let me see now . . . somewhere in Arabia . . . the *lieutenant* is in the *garrison* because he didn't fight

30. castle — *castle*, fairy tale . . . don't remember the sentry, remember the *castle* he guards

31. officer — the *lieutenant* is a *officer* in the . . . oh . . . he didn't obey the duties

32. destroyer — the *lieutenant* is an *officer*, *destroyer*, *mercenary* . . . the *lieutenant* is too much . . . he's a *destroyer*

33. jackknife — *jackknife*, in the summer you can use the *pond* to swim in and one of the things you can do is *jackknife* into it

34. widow — the mother is a *widow* in the *kitchen*, the *widowed* mother is in the *kitchen*

35. gambler — oh, another *city* you could think of is Las Vegas and Monte Carlo as opposed to New York

36. pumpkin — *pumpkin*, remember with *skeleton*, Hallowe'en . . . fun, *chestnuts*

37. sideburns — *sideburns*, the *lieutenant* has *sideburns*, the *dignitary* has a *beard*

38. skeleton — oops, oh, the *pumpkin* and the *skeleton*, right, *skeleton*

39. film — what I am looking at could be said to be a *film* or a *congregation* of objects

40. tattoo — *tattoo* . . . oh, 2 t's, 2 o's, spelled it wrong last time.

*Recall.* This is a complete transcription of the *S*'s remarks during the three minutes she had for recall. Italicized are those words that were written on the recall sheet.

Seeing as how I spelled it wrong last time — *t, a, t, t, o, o.* What I am looking at could be said to be a *film* of a *congregation* of objects. The *lieutenant* . . . lieu-ten-ant . . . is a *mercenary* with *sideburns* . . . *destroyer* . . . *officer* . . . who's in the *garrison* . . . and is being attacked by *vultures* and *scorpions* . . . and a *gambler's city* . . . called Las Vegas, Monte Carlo as opposed to a city where you have to use a *flashlight* like New York when it had the blackout. Let me see now . . . the mother, oops not mother but *kitchen* . . . kitchen, mother's in the kitchen using *pepper* . . . on the phone and she was visited by the *clergyman* . . . seeing as how she was recently *widowed* . . . she has many children who like to roast *chestnuts* . . . on the fire and tell fairy tales about *dragons* . . . mother *goose* fairy tales, that is, and ladies in *castles* being rescued . . . let me see now, afterward they go skating on a *pond*, that's during the winter, however they can use the *jackknife* during the summer . . . and they live in a valley between two *mountains* . . . and one time they were making the jackknife and they broke their *wrist*, one kid broke his wrist, right . . . and . . . let me see now, the lieutenant was a mercenary who had sideburns, the *dignitary* . . . was the guy who had the *beard* and he carried a *bowl* of flowers to the queen who was already in the castle . . . and . . . well, the lieutenant could be said to have a *skeleton* in his closet that he is reserving for Hallowe'en when he can use it with his *pumpkin* . . . oh, yes . . . let me see, what else can I remember about those nice people . . . the lieutenant could be said to have a skeleton in his closet . . . which he could use for Hallowe'en . . . let me see now, scorpion, gambler, city, flashlight . . . clergyman, widow, chestnut . . . goose, castle, pond, jackknife, wrist, dignitary, I am *present* and I am a *student* . . . oh, there is a word that I am not going to remember . . . because I remember it but I can't remember it, let me think . . . I am present and I am a student . . . *tub*, I remembered it . . . no, that's not the right one . . . tub, bath, pond . . . chestnuts roasting in an open fire . . . I'm not too sure I am not remembering the other 40 words.

## REFERENCES

Allen, M. Cueing and retrieval in free recall. *Journal of Experimental Psychology*, 1969, **81**, 29–35.

Battig, W. F., Allen, M., & Jensen, A. R. Priority of the free recall of newly learned items. *Journal of Verbal Learning and Verbal Behavior*, 1965, **4**, 175–179.

Battig, W. F., & Slaybaugh, G. D. Evidence that priority of free recall of newly learned items is not a recency artifact. *Journal of Verbal Learning and Verbal Behavior*, 1969, **8**, 536–538.

Bernbach, H. A. Decision processes in memory. *Psychological Review*, 1967, **74**, 462–480.

Bever, T. G., Fodor, J. A., & Garrett, M. A formal limitation of associationism. In T. R. Dixon & D. L. Horton (Eds.), *Verbal behavior and general behavior theory*. Englewood Cliffs, N.J.: Prentice-Hall, 1968.

Bierwisch, M. Some semantic universals of German adjectivals. *Foundations of Language*, 1967, **3**, 1–36.

Bolinger, D. The atomization of meaning. *Language*, 1965, **41**, 555–573.

Bousfield, W. A. The occurrence of clustering in recall of randomly arranged associates. *Journal of General Psychology*, 1953, **49**, 229–240.

Bousfield, W. A., & Cohen, B. H. The effects of reinforcement on the occurrence of clustering in the recall of randomly arranged associates. *Journal of Psychology*, 1953, **36**, 67–81.

Bousfield, W. A., & Cohen, B. H. Clustering in recall as a function of the number of word-categories in stimulus-word lists. *Journal of General Psychology*, 1956, **54**, 95–106.

Bousfield, W. A., Puff, C. R., & Cohen, B. H. The development of constancies in sequential organization during repeated free recall. *Journal of Verbal Learning and Verbal Behavior*, 1964, **3**, 489–495.

Bower, G. H. Analysis of a mnemonic device. *American Scientist*, 1970, **58**, 496–510.

Cofer, C. N. On some factors in the organizational characteristics of free recall. *American Psychologist*, 1965, **20**, 261–272.

Cofer, C. N. Does conceptual organization influence the amount retained in immediate free recall. In B. Kleinmutz (Ed.), *Concepts and the structure of memory*. New York: Wiley, 1967.

Cofer, C. N., Bruce, D. R., & Reicher, G. M. Clustering in free recall as a function of certain methodological variations. *Journal of Experimental Psychology*, 1966, **71**, 858–866.

Cohen, B. H., & Bousfield, W. A. The effects of a dual-level stimulus-word list on the occurrence of clustering in recall. *Journal of General Psychology*, 1956, **55**, 51–58.

Dallett, K. M. Number of categories and category information in free recall. *Journal of Experimental Psychology*, 1964, **68**, 1–12.

Deese, J. Influence of inter-item associative strength upon immediate free recall. *Psychological Reports*, 1959, 5, 305–312. (a)

Deese, J. On the prediction of occurrence of particular verbal intrusions in immediate recall. *Journal of Experimental Psychology*, 1959, 58, 17–22. (b)

Deese, J. Frequency of usage and number of words in free recall: The role of association. *Psychological Reports*, 1960, 7, 337–344.

Deese, J. *The structure of associations in language and thought*. Baltimore: Johns Hopkins Press, 1966.

Deese, J. Association and memory. In T. R. Dixon & D. L. Horton (Eds.), *Verbal behavior and general behavior theory*. Englewood Cliffs, N.J.: Prentice-Hall, 1968.

Dornbush, R. L., & Winnich, W. A. Short-term intentional and incidental learning. *Journal of Experimental Psychology*, 1967, 73, 608–611.

Eagle, M., & Leiter, E. Recall and recognition in intentional and incidental learning. *Journal of Experimental Psychology*, 1964, **68**, 58–63.

Glanzer, M. Distance between related words in free recall: Trace of the STS. *Journal of Verbal Learning and Verbal Behavior*, 1969, **8**, 105–111.

Glanzer, M., & Cunitz, A. R. Two storage mechanisms in free recall. *Journal of Verbal Learning and Verbal Behavior*, 1966, 5, 351–360.

Jenkins, J. J., and Russell, W. A. Associative clustering during recall. *Journal of Abnormal and Social Psychology*, 1952, 47, 818–821.

Katz, J. J., & Fodor, J. A. The structure of a semantic theory. *Language*, 1963, 39, 170–210.

Kintsch, W. Recognition and recall of organized lists. *Journal of Experimental Psychology*, 1968, **78**, 481–487.

Kintsch, W. Models for free recall and recognition. In D. A. Norman (Ed.), *Models of human memory*, New York: Academic Press, 1970.

Kiss, G. R. A test of the word selection model using multiple stimuli in word association. Paper presented at the conference of the British Psychological Society, London, 1967.

Lyons, J. *Introduction to theoretical linguistics*. London and New York: Cambridge University Press, 1969.

Mandler, G. Organization and memory. In K. W. Spence & J. T. Spence (Eds.), *The psychology of learning and motivation: Advances in research and theory*. Vol. 1. New York: Academic Press, 1967. Pp. 328–372.

Mandler, G., & Pearlstone, Z. Free and constrained concept learning and subsequent recall. *Journal of Verbal Learning and Verbal Behavior*, 1966, 5, 126–131.

Marshall, G. R. Effect of total association and conceptual cohesiveness among words on recall, clustering, and recognition association. *Psychological Reports*, 1967, **20**, 29–44.

Mathews, R. Recall as a function of number of classificatory categories. *Journal of Experimental Psychology*, 1954, 47, 241–247.

Melton, A. W. The situation with respect to the spacing of repetitions and memory. *Journal of Verbal Learning and Verbal Behavior*, 1970, 9, 596–606.

Miller, G. A. The magical number seven, plus or minus two: Some limits on our capacity to process information. *Psychological Review*, 1956, **63**, 81–97.

Murdock, B. B., Jr. The immediate retention of unrelated words. *Journal of Experimental Psychology*, 1960, **60**, 222–234.

Murdock, B. B., Jr. The serial position effect in free recall. *Journal of Experimental Psychology*, 1962, **64**, 482-488.

Norman, D. A. Toward a theory of memory and attention. *Psychological Review*, 1968, **75**, 522-536.

Pollio, H. R. Associative structure and verbal behavior. In T. R. Dixon & D. L. Horton (Eds.), *Verbal behavior and general behavior theory*. Englewood Cliffs, N.J.: Prentice-Hall, 1968.

Postman, L., Adams, P. A., & Phillips, L. W. Studies in incidental learning: II. The effects of association value and method of testing. *Journal of Experimental Psychology*, 1955, **49**, 1-10.

Postman, L., & Keppel, G. Conditions determining the priority of new items in free recall. *Journal of Verbal Learning and Verbal Behavior*, 1968, **7**, 260-263.

Postman, L., & Phillips, L. W. Short-term temporal changes in free recall. *Quarterly Journal of Experimental Psychology*, 1965, **17**, 132-138.

Puff, C. R. Role of clustering in free recall. *Journal of Experimental Psychology*, 1970, **86**, 384-386.

Quillian, M. R. *The teachable language comprehender: A simulation program and theory of language*. Project No. 8688. Cambridge, Mass.: Bolt, Beranek & Newman, 1969.

Rosner, S. R. The effects of presentation and recall trials on organization in multitrial free recall. *Journal of Verbal Learning and Verbal Behavior*, 1970, **9**, 69-74.

Schank, R. "Semantics" in conceptual analysis. Stanford A. I. Memo No. 122, May 1970, Computer Science Dept., Stanford University.

Shuell, T. J. Clustering and organization in free recall. *Psychological Bulletin*, 1969, **72**, 353-374.

Shuell, T. J., & Keppel, G. Item priority in free recall. *Journal of Verbal Learning and Verbal Behavior*, 1968, **7**, 969-971.

Slamecka, N. J. An examination of trace storage in free recall. *Journal of Experimental Psychology*, 1968, **76**, 504-513.

Slamecka, N. J. Testing for associative storage in multitrial free recall. *Journal of Experimental Psychology*, 1969, **81**, 557-560.

Tulving, E. Subjective organization in free recall of "unrelated" words. *Psychological Review*, 1962, **69**, 344-354.

Tulving, E. Theoretical issues in free recall. In T. R. Dixon & D. L. Horton (Eds.), *Verbal behavior and general behavior theory*. Englewood Cliffs, N.J.: Prentice-Hall, 1968.

Tulving, E., & Osler, S. Effectiveness of retrieval cues in memory for words. *Journal of Experimental Psychology*, 1968, **77**, 593-601.

Tulving, E., & Pearlstone, Z. Availability versus accessibility of information in memory for words. *Journal of Verbal Learning and Verbal Behavior*, 1966, **5**, 381-391.

Underwood, B. J. The representativeness of rote learning. In A. W. Melton (Ed.), *Categories of human learning*. New York: Academic Press, 1964. Pp. 47-78.

Waugh, N. C. Immediate memory as a function of repetition. *Journal of Verbal Learning and Verbal Behavior*, 1963, **2**, 107-112.

Waugh, N. C. Presentation time and free recall. *Journal of Experimental Psychology*, 1967, **73**, 39-44.

Waugh, N. C., & Norman, D. A. Stimulus and response interference in recognition-memory experiments. *Journal of Experimental Psychology*, 1968, **78**, 551-559.

# Author Index

Numbers in italics refer to the pages on which the complete references are listed.

# Subject Index

## L

Language processing, relation of short-term store to, 183–188
  auditory *vs.* visual presentation and, 184
  grouping effects and, 184–188
Latency, recruitment of habit and, 50–55
Learning, *see* Discrimination learning; Serial learning
Learning curve, for simulation model of free recall, 341
List(s),
  categorized, recall of, 362–368
  derived, in serial position effect, 302–309
List length,
  in serial learning, 275–276
  storage mechanisms and, 160–161
Long-term memory, *see also under* Storage mechanisms
  of free recall simulation model, 319–324

## M

Memory, *see* Finite-state decision model; Free recall; Short-term memory
Mnemonic relations, storage mechanisms and, 153–154, 182
Modality effects, in memory, 81–86

## O

Organization, *see under* Serial learning

## P

Paired associates,
  multitrial, 106–109
  single-trial, 100–106
Peak-shift, in discrimination learning, 225–236
  generality of, 228–229
  negative peak-shift, 227–228
  training conditions not producing, 235–236
  training conditions producing, 229–235
Presentation rate, storage mechanisms and, 159–160

## R

Recall, *see* Fixed-order recall; Free recall; Storage mechanisms
Recency, judgments of, 115–119
Recency effect, in memory, 76–78
Recognition, simulation model of free recall and, 368–370
Reinforcement,
  in differential conditioning to stimulus intensity, 33–36
  in discrimination learning, 211–215
  resistance to, 248–249
Repetitions, storage mechanisms and, 154–157
  number of, 161–162
  spacing of, 162
Responding, stimulus-produced decrement in, 245–248
Response evocation, decision theory of, *see* Decision theory

## S

Semantic markers, in long-term memory, 320–321
Serial learning, 267–314
  independence of sequence learning and the serial position effect in, 276–301
    absence of serial position effect and, 278–281
    dimensional *vs.* hierarchical organization and, 298–301
    generalization concerning, 286–298
    ubiquity of serial position effect and, 282–286
  information available after, 268–276
    item learning and contextual associations and, 269
    item location and interitem associations and, 269–275
    list length and, 275–276
    remote associations and Ebbinghaus' derived lists and, 302–309
    Von Restorff effect and end anchoring and, 301–302
Serial position curve,
  interactions with storage mechanisms, 132–136